Canadian Living
THE ULTIMATE
COOKBOOK

EXCLUSIVE DISTRIBUTOR FOR CANADA & USA

Simon & Schuster Canada
166 King Street East, Suite 300
Toronto ON M5A 1J3

Tel: 617-427-8882
Toll Free: 800-387-0446   **simonandschuster.ca**
Fax: 647-430-9446   **canadianliving.com/books**

Bibliothèque et Archives nationales du Québec
and Library and Archives Canada cataloguing
in publication

Main entry under title:

The ultimate cookbook
"Canadian living".
Includes index.
ISBN 978-1-988002-09-5
1. Cooking. 2. Cookbooks. I. Canadian Living Test
Kitchen. II. Title : Canadian living.
TX714.U47 2015   641.5   C2015-941642-6

Art director: Colin Elliott
Project editor: Tina Anson Mine
Copy editor: Lisa Fielding
Indexer: Beth Zabloski

08-15

Legal deposit: 2015
Bibliothèque et Archives nationales du Québec
Library and Archives Canada

Printed by Imprimerie Transcontinental, Beauceville, Canada

Government of Quebec – Tax credit for book publishing –
Administered by SODEC.

sodec.gouv.qc.ca

This publisher gratefully acknowledges the support
of the Société de développement des enterprises
culturelles du Québec.

Canada Council   Conseil des arts
for the Arts   du Canada

We gratefully acknowledge the support of the
Canada Council for the Arts for its publishing program.

We acknowledge the financial support of our
publishing activities by the Government of Canada
through the Canada Book Fund.

Canadian Living

THE ULTIMATE COOKBOOK

RECIPES FROM THE CANADIAN LIVING TEST KITCHEN

JUNIPER
PUBLISHING
A Quebecor Media Corporation

FROM OUR TEST KITCHEN

EVERYONE NEEDS THAT ONE GREAT REFERENCE COOKBOOK. It starts out stiff and crisp, smelling of fresh paper and ink. After a couple of years, you can easily pick out the most well-loved pages, which are dog-eared and stained with Worcestershire sauce or vanilla. After many more years, you'll find scribbles in the margins and discover that the book falls open almost automatically to certain places. It remains a cherished part of your collection because of what it represents: years of happy (or sometimes sad) moments, special occasions, lazy afternoons, rushed weeknights, first-ever attempts, joyful family traditions and, ultimately, a lifetime of food-focused memories. It's our honour to have created just such a book for Canadian cooks.

The Canadian Living Test Kitchen has been cooking right alongside Canadian families for 40 years now. Whether you've been with us since the magazine's first issue or have discovered our recipes more recently, you know Canadian Living is the most trusted recipe source in the country. We're proud to have earned that place in Canada's culinary heritage through our meticulous hard work—and a tremendous amount of trial and error.

Over the years, our recipe developers have created and fine-tuned every recipe until it's qualified to carry the Tested-Till-Perfect seal. It's a process we take very seriously. It means lugging countless bags from the grocery store and tracking down out-of-season items so that you can cook them in season when our long-in-progress magazines and cookbooks make their way to you. It means measuring and weighing every ingredient, timing every step with precision and occasionally setting off smoke alarms or barbecuing in our parkas and snow boots. Our copy team has edited each step to make sure it's clear and concise. We've ensured ingredients are readily available, equipment is common and methods are approachable. We've talked, tested and tasted our way through every single recipe we've ever published under the Canadian Living name.

To create this book, we dug into our hefty archives, choosing only the most essential and relevant recipes. We revised, updated and retested them along the way to ensure they remain as trustworthy as ever and, in some cases, so that they correspond with current-day package sizes and weights. We also developed many new recipes, each time aiming for the absolute best iteration—those winning dishes that just need to be in your repertoire—because we know you'll turn to them again and again, just like we do. What we've ended up with is the ultimate collection of Canadian Living's tried-and-true recipes. To us, these recipes reflect the cultural mosaic of our country and the past, present and future of our national cuisine.

This book is dedicated to you, dear Canadians. May we be in your kitchens, at your sides, making delicious memories for another 40 years.

Eat well and enjoy,

ANNABELLE WAUGH
FOOD DIRECTOR

"These recipes reflect the cultural mosaic of our country and the past, present and future of our national cuisine."

ANNABELLE WAUGH FOOD DIRECTOR

Our Tested-Till-Perfect guarantee means we've tested every recipe, using the same grocery store ingredients and household appliances as you do, until we're sure you'll get perfect results at home.

**CRUNCHY-TOPPED
MACARONI AND CHEESE**
page 253

Look for these helpful symbols throughout the book

 30 MINUTES OR LESS
In a hurry? These dishes are ready in half an hour or less

 VEGETARIAN
Need a meatless option? These dishes are vegetarian-friendly

 CANADIAN CLASSIC
These classic recipes are Canadian must-haves

 COMPLETE MEAL
These balanced meals contain protein, starch and vegetables

ULTIMATE CONTENTS

ULTIMATE APPETIZERS, DIPS & SPREADS | 1

"The appetizer has always been my favourite part of a meal. Not only do you have the hopeful anticipation of a great dinner ahead, but— for some reason—things always taste better when served in small amounts."

ANNABELLE WAUGH FOOD DIRECTOR

WILD MUSHROOM PÂTÉ

Making this rich, creamy spread ahead of time allows the wonderful flavours of the mushrooms to develop. Use any combination of exotic mushrooms you can find; in a pinch, opt for all cremini. Serve at room temperature with crackers or toast points.

HANDS-ON TIME
30 minutes

TOTAL TIME
45 minutes

MAKES
2½ cups

INGREDIENTS

2 tbsp	unsalted butter
675 g	mixed exotic mushrooms (such as shiitake, oyster or chanterelle), chopped
4	green onions, thinly sliced (light and dark green parts separated)
5	sprigs fresh thyme
3 tbsp	brandy
2 tsp	lemon juice
¼ tsp	each salt and pepper
1	pkg (250 g) cream cheese, softened (see tip, below)
2 tbsp	chopped fresh parsley

DIRECTIONS

In large nonstick skillet, melt butter over medium heat; cook mushrooms, light green parts of green onions and thyme, stirring occasionally, until mushrooms are tender and just beginning to brown, and no liquid remains, 12 to 15 minutes.

Add brandy; cook, stirring, until no liquid remains, about 2 minutes. Stir in lemon juice, salt and pepper; let cool completely. Discard thyme.

In food processor, pulse cream cheese until smooth. Add mushroom mixture; pulse, scraping down side of bowl often, until combined. Scrape into bowl; stir in dark green parts of green onions and parsley. Serve at room temperature. *(Make-ahead: Cover and refrigerate for up to 2 days. Bring to room temperature before serving.)*

NUTRITIONAL INFORMATION, PER 1 TBSP: about 32 cal, 1 g pro, 3 g total fat (2 g sat. fat), 1 g carb, trace fibre, 8 mg chol, 36 mg sodium, 90 mg potassium. % RDI: 1% calcium, 1% iron, 3% vit A, 2% vit C, 2% folate.

TIP FROM THE TEST KITCHEN
To soften cream cheese, let it stand on the counter at room temperature for about 1½ hours. If you're in a rush, microwave it on medium-low, 10 seconds at a time, until soft.

SPINACH AND CHEESE DIP

HANDS-ON TIME 20 minutes

TOTAL TIME 50 minutes

MAKES about 2 cups

INGREDIENTS

6 cups	packed baby spinach (about 200 g)
1 cup	shredded Swiss cheese
3 tbsp	grated Parmesan cheese
125 g	cream cheese (half 250 g pkg), softened
½ cup	mayonnaise
½ cup	sour cream
1	clove garlic, chopped
¼ tsp	each salt and pepper

DIRECTIONS

In saucepan of boiling lightly salted water, cook spinach until wilted, about 1 minute. Drain; let cool slightly. Using back of spoon, press out and discard excess liquid; chop spinach.

Combine Swiss with Parmesan; set aside.

In food processor, pulse spinach, cream cheese, mayonnaise, sour cream, garlic, salt and pepper, scraping down side of bowl often, until smooth.

Stir in all but 3 tbsp of the Swiss mixture. Scrape into 2-cup (500 mL) ovenproof dish; sprinkle with remaining Swiss mixture. *(Make-ahead: Cover and refrigerate for up to 24 hours. Add 10 minutes to baking time.)*

Bake on rimmed baking sheet in 350°F (180°C) oven until hot and bubbly, about 30 minutes. Broil until top is golden, about 1 minute. Let stand for 5 minutes before serving.

NUTRITIONAL INFORMATION, PER 1 TBSP: about 61 cal, 2 g pro, 6 g total fat (2 g sat. fat), 1 g carb, trace fibre, 10 mg chol, 86 mg sodium, 45 mg potassium. % RDI: 5% calcium, 2% iron, 9% vit A, 2% vit C, 5% folate.

VARIATION
KALE AND CHEESE DIP

Replace baby spinach with 6 cups packed baby kale (about 125 g).

EDAMAME WASABI SPREAD

HANDS-ON TIME 10 minutes

TOTAL TIME 10 minutes

MAKES 1½ cups

INGREDIENTS

2 cups	frozen shelled edamame
2 tbsp	lime juice
2 tbsp	vegetable oil
2	cloves garlic
1½ tsp	prepared wasabi (see tip, below)
1 tsp	sesame oil
¼ tsp	each salt and pepper

DIRECTIONS

In large pot of boiling water, cook edamame until slightly tender, about 3 minutes. Drain and rinse under cold water; drain well.

In food processor, purée together edamame, lime juice, vegetable oil, 1 tbsp water, garlic, wasabi, sesame oil, salt and pepper until smooth, about 2 minutes. *(Make-ahead: Refrigerate in airtight container for up to 3 days.)*

NUTRITIONAL INFORMATION, PER 1 TBSP: about 25 cal, 1 g pro, 2 g total fat (trace sat. fat), 1 g carb, 1 g fibre, 0 mg chol, 25 mg sodium, 48 mg potassium. % RDI: 1% calcium, 1% iron, 2% vit C, 15% folate.

TIP FROM THE TEST KITCHEN
Look for tubes of prepared wasabi in the Asian section or at the sushi counter of the supermarket.

CREAMY DILL DIP ③⓪ ◐

HANDS-ON TIME 5 minutes

TOTAL TIME 5 minutes

MAKES 1⅓ cups

INGREDIENTS

⅔ cup	light mayonnaise
½ cup	sour cream
¼ cup	chopped fresh dill
1 tsp	liquid honey
1	clove garlic, pressed or grated

DIRECTIONS

Stir together mayonnaise, sour cream, dill, honey and garlic. *(Make-ahead: Cover and refrigerate for up to 5 days.)*

NUTRITIONAL INFORMATION, PER 2 TBSP: about 70 cal, 1 g pro, 6 g total fat (2 g sat. fat), 3 g carb, trace fibre, 10 mg chol, 108 mg sodium, 32 mg potassium. % RDI: 2% calcium, 2% vit A.

VARIATIONS
RANCH DIP

Omit dill and honey. Stir together mayonnaise, sour cream and garlic as directed. Stir in 2 tbsp each chopped fresh chives and parsley, 2 tbsp minced or grated onion, 1 tsp Dijon mustard, dash cayenne-based hot pepper sauce (such as Frank's RedHot) and pinch pepper.

BLUE CHEESE DIP

Omit dill and garlic. Stir together mayonnaise, sour cream and honey as directed. Stir in ½ cup crumbled blue cheese, 1 tsp white wine vinegar and pinch pepper.

SESAME ALMOND DIP ③⓪ ◐

HANDS-ON TIME 10 minutes

TOTAL TIME 10 minutes

MAKES about 1¼ cups

INGREDIENTS

½ cup	smooth almond butter
3 tbsp	tahini
4 tsp	lime juice
1 tbsp	sodium-reduced soy sauce
1	piece (¾ inch/2 cm) fresh ginger, peeled and sliced
1 tsp	liquid honey
1	clove garlic
¼ tsp	each salt and pepper
	toasted sesame seeds (optional)

DIRECTIONS

In blender, purée together almond butter, ⅓ cup water, tahini, lime juice, soy sauce, ginger, honey, garlic, salt and pepper until smooth, adding up to 2 tbsp more water if needed to reach desired consistency.

Scrape into serving dish; sprinkle with sesame seeds (if using). *(Make-ahead: Cover and refrigerate for up to 24 hours. To serve, let stand at room temperature for 1 hour; whisk in more water, ½ tsp at a time, until mixture reaches desired consistency.)*

NUTRITIONAL INFORMATION, PER 1 TBSP: about 56 cal, 2 g pro, 5 g total fat (1 g sat. fat), 2 g carb, 1 g fibre, 0 mg chol, 90 mg sodium, 63 mg potassium. % RDI: 2% calcium, 3% iron, 1% vit C, 3% folate.

TIP FROM THE TEST KITCHEN
The dip gets thicker the longer it stands; thin it with a bit of water before serving, if needed.

CHICKEN LIVER MOUSSE

Clarified butter seals the mousse to keep out air and extend its shelf life. The butter also adds another layer of luxurious flavour. Chilling the spread for at least 24 hours before serving lets the flavours meld for maximum deliciousness.

HANDS-ON TIME
25 minutes

TOTAL TIME
25½ hours

MAKES
about 1 cup

INGREDIENTS

225 g	chicken livers
½ tsp	each salt and pepper
½ cup	unsalted butter
½ cup	chopped shallots
⅓ cup	thinly sliced peeled Granny Smith apple
1	clove garlic, finely chopped
1 tsp	finely chopped fresh thyme
3 tbsp	sherry or brandy
1 tsp	finely chopped fresh chives

DIRECTIONS

Separate lobes of livers, removing and discarding any connective tissue and fat; sprinkle livers with ¼ tsp each of the salt and pepper. In skillet, melt 1 tbsp of the butter over medium heat; cook shallots, apple, garlic and thyme, stirring often, until softened, 5 minutes. Push to 1 side of pan.

Add 2 tsp of the remaining butter to pan; melt over medium-high heat. Cook livers, turning once, until just a hint of pink remains in centre of thickest part, about 3 minutes. Add sherry; cook for 30 seconds.

Scrape into food processor; purée until smooth. Let cool slightly. Cut ¼ cup of the remaining butter into pieces. With motor running, drop butter into liver mixture, 1 piece at a time, waiting until combined before adding next piece. Sprinkle in remaining salt and pepper; process until shiny, about 1 minute.

Press through fine-mesh sieve into bowl. Scrape into two 6-oz (175 mL) ramekins or dishes. Cover with plastic wrap; refrigerate until set, about 1 hour. Remove plastic wrap; sprinkle with chives.

In small saucepan, melt remaining butter; skim off froth. Pour over chives, leaving any milky sediment behind. Cover and refrigerate until mousse is set and flavours meld, about 24 hours. *(Make-ahead: Cover with plastic wrap and refrigerate for up to 4 days.)*

NUTRITIONAL INFORMATION, PER 1 TBSP: about 78 cal, 3 g pro, 6 g total fat (4 g sat. fat), 2 g carb, trace fibre, 77 mg chol, 84 mg sodium, 57 mg potassium. % RDI: 1% calcium, 9% iron, 76% vit A, 7% vit C, 34% folate.

COUNTRY PÂTÉ

Seasoning is key to a good pâté. This recipe may appear to contain a lot of salt, pepper and spices, but they mellow as the pâté cures. Serve with Dijon mustard, baguette slices and cornichons for an authentic French appetizer.

HANDS-ON TIME
35 minutes

TOTAL TIME
33 hours

MAKES
10 servings

INGREDIENTS

PORK AND VEAL MIXTURE:

1 tsp	black peppercorns (or ground black pepper)
10	allspice berries (or 1 tsp ground allspice)
3	whole cloves (or pinch ground cloves)
450 g	lean ground pork
225 g	ground veal
½ cup	unsalted pistachios
¼ cup	finely chopped shallots
3 tbsp	cognac or brandy
1 tbsp	cornstarch
2½ tsp	coarse salt
2 tsp	chopped fresh thyme
1	clove garlic, minced

CHICKEN MIXTURE:

225 g	boneless skinless chicken thighs, halved lengthwise
170 g	chicken livers, trimmed and chopped
1 tbsp	cognac or brandy
½ tsp	salt
¼ tsp	pepper
450 g	bacon
115 g	piece Black Forest ham, cut in thick strips

DIRECTIONS

PORK AND VEAL MIXTURE: If using whole spices, in spice grinder or using mortar and pestle, finely grind together peppercorns, allspice berries and cloves. Pour ground spices into large bowl. Add pork, veal, pistachios, shallots, cognac, cornstarch, salt, thyme and garlic; stir to combine. Cover with plastic wrap; refrigerate for 3 hours. *(Make-ahead: Refrigerate for up to 24 hours.)*

CHICKEN MIXTURE: While pork mixture is chilling, in bowl, combine chicken thighs, chicken livers, cognac, salt and pepper. Cover with plastic wrap; refrigerate for 3 hours. *(Make-ahead: Refrigerate for up to 24 hours.)*

ASSEMBLY: Line terrine mould or 8- x 4-inch (1.5 L) loaf pan with bacon, leaving enough overhang to cover pâté completely.

Gently press one-third of the pork and veal mixture into mould. Arrange chicken thighs lengthwise in mould. Press half of the remaining pork and veal mixture over top. Arrange chicken livers in row down centre. Arrange ham strips down either side of livers. Gently press remaining pork and veal mixture over top, smoothing loaf. Fold bacon overhang over top to cover completely.

Place mould in centre of large double-thickness square of foil; bring sides up and over to cover mould, folding seam several times to seal. Place in roasting pan; pour enough warm water into pan to come halfway up sides of mould. Bake in 325°F (160°C) oven until instant-read thermometer inserted in centre reads 170°F (77°C), about 2½ hours.

Remove mould from water bath; unwrap and let cool for 30 minutes. Refrigerate until cold, about 3 hours. Wrap in plastic wrap and refrigerate for 24 hours. *(Make-ahead: Refrigerate for up to 4 days.)*

To serve, run knife around mould and invert pâté onto cutting board. Scrape away gelatin. (If crisp bacon is desired, brown loaf in skillet over medium heat until lightly browned, about 1 minute per side.) Slice with hot knife.

NUTRITIONAL INFORMATION, PER SERVING: about 421 cal, 28 g pro, 31 g total fat (15 g sat. fat), 5 g carb, 1 g fibre, 175 mg chol, 994 mg sodium, 498 mg potassium. % RDI: 2% calcium, 22% iron, 86% vit A, 10% vit C, 45% folate.

BAKED RHUBARB TOMATO CHUTNEY BRIE

Puff pastry is a great secret weapon to keep in the freezer for making easy appetizers. Here it only take a few minutes to wrap around Brie and a tangy rhubarb chutney, plus you can turn the leftovers into quick cheese straws (see tip, below).

HANDS-ON TIME
15 minutes

TOTAL TIME
1 hour

MAKES
4 to 6 servings

INGREDIENTS

1	round (4 inches/ 10 cm) Brie or Camembert cheese
1	sheet (half 450 g pkg) frozen butter puff pastry, thawed (see tip, below)
⅓ cup	Rhubarb Tomato Chutney (page 339)
1	egg, lightly beaten

DIRECTIONS

Cut Brie in half horizontally to make 2 equal rounds; set aside.

On lightly floured surface, roll out pastry to ⅛-inch (3 mm) thickness; cut into 10-inch (25 cm) round. Place 1 of the Brie rounds, cut side up, in centre. Spread chutney over Brie; top with remaining Brie round, cut side down. Fold pastry up over cheese, overlapping in centre and sealing with some of the egg; brush top with remaining egg. *(Make-ahead: Cover and refrigerate for up to 4 hours.)*

Place on rimmed baking sheet; bake in 400°F (200°C) oven until golden and puffed, 25 to 30 minutes. Let stand for 20 minutes. To serve, cut into wedges with serrated knife.

NUTRITIONAL INFORMATION, PER EACH OF 6 SERVINGS: about 280 cal, 9 g pro, 19 g total fat (7 g sat. fat), 19 g carb, 1 g fibre, 59 mg chol, 272 mg sodium. % RDI: 7% calcium, 8% iron, 7% vit A, 2% vit C, 16% folate.

TIP FROM THE TEST KITCHEN
Turn the leftover half-package of puff pastry into easy cheese straws! Roll out the pastry into a ⅛-inch (3 mm) thick rectangle. Brush it with a bit of Dijon mustard beaten with egg; sprinkle with some Parmesan cheese and a tiny bit of cayenne pepper. Cut the pastry lengthwise into ½-inch (1 cm) wide strips. Turn the ends of the strips in opposite directions to make twists. Bake them on a rimless baking sheet in a 425°F (220°C) oven until they're crisp, puffed and golden, about 14 minutes.

MARINATED ROASTED PEPPERS AND FETA

Serve these Mediterranean-inspired feta cubes and roasted peppers with sliced baguette or pita wedges to soak up the spicy, herb-infused oil. Crushing the fresh herbs before adding them to the oil mixture releases more of their pleasing aromas and flavours.

HANDS-ON TIME
15 minutes

TOTAL TIME
2¼ hours

MAKES
8 to 12 servings

INGREDIENTS

½ cup	chopped drained jarred roasted red peppers
½ cup	extra-virgin olive oil
4	sprigs each fresh oregano and thyme, crushed
¼ tsp	hot pepper flakes
280 g	feta cheese (see tip, right), cubed

DIRECTIONS

In shallow dish, stir together red peppers, oil, oregano, thyme and hot pepper flakes; stir in feta. Cover and refrigerate for 2 hours. *(Make-ahead: Refrigerate for up to 24 hours.)*

NUTRITIONAL INFORMATION, PER EACH OF 12 SERVINGS: about 145 cal, 4 g pro, 14 g total fat (5 g sat. fat), 2 g carb, trace fibre, 22 mg chol, 277 mg sodium, 31 mg potassium. % RDI: 11% calcium, 3% iron, 6% vit A, 17% vit C, 5% folate.

TIP FROM THE TEST KITCHEN
Feta cheese is brined to give it a salty flavour—rinse it you find it's too salty for your taste.

SAVOURY CHEDDAR CHEESECAKE SPREAD ◐

HANDS-ON TIME
20 minutes

TOTAL TIME
4½ hours

MAKES
about 2 cups

Sharp cheese, shallots and savoury spices make this velvety cheesecake an unexpected and tasty starter. Spread it on baguette slices, crostini or crackers.

INGREDIENTS

1	pkg (250 g) cream cheese, softened
1	egg
½ cup	shredded old Cheddar cheese
1	shallot, grated
¼ tsp	each cayenne pepper and smoked paprika
½ cup	chopped toasted pecans
½ cup	peach chutney

DIRECTIONS

In bowl, beat cream cheese until fluffy. On low speed, beat in egg, beating well and scraping down side of bowl often. Beat in Cheddar, shallot, cayenne pepper and smoked paprika.

Stir pecans with chutney; remove half and set aside. Stir remaining pecan mixture into cheesecake batter. Scrape into parchment paper–lined 5-inch (600 mL) springform pan. Spread reserved pecan mixture on top. Centre pan on large square of foil; press up side of pan.

Set springform pan in larger pan; pour enough hot water into larger pan to come 1 inch (2.5 cm) up side of springform pan. Bake in 300°F (150°C) oven until shine disappears and edge is set yet centre still jiggles slightly, about 1¼ hours. Turn off oven. Immediately run knife around edge of cake. Let cool in oven for 1 hour.

Remove springform pan from water and transfer to rack; remove foil and let cool completely. Refrigerate until chilled and set, about 2 hours. *(Make-ahead: Cover and refrigerate for up to 4 days.)*

NUTRITIONAL INFORMATION, PER 1 TBSP: about 57 cal, 1 g pro, 5 g total fat (2 g sat. fat), 3 g carb, trace fibre, 16 mg chol, 90 mg sodium, 26 mg potassium. % RDI: 2% calcium, 1% iron, 4% vit A, 1% folate.

MINI SMOKED SALMON DILL QUICHES

HANDS-ON TIME
20 minutes

TOTAL TIME
1½ hours

MAKES
24 pieces

Weighing down the crusts with pie weights or dried beans is worth the extra effort; this step prevents the pastry from puffing up and taking up the space you'll need for the quiche filling.

INGREDIENTS

1	batch Easy-Roll Pie Pastry (page 348), see tip, below
170 g	smoked salmon, chopped
125 g	cream cheese (half 250 g pkg), diced
4	eggs
1 cup	milk
2½ tbsp	chopped fresh dill
2	green onions, minced
¼ tsp	each salt and pepper

DIRECTIONS

On floured surface, roll out pastry to generous ⅛-inch (3 mm) thickness. Using 4-inch (10 cm) round pastry cutter, cut out 24 rounds. Fit into 24 muffin cups, without trimming. Prick all over with fork. Place on rimmed baking sheet; refrigerate for 30 minutes.

Line shells with foil; fill with pie weights or dried beans. Bake on bottom rack in 400°F (200°C) oven until rims are light golden, about 10 minutes. Remove weights and foil; let cool in pan on rack.

Sprinkle salmon and cream cheese into shells. Whisk together eggs, milk, dill, green onions, salt and pepper; pour into shells.

Bake in 375°F (190°C) oven until knife inserted in centre of several comes out clean, about 20 minutes. Let cool in pan on rack for 5 minutes. *(Make-ahead: Let cool. Layer between waxed paper in airtight container and refrigerate for up to 24 hours or freeze for up to 2 weeks. Thaw if frozen; reheat in 350°F/180°C oven for 10 minutes.)*

NUTRITIONAL INFORMATION, PER PIECE: about 151 cal, 4 g pro, 11 g total fat (5 g sat. fat), 9 g carb, trace fibre, 52 mg chol, 177 mg sodium, 63 mg potassium. % RDI: 2% calcium, 6% iron, 7% vit A, 13% folate.

TIP FROM THE TEST KITCHEN
Easy-Roll Pie Pastry is a Test Kitchen classic used for many of our pies and savouries—it's worth making and freezing extra to keep on hand for last-minute baking. To use frozen pastry, thaw it in the fridge so the butter stays cold—the little pockets of cold butter are what make the crust flaky.

SPICE MARKET BEEF AND LAMB CIGARS

HANDS-ON TIME
45 minutes

TOTAL TIME
1 hour

MAKES
20 pieces

In Morocco, these rich spiced meat–filled pastries are called betzel *and are made with a thin pastry called* warka. *Spring roll wrappers make an excellent, easy-to-find substitute.*

INGREDIENTS

115 g	each lean ground beef and lamb (or all beef)
1 tbsp	vegetable oil
1	onion, finely chopped
2	cloves garlic, minced
2 tbsp	lemon juice
½ tsp	each ground allspice and grated nutmeg
¼ tsp	each salt and pepper
1	egg, separated
¼ cup	minced fresh parsley
10	square (6-inch/ 15 cm) spring roll wrappers
	vegetable oil for deep-frying
	lemon wedges

DIRECTIONS

In large nonstick skillet, sauté beef and lamb over medium-high heat, breaking up with spoon, until no longer pink, about 5 minutes. Drain off any fat; transfer to bowl.

Add oil to skillet; heat over medium-high heat. Sauté onion and garlic until golden, about 5 minutes.

Return beef mixture to skillet. Add 1 cup water, lemon juice, allspice, nutmeg, salt and pepper; reduce heat, cover and simmer, stirring occasionally, until no liquid remains, about 20 minutes. Transfer to bowl; let cool slightly. Stir in egg yolk and parsley; let cool completely. *(Make-ahead: Cover and refrigerate for up to 24 hours.)*

In small bowl, whisk egg white until frothy. Cut spring roll wrappers in half. Place 1 tbsp filling in 3-inch (8 cm) strip along centre of 1 long edge of wrapper. Brush short edges with egg white; fold to meet in centre. Starting at filled edge, roll up tightly to resemble cigar. Repeat with remaining wrappers and filling. *(Make-ahead: Cover with plastic wrap and refrigerate on parchment paper–lined rimmed baking sheet for up to 8 hours.)*

Pour enough oil into large deep skillet to come 2 inches (5 cm) up side; heat until deep-fryer thermometer reads 325°F (160°C). Working in batches, deep-fry rolls, turning once, until golden and crispy, about 90 seconds per batch. Using slotted spoon, transfer to paper towel–lined plate; let drain. Serve hot with lemon wedges.

NUTRITIONAL INFORMATION, PER PIECE: about 102 cal, 4 g pro, 5 g total fat (1 g sat. fat), 10 g carb, trace fibre, 18 mg chol, 131 mg sodium. % RDI: 1% calcium, 6% iron, 1% vit A, 2% vit C, 8% folate.

VARIATIONS

SPICE MARKET BEEF AND LAMB TRIANGLES

Reduce spring roll wrappers to 5; cut each into 4 equal squares. Place 1 tbsp filling in centre of each. Brush edges with egg white; fold over and press edges together to form triangle.

MINT BEEF AND LAMB CIGARS

Replace allspice and nutmeg with 2 tsp each ground cumin and sweet paprika. Replace 2 tbsp of the parsley with 2 tbsp finely chopped fresh mint.

SMOKED TROUT AND SALMON RILLETTE

This smoky potted fish takes only a few minutes to put together. Spread on toasty crostini and topped with crispy garlic chips, it's a simple yet elegant party dish.

HANDS-ON TIME
35 minutes

TOTAL TIME
1¼ hours

MAKES
2 cups

INGREDIENTS

GARLIC CHIPS AND CROSTINI:

⅓ cup	olive oil
4	large cloves garlic, thinly sliced
1	baguette, thinly sliced

RILLETTE:

225 g	skinless salmon fillet
pinch	salt
⅓ cup	butter, melted and cooled
2 tbsp	olive oil
3 tbsp	finely chopped green onion
2 tbsp	finely chopped drained capers
4 tsp	chopped fresh parsley
4 tsp	lemon juice
170 g	smoked trout, skinned
¼ tsp	each pepper and sweet paprika

DIRECTIONS

GARLIC CHIPS AND CROSTINI: In small saucepan, heat oil over medium-low heat; fry garlic, stirring often, until golden and crisp, about 3 minutes. Using slotted spoon, transfer to paper towel–lined plate; let drain.

Brush 1 side of each baguette slice with garlic oil from pan; place on rimmed baking sheet. Bake in 350°F (180°C) oven, turning once, until golden and crisp, about 10 minutes. *(Make-ahead: Store garlic chips and crostini in airtight container for up to 4 days.)*

RILLETTE: Sprinkle salmon with salt; microwave on high until fish flakes easily when tested, about 2 minutes. Pat dry with paper towel.

In bowl, stir butter with oil; stir in green onion, capers, parsley and lemon juice. Using fork, flake salmon and trout; stir into butter mixture along with pepper and paprika.

Scrape rillette into serving dish; cover and refrigerate for 30 minutes. *(Make-ahead: Refrigerate for up to 2 days; let stand at room temperature for 30 minutes before serving.)* Serve on crostini topped with garlic chips.

NUTRITIONAL INFORMATION, PER 1 TBSP: about 91 cal, 4 g pro, 6 g total fat (2 g sat. fat), 5 g carb, trace fibre, 13 mg chol, 193 mg sodium, 69 mg potassium. % RDI: 1% calcium, 2% iron, 3% vit A, 2% vit C, 5% folate.

TIP FROM THE TEST KITCHEN
Instead of using a microwave, you can cook the salmon in a little oil in a skillet over medium heat.

GOUDA BACON GOUGÈRES

These small puffs are simply profiteroles studded with bacon and Gouda. This recipe can easily be halved, but the puffs freeze well, so you might as well make the whole batch and keep them on hand to share with friends who drop by for a drink.

HANDS-ON TIME
10 minutes

TOTAL TIME
45 minutes

MAKES
about 62 pieces

INGREDIENTS

½ cup	butter
pinch	salt
1¼ cups	all-purpose flour
4	eggs
1 cup	shredded Gouda cheese
¼ cup	crumbled cooked bacon (about 5 strips)
½ tsp	chopped fresh thyme

DIRECTIONS

In small heavy-bottomed saucepan, bring 1 cup water, butter and salt to boil. Remove from heat. Add flour all at once, stirring vigorously with wooden spoon until mixture forms smooth ball that pulls away from side of pan.

Return to medium-low heat; cook, stirring constantly, for 2 minutes. Remove from heat; let cool for 5 minutes.

Stirring vigorously with wooden spoon, beat in eggs, 1 at a time, beating well after each addition until smooth and shiny. Beat in Gouda, bacon and thyme.

Spoon dough into pastry bag fitted with ½-inch (1 cm) round tip or resealable plastic bag with corner snipped off. Pipe mounds, 1 inch (2.5 cm) in diameter and about 1 inch (2.5 cm) apart, onto greased or parchment paper–lined rimless baking sheets. Using wet fingertip, gently flatten peak of each mound.

Bake, 1 sheet at a time, in 400°F (200°C) oven until puffed, golden and crisp, about 16 minutes. *(Make-ahead: Let cool. Store in airtight container for up to 2 days. Or freeze for up to 1 month; thaw and bake in 350°F/180°C oven until hot, about 5 minutes.)*

NUTRITIONAL INFORMATION, PER PIECE: about 36 cal, 1 g pro, 3 g total fat (1 g sat. fat), 2 g carb, trace fibre, 19 mg chol, 41 mg sodium, 12 mg potassium. % RDI: 1% calcium, 1% iron, 2% vit A, 3% folate.

TIP FROM THE TEST KITCHEN
When you're frying bacon, make sure to turn the strips often to keep the ends from curling up.

SAUSAGE ROLLS ⊙
WITH HONEY MUSTARD DIP

If you really like heat, you might not find the hot Italian sausage all that fiery. Add a pinch of hot pepper flakes to the filling if you want a spicier roll.

HANDS-ON TIME
30 minutes

TOTAL TIME
1 hour

MAKES
about 63 pieces

INGREDIENTS

SAUSAGE ROLLS:

¼ cup	fresh bread crumbs (see tip, below)
2	eggs
¼ cup	milk
340 g	hot Italian sausages, casings removed
half	onion, minced
1	clove garlic, minced
½ tsp	each fennel seeds and dried oregano
3	sheets (one and a half 450 g pkg) frozen butter puff pastry, thawed

HONEY MUSTARD DIP:

¼ cup	prepared hot mustard
2 tbsp	liquid honey

DIRECTIONS

SAUSAGE ROLLS: In bowl, mix together bread crumbs, 1 of the eggs and milk until smooth; let stand for 5 minutes. Add sausages, onion, garlic, fennel seeds and oregano, combining with hands.

Cut each pastry sheet lengthwise into 3 equal strips. Spoon sausage mixture into piping bag fitted with ¾-inch (2 cm) plain tip; pipe along 1 long edge of each strip. Whisk remaining egg with 2 tsp water; brush over opposite edge and, starting at meat side, roll up. Cut into 1½-inch (4 cm) pieces.

Place, seam side down, on parchment paper–lined rimmed baking sheet; pierce top pastry of each piece with tip of sharp knife. *(Make-ahead: Layer between waxed paper in airtight container and freeze for up to 2 weeks; thaw in refrigerator.)* Bake in 425°F (220°C) oven until golden, about 18 minutes.

HONEY MUSTARD DIP: Whisk mustard with honey; serve with sausage rolls.

NUTRITIONAL INFORMATION, PER PIECE WITH DIP: about 67 cal, 2 g pro, 4 g total fat (2 g sat. fat), 5 g carb, trace fibre, 13 mg chol, 97 mg sodium, 22 mg potassium. % RDI: 1% calcium, 3% iron, 1% vit A.

TIP FROM THE TEST KITCHEN
Fresh bread crumbs are easy to make and freeze well. Place cubes of day-old bread in a food processor and process until they are in fine crumbs. Spoon them into a resealable freezer bag, press out as much air as possible and freeze the bag for up to 3 months.

ASPARAGUS AND RICOTTA CROSTINI ③⓪

Crostini are excellent for parties—they are simple to make and can be the base for a huge variety of different toppings. The three on these pages offer an array of tastes and textures to enjoy.

HANDS-ON TIME
15 minutes

TOTAL TIME
15 minutes

MAKES
15 pieces

INGREDIENTS

15	thick (¼-inch/5 mm) slices baguette
1 tsp	olive oil
1	clove garlic, halved
8	spears asparagus, trimmed
½ cup	ricotta cheese
2 tsp	chopped fresh chives
½ tsp	grated lemon zest
1 tbsp	lemon juice
¼ tsp	salt
pinch	pepper
½ cup	thinly sliced radishes

DIRECTIONS

On rimmed baking sheet, drizzle baguette slices with oil; bake in 400°F (200°C) oven until crispy and light golden, about 6 minutes. Rub tops with cut sides of garlic halves. Set aside. *(Make-ahead: Store in airtight container for up to 24 hours.)*

In saucepan of boiling salted water, cook asparagus for 1 minute; drain. Chill in ice water; drain and pat dry. Slice diagonally into 1-inch (2.5 cm) long pieces.

Stir together ricotta, chives, lemon zest, 2 tsp of the lemon juice, half of the salt and the pepper; set aside. *(Make-ahead: Refrigerate asparagus and ricotta mixture in separate airtight containers for up to 24 hours.)*

Toss together asparagus, radishes, and remaining lemon juice and salt. Top crostini with ricotta mixture, and then asparagus mixture.

NUTRITIONAL INFORMATION, PER PIECE: about 40 cal, 2 g pro, 2 g total fat (1 g sat. fat), 5 g carb, 1 g fibre, 4 mg chol, 144 mg sodium, 46 mg potassium. % RDI: 2% calcium, 2% iron, 2% vit A, 3% vit C, 9% folate.

TIP FROM THE TEST KITCHEN
A resealable plastic bag is fine for storing the crostini if you bake them ahead. Just make sure the crostini are completely cool, and press all the air out of the bag to keep the toasts nice and crisp.

PESTO WHITE BEAN CROSTINI 🗓 ◔

HANDS-ON TIME 15 minutes

TOTAL TIME 15 minutes

MAKES 15 pieces

INGREDIENTS

15	thick (¼-inch/5 mm) slices baguette
1 tsp	olive oil
1	clove garlic, halved
1 cup	drained canned white kidney or cannellini beans
pinch	each salt and pepper
1 tbsp	prepared pesto or Classic Pesto (page 330)
5	cherry tomatoes, cut in thirds

DIRECTIONS

On rimmed baking sheet, drizzle baguette slices with oil; bake in 400°F (200°C) oven until crispy and light golden, about 6 minutes. Rub tops with cut side of 1 garlic half. Set aside. *(Make-ahead: Store in airtight container for up to 24 hours.)*

In food processor, purée beans, remaining garlic half, salt and pepper until smooth. *(Make-ahead: Refrigerate in airtight container for up to 24 hours.)*

Spread bean mixture over crostini. Dot with pesto; top with tomatoes.

NUTRITIONAL INFORMATION, PER PIECE: about 39 cal, 2 g pro, 1 g total fat (trace sat. fat), 6 g carb, 1 g fibre, 0 mg chol, 89 mg sodium, 52 mg potassium. % RDI: 1% calcium, 3% iron, 1% vit A, 2% vit C, 5% folate.

PEAS AND PROSCIUTTO CROSTINI 🗓

HANDS-ON TIME 15 minutes

TOTAL TIME 15 minutes

MAKES 15 pieces

INGREDIENTS

15	thick (¼-inch/5 mm) slices baguette
1 tbsp	olive oil
4	cloves garlic
2	shallots, chopped
1 cup	frozen peas
pinch	each salt and pepper
¼ cup	soft goat cheese
3	slices prosciutto, coarsely chopped

DIRECTIONS

On rimmed baking sheet, drizzle baguette slices with 1 tsp of the oil; bake in 400°F (200°C) oven until crispy and light golden, about 6 minutes. Halve 1 of the garlic cloves; rub tops of baguette slices with cut sides. Discard garlic halves; set crostini aside. *(Make-ahead: Store in airtight container for up to 24 hours.)*

Meanwhile, chop remaining garlic cloves. In skillet, heat remaining oil over medium heat; cook shallots and garlic until softened, about 2 minutes. Add peas, salt and pepper; cook until peas are hot, about 5 minutes.

In food processor, purée pea mixture until smooth, about 1 minute. Add goat cheese; purée until smooth. *(Make-ahead: Refrigerate in airtight container for up to 24 hours.)*

Spread goat cheese mixture over crostini; top with chopped prosciutto.

NUTRITIONAL INFORMATION, PER PIECE: about 55 cal, 3 g pro, 2 g total fat (1 g sat. fat), 6 g carb, 1 g fibre, 5 mg chol, 137 mg sodium, 44 mg potassium. % RDI: 1% calcium, 4% iron, 3% vit A, 2% vit C, 5% folate.

VEGETABLE SAMOSAS ◐
WITH CILANTRO CHUTNEY

These potato-filled pastries have an authentic street-food appeal and are a fun project to make at home. You can fry or bake them; in either case, they're best freshly made, but you can freeze them for convenience.

HANDS-ON TIME
1½ hours

TOTAL TIME
1¾ hours

MAKES
24 pieces

INGREDIENTS

DOUGH:

2 cups	all-purpose flour
1 tsp	cumin seeds (preferably black)
½ tsp	salt
½ cup	cold butter, cubed
½ cup	milk

FILLING:

2 cups	diced peeled potatoes
½ cup	diced carrots
3 tbsp	vegetable oil
1 tsp	each fennel seeds and cumin seeds
1 tsp	brown or black mustard seeds
½ tsp	ground turmeric
½ tsp	each coriander seeds and fenugreek seeds
¼ tsp	cayenne pepper
1	onion, chopped
2	cloves garlic, minced
1 tbsp	grated fresh ginger
½ tsp	salt
½ cup	frozen peas
3 tbsp	lemon juice
2 tbsp	chopped fresh cilantro
	vegetable oil for deep-frying
	Cilantro Chutney (below)

DIRECTIONS

DOUGH: In food processor or bowl with pastry blender, combine flour, cumin seeds and salt; pulse or cut in butter until in fine crumbs. Pulse or stir in milk until ball begins to form. Press into disc; wrap and refrigerate for 30 minutes. *(Make-ahead: Refrigerate for up to 24 hours.)*

FILLING: In large saucepan of boiling salted water, cook potatoes and carrots until tender, about 10 minutes; drain.

While potatoes and carrots are cooking, in large skillet, heat oil over medium heat. Cook fennel, cumin and mustard seeds; turmeric; coriander and fenugreek seeds; and cayenne pepper just until cumin seeds begin to pop, about 1 minute.

Add onion, garlic, ginger and salt; cook until softened, about 3 minutes. Stir in potato mixture and peas. Stir in lemon juice and cilantro; let cool.

ASSEMBLY: Cut dough into 12 pieces; form each into flat round. On floured surface, roll out each piece into 6-inch (15 cm) circle; cut in half. Working with 1 piece at a time, moisten half of the cut edge with water. Form cone shape by overlapping cut edges by ¼ inch (5 mm). **PHOTO A**

Fill with rounded 1 tbsp potato mixture. Moisten top inside edges of pastry; press to seal. **PHOTO B**

Trim jagged edges of pastry; crimp edge with fork.

Pour enough oil into deep saucepan or pot to come 2 inches (5 cm) up side; heat until deep-fryer thermometer reads 350°F (180°C).

Working in batches, deep-fry samosas, turning often, until golden, about 4 minutes per batch; drain on paper towel–lined baking sheet. (Or bake in 425°F/220°C oven for 15 minutes.) Serve warm with Cilantro Chutney. *(Make-ahead: Let cool. Refrigerate in airtight container for up to 24 hours. Or freeze on waxed paper–lined baking sheet; transfer to airtight container and freeze for up to 2 weeks. Bake in 350°F/180°C oven until hot in centre, 10 to 20 minutes.)*

NUTRITIONAL INFORMATION, PER PIECE: about 133 cal, 2 g pro, 9 g total fat (3 g sat. fat), 12 g carb, 1 g fibre, 12 mg chol, 200 mg sodium. % RDI: 2% calcium, 6% iron, 11% vit A, 5% vit C, 8% folate.

CILANTRO CHUTNEY

In food processor, purée together 4 cups fresh cilantro leaves; ¼ cup water; half green finger hot pepper, seeded; 4 tsp lemon juice; and ¼ tsp salt until smooth. *(Make-ahead: Refrigerate in airtight container for up to 4 hours.)* **MAKES** ½ cup

A

B

SWEET-AND-SOUR MEATBALLS

HANDS-ON TIME
40 minutes

TOTAL TIME
40 minutes

MAKES
about 60 pieces

Grenadine gives the tangy sweet-and-sour sauce on these bite-size meatballs its signature bright red colour; look for this syrup in the drinks section of your grocery store.

INGREDIENTS

MEATBALLS:

¼ cup	dried bread crumbs
2	eggs, lightly beaten
2	green onions, finely chopped
3	cloves garlic, minced
1 tbsp	minced fresh ginger
1 tbsp	Worcestershire sauce
½ tsp	pepper
¼ tsp	salt
900 g	lean ground beef
2 tsp	vegetable oil

SWEET-AND-SOUR SAUCE:

⅔ cup	pineapple juice
½ cup	ketchup
⅓ cup	packed brown sugar
⅓ cup	grenadine
⅓ cup	vinegar
3 tbsp	cornstarch

DIRECTIONS

MEATBALLS: In bowl, stir together bread crumbs, eggs, green onions, garlic, ginger, Worcestershire sauce, pepper and salt; mix in beef. Roll by 1 tbsp into balls. *(Make-ahead: Cover and refrigerate for up to 12 hours.)*

In large nonstick skillet, heat oil over medium-high heat; working in batches, cook meatballs, turning occasionally, until browned and instant-read thermometer inserted into several reads 160°F (71°C), about 10 minutes per batch.

SWEET-AND-SOUR SAUCE: While meatballs are cooking, in small saucepan, whisk together ¾ cup water, pineapple juice, ketchup, brown sugar, grenadine and vinegar. Bring to boil over medium-high heat; reduce heat and simmer for 5 minutes.

Stir cornstarch with 2 tbsp water; whisk into sauce and simmer until thickened, about 30 seconds. Toss three-quarters of the sauce with meatballs. Arrange in serving dish; top with remaining sauce.

NUTRITIONAL INFORMATION, PER PIECE: about 45 cal, 3 g pro, 2 g total fat (1 g sat. fat), 4 g carb, trace fibre, 14 mg chol, 49 mg sodium, 57 mg potassium. % RDI: 1% calcium, 3% iron, 1% vit A, 2% vit C, 1% folate.

TIP FROM THE TEST KITCHEN
For a party, keep the meatballs hot in a small slow cooker set on warm or in a chafing dish set over a flame.

CRAB RANGOON–STUFFED MUSHROOM CAPS

This recipe reinvents two appetizer classics—creamy crab rangoon and crispy stuffed mushrooms—by melding them into one delicious nosh. They are incredibly hot when they come out of the oven, so resist the urge to pop one right into your mouth.

HANDS-ON TIME
25 minutes

TOTAL TIME
40 minutes

MAKES
30 pieces

INGREDIENTS

1	pkg (212 g) pasteurized crabmeat (see tip, below), drained
115 g	cream cheese, softened
3 tbsp	dried bread crumbs
2	green onions, finely chopped
1 tbsp	lemon juice
1	clove garlic, minced
1 tsp	Worcestershire sauce
¼ tsp	pepper
30	cremini mushrooms (about 675 g), stemmed
⅓ cup	panko bread crumbs
1 tbsp	butter, melted

DIRECTIONS

Stir together crabmeat, cream cheese, bread crumbs, green onions, lemon juice, garlic, Worcestershire sauce and pepper. Spoon 1 tbsp crabmeat mixture into each mushroom cap, pressing to flatten slightly. *(Make-ahead: Cover and refrigerate for up to 3 hours.)*

Place mushrooms on foil-lined rimmed baking sheet. Stir panko with butter; press ½ tsp onto filling in each mushroom. Bake in 400°F (200°C) oven until golden and mushrooms are tender, about 18 minutes.

Let cool for 5 minutes before serving.

NUTRITIONAL INFORMATION, PER PIECE: about 34 cal, 2 g pro, 2 g total fat (1 g sat. fat), 2 g carb, 1 g fibre, 12 mg chol, 44 mg sodium, 117 mg potassium. % RDI: 2% calcium, 1% iron, 2% vit A, 3% folate.

TIP FROM THE TEST KITCHEN
Look for plastic tubs of pasteurized crabmeat in the refrigerated area near the fish counter at your supermarket. While pasteurized, the crabmeat is not shelf stable, so be sure to keep it in the fridge and use it up within a day or so of opening.

SPICY HONEY-GARLIC BONELESS WINGS ㉚

HANDS-ON TIME 20 minutes

TOTAL TIME 20 minutes

MAKES 10 to 12 servings

INGREDIENTS

⅓ cup	liquid honey
3 tbsp	sesame oil
2 tbsp	sesame seeds, toasted
3	cloves garlic, grated or pressed
5 tsp	cayenne-based hot pepper sauce, such as Frank's RedHot Original
¼ tsp	each salt and pepper
2 tbsp	cornstarch
900 g	boneless skinless chicken breasts, cut in 1-inch (2.5 cm) chunks
2 tsp	olive oil
2	green onions, sliced

DIRECTIONS

Stir together ⅓ cup water, honey, sesame oil, sesame seeds, garlic, hot pepper sauce, salt and pepper. Set aside.

Sprinkle cornstarch over chicken; toss to coat. In large nonstick skillet, heat olive oil over medium-high heat; cook chicken, stirring, until light golden, about 5 minutes.

Stir in honey mixture; cook, stirring occasionally, until sauce is thick and coats chicken completely, and chicken is no longer pink inside, about 6 minutes.

Scrape into serving dish; sprinkle with sliced green onions.

NUTRITIONAL INFORMATION, PER EACH OF 12 SERVINGS: about 166 cal, 18 g pro, 6 g total fat (1 g sat. fat), 10 g carb, trace fibre, 44 mg chol, 166 mg sodium, 236 mg potassium. % RDI: 1% calcium, 4% iron, 1% vit A, 2% vit C, 2% folate.

CRAB CAKES
WITH CHIPOTLE MAYO

HANDS-ON TIME 35 minutes

TOTAL TIME 35 minutes

MAKES 16 pieces

INGREDIENTS

CHIPOTLE MAYO:

2	canned chipotle peppers in adobo sauce, finely chopped
½ cup	light mayonnaise
1 tbsp	adobo sauce from canned chipotles
dash	Worcestershire sauce

CRAB CAKES:

1	pkg (200 g) frozen crabmeat, thawed
⅓ cup	finely diced sweet red pepper
¼ cup	finely diced sweet green pepper
¼ cup	chopped green onions
1	egg, lightly beaten
1¼ cups	dried bread crumbs
2 tbsp	vegetable oil

DIRECTIONS

CHIPOTLE MAYO: Mix together chipotles, mayonnaise, adobo sauce and Worcestershire sauce; set aside.

CRAB CAKES: In fine-mesh sieve, pick through crabmeat to remove any cartilage; press to remove liquid. Transfer to large bowl; stir in red and green peppers, onions, egg, 2 tbsp of the bread crumbs and 3 tbsp of the chipotle mayo. Form by rounded 1 tbsp into balls; roll in remaining bread crumbs to lightly coat. Place on waxed paper–lined baking sheet; flatten to 2-inch (5 cm) diameter. *(Make-ahead: Cover and refrigerate for up to 24 hours.)*

In nonstick skillet, heat half of the oil over medium-high heat; in batches, fry crab cakes, adding remaining oil as necessary, until golden, 3 minutes per side. Serve with remaining chipotle mayo.

NUTRITIONAL INFORMATION, PER PIECE: about 93 cal, 5 g pro, 5 g total fat (trace sat. fat), 8 g carb, trace fibre, 22 mg chol, 214 mg sodium. % RDI: 2% calcium, 6% iron, 3% vit A, 13% vit C, 5% folate.

VARIATION

CURRIED MANGO CHUTNEY MAYO

Substitute 1 tbsp mango chutney and 1 tsp mild or hot curry paste for the chipotles and adobo sauce.

**NOVA SCOTIA
SEAFOOD CHOWDER**
page 57

ULTIMATE SOUPS | 2

"I love to cook for people, and soups are my go-to if I'm making food for friends and family. They are easy to make for a crowd and just have this way of warming you up like nothing else."

IRENE FONG SENIOR FOOD SPECIALIST

BEET BORSCHT ◗

This big-batch, veggie-dense soup is naturally vegan, but it tastes even better served with a dollop of sour cream (or plain Greek yogurt) and a sprinkle of fresh dill. This sweet yet tangy soup is terrific hot or cold, so you can enjoy it year-round.

HANDS-ON TIME
35 minutes

TOTAL TIME
1¼ hours

MAKES
10 to 12 servings

INGREDIENTS

2 tbsp	vegetable oil
1	onion, diced
3	cloves garlic, minced
½ tsp	caraway seeds
675 g	beets, peeled and diced
5 cups	diced green cabbage
2	small white potatoes (about 280 g), cubed
2	ribs celery, diced
1	carrot, diced
2	bay leaves
1¾ tsp	salt
½ tsp	pepper
1	can (156 mL) tomato paste
1 tbsp	packed brown sugar
3 tbsp	vinegar

DIRECTIONS

In large Dutch oven, heat oil over medium-high heat; cook onion, garlic and caraway seeds, stirring occasionally, until onion is softened and light golden, about 4 minutes.

Reduce heat to medium. Stir in beets, cabbage, potatoes, celery, carrot, bay leaves, salt and pepper; cook, stirring often, until beets are just starting to soften, about 10 minutes.

Stir in tomato paste and brown sugar; cook, stirring, for 2 minutes. Stir in 10 cups water; bring to boil. Reduce heat and simmer, stirring occasionally, until vegetables are tender, about 40 minutes.

Stir in vinegar; discard bay leaves. *(Make-ahead: Freeze in airtight container for up to 2 weeks.)*

NUTRITIONAL INFORMATION, PER EACH OF 12 SERVINGS: about 85 cal, 2 g pro, 2 g total fat (trace sat. fat), 12 g carb, 3 g fibre, 0 mg chol, 398 mg sodium, 425 mg potassium. % RDI: 3% calcium, 8% iron, 14% vit A, 23% vit C, 20% folate.

GOLDEN GAZPACHO ◐

HANDS-ON TIME 30 minutes

TOTAL TIME 4½ hours

MAKES 4 to 6 servings

INGREDIENTS

8	yellow tomatoes (about 900 g)
1¼ cups	diced seeded peeled cucumber
½ cup	diced red onion
1	sweet yellow pepper, chopped
1	clove garlic, minced
⅓ cup	white wine
3 tbsp	extra-virgin olive oil
2 tbsp	white wine vinegar or unseasoned rice vinegar
½ tsp	salt
¼ tsp	hot pepper sauce (optional)

DIRECTIONS

Halve tomatoes crosswise; squeeze juice and seeds into strainer set over bowl, pressing on pulp to extract juice. Reserve juice; discard seeds. Core and dice tomatoes.

Combine ¼ cup of the tomatoes, ¼ cup of the cucumber and 2 tbsp of the onion; set aside for garnish. *(Make-ahead: Cover and refrigerate for up to 2 days.)*

In blender, blend remaining tomatoes and reserved juice, remaining cucumber, remaining onion, yellow pepper, garlic, wine, oil, vinegar, salt, and hot pepper sauce (if using) until smooth. Cover and refrigerate for 4 hours. *(Make-ahead: Refrigerate in airtight container for up to 2 days.)*

Serve topped with reserved vegetable garnish.

NUTRITIONAL INFORMATION, PER EACH OF 6 SERVINGS: about 104 cal, 2 g pro, 7 g total fat (1 g sat. fat), 8 g carb, 2 g fibre, 0 mg chol, 225 mg sodium. % RDI: 2% calcium, 7% iron, 1% vit A, 85% vit C, 24% folate.

VARIATION
SCARLET GAZPACHO

Substitute red tomatoes for the yellow tomatoes, and a sweet red pepper for the sweet yellow pepper.

VELVETY SPINACH SOUP

HANDS-ON TIME 30 minutes

TOTAL TIME 45 minutes

MAKES 4 to 6 servings

INGREDIENTS

¼ cup	butter
2	shallots, thinly sliced
2	cloves garlic, minced
½ tsp	salt
¼ tsp	pepper
450 g	russet potatoes, peeled and chopped
3 cups	sodium-reduced chicken broth
280 g	baby spinach

DIRECTIONS

In large saucepan, melt butter over medium heat; cook shallots, garlic, salt and pepper, stirring occasionally, until softened and light golden, about 4 minutes.

Add potatoes; cook, stirring, for 2 minutes. Add 4 cups water and broth; bring to boil. Reduce heat and simmer until potatoes are tender, 15 to 20 minutes.

Turn off heat. Stir in spinach; let stand on burner for 5 minutes. Working in batches, in blender, purée soup until smooth.

NUTRITIONAL INFORMATION, PER EACH OF 6 SERVINGS: about 141 cal, 4 g pro, 8 g total fat (5 g sat. fat), 15 g carb, 2 g fibre, 20 mg chol, 580 mg sodium, 428 mg potassium. % RDI: 7% calcium, 14% iron, 55% vit A, 15% vit C, 33% folate.

CREAM OF MUSHROOM SOUP
WITH MULTIGRAIN GARLIC CROUTONS

Restaurant and packaged soups can contain as much as 1,000 mg of sodium per bowl. We've reduced that amount by more than half by using sodium-reduced chicken broth and less salt—without sacrificing any of this soup's flavour.

HANDS-ON TIME
45 minutes

TOTAL TIME
1½ hours

MAKES
6 to 8 servings

INGREDIENTS

CREAM OF MUSHROOM SOUP:

1	pkg (14 g) dried mixed mushrooms
1 cup	boiling water
2 tbsp	extra-virgin olive oil
2	leeks (white and light green parts only), sliced
1 tsp	dried thyme
¾ tsp	salt
¼ tsp	each dried dillweed and pepper
2	russet potatoes, peeled and cubed (about 450 g)
340 g	white mushrooms, sliced
2 cups	sodium-reduced chicken broth or vegetable broth
1 tsp	Dijon mustard
½ cup	10% cream

MULTIGRAIN GARLIC CROUTONS:

3 cups	cubed multigrain bread
2 tbsp	butter, melted
1	small clove garlic, minced
1 tbsp	chopped fresh parsley

DIRECTIONS

CREAM OF MUSHROOM SOUP: Soak dried mushrooms in boiling water; set aside.

Meanwhile, in large saucepan, heat oil over medium heat; cook leeks, thyme, salt, dillweed and pepper, stirring occasionally, until softened, about 6 minutes.

Add potatoes and white mushrooms; cook, stirring, for 3 minutes. Stir in broth, mustard, dried mushrooms with soaking liquid and 6 cups water; bring to boil. Reduce heat, cover and simmer until potatoes are tender, about 30 minutes. Let stand for 10 minutes.

Working in batches, in blender, purée soup. *(Make-ahead: Refrigerate in airtight container for up to 4 days or freeze for up to 1 month.)*

Transfer soup to clean pot. Stir in cream; heat over medium heat until steaming but not boiling.

MULTIGRAIN GARLIC CROUTONS: While soup is steaming, toss together bread, butter, garlic and parsley. Spread on foil-lined rimmed baking sheet; bake in 375°F (190°C) oven until crisp and golden, 15 to 20 minutes. *(Make-ahead: Store in airtight container for up to 4 days.)* Sprinkle over soup.

NUTRITIONAL INFORMATION, PER EACH OF 8 SERVINGS: about 162 cal, 4 g pro, 8 g total fat (3 g sat. fat), 19 g carb, 2 g fibre, 12 mg chol, 443 mg sodium, 332 mg potassium. % RDI: 4% calcium, 11% iron, 4% vit A, 10% vit C, 10% folate.

HERE'S HOW

A

B

SHRIMP BISQUE

A bisque is an elegant puréed soup featuring seafood and cream. Shrimp stock created from the shells enriches every spoonful with luscious flavour.

HANDS-ON TIME
50 minutes

TOTAL TIME
1½ hours

MAKES
8 to 12 servings

INGREDIENTS

675 g	raw small shrimp (40 to 44 count)
3 tbsp	butter
3	ribs celery, finely chopped
2	carrots, finely chopped
1	onion, finely chopped
3	large sprigs fresh thyme (or 2 tsp dried)
½ cup	sherry, brandy or clam juice
1	bay leaf
3 tbsp	long-grain rice
3 tbsp	tomato paste
1 tsp	salt
¼ tsp	cayenne pepper
1 cup	whipping cream (35%)
2 tbsp	lemon juice
2 tbsp	chopped fresh chives

DIRECTIONS

Reserving shells, peel and devein shrimp; refrigerate shrimp and set shells aside. In Dutch oven, melt half of the butter over medium heat; cook celery, carrots, onion and thyme, stirring occasionally, until softened, about 5 minutes. Add shrimp shells; cook, stirring, until pink, about 2 minutes. **PHOTO A**

Add sherry; bring to boil, scraping up any browned bits from bottom of pan. Add 6 cups water and bay leaf; bring to boil. Reduce heat, cover and simmer for 30 minutes.

Pour through fine-mesh sieve or cheesecloth-lined strainer into bowl, pressing solids to extract liquid. **PHOTO B**

Return stock to pan. Whisk in rice, tomato paste, salt and cayenne pepper; cover and simmer until rice is tender, about 20 minutes.

Meanwhile, in skillet, melt remaining butter over medium-high heat; sauté shrimp until pink and opaque, about 4 minutes.

Working in 4 batches, in blender, purée soup with shrimp until smooth. *(Make-ahead: Let cool for 30 minutes; refrigerate, uncovered, in airtight container until cold. Cover and refrigerate for up to 2 days; reheat before proceeding with recipe.)*

Pour soup into clean Dutch oven. Whisk in cream and bring to barely a simmer over low heat (soup should be heated through but not boiling). Stir in lemon juice. Ladle bisque into warmed bowls; sprinkle with chopped chives.

NUTRITIONAL INFORMATION, PER EACH OF 12 SERVINGS: about 155 cal, 10 g pro, 11 g total fat (6 g sat. fat), 5 g carb, trace fibre, 99 mg chol, 298 mg sodium. % RDI: 4% calcium, 9% iron, 12% vit A, 7% vit C, 2% folate.

FRESH TOMATO SOUP ◐
WITH HERBED FRESH CHEESE

Herbed soft cheese, such as Boursin, comes nicely seasoned with garlic and herbs.
If you use plain soft goat cheese instead of seasoned, garnish the soup with some minced
fresh chives and parsley to give it the same flavour notes.

HANDS-ON TIME
30 minutes

TOTAL TIME
45 minutes

MAKES
4 to 6 servings

INGREDIENTS

1.8 kg	tomatoes (see tip, below)
¼ cup	extra-virgin olive oil
2	onions, finely chopped
1	rib celery, finely chopped
2	cloves garlic, minced
2	sprigs fresh thyme (or ¼ tsp dried)
1 tsp	salt
¼ tsp	pepper
170 g	garlic-and-herb soft cheese, such as Boursin, or soft goat cheese

DIRECTIONS

Using sharp knife, score X in bottom of each tomato. In large pot of boiling water, blanch tomatoes until skins begin to split, 20 to 30 seconds. Using slotted spoon, transfer to bowl of ice water; let cool for 1 minute.

Drain tomatoes and peel off skins. Halve tomatoes crosswise; squeeze out seeds and liquid into fine-mesh sieve set over bowl, adding enough water to juice to make 2 cups. Reserve liquid; discard seeds. Core and coarsely chop tomatoes.

In saucepan, heat 2 tbsp of the oil over medium-low heat; cook onions and celery, stirring occasionally and reducing heat if necessary to prevent browning, until tender, about 10 minutes.

Stir in tomatoes, reserved tomato liquid, garlic, thyme, salt and pepper. Bring to boil; reduce heat, cover and simmer for 20 minutes. Stir in remaining oil. Remove thyme.

Ladle soup into bowls; top with dollops of garlic-and-herb cheese.

NUTRITIONAL INFORMATION, PER EACH OF 6 SERVINGS: about 221 cal, 8 g pro, 16 g total fat (6 g sat. fat), 16 g carb, 4 g fibre, 13 mg chol, 517 mg sodium. % RDI: 6% calcium, 14% iron, 23% vit A, 83% vit C, 18% folate.

TIP FROM THE TEST KITCHEN
Plum tomatoes are a great choice for cooking. They have dense flesh and not too many seeds.

SLOW COOKER BEEF STOCK

Homemade stock couldn't be simpler to make—your slow cooker does all the work. It's far more delicious than store-bought and contains no added salt, giving you better control over the amount of sodium you add to recipes.

HANDS-ON TIME
10 minutes

TOTAL TIME
25 hours

MAKES
about 9 cups

INGREDIENTS

2.25 kg	beef soup bones
12 cups	cold water
2	onions, coarsely chopped
3	ribs celery, coarsely chopped
10	sprigs parsley or leftover parsley stems
2	bay leaves
½ tsp	black peppercorns

DIRECTIONS

Arrange bones in large roasting pan; roast in 450°F (230°C) oven, turning once, until browned, about 45 minutes.

Transfer bones to slow cooker. Drain fat from roasting pan; discard. Stir 1 cup of the cold water into roasting pan; bring to boil over medium heat. Continue to boil for 1 minute, scraping up any browned bits from bottom of pan; transfer to slow cooker.

Add onions, celery, parsley, bay leaves and peppercorns to slow cooker. Pour in remaining cold water. Cover and cook on low for 24 hours.

Strain through cheesecloth-lined fine-mesh sieve into large bowl. Let cool for 30 minutes. Skim off fat and discard. *(Make-ahead: Refrigerate in airtight containers for up to 3 days or freeze for up to 2 months.)*

NUTRITIONAL INFORMATION, PER 1 CUP: about 14 cal, 1 g pro, 1 g total fat (0 g sat. fat), 0 g carb, 0 g fibre, 0 mg chol, 4 mg sodium, 14 mg potassium. % RDI: 2% folate.

VARIATIONS

SLOW COOKER CHICKEN STOCK

Omit beef soup bones. In slow cooker, combine 900 g cooked or raw chicken bones (about 3 carcasses with wings), onions, celery, parsley, bay leaves and peppercorns. Pour in cold water. Proceed with recipe as directed.

SLOW COOKER TURKEY STOCK

Omit beef soup bones. In slow cooker, combine 1 cooked or raw turkey carcass, broken into 3 or 4 pieces; onions; celery; parsley; bay leaves; and peppercorns. Pour in cold water. Proceed with recipe as directed.

SLOW COOKER SEAFOOD STOCK

Omit beef soup bones and onions. In slow cooker, combine 225 g shrimp shells; 1 leek, sliced; and 2 bottles (each 236 mL) clam juice. Add celery, parsley, bay leaves and peppercorns; pour in cold water. Cover and cook on low for 6 hours. Proceed with recipe as directed.

SLOW COOKER VEGETABLE STOCK

Omit beef soup bones and onions. In slow cooker, combine 1 leek, chopped; 1 cup sliced mushrooms (stems and/or caps); 1 carrot, chopped; and 3 sprigs fresh thyme. Add celery, parsley, bay leaves and peppercorns; pour in cold water. Cover and cook on low for 6 hours. Proceed with recipe as directed.

TIP FROM THE TEST KITCHEN
Skimming the fat off the finished stock isn't hard, but it does take a bit of time. Refrigerate the finished stock, uncovered, until the fat hardens on the surface, about 8 hours. Then simply lift it off.

SLOW COOKER POTATO, CHEDDAR AND CHIVE SOUP

This hearty soup has all the flavours of a stuffed baked potato. The stock is the key to its taste, so homemade is best. But if you don't have any in your freezer, the soup is still yummy made with no-salt-added broth.

HANDS-ON TIME
20 minutes

TOTAL TIME
5½ hours

MAKES
6 to 8 servings

INGREDIENTS

POTATO SOUP:

5	russet potatoes (about 900 g), peeled and chopped (see tip, below)
1	sweet onion (such as Vidalia), chopped
4	strips bacon (115 g total), chopped
2	cloves garlic, chopped
¾ tsp	salt
½ tsp	pepper
¼ tsp	dried rosemary
4 cups	Slow Cooker Chicken Stock (page 45) or no-salt-added chicken broth

GARNISH:

¼ cup	sour cream
1 cup	shredded old Cheddar cheese
¼ cup	crumbled cooked bacon (about 5 strips)
¼ cup	chopped fresh chives

DIRECTIONS

POTATO SOUP: In slow cooker, combine potatoes, onion, bacon, garlic, salt, pepper and rosemary. Pour in stock. Cover and cook on low for 5 to 8 hours. Skim off fat. Using immersion blender, purée soup until smooth.

GARNISH: Ladle soup into bowls; top with sour cream. Sprinkle with Cheddar, bacon and chives.

NUTRITIONAL INFORMATION, PER EACH OF 8 SERVINGS: about 253 cal, 11 g pro, 13 g total fat (7 g sat. fat), 23 g carb, 2 g fibre, 30 mg chol, 492 mg sodium, 521 mg potassium. % RDI: 12% calcium, 7% iron, 6% vit A, 17% vit C, 10% folate.

TIP FROM THE TEST KITCHEN

When you're cooking potatoes to mash or purée, it's best to use floury russets. If you choose new potatoes or red-skinned potatoes, you may end up with a gluey texture.

QUÉBÉCOIS-STYLE PEA SOUP ✪ 🍴

Look for an unsmoked ham hock in the meat department of your local supermarket. If you can't find one, a smoked ham hock will work; simply reduce the salt in the recipe to ¼ tsp.

HANDS-ON TIME
30 minutes

TOTAL TIME
2½ hours

MAKES
4 to 6 servings

INGREDIENTS

PEA SOUP:

450 g	unsmoked ham hock
2 tbsp	butter
2	carrots, diced
2	ribs celery, diced
1	onion, diced
2	cloves garlic, minced
1¾ cups	dried yellow split peas
2	bay leaves
1 tsp	dried savory or thyme
¾ tsp	salt
¼ tsp	pepper

GARLIC TOASTS:

1	demi-baguette (or half baguette)
2 tbsp	butter, softened
1	large clove garlic, halved
¼ tsp	coarse sea salt

DIRECTIONS

PEA SOUP: Trim off and discard skin from ham hock; set hock aside. In large Dutch oven, melt butter over medium heat; cook carrots, celery, onion and garlic, stirring occasionally, until softened and golden, 15 minutes.

Stir in split peas, bay leaves, savory, salt and pepper; cook, stirring, for 2 minutes. Stir in 8 cups water; add ham hock. Bring to boil; reduce heat, cover and simmer, stirring occasionally, until peas are very soft and soup is thickened, 1½ to 2 hours.

Discard bay leaves. Transfer ham hock to plate; let cool enough to handle. Discarding bone and any fat, dice meat and return to soup; cook until heated through.

GARLIC TOASTS: While soup is simmering, cut baguette into 12 slices; spread with butter. Broil on rimmed baking sheet until golden, about 2 minutes. Rub with cut sides of garlic halves; sprinkle with salt. Serve with soup.

NUTRITIONAL INFORMATION, PER EACH OF 6 SERVINGS: about 446 cal, 28 g pro, 14 g total fat (7 g sat. fat), 54 g carb, 7 g fibre, 51 mg chol, 994 mg sodium, 951 mg potassium. % RDI: 7% calcium, 26% iron, 50% vit A, 5% vit C, 63% folate.

VARIATION

SLOW COOKER QUÉBÉCOIS-STYLE PEA SOUP

Follow first paragraph as directed, substituting large saucepan for Dutch oven. Transfer to slow cooker. Add split peas, bay leaves, savory, salt, pepper, 8 cups water and ham hock. Cover and cook on low for 8 to 10 hours. Proceed with recipe as directed.

COZY CHICKEN AND RICE SOUP

HANDS-ON TIME 32 minutes

TOTAL TIME 45 minutes

MAKES 4 servings

INGREDIENTS

1 tbsp	olive oil
340 g	boneless skinless chicken thighs
1	leek, diced
2	each ribs celery and carrots, diced
1	yellow-fleshed potato, peeled and diced
half	sweet potato, peeled and diced
3	sprigs each fresh thyme and parsley
¼ tsp	each salt and pepper
4 cups	sodium-reduced chicken broth (see tip, page 52)
½ cup	basmati rice, rinsed
1 cup	frozen peas

DIRECTIONS

In large Dutch oven, heat oil over medium-high heat; brown chicken, 4 to 5 minutes. Transfer chicken to cutting board; cut into chunks. Set aside.

Add leek and celery to pan; cook over medium heat until softened, about 2 minutes. Add carrots, yellow-fleshed potato, sweet potato, thyme, parsley, salt and pepper; cook, stirring often, for 3 minutes.

Return chicken to pan along with any accumulated juices. Stir in broth and 4 cups water; bring to boil. Reduce heat and simmer for 5 minutes.

Stir in rice; cook until vegetables and rice are tender, about 13 minutes. Add peas; cook until hot, about 1 minute. Discard thyme and parsley.

NUTRITIONAL INFORMATION, PER SERVING: about 345 cal, 25 g pro, 8 g total fat (2 g sat. fat), 43 g carb, 5 g fibre, 71 mg chol, 887 mg sodium, 625 mg potassium. % RDI: 7% calcium, 17% iron, 117% vit A, 27% vit C, 21% folate.

CALDO VERDE

HANDS-ON TIME 25 minutes

TOTAL TIME 45 minutes

MAKES 6 to 8 servings

INGREDIENTS

250 g	mild dry-cured chorizo sausages, halved lengthwise and sliced
1	Spanish onion, sliced
4	cloves garlic, sliced
450 g	yellow-fleshed potatoes, peeled, halved lengthwise and sliced
2	bay leaves
1 tsp	sweet paprika
½ tsp	salt
¼ tsp	pepper
4 cups	sodium-reduced chicken broth (see tip, page 52)
1	bunch kale, trimmed and shredded

DIRECTIONS

In Dutch oven, brown chorizo over medium-high heat, about 2 minutes. Transfer to bowl; set aside. Drain fat from pan (do not wipe clean); reduce heat to medium. Add onion and garlic; cook, stirring often, until softened and light golden, about 8 minutes.

Add potatoes, bay leaves, paprika, salt and pepper; stir in broth and 4 cups water. Bring to boil; reduce heat, cover and simmer until potatoes are tender, 10 minutes. Discard bay leaves. Transfer as many chorizo pieces as possible to bowl; set aside.

Add kale; cover and simmer until tender, about 10 minutes. Using immersion blender, purée soup until almost smooth with a few chunks remaining. Stir in reserved chorizo. *(Make-ahead: Freeze in airtight container for up to 2 weeks.)*

NUTRITIONAL INFORMATION, PER EACH OF 8 SERVINGS: about 213 cal, 11 g pro, 11 g total fat (4 g sat. fat), 18 g carb, 2 g fibre, 25 mg chol, 817 mg sodium, 515 mg potassium. % RDI: 8% calcium, 11% iron, 60% vit A, 82% vit C, 10% folate.

VEGETABLE BEEF NOODLE SOUP

HANDS-ON TIME
30 minutes

TOTAL TIME
2½ hours

MAKES
6 servings

If you have Slow Cooker Beef Stock (page 45), use it in place of the broth and check the seasoning at the end of cooking.

INGREDIENTS

450 g	stewing beef cubes
½ tsp	pepper
¼ tsp	salt
1 tbsp	vegetable oil
3	carrots, chopped
2	ribs celery, chopped
1	onion, chopped
3	cloves garlic, minced
1	pkg (900 mL) sodium-reduced beef broth
2 tbsp	tomato paste
1 tsp	herbes de Provence
½ tsp	red wine vinegar
1 cup	large curly egg noodles
½ cup	frozen peas
3 cups	baby spinach

DIRECTIONS

Sprinkle beef with pepper and salt. In Dutch oven or large heavy-bottomed saucepan, heat oil over medium-high heat; cook beef, stirring occasionally, until browned, about 6 minutes. Stir in carrots, celery, onion and garlic; cook, stirring occasionally, until vegetables are softened, about 6 minutes.

Stir in broth, 3 cups water, tomato paste, herbes de Provence and vinegar. Bring to boil; reduce heat, partially cover and simmer, stirring occasionally, until beef is tender, about 2 hours.

Stir in noodles and peas; cook over medium heat until noodles are tender, about 5 minutes. Stir in spinach.

NUTRITIONAL INFORMATION, PER SERVING: about 226 cal, 20 g pro, 10 g total fat (3 g sat. fat), 14 g carb, 3 g fibre, 50 mg chol, 593 mg sodium, 519 mg potassium. % RDI: 7% calcium, 20% iron, 83% vit A, 12% vit C, 20% folate.

TIP FROM THE TEST KITCHEN
Cooking the noodles in the soup thickens the broth and gives the dish that "stick to your ribs" feeling. They do soak up some of the broth, though, so you may want to add a bit of water to any leftovers before reheating to make them soupy again.

SLOW COOKER HEARTY THICK TURKEY BARLEY SOUP

HANDS-ON TIME
20 minutes

TOTAL TIME
7 hours

MAKES
6 servings

Smoked turkey adds richness to this filling root vegetable soup. It freezes well, so you can make a double batch and keep it to enjoy as an easy meal later on. Pot barley is a whole grain, so it adds healthy fibre to the soup; pearl barley is refined, but still very tasty.

INGREDIENTS

1	smoked turkey thigh or drumstick (about 450 g)
2	carrots, diced
2	ribs celery, diced
450 g	mini red potatoes, scrubbed and quartered
340 g	white turnips, peeled and diced
2	parsnips, peeled and diced
1	onion, diced
1 tsp	dried thyme
½ tsp	salt
¼ tsp	pepper
4 cups	sodium-reduced chicken broth
½ cup	pot barley or pearl barley
¼ cup	chopped fresh parsley

DIRECTIONS

Remove skin and meat from turkey. Reserve bone; discard skin. Cut meat into bite-size pieces; set aside.

In slow cooker, combine turkey bone, carrots, celery, potatoes, turnips, parsnips, onion, thyme, salt and pepper. Stir in broth and 3 cups water. Cover and cook on low until vegetables are tender, 6 to 8 hours.

Stir in barley; cover and cook on high until barley is tender, about 30 minutes.

Stir in reserved turkey meat and parsley; cover and cook on high until turkey is heated through, about 5 minutes.

NUTRITIONAL INFORMATION, PER SERVING: about 301 cal, 22 g pro, 8 g total fat (2 g sat. fat), 36 g carb, 6 g fibre, 54 mg chol, 1,215 mg sodium, 916 mg potassium. % RDI: 9% calcium, 22% iron, 45% vit A, 50% vit C, 31% folate.

TIP FROM THE TEST KITCHEN

In the Test Kitchen, we often dilute commercial broth (even sodium-reduced) with water when making soup to reduce the salt. If you use Slow Cooker Chicken Stock (page 45) instead, substitute it for the total amount of broth and water (here, that's 7 cups). Check the soup and season it with salt at the end if necessary.

PARMESAN CRISPS

Divide ⅔ cup grated Parmesan cheese into 16 mounds on parchment paper–lined rimless baking sheet; spread each to 2-inch (5 cm) circle. Bake in 400°F (200°C) oven until bottoms are light golden, about 5 minutes. Immediately drape over rolling pin to create curve; let cool. *(Make-ahead: Store in airtight container for up to 2 days.)* **MAKES** 16 crisps

HEARTY MINESTRONE 🍽

*A piece of Parmesan cheese rind adds incredible flavour to minestrone.
If you need to get dinner on the table more quickly, garnish the soup with
store-bought pesto and omit the Parmesan Crisps.*

HANDS-ON TIME
45 minutes

TOTAL TIME
2½ hours

MAKES
8 servings

INGREDIENTS

CROSTINI:

2½ cups	cubed trimmed Italian bread
3 tbsp	extra-virgin olive oil
½ tsp	coarsely cracked pepper

MINESTRONE:

1 tbsp	extra-virgin olive oil
1	large onion, chopped
3	each ribs celery and carrots, sliced
3	cloves garlic, minced
2	bay leaves
½ tsp	each salt and pepper
1	can (156 mL) tomato paste
450 g	smoked ham hock
1	piece Parmesan cheese rind (optional)
1	large white potato, peeled and cubed
1	sweet red pepper, diced
1	small zucchini
1 cup	dried pasta (such as garganelli, radiatori or macaroni)
1 cup	each rinsed drained canned red and white kidney beans

QUICK PESTO:

½ cup	packed fresh basil leaves
¼ cup	extra-virgin olive oil
1 tbsp	pine nuts, toasted
¼ tsp	each salt and pepper
1	clove garlic, minced
	Parmesan Crisps (opposite)

DIRECTIONS

CROSTINI: While crisps are cooling, in bowl, toss together bread, oil and pepper; spread on rimmed baking sheet. Bake in 400°F (200°C) oven, tossing once, until golden and crisp, 6 to 8 minutes. *(Make-ahead: Let cool and store in airtight container for up to 24 hours.)*

MINESTRONE: In Dutch oven, heat oil over medium heat; cook onion, celery, carrots, garlic, bay leaves, salt and pepper, stirring often, until softened, about 4 minutes. Add tomato paste; cook, stirring, for 2 minutes. Add ham hock, Parmesan rind (if using) and 8 cups water; bring to boil. Reduce heat to low; cover and simmer for 30 minutes. Skim off foam. Add potato and red pepper; cover and simmer for 1 hour.

Remove ham hock; let cool enough to handle. Discard skin, fat and bone. Using fork or fingers, shred ham and return to soup. Discard bay leaves and Parmesan rind. *(Make-ahead: Let cool for 30 minutes; refrigerate, uncovered, until cold. Refrigerate in airtight container for up to 2 days.)*

Cut zucchini in half lengthwise; slice crosswise. Add pasta, red and white kidney beans and zucchini to soup; bring to boil. Reduce heat and simmer until pasta is al dente, about 12 minutes.

QUICK PESTO: While soup is simmering, in food processor, purée together basil, oil, pine nuts, salt, pepper and garlic. *(Make-ahead: Refrigerate in airtight container for up to 2 days.)*

TO FINISH: Ladle soup into bowls; garnish with pesto, crostini and crisps.

NUTRITIONAL INFORMATION, PER SERVING: about 361 cal, 12 g pro, 18 g total fat (4 g sat. fat), 40 g carb, 7 g fibre, 10 mg chol, 715 mg sodium. % RDI: 13% calcium, 20% iron, 81% vit A, 68% vit C, 34% folate.

VARIATION

SLOW COOKER HEARTY MINESTRONE

MINESTRONE: Increase salt and pepper to 1 tsp. Cook onion, celery, carrots, garlic, bay leaves, salt and pepper as directed. Add to slow cooker along with tomato paste, ham hock, Parmesan rind (if using), potato, red and white beans and 8 cups water. Cover and cook on low until ham pulls off bone easily, 6 to 8 hours. Discard bay leaves and Parmesan. Increase heat to high. Stir in red pepper and zucchini; cover and cook for 20 minutes. Meanwhile, cook pasta according to package instructions until al dente; stir into soup. Garnish and serve as directed.

CURRIED CHICKEN AND LENTIL SOUP ㉚ 🍴

This satisfying spiced soup is packed with protein and will keep hunger at bay for hours. A piece of warm Naan (page 316) would be a tasty accompaniment.

HANDS-ON TIME
15 minutes

TOTAL TIME
30 minutes

MAKES
4 servings

INGREDIENTS

2 tbsp	olive oil
1	onion, chopped
1	rib celery, diced
2	cloves garlic, minced
2 tsp	curry powder
1 tsp	minced fresh ginger
¼ tsp	each ground coriander, ground cumin and pepper
2	boneless skinless chicken breasts (about 450 g total)
1	pkg (900 mL) sodium-reduced chicken broth
1	can (796 mL) no-salt-added diced tomatoes
2 cups	diced peeled sweet potato (about 1 large)
⅔ cup	dried green lentils, rinsed
¼ cup	chopped fresh cilantro
½ tsp	salt

DIRECTIONS

In large saucepan, heat oil over medium heat; cook onion and celery, stirring occasionally, until softened, about 2 minutes. Add garlic, curry powder, ginger, coriander, cumin and pepper; cook, stirring, until fragrant, about 1 minute.

Stir in chicken, broth, tomatoes, sweet potato and lentils; bring to boil. Reduce heat, cover and simmer until lentils are tender, 15 to 20 minutes.

Transfer chicken to plate; using 2 forks, shred meat. Return chicken to soup; stir in cilantro and salt.

NUTRITIONAL INFORMATION, PER SERVING: about 418 cal, 40 g pro, 9 g total fat (1 g sat. fat), 45 g carb, 8 g fibre, 65 mg chol, 975 mg sodium, 1,350 mg potassium. % RDI: 16% calcium, 40% iron, 119% vit A, 45% vit C, 83% folate.

TIP FROM THE TEST KITCHEN
To make the soup even quicker to prepare, substitute about 2 cups leftover shredded cooked chicken and 2 cups cooled cooked lentils (or one 540 mL can of lentils, drained and rinsed). Just simmer until the sweet potato is tender, about 10 minutes.

ASPARAGUS SOUP 30 ◑
WITH HOMEMADE CROUTONS

HANDS-ON TIME	30 minutes
TOTAL TIME	30 minutes
MAKES	4 servings

This delicately flavoured soup is a wonderful vegetarian dish that's quick and easy to make. Crème fraîche on top adds richness; substitute sour cream or Greek yogurt if you like.

INGREDIENTS

1 tbsp	olive oil
3	shallots, chopped
4	cloves garlic, minced
1	leek (white and light green parts only), thinly sliced
675 g	asparagus (see tip, below), trimmed and cut in 1½-inch (4 cm) pieces
¼ tsp	each salt and pepper
1	pkg (900 mL) vegetable broth
⅓ cup	whipping cream (35%)
1 tbsp	lemon juice
3 cups	cubed crusty whole grain bread
½ cup	crème fraîche, sour cream or Greek yogurt
2 tbsp	chopped fresh chives

DIRECTIONS

In large heavy-bottomed saucepan, heat 1½ tsp of the oil over medium heat; cook shallots and three-quarters of the garlic, stirring occasionally, until shallots are softened, about 3 minutes. Add leek; cook, stirring, until softened, about 6 minutes.

Stir in asparagus, salt and pepper; cook for 2 minutes. Add broth and bring to boil; reduce heat and simmer until asparagus is tender, about 5 minutes.

Working in batches, in blender, purée soup until smooth. Return to saucepan over medium-low heat; stir in cream and lemon juice.

Meanwhile, toss bread with remaining oil and garlic; spread on parchment paper–lined rimmed baking sheet. Bake in 450°F (230°C) oven until golden, about 8 minutes.

Ladle soup into bowls. Combine crème fraîche with chives; spoon onto soup. Sprinkle with croutons.

NUTRITIONAL INFORMATION, PER SERVING: about 331 cal, 8 g pro, 24 g total fat (13 g sat. fat), 26 g carb, 5 g fibre, 79 mg chol, 1,024 mg sodium, 424 mg potassium. % RDI: 7% calcium, 18% iron, 46% vit A, 23% vit C, 91% folate.

TIP FROM THE TEST KITCHEN
Choose asparagus stalks that are thick, smooth, plump and unblemished. They have the best flavour.

NOVA SCOTIA SEAFOOD CHOWDER ✪

This rich soup is inspired by a similar seafood chowder served at the Masstown Market, near Truro, N.S.

HANDS-ON TIME
35 minutes

TOTAL TIME
1¼ hours

MAKES
12 servings

INGREDIENTS

900 g	mussels
⅔ cup	dry white wine
3 tbsp	butter
3	ribs celery, thinly sliced
2	onions, chopped
½ tsp	each salt and sweet paprika
¼ tsp	cayenne pepper
3 tbsp	all-purpose flour
1	bottle (240 mL) clam juice
2	yellow-fleshed potatoes, peeled and cubed
340 g	haddock or other firm-fleshed fish fillets, cut in 2-inch (5 cm) chunks
340 g	sea scallops, halved horizontally
1	can (320 g) frozen lobster meat, thawed and drained
3 cups	10% cream
¼ cup	chopped fresh parsley

DIRECTIONS

Scrub mussels; remove any beards. Discard any mussels that do not close when tapped.

In saucepan, bring mussels and wine to boil over high heat. Reduce heat, cover and simmer until mussels open, about 5 minutes. Reserving broth, strain mussels; discard any that do not open. Let cool enough to handle. Remove and discard shells; set mussels and broth aside.

In Dutch oven, melt butter over medium heat; cook celery, onions, salt, paprika and cayenne pepper, stirring occasionally, until softened, about 6 minutes. Stir in flour; cook, stirring constantly, for 1 minute.

Stir in reserved mussel broth, clam juice and 1½ cups water, scraping up any browned bits from bottom of pan. Add potatoes; bring to boil. Reduce heat, cover and simmer, stirring occasionally, until potatoes are tender, about 15 minutes.

Stir in haddock, scallops and lobster; bring to boil. Reduce heat and simmer for 5 minutes. Stir in cream, mussels and parsley. Cook, stirring, until heated through, about 2 minutes. *(Make-ahead: Let cool. Refrigerate in airtight containers for up to 2 days.)*

NUTRITIONAL INFORMATION, PER SERVING: about 236 cal, 21 g pro, 10 g total fat (6 g sat. fat), 14 g carb, 1 g fibre, 78 mg chol, 405 mg sodium, 582 mg potassium. % RDI: 11% calcium, 13% iron, 12% vit A, 12% vit C, 14% folate.

SHOW-OFF CAESAR SALAD
page 62

ULTIMATE SALADS | 3

"Salads are where I let my creativity shine for fast suppers. A little crunch, a killer flavour combination and a homemade tangy vinaigrette open up so many tasty possibilities."

JENNIFER BARTOLI FOOD SPECIALIST

JICAMA AND APPLE SPINACH SALAD ③⓪
WITH HONEY-DIJON DRESSING

Jicama (pronounced hee-kah-ma) is a root vegetable with a sweet flavour and crunchy texture that's best enjoyed raw, making it a perfect salad ingredient. Look for firm, blemish-free jicama in the root vegetable section of your grocery store.

HANDS-ON TIME
20 minutes

TOTAL TIME
20 minutes

MAKES
12 servings

INGREDIENTS

HONEY-DIJON DRESSING:

3 tbsp	cider vinegar
2 tbsp	finely chopped fresh chives
1 tbsp	liquid honey
2 tsp	Dijon mustard
1	small clove garlic, pressed
¼ tsp	each salt and pepper
⅓ cup	extra-virgin olive oil

JICAMA AND APPLE SPINACH SALAD:

10	thin slices pancetta, chopped
2	pkg (each 142 g) baby spinach
2	Gala or Empire apples, chopped
1	jicama (about 650 g), peeled and cut in ¼-inch (5 mm) wide sticks

DIRECTIONS

HONEY-DIJON DRESSING: In small bowl, whisk together vinegar, chives, honey, mustard, garlic, salt and pepper; gradually whisk in oil until combined. *(Make-ahead: Refrigerate in airtight container for up to 24 hours; whisk well before using.)*

JICAMA AND APPLE SPINACH SALAD: In small dry skillet, cook pancetta over medium heat, stirring occasionally, until crisp, about 5 minutes. Transfer to paper towel–lined plate; let drain.

In large bowl, toss together spinach, apples, jicama and dressing; top with pancetta.

NUTRITIONAL INFORMATION, PER SERVING: about 147 cal, 5 g pro, 10 g total fat (2 g sat. fat), 10 g carb, 4 g fibre, 18 mg chol, 349 mg sodium, 240 mg potassium. % RDI: 3% calcium, 8% iron, 23% vit A, 30% vit C, 24% folate.

VARIATION

FENNEL AND APPLE SPINACH SALAD
WITH HONEY-DIJON DRESSING

Substitute 1 bulb fennel, cored and thinly sliced, for the jicama.

SHOW-OFF CAESAR SALAD ⓻

This classic salad is traditionally assembled tableside at fine-dining restaurants. At home, prep the ingredients and set them out on a tray alongside a wooden serving bowl; take the tray to the table and assemble the salad as your guests watch in awe.

HANDS-ON TIME
25 minutes

TOTAL TIME
25 minutes

MAKES
8 to 10 servings

INGREDIENTS

1	egg (unshelled)
1	clove garlic, halved
1	pkg (50 g) anchovy fillets, drained, rinsed and chopped
¼ cup	lemon juice
1 tsp	each Worcestershire sauce and salt
½ tsp	each dry mustard and pepper
½ cup	olive oil or vegetable oil
2	heads romaine lettuce, torn in bite-size pieces
2 cups	Buttery Croutons (right)
½ cup	freshly grated Parmesan cheese

DIRECTIONS

In saucepan of gently simmering water, cook egg for 1 minute. Drain and rinse under cold water. Set aside.

Rub inside of wooden serving bowl with cut sides of garlic halves; discard garlic. Add anchovies to bowl; using fork, mash into paste. Crack egg into bowl; add lemon juice, Worcestershire sauce, salt, mustard and pepper. Gradually whisk in oil in thin steady stream until blended.

Add lettuce; toss to coat. Add croutons and Parmesan; toss to combine. Serve immediately.

NUTRITIONAL INFORMATION, PER EACH OF 10 SERVINGS: about 226 cal, 6 g pro, 18 g total fat (5 g sat. fat), 11 g carb, 3 g fibre, 37 mg chol, 554 mg sodium, 369 mg potassium. % RDI: 11% calcium, 14% iron, 115% vit A, 53% vit C, 85% folate.

BUTTERY CROUTONS

Cut 4 slices bread (such as white, brown, cracked wheat, whole wheat, egg or cheese) into small cubes. Place on rimmed baking sheet; broil until browned on 1 side, 1 to 1½ minutes. Remove from oven; add ¼ cup butter, cut in pieces, to hot bread cubes and toss until butter is melted. Turn cubes browned side down. Return to oven; broil until tops are browned, 1 minute. Let cool on pan on rack. **MAKES** about 2 cups

TIP FROM THE TEST KITCHEN
When properly handled, raw, refrigerated Canada Grade 'A' eggs with clean, uncracked shells are fine for healthy people to eat—only those with compromised immune systems, very young children, the elderly and pregnant women should avoid them. Be sure to eat the salad immediately after it's prepared and don't save leftovers.

GREEN GODDESS WEDGE SALAD ㉚

Use a knife and fork to dig into this retro crispy steakhouse salad. A wedge makes a beautiful presentation and is actually easier to make than a salad with torn greens.

HANDS-ON TIME
20 minutes

TOTAL TIME
20 minutes

MAKES
6 servings

INGREDIENTS

GREEN GODDESS DRESSING:

4	strips bacon
⅓ cup	mayonnaise
⅓ cup	sour cream
¼ cup	minced fresh parsley
1	green onion, finely chopped
1	small clove garlic, pressed or grated
1 tbsp	white wine vinegar
1 tbsp	Dijon mustard
1 tsp	Worcestershire sauce
pinch	salt

WEDGE SALAD:

2	eggs (unshelled)
1	head iceberg lettuce, cored and cut in 6 wedges
2	vine-ripened tomatoes, seeded and diced
half	English cucumber, seeded and diced
6	radishes, diced
1	green onion, sliced

DIRECTIONS

GREEN GODDESS DRESSING: In large skillet, cook bacon over medium heat, turning once, until browned and crisp, about 7 minutes. Reserving fat in pan, transfer bacon to paper towel–lined plate; let drain. Chop bacon; set aside for garnish.

Spoon 2 tsp of the bacon fat into small bowl; discard remainder or save for another use. Whisk in mayonnaise, sour cream, parsley, green onion, garlic, vinegar, mustard, Worcestershire sauce and salt. Set aside.

WEDGE SALAD: While bacon is cooking, place eggs in single layer in saucepan; add enough water to cover by at least 1 inch (2.5 cm). Bring to boil; reduce heat and simmer for 4 minutes. Remove from heat; let stand for 4 minutes. Drain; rinse eggs under cold water for 2 minutes and drain well. Peel off shells; chop eggs. Set aside.

Arrange 1 wedge of the lettuce, cut side up, on each of 6 plates; press down lightly to stabilize. Drizzle with dressing; sprinkle with tomatoes, cucumber, radishes, green onion, chopped eggs and reserved bacon.

NUTRITIONAL INFORMATION, PER SERVING: about 202 cal, 6 g pro, 17 g total fat (4 g sat. fat), 7 g carb, 2 g fibre, 79 mg chol, 258 mg sodium, 405 mg potassium. % RDI: 6% calcium, 9% iron, 15% vit A, 25% vit C, 35% folate.

VARIATION

RUSSIAN WEDGE SALAD

Omit Green Goddess Dressing. Whisk together ⅔ cup mayonnaise, 2 tbsp tomato-based chili sauce, 1 tbsp grated onion, 1 tbsp drained prepared horseradish, 1 tsp water, ¾ tsp Worcestershire sauce, ½ tsp hot pepper sauce and pinch sweet paprika. Proceed with recipe as directed.

PEA, FENNEL AND GOAT CHEESE SALAD ③⓪

This simple salad makes great use of fresh spring peas and baby greens. Feel free to skip the spinach and swap in whatever greens you love or have on hand.

HANDS-ON TIME
10 minutes

TOTAL TIME
10 minutes

MAKES
4 servings

INGREDIENTS

DRESSING:

2 tbsp	extra-virgin olive oil
1 tbsp	lemon juice
pinch	each salt and pepper
pinch	granulated sugar

SALAD:

1½ cups	shelled fresh peas
6 cups	lightly packed baby spinach
1	bulb fennel, thinly sliced
⅓ cup	crumbled soft goat cheese

DIRECTIONS

DRESSING: In large bowl, whisk together oil, lemon juice, salt, pepper and sugar. Set aside.

SALAD: In saucepan of boiling salted water, cook peas until tender-crisp, about 2 minutes. Drain and pat dry.

Add spinach, fennel and peas to dressing; gently toss to coat. Sprinkle with goat cheese.

NUTRITIONAL INFORMATION, PER SERVING: about 166 cal, 7 g pro, 10 g total fat (3 g sat. fat), 14 g carb, 6 g fibre, 6 mg chol, 238 mg sodium, 642 mg potassium. % RDI: 10% calcium, 19% iron, 51% vit A, 46% vit C, 63% folate.

TIP FROM THE TEST KITCHEN
When fresh peas are not in season, substitute frozen peas.

FROM TOP:
PEA, FENNEL AND GOAT CHEESE SALAD
opposite

HEIRLOOM CARROT SALAD
page 66

KOHLRABI AND RUTABAGA SLAW
page 67

HEIRLOOM CARROT SALAD ③⓪ ◐

Paper-thin ribbons of orange, yellow and purple heirloom carrots make a stunning salad. If you don't have a multihued bunch on hand, orange carrots are just as delicious.

HANDS-ON TIME
15 minutes

TOTAL TIME
15 minutes

MAKES
4 servings

INGREDIENTS

ORANGE-CUMIN VINAIGRETTE:

¼ tsp	cumin seeds, crushed
2 tbsp	orange juice
1 tbsp	vegetable oil
1 tbsp	lemon juice
½ tsp	ground coriander
½ tsp	liquid honey
pinch	each salt and pepper

CARROT SALAD:

450 g	multicoloured heirloom carrots (about 3)
12	sprigs fresh cilantro
¼ cup	toasted unsalted pepitas (see tip, right)
¼ cup	crumbled feta cheese

DIRECTIONS

ORANGE-CUMIN VINAIGRETTE: In small dry skillet over medium-high heat, toast cumin seeds until darkened and just beginning to pop, about 30 seconds. Transfer to large bowl. Whisk in orange juice, oil, lemon juice, coriander, honey, salt and pepper. Set aside.

CARROT SALAD: Using mandoline or vegetable peeler, slice carrots lengthwise into paper-thin strips. Chill carrot strips and cilantro in ice water; let stand for 3 minutes. Drain and pat dry.

Add carrots, cilantro and pepitas to vinaigrette; toss to coat. Sprinkle with feta.

NUTRITIONAL INFORMATION, PER SERVING: about 185 cal, 7 g pro, 12 g total fat (3 g sat. fat), 15 g carb, 5 g fibre, 9 mg chol, 190 mg sodium, 542 mg potassium. % RDI: 9% calcium, 20% iron, 196% vit A, 22% vit C, 19% folate.

TIP FROM THE TEST KITCHEN
Pepitas are hulled green pumpkin seeds. You can buy them in many forms: unsalted, salted, roasted or raw. Unsalted raw pepitas are the best choice for toasting and adding to this salad.

GREEK SALAD 30 ⬤

HANDS-ON TIME 15 minutes

TOTAL TIME 15 minutes

MAKES 8 servings

INGREDIENTS

1	English cucumber
2	sweet green peppers
2	large ripe tomatoes
1	red onion, chopped
1 cup	Kalamata olives
¼ cup	extra-virgin olive oil
3 tbsp	red wine vinegar
2 tbsp	chopped fresh oregano (or 2 tsp dried)
¼ tsp	each salt and pepper
170 g	feta cheese, cut in 8 slices

DIRECTIONS

Quarter cucumber lengthwise and cut into ¾-inch (2 cm) chunks. Cut green peppers into same-size pieces. Place in large bowl. *(Make-ahead: Cover and refrigerate for up to 4 hours.)*

Cut tomatoes into same-size chunks. Add to bowl along with onion and olives. Sprinkle with oil, vinegar, oregano, salt and pepper; toss to combine. Top each serving with 1 slice of the feta.

NUTRITIONAL INFORMATION, PER SERVING: about 214 cal, 5 g pro, 18 g total fat (5 g sat. fat), 11 g carb, 3 g fibre, 20 mg chol, 808 mg sodium. % RDI: 13% calcium, 8% iron, 9% vit A, 67% vit C, 15% folate.

KOHLRABI AND RUTABAGA SLAW 30 ⬤

HANDS-ON TIME 15 minutes

TOTAL TIME 15 minutes

MAKES 4 to 6 servings

INGREDIENTS

¼ cup	light mayonnaise
¼ cup	Balkan-style plain yogurt
1 tbsp	lemon juice
2 tsp	Dijon mustard
¼ tsp	each salt and pepper
2 cups	julienned peeled kohlrabi
2 cups	julienned peeled rutabaga
¼ cup	chopped fresh parsley

DIRECTIONS

In large bowl, whisk together mayonnaise, yogurt, lemon juice, mustard, salt and pepper. Add kohlrabi, rutabaga and parsley; toss to coat. *(Make-ahead: Refrigerate in airtight container for up to 3 days. Toss just before serving.)*

NUTRITIONAL INFORMATION, PER EACH OF 6 SERVINGS: about 70 cal, 2 g pro, 4 g total fat (1 g sat. fat), 8 g carb, 3 g fibre, 5 mg chol, 208 mg sodium, 325 mg potassium. % RDI: 5% calcium, 4% iron, 3% vit A, 63% vit C, 9% folate.

TIP FROM THE TEST KITCHEN
This dressing is equally tasty over julienned celeriac or broccoli stems, or shredded brussels sprouts.

CLASSIC CREAMY COLESLAW ◖

Creamy coleslaw is a summertime favourite with just about anything grilled. The extra step of draining the shredded cabbage helps the salad last longer without getting watery.

HANDS-ON TIME
30 minutes

TOTAL TIME
2½ hours

MAKES
8 servings

INGREDIENTS

COLESLAW MIX:

8 cups	shredded cabbage
1¼ tsp	salt
3 cups	grated carrots
half	red onion, thinly sliced

CREAMY DRESSING:

¾ cup	mayonnaise
2 tbsp	vinegar
1 tsp	granulated sugar
1 tsp	dry mustard
½ tsp	celery seeds
¼ cup	chopped fresh parsley

DIRECTIONS

COLESLAW MIX: In large bowl, toss cabbage with 1 tsp of the salt. In separate bowl, toss together carrots, onion and remaining salt. Let both stand for 1 hour.

In colander, drain cabbage. By handfuls, squeeze out excess moisture and return to bowl. Repeat with carrot mixture; add to cabbage and toss to combine.

CREAMY DRESSING: Whisk together mayonnaise, vinegar, sugar, mustard and celery seeds.

TO FINISH: Toss together coleslaw mix, dressing and parsley. Cover and refrigerate for 1 hour. *(Make-ahead: Cover and refrigerate for up to 3 days.)*

NUTRITIONAL INFORMATION, PER SERVING: about 193 cal, 2 g pro, 17 g total fat (2 g sat. fat), 11 g carb, 3 g fibre, 8 mg chol, 268 mg sodium, 343 mg potassium. % RDI: 5% calcium, 6% iron, 73% vit A, 47% vit C, 21% folate.

VARIATION

CLASSIC TANGY COLESLAW

Omit Creamy Dressing. Whisk together ⅓ cup vinegar, 2 tbsp vegetable oil, 4 tsp granulated sugar, 1 tsp dry mustard and ½ tsp celery seeds; toss with coleslaw mix and parsley. Refrigerate as directed. This slaw is an ideal side with fried fish.

CLASSIC CREAMY POTATO SALAD

Fresh herbs give this potato salad lots of bright flavour. Cooking the potatoes whole, with the skin on, keeps them from getting soggy and gives them the best texture.

HANDS-ON TIME
20 minutes

TOTAL TIME
1½ hours

MAKES
6 to 8 servings

INGREDIENTS

1.6 kg	white potatoes (about 7), each about 3 inches (8 cm) long, scrubbed (see tip, below)
1 cup	sour cream
¾ cup	chopped dill pickles (about 2)
¾ cup	mayonnaise
½ cup	chopped fresh parsley
⅓ cup	chopped fresh chives
1 tbsp	drained capers, finely chopped
1 tbsp	Dijon mustard
2 tsp	lemon juice
½ tsp	each salt and pepper
4	hard-cooked eggs (optional), peeled and chopped

DIRECTIONS

In large pot of boiling salted water, cook potatoes until they easily slide off knife when pierced in centre, about 25 minutes. Drain and let cool slightly; peel. Cover and refrigerate until completely cooled, about 1 hour; cut into chunks.

In large bowl, whisk together sour cream, pickles, mayonnaise, parsley, chives, capers, mustard, lemon juice, salt and pepper; add potatoes and stir to coat. Stir in egg, if using. *(Make-ahead: Cover and refrigerate for up to 24 hours.)*

NUTRITIONAL INFORMATION, PER EACH OF 8 SERVINGS: about 339 cal, 5 g pro, 21 g total fat (5 g sat. fat), 34 g carb, 3 g fibre, 18 mg chol, 822 mg sodium, 684 mg potassium. % RDI: 6% calcium, 6% iron, 10% vit A, 45% vit C, 13% folate.

TIP FROM THE TEST KITCHEN
White potatoes have a waxy texture that works very well in cold salads. Save fluffier russets for baking, mashing or making fries.

DILLED POTATO AND GRILLED CORN SALAD ③⓿ ◐

HANDS-ON TIME 15 minutes

TOTAL TIME 30 minutes

MAKES 6 to 8 servings

INGREDIENTS

4	cobs corn, husked
3 tbsp	vegetable oil
900 g	small red or white potatoes (about 30), peeled
4	green onions, sliced
2 tsp	grainy mustard
½ tsp	salt
¼ tsp	pepper
¼ cup	red wine vinegar
2 tbsp	chopped fresh dill (see tip, below)

DIRECTIONS

Brush corn with 1 tbsp of the oil. Place on greased grill over medium-high heat; close lid and grill, turning occasionally, until tender and slightly charred, 10 to 15 minutes. Let cool. Cut off kernels and place in large bowl.

While corn is grilling, in large saucepan of boiling salted water, cook potatoes until tender, about 15 minutes. Drain and halve; add to bowl.

Add green onions, mustard, salt and pepper; sprinkle with vinegar and toss to coat. Let cool.

Add remaining oil and dill; toss to coat.

NUTRITIONAL INFORMATION, PER EACH OF 8 SERVINGS: about 197 cal, 4 g pro, 6 g total fat (1 g sat. fat), 34 g carb, 4 g fibre, 0 mg chol, 400 mg sodium, 641 mg potassium. % RDI: 2% calcium, 10% iron, 2% vit A, 37% vit C, 22% folate.

TIP FROM THE TEST KITCHEN
This salad is equally delicious with other tender, leafy herbs. Change them up to suit your menu. Try tarragon for a French theme, or cilantro for an Asian- or Latin American–inspired menu.

ROASTED BEET AND FETA SALAD ◐

HANDS-ON TIME 17 minutes

TOTAL TIME 1¼ hours

MAKES 4 servings

INGREDIENTS

6	baby beets, trimmed
3 tbsp	extra-virgin olive oil
2 tbsp	red wine vinegar
½ tsp	Dijon mustard
pinch	each salt and pepper
6 cups	loosely packed baby greens
¼ cup	thinly sliced red onion
2 tbsp	each chopped fresh parsley, dill and chives
½ cup	crumbled feta cheese (see tip, page 19)

DIRECTIONS

Arrange beets on double-thickness piece of foil; seal to form package. Roast on rimmed baking sheet in 425°F (220°C) oven until tender, about 45 minutes. Let cool enough to handle. Remove skins; cut beets into wedges. Set aside.

In large bowl, whisk together oil, vinegar, mustard, salt and pepper. Add beets, greens, onion, parsley, dill and chives; toss to coat. Sprinkle with feta.

NUTRITIONAL INFORMATION, PER SERVING: about 184 cal, 5 g pro, 15 g total fat (4 g sat. fat), 10 g carb, 3 g fibre, 17 mg chol, 287 mg sodium, 466 mg potassium. % RDI: 15% calcium, 11% iron, 23% vit A, 30% vit C, 59% folate.

VARIATION

ROASTED BEET AND GOAT CHEESE SALAD
Substitute crumbled soft goat cheese for the feta cheese.

CREAMY CUCUMBER SALAD

This easy-to-prepare Scandinavian-style salad is full of lively flavours. Salting and draining the cucumber is essential to prevent the dish from getting watery.

HANDS-ON TIME
15 minutes

TOTAL TIME
1 hour

MAKES
4 servings

INGREDIENTS

3 cups	thinly sliced peeled English cucumber
1 tsp	salt
½ cup	thinly sliced red onion
¼ cup	light or regular sour cream
1 tbsp	chopped fresh dill (or 1 tsp dried dillweed)
1 tbsp	white wine vinegar
1 tsp	granulated sugar

DIRECTIONS

In colander, sprinkle cucumber with salt; let drain for 30 minutes. Pat dry.

Meanwhile, soak onion in cold water for 15 minutes; drain and pat dry.

In bowl, whisk together sour cream, dill, vinegar and sugar. Add cucumber and onion; toss to coat.

NUTRITIONAL INFORMATION, PER SERVING: about 38 cal, 2 g pro, 1 g total fat (1 g sat. fat), 6 g carb, 1 g fibre, 2 mg chol, 302 mg sodium. % RDI: 4% calcium, 1% iron, 1% vit A, 7% vit C, 7% folate.

TIP FROM THE TEST KITCHEN

You can also use a regular field cucumber to make this salad. Once you've peeled it, slice the cucumber in half lengthwise. Run a small spoon down the centre to scoop out the tough seeds, and then slice the cucumber.

TABBOULEH

HANDS-ON TIME 20 minutes

TOTAL TIME 40 minutes

MAKES 4 servings

INGREDIENTS

½ cup	medium bulgur
3 cups	chopped seeded tomatoes
1 cup	minced fresh parsley
¼ cup	minced fresh mint
4	green onions, minced
½ cup	lemon juice
¼ cup	extra-virgin olive oil
¼ tsp	each salt and pepper

DIRECTIONS

Place bulgur in fine-mesh sieve; rinse several times under running water. Transfer to bowl; cover with ½ inch (1 cm) water and let stand for 20 minutes. Drain; by handfuls, squeeze bulgur to remove excess water.

In large bowl, combine bulgur, tomatoes, parsley, mint and green onions. Whisk together lemon juice, oil, salt and pepper; add to bulgur mixture and toss to coat. *(Make-ahead: Cover and refrigerate for up to 8 hours.)*

NUTRITIONAL INFORMATION, PER SERVING: about 223 cal, 4 g pro, 14 g total fat (2 g sat. fat), 23 g carb, 6 g fibre, 0 mg chol, 178 mg sodium. % RDI: 6% calcium, 20% iron, 28% vit A, 82% vit C, 30% folate.

TIP FROM THE TEST KITCHEN

Bulgur is wheat that has had just a bit of the bran removed; it is still considered a whole grain because it contains most of the nutrients in the whole kernel. Bulgur comes in different grinds; medium has the right texture for salads like this.

MEDITERRANEAN KALE SALAD

HANDS-ON TIME 10 minutes

TOTAL TIME 2¼ hours

MAKES 8 to 10 servings

INGREDIENTS

3 tbsp	extra-virgin olive oil
2 tbsp	balsamic vinegar
1 tsp	liquid honey
2	cloves garlic, minced
½ tsp	pepper
pinch	salt
10 cups	stemmed kale, thinly sliced
2 cups	cherry tomatoes, halved
1	can (398 mL) water-packed artichoke hearts, drained, rinsed and thinly sliced
1 cup	shaved Pecorino-Romano or Parmesan cheese (about 80 g)

DIRECTIONS

In large bowl, whisk together oil, vinegar, honey, garlic, pepper and salt. Add kale, tomatoes and artichoke hearts; toss to coat.

Cover and refrigerate, tossing occasionally, until kale begins to soften slightly, about 2 hours. *(Make-ahead: Refrigerate for up to 24 hours.)*

Toss salad just before serving; sprinkle with Pecorino-Romano.

NUTRITIONAL INFORMATION, PER EACH OF 10 SERVINGS: about 125 cal, 6 g pro, 7 g total fat (2 g sat. fat), 12 g carb, 3 g fibre, 8 mg chol, 213 mg sodium, 476 mg potassium. % RDI: 18% calcium, 12% iron, 64% vit A, 145% vit C, 17% folate.

BLACK AND WHITE
BEAN AND QUINOA SALAD ㉚ ◖

This salad packs a protein punch along with good amounts of fibre and iron.
Plus, it looks beautiful on the table, with its mix of pale green cukes, purplish-red onion,
and black and white beans.

HANDS ON TIME
15 minutes

TOTAL TIME
30 minutes

MAKES
4 servings

INGREDIENTS

DRESSING:

¼ cup	vegetable oil
2 tbsp	lime juice
1 tbsp	cider vinegar
1	clove garlic, minced
1 tsp	each chili powder and ground coriander
½ tsp	dried oregano
¼ tsp	each salt and pepper

BEAN AND QUINOA SALAD:

⅓ cup	quinoa, rinsed
1	can (540 mL) black beans, drained and rinsed
1	can (540 mL) navy beans, drained and rinsed
1 cup	diced English cucumber
¼ cup	diced red onion
1	jalapeño pepper, seeded and minced
¼ cup	chopped fresh cilantro

DIRECTIONS

DRESSING: In large bowl, whisk together oil, lime juice, vinegar, garlic, chili powder, coriander, oregano, salt and pepper. Set aside.

BEAN AND QUINOA SALAD: In saucepan of boiling salted water, cook quinoa until tender, about 12 minutes. Drain and rinse; drain well.

Add quinoa, black beans, navy beans, cucumber, onion, jalapeño pepper and cilantro to dressing; toss to combine.

NUTRITIONAL INFORMATION, PER SERVING: about 415 cal, 17 g pro, 16 g total fat (1 g sat. fat), 55 g carb, 11 g fibre, 0 mg chol, 984 mg sodium. % RDI: 9% calcium, 38% iron, 3% vit A, 13% vit C, 59% folate.

WILD RICE AND LENTIL SALAD

Wild rice is a tasty, nutritious ingredient (see tip, below). Blending it with Indian spices, sweet currants and crunchy almonds makes a salad that's ideal any time of year.

HANDS-ON TIME
5 minutes

TOTAL TIME
1 hour

MAKES
8 to 10 servings

INGREDIENTS

1 cup	wild rice, rinsed and drained
1 tsp	each ground coriander and ground cumin
½ tsp	each turmeric and granulated sugar
¼ tsp	each cinnamon, salt and pepper
¼ cup	vinegar
¼ cup	olive oil
1	can (540 mL) lentils, drained and rinsed
1 cup	diced red onion
½ cup	chopped fresh parsley
¼ cup	dried currants
½ cup	sliced almonds, toasted

DIRECTIONS

In small saucepan, bring 4 cups water and wild rice to boil; reduce heat, cover and simmer until most of the rice is split and tender, about 45 minutes. Remove from heat; let stand, covered, for 5 minutes. Drain; transfer to large bowl.

While rice is standing, in separate large bowl, whisk together coriander, cumin, turmeric, sugar, cinnamon, salt and pepper; whisk in vinegar and oil. Stir in rice, lentils, onion, parsley and currants. *(Make-ahead: Refrigerate in airtight container for up to 2 days.)*

Stir in almonds just before serving.

NUTRITIONAL INFORMATION, PER EACH OF 10 SERVINGS: about 199 cal, 7 g pro, 8 g total fat (1 g sat. fat), 26 g carb, 4 g fibre, 0 mg chol, 159 mg sodium, 316 mg potassium. % RDI: 3% calcium, 18% iron, 3% vit A, 10% vit C, 44% folate.

TIP FROM THE TEST KITCHEN

There are good reasons to add wild rice to your menu regularly. It is high in fibre and protein (with double that of brown rice) and is a rich source of iron, thiamine, riboflavin, niacin, calcium, phosphorus and carbohydrates. It's also naturally gluten-free, but make sure to check the label on the package to ensure that your wild rice has been processed in a gluten-free facility to prevent cross-contamination with wheat or other gluten-containing grains.

BEAN, MUSHROOM AND WILTED SPINACH SALAD 30

Baby greens are the solution when you want to make a salad without a lot of prep. They have tender stems, so you don't have to trim them—plus the leaves are already bite-size!

HANDS-ON TIME
25 minutes

TOTAL TIME
25 minutes

MAKES
4 servings

INGREDIENTS

225 g	yellow or green beans, trimmed
1	bag (170 g) baby spinach
3 tbsp	extra-virgin olive oil
1	small red or sweet onion, thinly sliced
225 g	cremini mushrooms
1	clove garlic, minced
¼ tsp	each salt and pepper
¼ tsp	dried thyme
1 cup	rinsed drained canned chickpeas
3 tbsp	white wine vinegar
4	hard-cooked eggs, quartered
3 tbsp	shaved Asiago cheese

DIRECTIONS

In saucepan of boiling water, blanch beans until tender-crisp, about 2 minutes. Drain and set aside.

Meanwhile, place spinach in large bowl; set aside.

In large skillet, heat oil over medium-high heat; sauté onion until tender, about 5 minutes. Add mushrooms, garlic, salt, pepper and thyme; cook, stirring occasionally, until mushrooms are tender and no liquid remains, about 7 minutes.

Add beans, chickpeas and vinegar to skillet; cook until heated through, about 3 minutes. Add to spinach, tossing to wilt and coat.

Arrange salad on plates. Top with eggs; sprinkle with Asiago.

NUTRITIONAL INFORMATION, PER SERVING: about 352 cal, 18 g pro, 18 g total fat (4 g sat. fat), 32 g carb, 10 g fibre, 190 mg chol, 530 mg sodium, 814 mg potassium. % RDI: 18% calcium, 31% iron, 51% vit A, 15% vit C, 76% folate.

TIP FROM THE TEST KITCHEN
Sweet onions aren't as pungent as cooking, white or red onions, which makes them a great choice for delicately flavoured salads. There are many varieties; Vidalia and Walla Walla are common ones.

ORANGE, SALMON AND ORZO SALAD ㉚ ◉

HANDS-ON TIME
25 minutes

TOTAL TIME
30 minutes

MAKES
4 servings

This pasta salad makes a scrumptious main dish, but you can serve smaller portions as a side.

INGREDIENTS

ORANGE-CHIVE DRESSING:

½ tsp	grated orange zest
3 tbsp	orange juice
2 tbsp	chopped fresh chives
2 tsp	Dijon mustard
1 tsp	liquid honey
1	clove garlic, finely grated or pressed
½ tsp	each salt and pepper
⅓ cup	vegetable oil

SALAD:

450 g	skinless salmon fillet
pinch	each salt and pepper
¼ cup	chopped fresh parsley
4 tsp	Dijon mustard
2 tsp	grated orange zest
1½ cups	orzo
2 cups	snow peas, trimmed and sliced diagonally
8 cups	baby arugula
2 cups	watercress

DIRECTIONS

ORANGE-CHIVE DRESSING: In small bowl, whisk together orange zest, orange juice, chives, mustard, honey, garlic, salt and pepper; slowly whisk in oil until blended. Set aside.

SALAD: Sprinkle salmon with salt and pepper. Stir together parsley, mustard and orange zest; spread over salmon. Place on lightly greased foil-lined rimmed baking sheet. Bake in 400°F (200°C) oven until fish flakes easily when tested, about 15 minutes. Transfer to cutting board; chop or break into large chunks.

While salmon is baking, in large saucepan of boiling salted water, cook orzo until almost al dente, about 8 minutes. Add snow peas and cook until orzo is al dente and peas are bright green and tender-crisp, about 30 seconds. Drain.

In large bowl, toss together orzo mixture, arugula, watercress and dressing. Gently fold in salmon.

NUTRITIONAL INFORMATION, PER SERVING: about 635 cal, 32 g pro, 31 g total fat (4 g sat. fat), 56 g carb, 4 g fibre, 55 mg chol, 714 mg sodium, 721 mg potassium. % RDI: 11% calcium, 21% iron, 20% vit A, 75% vit C, 43% folate.

PANCETTA AND EGGS ON HEARTY GREENS ㉚ 🍴

You'll find versions of this satisfying dinner salad in small bistros all over France. If you like fresh black pepper, grind some over the poached eggs just before serving.

HANDS-ON TIME
30 minutes

TOTAL TIME
30 minutes

MAKES
4 servings

INGREDIENTS

CAPER DRESSING:

⅓ cup	thinly sliced shallots
2 tbsp	white wine vinegar
1 tbsp	drained capers, finely chopped
2 tsp	Dijon mustard
pinch	each granulated sugar, salt and pepper
⅓ cup	extra-virgin olive oil

POACHED EGGS:

1 tbsp	vinegar
4	eggs (unshelled)

SALAD:

1 tbsp	extra-virgin olive oil
8	thin slices pancetta
1	pkg (340 g) mixed mushrooms, sliced
pinch	each salt and pepper
1	head curly endive, torn (about 10 cups)
1	head radicchio, torn (about 4 cups)

DIRECTIONS

CAPER DRESSING: In bowl, combine shallots, vinegar, capers, mustard, sugar, salt and pepper; slowly whisk in oil until blended. Set aside.

POACHED EGGS: In large saucepan or deep skillet, heat 2 to 3 inches (5 to 8 cm) water over medium heat until simmering. Add vinegar. One at a time, crack eggs into custard cup or small bowl; gently slide into simmering water. Reduce heat to low; cook until whites are set and yolks are still soft, about 3 minutes. Using slotted spoon, transfer to paper towel–lined tray; keep warm.

SALAD: While eggs are poaching, in large skillet, heat oil over medium-high heat; cook pancetta until crisp, about 4 minutes. Transfer to paper towel–lined plate; let drain.

Drain off all but 2 tbsp fat from pan. Add mushrooms, salt and pepper; cook, stirring occasionally, over medium heat, until tender and no liquid remains, about 6 minutes.

In large bowl, toss together endive, radicchio, mushroom mixture and dressing. Divide among 4 plates; top each with pancetta and poached egg.

NUTRITIONAL INFORMATION, PER SERVING: about 395 cal, 16 g pro, 33 g total fat (6 g sat. fat), 13 g carb, 4 g fibre, 206 mg chol, 498 mg sodium, 976 mg potassium. % RDI: 11% calcium, 22% iron, 35% vit A, 22% vit C, 113% folate.

THAI STEAK, MANGO AND PEPPER SALAD ㉚ ◑

When the Test Kitchen calls for lime or other citrus juice, we always mean freshly squeezed, because it has the best flavour.

HANDS-ON TIME
30 minutes

TOTAL TIME
30 minutes

MAKES
4 servings

INGREDIENTS

STEAK:

450 g	beef top sirloin grilling steak (¾ inch/2 cm thick)
2 tbsp	each fish sauce and lime juice
1 tbsp	vegetable oil
2 tsp	grated fresh ginger

MANGO AND PEPPER SALAD:

3 tbsp	vegetable oil
2 tbsp	lime juice
1 tsp	fish sauce
¼ tsp	Asian chili sauce (such as sriracha)
1	mango, peeled, pitted and cut in matchsticks
1	sweet red pepper, cut in matchsticks
⅓ cup	sliced sweet onion
¼ cup	fresh cilantro leaves, chopped
¼ cup	roasted peanuts, chopped
half	pkg (454 g pkg) dried rice stick noodles (¼ inch/ 5 mm wide)

DIRECTIONS

STEAK: Place steak in shallow dish. Whisk together fish sauce, lime juice, oil and ginger; pour over steak, turning to coat. Let stand for 10 minutes.

Reserving marinade, place steak on greased grill over medium-high heat; close lid and grill, turning and brushing with reserved marinade halfway through, until medium-rare, about 10 minutes. Transfer to cutting board; cover loosely with foil and let rest for 5 minutes before thinly slicing across the grain.

MANGO AND PEPPER SALAD: While steak is grilling, in large bowl, whisk together oil, lime juice, fish sauce and chili sauce. Add mango, red pepper, onion, cilantro and peanuts; toss to combine.

TO FINISH: Prepare noodles according to package instructions. Drain well; top with salad and steak.

NUTRITIONAL INFORMATION, PER SERVING: about 565 cal, 27 g pro, 23 g total fat (4 g sat. fat), 62 g carb, 4 g fibre, 52 mg chol, 901 mg sodium, 550 mg potassium. % RDI: 3% calcium, 21% iron, 14% vit A, 97% vit C, 23% folate.

TIP FROM THE TEST KITCHEN
This salad is naturally gluten-free, but be sure to check the ingredient list on your container of peanuts. Roasted varieties sometimes contain gluten.

ULTRA-CRISPY
ROASTED POTATOES
page 90

ULTIMATE SIDE DISHES | 4

"To me, a meal isn't complete without lots of delicious sides. Sometimes I find myself looking forward to them even more than the main event."

AMANDA BARNIER FOOD SPECIALIST

CREAMY POTATO AND CHEESE GRATIN

The dark green parts of leeks are unpleasantly chewy, so we don't include them in most recipes. They are, however, great for flavouring homemade stocks (page 45), so save them; simply remove and set them aside before slicing the white and light green parts.

HANDS-ON TIME
50 minutes

TOTAL TIME
1½ hours

MAKES
8 to 10 servings

INGREDIENTS

POTATO GRATIN:

1 tbsp	extra-virgin olive oil
1	leek (white and light green parts only), halved and thinly sliced
4	strips bacon (see tip, below)
1.35 kg	yellow-fleshed potatoes, peeled and cut in ¼-inch (5 mm) thick slices
1½ cups	sodium-reduced chicken broth
1 cup	whipping cream (35%)
½ cup	milk
3	sprigs fresh thyme
2	cloves garlic, thinly sliced
½ tsp	each salt and pepper
pinch	nutmeg
1 cup	shredded Gruyère cheese

TOPPING:

1 cup	fresh bread crumbs
½ cup	shredded Gruyère cheese
2 tbsp	unsalted butter, melted

DIRECTIONS

POTATO GRATIN: In large skillet, heat oil over medium heat; cook leek, stirring occasionally, until softened and light golden, about 4 minutes. Transfer to bowl; set aside.

In same skillet over medium heat, cook bacon until crisp, 6 to 8 minutes. Transfer to paper towel–lined plate; let drain. Chop bacon; set aside.

Drain fat from pan; wipe clean. Add potatoes, broth, cream, milk, thyme, garlic, salt, pepper and nutmeg; bring just to simmer over medium heat, about 10 minutes. Reduce heat to medium-low; partially cover and simmer, stirring occasionally, until potatoes are fork-tender but still hold their shape, about 12 minutes. Discard thyme.

Using slotted spoon, transfer half of the potatoes to greased 13- x 9-inch (3 L) baking dish. Sprinkle with Gruyère, leek and bacon; top with remaining potatoes. Scrape cooking liquid over top.

TOPPING: Stir together bread crumbs, Gruyère and butter; sprinkle over potato mixture.

Bake in 400°F (200°C) oven until sauce is bubbly and topping is crisp and golden, 25 to 30 minutes.

NUTRITIONAL INFORMATION, PER EACH OF 10 SERVINGS: about 295 cal, 9 g pro, 18 g total fat (10 g sat. fat), 25 g carb, 2 g fibre, 56 mg chol, 319 mg sodium, 686 mg potassium. % RDI: 20% calcium, 9% iron, 17% vit A, 30% vit C, 10% folate.

TIP FROM THE TEST KITCHEN
Don't want the bacon? Just leave it out. The gratin will still be creamy, indulgent and totally delicious.

BEST-EVER FRENCH FRIES ⊙

Blanching the potatoes in oil, letting them drain, and then frying them until golden ensures the crispiest fries. The oil temperature will fluctuate, so you may need to adjust the heat. Top with Poutine Gravy (below) and cheese curds to make our national snack obsession—poutine.

HANDS-ON TIME
1 hour

TOTAL TIME
1 hour

MAKES
8 servings

INGREDIENTS

| | vegetable oil for deep-frying |
| 1.8 kg | baking potatoes (such as russet) |

DIRECTIONS

Pour enough oil into deep fryer or deep saucepan to come no more than halfway up side; heat until deep-fryer thermometer reads 375°F (190°C).

Meanwhile, scrub potatoes; cut lengthwise into ¼-inch (5 mm) thick slices. Stacking 2 or 3 slices at a time, cut lengthwise into ¼-inch (5 mm) wide sticks. Pat dry.

Working in small batches, blanch potatoes in oil until barely golden, 30 to 45 seconds per batch. Transfer to paper towel–lined baking sheet; let drain and cool slightly. *(Make-ahead: Let stand for 1 hour.)*

Working in batches, return potatoes to oil and fry until tender and golden, 4 to 5 minutes per batch. Transfer to paper towel–lined baking sheet; let drain.

NUTRITIONAL INFORMATION, PER SERVING: about 317 cal, 5 g pro, 16 g total fat (1 g sat. fat), 41 g carb, 3 g fibre, 0 mg chol, 11 mg sodium, 844 mg potassium. % RDI: 3% calcium, 13% iron, 55% vit C, 13% folate

POUTINE GRAVY

In small bowl, pour ⅓ cup warm water over 2 dried morel mushrooms; let stand until softened, about 15 minutes. Meanwhile, in Dutch oven, heat 4 tsp vegetable oil over medium heat. Cook 1 onion, chopped; 2 shallots, chopped; 2 cloves garlic, minced; 2 tbsp tomato paste; and 6 sprigs fresh thyme until onions and shallots are softened and golden, about 5 minutes.

Stir in 3 cups sodium-reduced beef broth, 2 cups sodium-reduced chicken broth, 1 tbsp mixed whole peppercorns, 2 tsp cider vinegar, ½ tsp each granulated sugar and Worcestershire sauce, and pinch each dried sage leaves and salt. Add mushrooms and soaking liquid; bring to boil. Reduce heat and simmer, stirring occasionally, for 15 minutes. Strain through fine-mesh sieve into large glass measure. Discard onion mixture.

In same Dutch oven, melt ⅓ cup butter over medium heat; add ½ cup all-purpose flour, whisking constantly, until mixture forms smooth paste and is pale butterscotch colour, about 4 minutes. Whisk in reserved broth mixture; bring to boil. Reduce heat and simmer, whisking constantly, until thickened, about 5 minutes. **MAKES** 4 cups.

SMOOTH AND CREAMY MASHED POTATOES ③⓪

Russet potatoes cook up to be super-fluffy, and pressing them through a ricer is the key to creating the smoothest mashed potatoes. You can boil and rice the potatoes a day ahead, which makes this side dish easy to finish at the last minute.

HANDS-ON TIME
15 minutes

TOTAL TIME
30 minutes

MAKES
8 to 10 servings

INGREDIENTS

2.25 kg	russet potatoes, peeled and cut in chunks
1¼ cups	10% cream
¼ cup	butter
1 tsp	salt
¼ tsp	pepper

DIRECTIONS

In large pot of boiling salted water, cook potatoes until fork-tender, about 15 minutes. Drain well. Press potatoes through ricer; spread on parchment paper–lined rimmed baking sheet. *(Make-ahead: Let cool. Cover and refrigerate for up to 24 hours. Continue with recipe, adding 8 minutes to cooking time.)*

In large saucepan, heat cream, butter, salt and pepper over medium heat until butter is melted; stir in riced potatoes. Cook, stirring often, until smooth and hot, about 4 minutes.

NUTRITIONAL INFORMATION, PER EACH OF 10 SERVINGS: about 219 cal, 5 g pro, 8 g total fat (5 g sat. fat), 34 g carb, 2 g fibre, 22 mg chol, 708 mg sodium, 718 mg potassium. % RDI: 5% calcium, 11% iron, 6% vit A, 45% vit C, 10% folate.

TIP FROM THE TEST KITCHEN
Don't have a ricer? A standard potato masher will also work in a pinch. Mash thoroughly and spread the potatoes out as directed.

ULTRA-CRISPY ROASTED POTATOES

Fluffy on the inside and crispy on the outside, these roasted potatoes are incredible. Duck fat is the secret to their rich flavour, but you can customize the taste by switching up the type of fat you use.

HANDS-ON TIME
20 minutes

TOTAL TIME
1½ hours

MAKES
4 servings

INGREDIENTS

1 kg	russet potatoes, peeled and cut in 1½-inch (4 cm) pieces
¼ cup	duck, goose, beef or chicken fat (or 2 tbsp each olive oil and melted unsalted butter)
½ tsp	salt
pinch	pepper

DIRECTIONS

In large saucepan of boiling salted water, cook potatoes just until fork-tender, about 6 minutes. Drain well.

In roasting pan, heat duck fat in 450°F (230°C) oven just until beginning to smoke, about 4 minutes. Remove from oven; standing back and averting face, add potatoes. Sprinkle with salt and pepper; stir to coat. Roast, turning potatoes every 20 minutes, until golden, 50 to 60 minutes.

NUTRITIONAL INFORMATION, PER SERVING: about 277 cal, 4 g pro, 13 g total fat (4 g sat. fat), 37 g carb, 3 g fibre, 13 mg chol, 780 mg sodium, 766 mg potassium. % RDI: 2% calcium, 12% iron, 50% vit C, 12% folate.

TIP FROM THE TEST KITCHEN
If you don't have a roasting pan big enough to fit the potatoes, a large rimmed baking sheet will also work. Just be careful when stirring and lifting the pan out of the oven so none of the hot fat spills onto your oven floor.

SAVOURY SLOW COOKER STUFFING

HANDS-ON TIME
15 minutes

TOTAL TIME
6¼ hours

MAKES
8 servings

If you like moist stuffing, this recipe is for you—and it requires absolutely no oven space. Choose an apple that holds its shape when cooked, such as Cortland, Braeburn or Crispin.

INGREDIENTS

12 cups	cubed day-old bread (see tip, below)
1	onion, diced
2	ribs celery, diced
1	cooking apple, peeled, cored and diced
1½ tsp	crumbled dried sage
1 tsp	crumbled dried thyme
¼ tsp	each salt and pepper
½ cup	sodium-reduced chicken broth
2 tbsp	unsalted butter, melted

DIRECTIONS

In large bowl, toss together bread, onion, celery, apple, sage, thyme, salt and pepper. Drizzle with broth and butter; toss to moisten. Transfer to slow cooker.

Cover and cook on low, stirring once, until vegetables are tender, about 6 hours.

NUTRITIONAL INFORMATION, PER SERVING: about 174 cal, 5 g pro, 5 g total fat (2 g sat. fat), 29 g carb, 2 g fibre, 8 mg chol, 385 mg sodium, 124 mg potassium. % RDI: 6% calcium, 13% iron, 3% vit A, 3% vit C, 23% folate.

TIP FROM THE TEST KITCHEN
Be sure to use day-old bread that is firm (but not dry like croutons) instead of fresh bread. It will mean the difference between a moist or soggy stuffing.

BASMATI RICE ㉚
WITH PESTO

Store-bought flavoured rice packages contain astronomical amounts of sodium per serving. Homemade rice dishes like this not only taste great but also lean way less on salt as a flavour enhancer. Here, fragrant, garlicky pesto does the trick.

HANDS-ON TIME
20 minutes

TOTAL TIME
30 minutes

MAKES
4 servings

INGREDIENTS

1½ cups	basmati rice (see tip, below)
½ cup	fresh basil leaves
2 tbsp	each extra-virgin olive oil and lemon juice
1	small clove garlic, minced
¼ tsp	each salt and pepper

DIRECTIONS

Wash rice in 3 changes of cold water; drain and transfer to saucepan. Add 1¾ cups water; bring to boil. Reduce heat, cover and simmer over low heat until water is completely absorbed, about 15 minutes. Let stand, covered, for 5 minutes.

Meanwhile, in food processor, pulse together basil, oil, lemon juice, garlic, salt and pepper until slightly chunky. Stir into rice.

NUTRITIONAL INFORMATION, PER SERVING: about 317 cal, 6 g pro, 7 g total fat (1 g sat. fat), 56 g carb, 1 g fibre, 0 mg chol, 147 mg sodium. % RDI: 3% calcium, 5% iron, 3% vit A, 3% vit C, 4% folate.

TIP FROM THE TEST KITCHEN
Any long-grain white rice will work in this recipe. Try jasmine rice for a completely different aromatic note.

RISOTTO MILANESE

Saffron is an essential ingredient in this Italian dish, giving it both a wonderful flavour and a beautiful colour. Beef broth is traditionally added to this recipe, but we use chicken broth instead to give the rice a prettier golden hue.

HANDS-ON TIME
30 minutes

TOTAL TIME
40 minutes

MAKES
6 servings

INGREDIENTS

½ cup	dry white wine
½ tsp	saffron threads, crumbled
3 cups	sodium-reduced chicken broth
¼ cup	butter
1	onion, chopped
¼ tsp	each salt and pepper
2 cups	arborio rice
½ cup	grated Parmesan cheese
2 tbsp	chopped fresh parsley

DIRECTIONS

Stir wine with saffron; let stand for 10 to 20 minutes.

In saucepan, bring broth and 3 cups water to simmer; keep warm.

In large skillet, melt 2 tbsp of the butter over medium heat; cook onion, salt and pepper, stirring occasionally, until onion is translucent, about 5 minutes. Stir in rice until coated.

Stir in saffron mixture; cook, stirring, until no liquid remains. Reduce heat to medium-low. Stir in warm broth, ½ cup at a time and adding more broth when completely absorbed, until rice is creamy and tender, about 20 minutes.

Stir in remaining butter, half of the Parmesan and the parsley. Sprinkle with remaining Parmesan.

NUTRITIONAL INFORMATION, PER SERVING: about 364 cal, 9 g pro, 11 g total fat (6 g sat. fat), 56 g carb, 1 g fibre, 28 mg chol, 584 mg sodium. % RDI: 10% calcium, 5% iron, 9% vit A, 3% vit C, 4% folate.

TIP FROM THE TEST KITCHEN
If you love a little extra colour and texture in your risotto, add 1 cup frozen peas in the last 2 minutes of cooking, before adding the butter.

CRISPY SPAGHETTI SQUASH BAKE ◖

Sweet spaghetti squash, roasted then baked with a savoury bread crumb and Parmesan topping, is a great partner to roast turkey.

HANDS-ON TIME
25 minutes

TOTAL TIME
2 hours

MAKES
10 to 12 servings

INGREDIENTS

2	spaghetti squash (2 kg total)
¼ tsp	each salt and pepper
2 tbsp	olive oil
1	onion, thinly sliced
1 tbsp	chopped fresh sage
1¼ cups	fresh bread crumbs (see tip, page 27)
¼ cup	grated Parmesan cheese
2 tbsp	butter, melted

DIRECTIONS

Using fork, pierce squash all over. Roast in roasting pan in 375°F (190°C) oven, turning twice, until tender when pressed, about 1 hour. Let cool slightly.

Cut squash in half lengthwise and scoop out seeds. Using fork, pull strands apart and place in colander. Drain for 30 minutes. Transfer to bowl; stir in salt and pepper.

While squash is draining, in large skillet, heat oil over medium heat; cook onion, stirring often, until golden, about 15 minutes. Add sage and toss to combine. Add to squash; gently stir to combine. Scrape into 8-inch (2 L) square baking dish. *(Make-ahead: Cover and refrigerate for up to 24 hours; bake, uncovered, for 25 minutes before continuing.)*

Combine bread crumbs, Parmesan and butter; spread over squash mixture. Bake in 400°F (200°C) oven until topping is golden, about 15 minutes.

NUTRITIONAL INFORMATION, PER EACH OF 12 SERVINGS: about 99 cal, 2 g pro, 5 g total fat (2 g sat. fat), 12 g carb, 2 g fibre, 7 mg chol, 141 mg sodium, 187 mg potassium. % RDI: 6% calcium, 6% iron, 4% vit A, 8% vit C, 7% folate.

BAKED BEANS

A little sweet, a little smoky and totally delish, baked beans are a must at any barbecue. They do require quite a bit of cooking time, but it's almost all hands-off.

HANDS ON TIME
15 minutes

TOTAL TIME
12¾ hours

MAKES
8 servings

INGREDIENTS

450 g	dried navy beans
⅔ cup	bottled strained tomatoes (passata)
⅓ cup	packed brown sugar
⅓ cup	cooking or blackstrap molasses (see tip, below)
1 tbsp	sodium-reduced soy sauce
1 tsp	dry mustard
½ tsp	salt
1	sweet onion, chopped
125 g	slab bacon, diced
60 g	salt pork, diced

DIRECTIONS

Rinse and soak beans overnight (8 to 12 hours) in 3 times their volume of water. (Or for quick-soak method, bring to boil; boil gently for 2 minutes. Remove from heat; cover and let stand for 1 hour.) Drain.

In saucepan, cover beans again with 3 times their volume of water and bring to boil. Reduce heat, cover and simmer until tender, 30 to 40 minutes. Reserving 2 cups of the cooking liquid, drain beans. Set aside.

Whisk together tomatoes, brown sugar, molasses, soy sauce, mustard and salt.

In bean pot or 16-cup (4 L) casserole dish, combine beans, reserved cooking liquid, tomato mixture, onion, bacon and salt pork. Cover and bake in 300°F (150°C) oven for 2 hours.

Uncover and bake until sauce is thickened and coats beans, about 2 hours. *(Make-ahead: Refrigerate in airtight container for up to 3 days.)*

NUTRITIONAL INFORMATION, PER SERVING: about 403 cal, 14 g pro, 13 g total fat (6 g sat. fat), 59 g carb, 10 g fibre, 16 mg chol, 462 mg sodium, 812 mg potassium. % RDI: 13% calcium, 34% iron, 5% vit C, 89% folate.

TIP FROM THE TEST KITCHEN
Blackstrap and cooking molasses both have a stronger flavour than fancy molasses. If you prefer a milder taste, feel free to use fancy molasses instead.

CHANA MASALA ③⓪ ◐

This chickpea dish is a common vegetarian main in India, but it makes a fine side dish too. If you're a fan of spice, add a finely chopped red finger hot pepper or two along with the garlic.

HANDS ON TIME
15 minutes

TOTAL TIME
30 minutes

MAKES
6 servings

INGREDIENTS

3 tbsp	olive oil
2	onions, chopped
6	cloves garlic, minced
2 tbsp	grated fresh ginger
2 tsp	each chili powder, ground coriander, ground cumin and garam masala
2	cans (each 540 mL) chickpeas, drained and rinsed
½ cup	tomato paste
2 tsp	packed brown sugar
¼ tsp	salt
2 tbsp	lemon juice

DIRECTIONS

In saucepan, heat oil over medium-high heat; cook onions, stirring occasionally, until softened, about 5 minutes.

Add garlic and ginger; cook for 1 minute. Stir in chili powder, coriander, cumin and garam masala; cook until fragrant, about 1 minute.

Stir in 1 cup water, chickpeas, tomato paste, brown sugar and salt, scraping up any browned bits from bottom of pan. Reduce heat, cover and simmer until thickened slightly, about 15 minutes. Stir in lemon juice.

NUTRITIONAL INFORMATION, PER SERVING: about 293 cal, 9 g pro, 9 g total fat (1 g sat. fat), 46 g carb, 9 g fibre, 0 mg chol, 518 mg sodium, 580 mg potassium. % RDI: 7% calcium, 25% iron, 6% vit A, 23% vit C, 43% folate.

TIP FROM THE TEST KITCHEN

Naan makes a great accompaniment, but the store-bought variety can be rather high in sodium. If you're watching your salt intake, steamed rice is a better choice.

SMASHED PEAS 30
WITH BACON AND BASIL

Fresh peas are so good, and this recipe shows off their natural sweetness. Serve with baked ham, roast chicken or steamed fish. Or spoon onto crostini and drizzle with your favourite extra-virgin olive oil to make a quick appetizer.

HANDS-ON TIME
15 minutes

TOTAL TIME
15 minutes

MAKES
4 servings

INGREDIENTS

3	strips bacon
3 cups	fresh or frozen peas
1 tbsp	olive oil
2	cloves garlic, minced
1	shallot, finely diced
¼ cup	2% plain Greek yogurt
1 tbsp	lemon juice
¼ tsp	each salt and pepper
4	fresh basil leaves, thinly sliced

DIRECTIONS

In nonstick skillet, cook bacon over medium-high heat until crisp, about 5 minutes. Transfer to paper towel–lined plate; let drain. Drain fat from pan.

Meanwhile, in saucepan of boiling lightly salted water, cook peas until softened, about 4 minutes for fresh or 1 minute for frozen. Drain; transfer to food processor.

Add oil to skillet; heat over medium heat. Cook garlic and shallot, stirring often, until shallot is softened, about 3 minutes. Add to food processor.

Add yogurt, lemon juice, salt and pepper to food processor; pulse until coarsely puréed. Stir in basil. Transfer to serving dish; crumble bacon over top.

NUTRITIONAL INFORMATION, PER SERVING: about 184 cal, 8 g pro, 9 g total fat (3 g sat. fat), 19 g carb, 7 g fibre, 9 mg chol, 514 mg sodium, 333 mg potassium. % RDI: 5% calcium, 13% iron, 9% vit A, 28% vit C, 31% folate.

TIP FROM THE TEST KITCHEN
After cutting a lemon, wash or rinse your knife as soon as possible. The acid can discolour and damage your blade if left to dry on it.

BALSAMIC-GLAZED SQUASH

This easy recipe has so few ingredients and takes so little time to prepare that you might want to consider keeping some extra squash around for spur-of-the-moment get-togethers.

HANDS-ON TIME
15 minutes

TOTAL TIME
1 hour

MAKES
8 servings

INGREDIENTS

2	acorn squash (1.8 kg total), halved, seeded and cut in 1-inch (2.5 cm) thick semicircles (see tip, below)
3	shallots, diced
⅓ cup	packed brown sugar
⅓ cup	balsamic vinegar
¼ cup	butter, melted
¼ tsp	each salt and pepper

DIRECTIONS

Arrange squash in 13- x 9-inch (3 L) casserole dish. Whisk together shallots, brown sugar, vinegar, butter, salt and pepper; pour over squash.

Bake on bottom rack in 400°F (200°C) oven, turning every 15 minutes, until tender when pierced with fork and glaze is thickened, 50 to 60 minutes.

NUTRITIONAL INFORMATION, PER SERVING: about 168 cal, 2 g pro, 6 g total fat (4 g sat. fat), 30 g carb, 3 g fibre, 15 mg chol, 124 mg sodium, 608 mg potassium. % RDI: 6% calcium, 11% iron, 11% vit A, 23% vit C, 11% folate.

TIP FROM THE TEST KITCHEN
Unlike some of its tougher winter-squash cousins, acorn squash has tender skin that can be left on and eaten.

BRAISED CABBAGE AND BEETS

HANDS-ON TIME
25 minutes

TOTAL TIME
1¼ hours

MAKES
8 to 10 servings

The festive red colour of this stove-top side dish is dazzling on a holiday table. The beets turns a bit sweet when cooked, so they are a good counterbalance to the earthy cabbage.

INGREDIENTS

2	strips bacon, thinly sliced
1	onion, thinly sliced
8 cups	shredded red cabbage
450 g	beets, peeled, halved and thinly sliced
2	bay leaves
½ tsp	salt
¼ tsp	pepper
⅓ cup	no-salt-added chicken broth
2 tbsp	packed brown sugar
2 tbsp	red wine vinegar
2 tbsp	tomato paste (see tip, below)
¼ cup	chopped fresh parsley

DIRECTIONS

In Dutch oven, cook bacon over medium heat until slightly crisp, about 4 minutes.

Stir in onion; cook, stirring occasionally, until softened, about 3 minutes. Stir in cabbage, beets, bay leaves, salt and pepper; cook, stirring, for 1 minute.

Stir in broth, ⅓ cup water, brown sugar, vinegar and tomato paste; bring to boil. Reduce heat, cover and simmer until vegetables are tender, about 50 minutes.

Discard bay leaves; stir in parsley.

NUTRITIONAL INFORMATION, PER EACH OF 10 SERVINGS: about 69 cal, 2 g pro, 2 g total fat (1 g sat. fat), 11 g carb, 2 g fibre, 3 mg chol, 178 mg sodium, 307 mg potassium. % RDI: 3% calcium, 6% iron, 2% vit A, 17% vit C, 19% folate.

TIP FROM THE TEST KITCHEN
You only need a small amount of tomato paste for this recipe. Freeze the leftover paste in 1 tbsp portions to use another time.

CLOCKWISE FROM TOP LEFT:
SMOOTH AND CREAMY MASHED POTATOES
page 89
SAUTÉED SPINACH AND MUSHROOMS
page 104
BRAISED CABBAGE AND BEETS
this page

SAUTÉED SPINACH AND MUSHROOMS ㉚ ◐

Meaty oyster mushrooms and fresh spinach come together for a super-quick side dish that complements any roast. Not a huge garlic fan? Remove the cloves before serving— they will impart a subtle flavour.

HANDS-ON TIME
20 minutes

TOTAL TIME
20 minutes

MAKES
6 servings

INGREDIENTS

2	bags (each 225 g) baby spinach (see tip, below)
2 tbsp	olive oil
3	cloves garlic, smashed
450 g	oyster mushrooms, trimmed and torn
1 tsp	lemon juice
¼ tsp	each salt and pepper

DIRECTIONS

Working in batches, in large pot of boiling water, blanch spinach for 30 seconds. Using slotted spoon, transfer to bowl of ice water; let cool. Drain well; squeeze out excess water. Coarsely chop; set aside. *(Make-ahead: Refrigerate in airtight container for up to 24 hours.)*

In large skillet, heat oil over medium-high heat; cook garlic until golden and fragrant, about 1 minute. Stir in mushrooms; cook, stirring often, until tender and light golden, about 7 minutes.

Stir in spinach, lemon juice, salt and pepper; cook, stirring, for 1 minute.

NUTRITIONAL INFORMATION, PER SERVING: about 85 cal, 5 g pro, 5 g total fat (1 g sat. fat), 8 g carb, 4 g fibre, 0 mg chol, 160 mg sodium, 659 mg potassium. % RDI: 9% calcium, 26% iron, 76% vit A, 13% vit C, 54% folate.

TIP FROM THE TEST KITCHEN
Any tender greens will work in this flavourful mixture. Try baby kale or dandelion greens for a change of pace.

TURNIP, POTATO AND SWISS CHARD HASH

HANDS-ON TIME
30 minutes

TOTAL TIME
40 minutes

MAKES
6 to 8 servings

The humble turnip becomes a superstar in this mildly spicy dish. If you don't have a large enough skillet, divide the mixture between two smaller ones.

INGREDIENTS

450 g	white turnip
450 g	yellow-fleshed potatoes
4 cups	packed chopped Swiss chard (with stems)
3 tbsp	olive oil
115 g	ham steak (see tip, below), cubed
1	onion, diced
3	cloves garlic, minced
2 tsp	chopped fresh thyme
½ tsp	salt
¼ tsp	hot pepper flakes, crushed

DIRECTIONS

Peel and cut turnip and potatoes into ½-inch (1 cm) cubes. In large saucepan of boiling salted water, cook turnip for 3 minutes. Using slotted spoon, transfer to bowl.

Add potatoes to saucepan; cook for 3 minutes. Using slotted spoon, add to turnip.

Add Swiss chard to saucepan; cook for 1 minute. Drain and set aside.

In deep 12-inch (30 cm) nonstick skillet, heat 1 tbsp of the oil over medium-high heat; cook ham, stirring often, until browned, 3 to 4 minutes. Add to turnip mixture.

Add remaining oil to pan; cook onion, stirring often, until softened, about 3 minutes. Add garlic, thyme, salt and hot pepper flakes; cook, stirring occasionally, until onion is light golden, about 3 minutes.

Add turnip mixture; cook, stirring occasionally, until vegetables are tender and edges are crisp, about 12 minutes.

Stir in Swiss chard; cook, stirring occasionally, for 3 minutes.

NUTRITIONAL INFORMATION, PER EACH OF 8 SERVINGS: about 125 cal, 5 g pro, 6 g total fat (1 g sat. fat), 15 g carb, 2 g fibre, 6 mg chol, 641 mg sodium, 399 mg potassium. % RDI: 3% calcium, 6% iron, 10% vit A, 23% vit C, 6% folate.

TIP FROM THE TEST KITCHEN
A smoky kielbasa or turkey kielbasa makes a lovely substitution for the ham in this dish.

CHINESE BROCCOLI AMANDINE ㉚

Also known as gai lan, *or Chinese kale, this vegetable has long, thin stalks topped with buds or florets, similar to broccolini (which makes a good substitute if you can't find it). The healthy fats in the olive oil and almonds help your body absorb antioxidants from the leafy greens.*

HANDS-ON TIME
15 minutes

TOTAL TIME
15 minutes

MAKES
4 servings

INGREDIENTS

2 tbsp	slivered almonds (see tip, below)
2	bunches Chinese broccoli (about 375 g total)
2 tbsp	extra-virgin olive oil
1	clove garlic, sliced
¼ tsp	salt
1 tsp	grated lemon zest
1 tbsp	lemon juice

DIRECTIONS

In large dry skillet, toast almonds over medium heat until light golden, about 3 minutes. Set aside.

Trim tough ends from broccoli. In same skillet, heat oil over medium-high heat; sauté garlic and salt until fragrant, about 1 minute.

Add broccoli, ¼ cup water and lemon zest; cover and steam until broccoli is tender and no water remains, about 6 minutes. Stir in lemon juice and almonds.

NUTRITIONAL INFORMATION, PER SERVING: about 99 cal, 2 g pro, 9 g total fat (1 g sat. fat), 4 g carb, 2 g fibre, 0 mg chol, 150 mg sodium. % RDI: 8% calcium, 4% iron, 13% vit A, 42% vit C, 36% folate.

TIP FROM THE TEST KITCHEN
For a nut-free version of this dish, swap in pepitas or shelled sunflower seeds for the slivered almonds.

CREAMED BRUSSELS SPROUTS ⑳

HANDS-ON TIME 25 minutes

TOTAL TIME 25 minutes

MAKES 12 to 16 servings

INGREDIENTS

1 tbsp	butter
3	cloves garlic, minced
2	shallots, thinly sliced
900 g	brussels sprouts, trimmed and thinly sliced lengthwise
½ cup	sodium-reduced chicken broth or vegetable broth
⅔ cup	whipping cream (35%)
½ tsp	each salt and pepper

DIRECTIONS

In Dutch oven or large skillet, heat butter over medium heat; cook garlic and shallots, stirring often, until fragrant and shallots are softened, about 2 minutes.

Add brussels sprouts and broth; cook, stirring often, until softened, about 5 minutes.

Stir in cream, salt and pepper; cook, stirring, until liquid is reduced and brussels sprouts are tender, about 3 minutes.

NUTRITIONAL INFORMATION, PER EACH OF 16 SERVINGS: about 61 cal, 2 g pro, 5 g total fat (3 g sat. fat), 5 g carb, 2 g fibre, 14 mg chol, 110 mg sodium, 192 mg potassium. % RDI: 3% calcium, 5% iron, 8% vit A, 58% vit C, 16% folate.

VARIATION
CREAMED CABBAGE

Substitute green cabbage for the brussels sprouts.

CREAMED CORN ⑳ ◗

HANDS-ON TIME 20 minutes

TOTAL TIME 20 minutes

MAKES 6 to 8 servings

INGREDIENTS

2 tbsp	butter
3	green onions, sliced
1	clove garlic, crushed
1	bay leaf
4 cups	frozen or fresh corn kernels
¼ tsp	each salt and pepper
1 tbsp	all-purpose flour
1 cup	10% cream

DIRECTIONS

In saucepan, melt butter over medium heat; cook green onions, garlic and bay leaf, stirring often, until fragrant, about 2 minutes.

Stir in corn, salt and pepper; cook, stirring often, until tender, about 5 minutes for frozen corn or 7 minutes for fresh.

Sprinkle with flour; cook, stirring, for 1 minute. Whisk in cream; simmer until thickened, about 3 minutes. Discard bay leaf.

Transfer one-third to blender; purée until smooth. Return to saucepan and stir to combine.

NUTRITIONAL INFORMATION, PER EACH OF 8 SERVINGS: about 131 cal, 3 g pro, 7 g total fat (4 g sat. fat), 18 g carb, 2 g fibre, 17 mg chol, 106 mg sodium, 243 mg potassium. % RDI: 4% calcium, 4% iron, 7% vit A, 7% vit C, 15% folate.

SAUTÉED ZUCCHINI AND TOMATOES ③⓪ ◐

HANDS-ON TIME 15 minutes

TOTAL TIME 15 minutes

MAKES 4 servings

INGREDIENTS

1 tbsp	extra-virgin olive oil
2	zucchini, cut in 1-inch (2.5 cm) pieces
1	clove garlic, minced
¼ tsp	each dried oregano and salt
pinch	hot pepper flakes
1½ cups	cherry or grape tomatoes, halved
pinch	granulated sugar
1 tbsp	thinly sliced green part of green onion
2 tsp	red wine vinegar

DIRECTIONS

In large skillet, heat oil over medium-high heat; sauté zucchini, garlic, oregano, salt and hot pepper flakes until softened, about 3 minutes.

Add tomatoes and sugar; cook until tomatoes are shrivelled, about 5 minutes.

Stir in green onion and vinegar.

NUTRITIONAL INFORMATION, PER SERVING: about 55 cal, 1 g pro, 4 g total fat (1 g sat. fat), 6 g carb, 2 g fibre, 0 mg chol, 149 mg sodium. % RDI: 2% calcium, 4% iron, 14% vit A, 18% vit C, 10% folate.

BRAISED BOK CHOY ③⓪

HANDS-ON TIME 20 minutes

TOTAL TIME 20 minutes

MAKES 4 servings

INGREDIENTS

¼ cup	sodium-reduced chicken broth
1 tsp	cornstarch
¼ tsp	salt
pinch	each granulated sugar and pepper
2 tbsp	vegetable oil
1	clove garlic, thinly sliced
450 g	baby bok choy, halved lengthwise
1 tsp	sesame oil
½ tsp	sesame seeds

DIRECTIONS

Whisk together broth, cornstarch, salt, sugar and pepper; set aside.

In wok or large skillet, heat vegetable oil over medium-high heat; stir-fry garlic for 5 seconds. Add bok choy; stir-fry until bright green, about 2 minutes. Cover and steam, stirring occasionally, until stalks are tender-crisp, 4 to 8 minutes.

Stir in broth mixture; bring to boil. Reduce heat; simmer, uncovered, until almost no liquid remains, about 2 minutes.

Transfer to plate; drizzle with sesame oil. Sprinkle with sesame seeds.

NUTRITIONAL INFORMATION, PER SERVING: about 60 cal, 1 g pro, 5 g total fat (trace sat. fat), 2 g carb, 1 g fibre, 0 mg chol, 149 mg sodium. % RDI: 7% calcium, 6% iron, 35% vit A, 35% vit C, 15% folate.

GRILLED VEGETABLES 30 ⬤
WITH CHIMICHURRI SAUCE

HANDS-ON TIME
15 minutes

TOTAL TIME
25 minutes

MAKES
6 servings

The herbaceous dressing adds an aromatic freshness to summery grilled vegetables. Increase the hot pepper flakes for a spicier bite.

INGREDIENTS

CHIMICHURRI SAUCE:

1 cup	packed fresh basil leaves
½ cup	fresh parsley leaves
⅓ cup	fresh mint leaves
1	clove garlic, minced
¼ tsp	each salt and pepper
pinch	hot pepper flakes
¼ cup	extra-virgin olive oil
1 tbsp	red wine vinegar

GRILLED VEGETABLES:

4	sweet red, yellow or orange peppers (or a combination)
4	zucchini, cut lengthwise in ½-inch (1 cm) thick slices
pinch	each salt and pepper

DIRECTIONS

CHIMICHURRI SAUCE: In food processor, pulse together basil, parsley, mint, garlic, salt, pepper and hot pepper flakes. Add oil, 2 tbsp water and vinegar; pulse until mixture becomes smooth paste. Set aside.

GRILLED VEGETABLES: Halve and seed peppers; cut each half into thirds. Sprinkle peppers and zucchini with salt and pepper.

Place peppers and zucchini on greased grill over medium-high heat; close lid and grill, turning once, until tender, 12 to 15 minutes.

Brush vegetables with half of the chimichurri sauce; serve with remaining sauce.

NUTRITIONAL INFORMATION, PER SERVING: about 125 cal, 3 g pro, 10 g total fat (1 g sat. fat), 9 g carb, 3 g fibre, 0 mg chol, 106 mg sodium, 539 mg potassium. % RDI: 5% calcium, 14% iron, 29% vit A, 238% vit C, 29% folate.

TIP FROM THE TEST KITCHEN
Chimichurri is a classic Argentinean sauce that also pairs deliciously with grilled meat or fish.

ROASTED CAULIFLOWER ◯

HANDS-ON TIME 10 minutes

TOTAL TIME 40 minutes

MAKES 4 servings

INGREDIENTS

3 tbsp	extra-virgin olive oil
¼ tsp	salt
1	head cauliflower (about 1.5 kg)

DIRECTIONS

In large casserole dish, stir oil with salt; set aside. Cut cauliflower into florets; add to paprika mixture and toss to coat.

Roast in 400°F (200°C) oven, stirring once, until tender and browned, 30 to 35 minutes.

NUTRITIONAL INFORMATION, PER SERVING: about 135 cal, 4 g pro, 11 g total fat (2 g sat. fat), 8 g carb, 5 g fibre, 0 mg chol, 173 mg sodium. % RDI: 3% calcium, 6% iron, 2% vit A, 143% vit C, 39% folate.

VARIATION

PAPRIKA-ROASTED CAULIFLOWER

Stir ½ tsp smoked or sweet paprika into oil mixture before tossing with cauliflower.

OVEN-ROASTED GRAPE TOMATOES ㉚ ◯

HANDS-ON TIME 5 minutes

TOTAL TIME 30 minutes

MAKES 8 servings

INGREDIENTS

4 cups	grape tomatoes (or halved cherry tomatoes)
2 tbsp	extra-virgin olive oil
2	cloves garlic, sliced
½ tsp	dried oregano
¼ tsp	salt
pinch	hot pepper flakes (optional)

DIRECTIONS

In 13- x 9-inch (3 L) baking dish, toss together tomatoes, oil, garlic, oregano, salt, and hot pepper flakes (if using).

Roast in 400°F (200°C) oven, stirring occasionally, until shrivelled, about 25 minutes.

NUTRITIONAL INFORMATION, PER SERVING: about 45 cal, 1 g pro, 4 g total fat (1 g sat. fat), 3 g carb, 1 g fibre, 0 mg chol, 76 mg sodium, 181 mg potassium. % RDI: 1% calcium, 2% iron, 6% vit A, 15% vit C, 4% folate.

GREEN BEANS ③⓪ ◗
WITH SHERRIED MUSHROOMS

Green beans are one of those sides that almost everyone can agree on.
Here, they're dressed up with seasoned mushrooms and a hint of dry sherry
to make them perfect alongside a slightly fancier meal.

HANDS-ON TIME
20 minutes

TOTAL TIME
20 minutes

MAKES
4 servings

INGREDIENTS

450 g	green beans, trimmed
1 tbsp	extra-virgin olive oil
250 g	button mushrooms
1	clove garlic, minced
1 tsp	dried thyme
¼ tsp	each salt and pepper
1 tbsp	dry sherry
1 tbsp	butter

DIRECTIONS

In skillet of boiling water, blanch beans until tender-crisp, about 5 minutes. Drain and pat dry.

Wipe out skillet. Add oil; heat over medium-high heat. Sauté mushrooms, garlic, thyme, salt and pepper until softened and golden, about 6 minutes.

Add sherry; cook until no liquid remains. Add beans and butter; cook, stirring, until beans are hot and butter is melted.

NUTRITIONAL INFORMATION, PER SERVING: about 105 cal, 3 g pro, 7 g total fat (2 g sat. fat), 10 g carb, 4 g fibre, 8 mg chol, 166 mg sodium. % RDI: 5% calcium, 12% iron, 9% vit A, 18% vit C, 17% folate.

TIP FROM THE TEST KITCHEN
For a vegan alternative, replace the butter with an extra 1 tbsp of olive oil.

GRILLED CORN
WITH CHIPOTLE LIME BUTTER

You can use unsalted butter if you prefer; just add a pinch of salt to season the mixture. If you're not into chipotle, this corn is also amazing with any of our flavoured butters from page 233.

HANDS-ON TIME
20 minutes

TOTAL TIME
1½ hours

MAKES
6 servings

INGREDIENTS

CHIPOTLE LIME BUTTER:

⅓ cup	butter, softened
½ tsp	grated lime zest
2 tsp	lime juice
1	canned chipotle pepper in adobo sauce, finely diced
1 tbsp	chopped fresh cilantro

GRILLED CORN:

6	cobs corn, husked

DIRECTIONS

CHIPOTLE LIME BUTTER: Mash together butter, lime zest, lime juice, chipotle pepper and cilantro. On waxed paper or plastic wrap, form into 6-inch (15 cm) long log. Wrap and refrigerate until firm, about 1 hour. *(Make-ahead: Refrigerate for up to 3 days or freeze for up to 1 month.)*

GRILLED CORN: Place corn on greased grill over medium-high heat; close lid and grill, turning occasionally, until grill-marked and tender, 10 to 15 minutes.

Cut butter log into 12 pieces; place on corn cobs to melt.

NUTRITIONAL INFORMATION, PER SERVING: about 222 cal, 4 g pro, 12 g total fat (7 g sat. fat), 31 g carb, 3 g fibre, 27 mg chol, 107 mg sodium, 305 mg potassium. % RDI: 1% calcium, 6% iron, 13% vit A, 13% vit C, 25% folate.

TIP FROM THE TEST KITCHEN

We love the smoky flavour that comes from cooking corn directly on the grill. If you prefer a less-smoky taste, fold the husks back over the corn to cover it. Soak the cobs in a large bowl of water for 30 minutes before grilling as directed. Husk the corn before serving.

ROASTED CARROTS AND RADISHES
WITH DILL BUTTER

Roasting may not be the first thing that comes to mind when you're dealing with radishes, but these crunchy roots turn incredibly sweet and mild when cooked this way.

HANDS-ON TIME
15 minutes

TOTAL TIME
55 minutes

MAKES
8 servings

INGREDIENTS

ROASTED CARROTS AND RADISHES:

3	bunches carrots (900 g total), trimmed and peeled
450 g	radishes
1 tbsp	olive oil
½ tsp	salt
¼ tsp	pepper

DILL BUTTER:

3 tbsp	butter
3	shallots, diced
¼ cup	chopped fresh dill (see tip, below)

DIRECTIONS

ROASTED CARROTS AND RADISHES: Cut carrots in half crosswise; cut lengthwise in half or in quarters (if carrots are small, only halve lengthwise). Cut large radishes in half, leaving bite-size ones whole.

In large bowl, toss together carrots, radishes, oil, salt and pepper; spread on rimmed baking sheet. Bake in 400°F (200°C) oven for 30 minutes; toss. Bake until tender, about 15 minutes.

DILL BUTTER: While carrots and radishes are roasting, in small skillet, melt butter over medium heat; cook shallots, stirring occasionally, until softened, about 5 minutes. Remove from heat. Stir in dill. Toss with carrots and radishes.

NUTRITIONAL INFORMATION, PER SERVING: about 93 cal, 1 g pro, 6 g total fat (3 g sat. fat), 9 g carb, 3 g fibre, 11 mg chol, 242 mg sodium, 329 mg potassium. % RDI: 4% calcium, 4% iron, 144% vit A, 15% vit C, 10% folate.

TIP FROM THE TEST KITCHEN
You can switch up the flavour of these vegetables by using 2 tbsp chopped fresh thyme instead of the dill in the butter mixture.

KALE AND PANCETTA ③⓪
WITH CRISPY SHALLOTS

Shallots become bitter when overcooked, so stir them constantly and take them out of the pan as soon as they turn golden brown.

HANDS-ON TIME
20 minutes

TOTAL TIME
20 minutes

MAKES
4 to 6 servings

INGREDIENTS

CRISPY SHALLOTS:

3 tbsp	olive oil
3	shallots, thinly sliced and separated in rings

KALE AND PANCETTA:

¼ cup	diced pancetta
3	cloves garlic, sliced
16 cups	torn kale leaves (about 2 bunches)
¼ tsp	pepper
pinch	salt

DIRECTIONS

CRISPY SHALLOTS: In small nonstick skillet, heat oil over medium heat; cook shallots, stirring constantly, until golden, about 3 minutes. Using slotted spoon, transfer to paper towel–lined plate; let drain. *(Make-ahead: Let cool. Store in airtight container at room temperature for up to 6 hours.)*

KALE AND PANCETTA: In nonstick skillet, cook pancetta over medium-high heat until crisp, about 5 minutes. Using slotted spoon, transfer to paper towel–lined plate; let drain.

Drain all but 2 tsp fat from pan. Add garlic; cook until fragrant, about 30 seconds. Add one-third of the kale, the pepper and salt; cook, stirring, until kale is slightly wilted, about 3 minutes. Transfer to bowl. Working in 2 batches, repeat with remaining kale. Toss pancetta with kale; sprinkle with shallots.

NUTRITIONAL INFORMATION, PER EACH OF 6 SERVINGS: about 178 cal, 10 g pro, 67 g total fat (2 g sat. fat), 23 g carb, 5 g fibre, 7 mg chol, 218 mg sodium, 1,026 mg potassium. % RDI: 28% calcium, 28% iron, 310% vit A, 380% vit C, 25% folate.

TIP FROM THE TEST KITCHEN
To add a hint of smoky flavour, replace the pancetta with 3 strips of bacon, chopped.

GRILLED ASPARAGUS ㉚ ◐
WITH FINES HERBES SAUCE

HANDS-ON TIME 25 minutes

TOTAL TIME 25 minutes

MAKES 8 servings

INGREDIENTS

FINES HERBES SAUCE:

1	egg yolk
2 tbsp	lemon juice
1 tbsp	white wine vinegar
1	small clove garlic, minced
1 tsp	Dijon mustard
pinch	each salt and pepper
½ cup	extra-virgin olive oil
1 tbsp	each chopped fresh chives and fresh tarragon
1 tbsp	chopped fresh chervil or fresh parsley

GRILLED ASPARAGUS:

900 g	asparagus, trimmed
1 tbsp	olive oil or vegetable oil
¼ tsp	salt

DIRECTIONS

FINES HERBES SAUCE: In heatproof bowl set over saucepan of gently simmering water, whisk together egg yolk, lemon juice and vinegar until slightly thickened, about 2 minutes. Remove from heat; whisk in garlic, mustard, salt and pepper. Whisking constantly, drizzle in olive oil, a few drops at a time, until thick and opaque. Whisk in chives, tarragon and chervil. Keep warm.

GRILLED ASPARAGUS: Toss together asparagus, oil and salt. Place on greased grill over medium-high heat; close lid and grill, turning occasionally, until tender-crisp, about 6 minutes.

Transfer asparagus to platter; spoon fines herbes sauce over top.

NUTRITIONAL INFORMATION, PER SERVING: about 104 cal, 3 g pro, 9 g total fat (1 g sat. fat), 4 g carb, 1 g fibre, 25 mg chol, 90 mg sodium. % RDI: 2% calcium, 6% iron, 6% vit A, 18% vit C, 55% folate.

ROASTED LEEK AND ENDIVE ◐
WITH CITRUS DRESSING

HANDS-ON TIME 20 minutes

TOTAL TIME 45 minutes

MAKES 12 to 16 servings

INGREDIENTS

CITRUS DRESSING:

2 tbsp	chopped fresh parsley
2 tbsp	olive oil
2 tsp	grated orange zest
1 tbsp	each orange juice and lemon juice
2 tsp	liquid honey
1	clove garlic, grated or pressed
¼ tsp	each salt and pepper

BRAISED LEEKS AND ENDIVE:

8	leeks (white and light green parts only), trimmed and halved lengthwise
5	heads Belgian endive, halved lengthwise
2 tbsp	olive oil
pinch	each salt and pepper

DIRECTIONS

CITRUS DRESSING: Whisk together parsley, oil, orange zest, orange juice, lemon juice, honey, garlic, salt and pepper. Set aside. *(Make-ahead: Refrigerate in airtight container for up to 24 hours.)*

BRAISED LEEKS AND ENDIVE: In large bowl, toss together leeks, endive, oil, salt and pepper. Spread on foil-lined rimmed baking sheet. Roast in 425°F (220°C) oven, turning once, until tender and light golden, about 25 minutes. Let cool for 5 minutes.

In large bowl, toss dressing with leek mixture. Transfer to serving platter.

NUTRITIONAL INFORMATION, PER EACH OF 16 SERVINGS: about 55 cal, 1 g pro, 4 g total fat (1 g sat. fat), 6 g carb, 1 g fibre, 0 mg chol, 43 mg sodium, 94 mg potassium. % RDI: 2% calcium, 6% iron, 1% vit A, 8% vit C, 9% folate.

**EXTRA-CRISPY
FRIED CHICKEN**
page 135

ULTIMATE POULTRY | 5

"The very first recipe I made for my now-husband was a chicken stew from scratch. There's something so satisfying about transforming a whole chicken into a hearty, comforting meal to share with those you love."

GILEAN WATTS ARTICLES EDITOR, FOOD

SKILLET CHICKEN COBBLER

This is a lot like chicken pot pie—only easier and faster. If your nonstick pan has a plastic handle, wrap it in a double layer of foil to make it ovenproof.

HANDS-ON TIME
35 minutes

TOTAL TIME
1 hour

MAKES
6 servings

INGREDIENTS

CHICKEN STEW:

1 tbsp	each vegetable oil and unsalted butter
1	onion, chopped
225 g	button mushrooms, quartered
450 g	boneless skinless chicken thighs, cut in bite-size pieces
1	clove garlic, minced
¼ tsp	each salt and pepper
2 tbsp	all-purpose flour
1 cup	sodium-reduced chicken broth
2	ribs celery, chopped
2	carrots, thinly sliced
1	bay leaf
1	sprig fresh thyme
1 cup	frozen peas

BISCUIT TOPPING:

1 cup + 2 tbsp	all-purpose flour
1 tsp	baking powder
¼ tsp	salt
3 tbsp	cold unsalted butter, cubed
½ cup	buttermilk (approx), see tip, right

DIRECTIONS

CHICKEN STEW: In ovenproof 10-inch (25 cm) nonstick skillet, heat oil and butter over medium-high heat; cook onion and mushrooms, stirring often, until mushrooms are lightly browned, 5 to 6 minutes.

Add chicken, garlic, salt and pepper; cook, stirring, until chicken is browned, 2 to 3 minutes. Stir in flour and cook for 1 minute. Add broth and bring to boil, stirring.

Stir in celery, carrots, bay leaf and thyme; reduce heat, cover and simmer until thickened and vegetables are tender-crisp, 3 to 5 minutes. Stir in peas. Discard bay leaf and thyme. Remove from heat and set aside.

BISCUIT TOPPING: In bowl, whisk together flour, baking powder and salt. Using pastry blender or 2 knives, cut in butter until crumbly. Drizzle in buttermilk, stirring just until soft sticky dough forms. Turn out onto floured surface; knead 6 times or just until smooth. Roll out into 6-inch (15 cm) square; brush with 2 tsp more buttermilk. Cut into 6 biscuits. Arrange over stew in skillet.

TO FINISH: Bake in 375°F (190°C) oven until biscuits are golden and stew is bubbly, 30 to 35 minutes. Let stand for 5 minutes before serving.

NUTRITIONAL INFORMATION, PER SERVING: about 337 cal, 21 g pro, 15 g total fat (6 g sat. fat), 30 g carb, 3 g fibre, 85 mg chol, 466 mg sodium, 481 mg potassium. % RDI: 8% calcium, 21% iron, 56% vit A, 12% vit C, 39% folate.

TIP FROM THE TEST KITCHEN

If you're out of buttermilk, you can still make these biscuits. Pour 1 tbsp lemon juice or vinegar into a glass measuring cup then fill to the 1-cup mark with milk. Let stand for five minutes to thicken. Voilà—easy homemade buttermilk substitute.

BASQUE ROAST CHICKEN

Espelette chili powder is a special spice found in the Basque region of Spain, and it's hard to buy here. A good substitute is a mix of sweet paprika, smoked paprika and cayenne pepper, which we've used in this take on a typical Basque chicken dish.

HANDS-ON TIME
25 minutes

TOTAL TIME
1¼ hours

MAKES
4 to 6 servings

INGREDIENTS

3	sweet red peppers, halved and cored
1	sweet onion, thickly sliced
1	can (796 mL) whole tomatoes, drained
140 g	dry-cured chorizo (see tip, below), cut in chunks
10	cloves garlic
8	small bone-in skin-on chicken pieces (half-breasts, thighs and/or drumsticks), about 1.25 kg total
2 tbsp	olive oil
1¾ tsp	chopped fresh thyme
½ tsp	salt
½ tsp	each sweet and smoked paprika
¼ tsp	cayenne pepper

DIRECTIONS

On rimmed baking sheet, broil red peppers, cut sides down, until blackened, about 12 minutes. Let cool enough to handle. Peel off blackened skins. *(Make-ahead: Refrigerate in airtight container for up to 2 days.)*

In roasting pan, combine red peppers, onion, tomatoes, chorizo and garlic cloves.

Toss chicken with oil to coat. Combine thyme, salt, sweet paprika, smoked paprika and cayenne pepper; rub all over chicken. Place, skin side up, on vegetable mixture in pan.

Roast in 450°F (230°C) oven, basting halfway through, until juices run clear when chicken is pierced, about 45 minutes.

NUTRITIONAL INFORMATION, PER EACH OF 6 SERVINGS: about 415 cal, 28 g pro, 28 g total fat (8 g sat. fat), 14 g carb, 2 g fibre, 95 mg chol, 668 mg sodium, 690 mg potassium. % RDI: 6% calcium, 19% iron, 25% vit A, 175% vit C, 13% folate.

TIP FROM THE TEST KITCHEN
Look for dry-cured Spanish chorizo or Portuguese chouriço in the deli section of the supermarket, near the cured meat. South American fresh chorizo is an uncooked sausage; don't substitute it for the dry-cured.

MAPLE BUTTERMILK GRILLED CHICKEN ✪

Make this dish with a variety of white and dark meat so everyone at the table gets a favourite piece. For a juicy garnish, cut a lime in half to grill alongside the chicken for the last 10 minutes. Squeeze the warm juice over the finished chicken.

HANDS ON TIME
45 minutes

TOTAL TIME
2¾ hours

MAKES
10 to 12 servings

INGREDIENTS

2 cups	buttermilk
2	green onions, chopped
4	cloves garlic, minced
½ tsp	pepper
¼ tsp	each cinnamon and crushed hot pepper flakes
20	small bone-in skin-on chicken pieces (about 1.125 kg), see tip, below
½ tsp	salt
¼ cup	maple syrup

DIRECTIONS

In large bowl, combine buttermilk, green onions, garlic, pepper, cinnamon and hot pepper flakes. Add chicken, turning to coat. Cover and refrigerate for 2 hours. *(Make-ahead: Refrigerate for up to 24 hours.)*

Remove chicken from marinade; discard marinade. Sprinkle chicken with salt. Place on greased grill over medium-high heat; close lid and grill, turning occasionally, until instant-read thermometer inserted in thickest parts of pieces reads 165°F (74°C), about 35 minutes.

Grill, brushing with maple syrup and turning occasionally, until glossy and coated, about 5 minutes.

NUTRITIONAL INFORMATION, PER EACH OF 12 SERVINGS: about 113 cal, 10 g pro, 5 g total fat (2 g sat. fat), 6 g carb, trace fibre, 34 mg chol, 149 mg sodium, 157 mg potassium. % RDI: 3% calcium, 2% iron, 2% vit A, 2% folate.

TIP FROM THE TEST KITCHEN

When you're using a mix of white and dark meat, be sure to cut any chicken breasts in half crosswise, through the bone, to make them similar in size to the thighs and drumsticks. That way, everything will cook through in the same amount of time.

KUNG PAO CHICKEN ㉚

Chili garlic sauce adds a nice spiciness to this stir-fry—add as much or as little as you like. Serve with hot cooked rice or egg noodles.

HANDS-ON TIME
25 minutes

TOTAL TIME
25 minutes

MAKES
4 servings

INGREDIENTS

1 tbsp	vegetable oil
450 g	boneless skinless chicken breasts, sliced
1	onion, sliced
225 g	green beans, trimmed
2 tsp	grated fresh ginger
2	cloves garlic, minced
2 tbsp	oyster sauce
2 tsp	cornstarch
2 tsp	chili garlic sauce or sambal oelek (see tip, below)
1	sweet red pepper, thinly sliced
½ cup	unsalted roasted peanuts

DIRECTIONS

In large nonstick skillet or wok, heat 1 tsp of the oil over medium-high heat; stir-fry chicken until lightly browned, about 5 minutes. Transfer to plate.

Add remaining oil to pan; stir-fry onion, green beans, ginger and garlic until fragrant, about 2 minutes. Add ⅓ cup water; cover and cook, stirring often, over medium heat until no liquid remains and beans are slightly softened, about 3 minutes.

Whisk together oyster sauce, cornstarch, chili garlic sauce and ¼ cup water; set aside.

Add red pepper to pan; stir-fry over medium-high heat until tender-crisp, about 3 minutes. Pour in oyster sauce mixture. Return chicken to pan; stir-fry until chicken is no longer pink inside, about 2 minutes. Sprinkle with peanuts.

NUTRITIONAL INFORMATION, PER SERVING: about 303 cal, 32 g pro, 14 g total fat (2 g sat. fat), 15 g carb, 3 g fibre, 66 mg chol, 342 mg sodium, 614 mg potassium. % RDI: 5% calcium, 9% iron, 15% vit A, 93% vit C, 22% folate.

TIP FROM THE TEST KITCHEN
Chili garlic sauce offers both the spiciness of hot peppers and the fragrant zip of garlic. Sambal oelek is more of a pure pepper purée; if you use it, you won't have quite as big a hit of garlic. Both are good options in this recipe.

GRILLED SPATCHCOCK CHICKEN
WITH BUTTERY BARBECUE SAUCE

HANDS-ON TIME
40 minutes

TOTAL TIME
1½ hours

MAKES
4 to 6 servings

"Spatchcocking" a chicken means flattening it after removing the backbone. This decreases cooking time and, along with the super-flavourful basting sauce, keeps the meat juicy.

INGREDIENTS

BUTTERY BARBECUE SAUCE:

¼ cup	butter
2 cups	finely diced onion
¼ cup	cider vinegar
1	clove garlic, minced
⅔ cup	ketchup
¼ cup	liquid honey
2 tbsp	packed brown sugar
2 tsp	dry mustard
1 tsp	smoked hot paprika (see tip, below)
¼ tsp	cayenne pepper

SPATCHCOCK CHICKEN:

1	whole chicken (about 1.35 kg)
1 tbsp	butter, melted
½ tsp	each salt and pepper

DIRECTIONS

BUTTERY BARBECUE SAUCE: In saucepan, heat 1 tbsp of the butter over medium heat; cook onion, stirring often, until golden, about 8 minutes. Add vinegar and garlic; cook until no liquid remains, about 30 seconds.

Stir in ketchup, honey, brown sugar, mustard, paprika and cayenne pepper; bring to boil. Reduce heat and simmer, stirring occasionally, until as thick as ketchup, about 25 minutes. Remove from heat. Stir in remaining butter. *(Make-ahead: Refrigerate in airtight container for up to 1 month; warm gently before using.)*

SPATCHCOCK CHICKEN: Remove giblets and neck (if any) from chicken. Using kitchen shears, cut chicken down each side of backbone; remove backbone. Turn chicken breast side up; press firmly on breastbone to flatten.

Brush chicken with butter; sprinkle with salt and pepper. Place, bone side down, on greased grill over medium heat; close lid and grill, turning once, for 35 minutes. Grill, brushing with ½ cup of the barbecue sauce, until instant-read thermometer inserted in thickest part of thigh reads 185°F (85°C), 10 to 15 more minutes.

Transfer chicken to cutting board; cover loosely with foil and let rest for 10 minutes before cutting into pieces.

NUTRITIONAL INFORMATION, PER EACH OF 6 SERVINGS: about 297 cal, 22 g pro, 18 g total fat (7 g sat. fat), 12 g carb, 1 g fibre, 93 mg chol, 417 mg sodium, 340 mg potassium. % RDI: 2% calcium, 7% iron, 10% vit A, 3% vit C, 4% folate.

TIP FROM THE TEST KITCHEN
Smoked paprika comes in hot and mild varieties. We've used hot to give the barbecue sauce some bite, but you can substitute mild if you prefer.

CHICKEN STEW 🍴
WITH HERBED DUMPLINGS

This one-pot meal has everything you could want in a stew: juicy chicken, hearty potatoes, tender-crisp vegetables and smoky bacon. The dumplings, which are just tender steamed biscuits, help soak up all that creamy sauce.

HANDS-ON TIME
1¼ hours

TOTAL TIME
1½ hours

MAKES
8 servings

INGREDIENTS

CHICKEN STEW:

6	strips bacon, chopped
2 tsp	olive oil (approx)
1	pkg (227 g) cremini mushrooms, quartered
900 g	boneless skinless chicken thighs
3	each carrots and ribs celery, chopped
2	onions, chopped
3	cloves garlic, minced
½ cup	all-purpose flour
4 cups	sodium-reduced chicken broth
1 cup	dry white wine
500 g	yellow-fleshed potatoes, peeled and cubed
1	bay leaf
½ tsp	each dried marjoram leaves, dried savory leaves and pepper
¼ tsp	salt
1 cup	frozen peas
⅔ cup	whipping cream (35%)
½ cup	frozen corn kernels
¼ cup	chopped fresh parsley

HERBED DUMPLINGS:

1½ cups	all-purpose flour
2 tbsp	each chopped fresh parsley and chives
1 tsp	chopped fresh thyme
1 tsp	baking powder
¼ tsp	each baking soda and salt
2 tbsp	cold butter, cubed
⅔ cup	buttermilk

DIRECTIONS

CHICKEN STEW: In large Dutch oven or heavy-bottomed saucepan, cook bacon over medium heat, stirring occasionally, until crisp, about 6 minutes. Using slotted spoon, transfer bacon to bowl. Drain fat from pan, reserving 3 tbsp (add extra olive oil to make 3 tbsp if not enough fat remains in pan).

Add oil to pan; heat over medium heat. Cook mushrooms, stirring occasionally, until softened and no liquid remains, about 7 minutes. Add to bacon.

Working in 2 batches and using half of the reserved fat, brown chicken over medium heat, about 3 minutes per side. Transfer to separate bowl. Add 2 tbsp water to pan and scrape up browned bits from bottom; pour into bowl with chicken.

Add remaining reserved fat to pan; cook carrots, celery and onions, stirring occasionally, until onions are softened, about 10 minutes. Add garlic; cook, stirring, until fragrant, about 1 minute. Stir in flour. Cook, stirring often, until light golden, about 2 minutes.

Add broth and wine, stirring until smooth. Add chicken mixture, potatoes, bay leaf, marjoram, savory, pepper and salt; bring to boil. Reduce heat to medium-low; simmer, stirring occasionally, until potatoes are fork-tender, about 20 minutes.

Discard bay leaf. Using slotted spoon, transfer chicken to cutting board; using 2 forks, shred meat and return to pan. Stir in peas, cream, corn, parsley and mushroom mixture. Return to simmer.

HERBED DUMPLINGS: While stew is returning to simmer, in bowl, whisk together flour, parsley, chives, thyme, baking powder, baking soda and salt. Using pastry blender or 2 knives, cut in butter until mixture resembles fine crumbs with a few larger pieces. Using fork, stir in buttermilk to make soft sticky dough. On parchment paper, roll dough into 7-inch (18 cm) log; cut crosswise into eight generous ¾-inch (2 cm) thick rounds, reshaping if necessary.

Arrange dumplings over simmering stew; cover and cook, without lifting lid, until dumplings are no longer doughy underneath, about 15 minutes.

NUTRITIONAL INFORMATION, PER SERVING: about 568 cal, 34 g pro, 25 g total fat (11 g sat. fat), 50 g carb, 6 g fibre, 138 mg chol, 874 mg sodium, 1,000 mg potassium. % RDI: 12% calcium, 29% iron, 83% vit A, 30% vit C, 44% folate.

CHICKEN POT PIE ⦿
WITH FLAKY BUTTER HERB PASTRY

HANDS-ON TIME	1¼ hours
TOTAL TIME	3 hours
MAKES	12 servings

This classic creamy casserole packs buttery herb-flecked pastry and rich, savoury chicken in every scrumptious bite.

INGREDIENTS

FILLING:

3 tbsp	unsalted butter
1.125 kg	boneless skinless chicken breasts or thighs, cubed
1	pkg (227 g) button mushrooms, quartered
10	shallots, halved lengthwise and thinly sliced crosswise (about 2 cups)
5	sprigs fresh thyme
1	bay leaf
½ cup	dry white wine
1	rutabaga (about 915 g), peeled and cut in ¾-inch (2 cm) chunks
375 g	mini red-skinned potatoes, quartered
2	carrots, cut in ½-inch (1 cm) chunks
1 tsp	salt
½ tsp	pepper
3 cups	sodium-reduced chicken broth
½ cup	all-purpose flour
¾ cup	frozen peas
¼ cup	chopped fresh parsley
¼ cup	whipping cream (35%)
1 tbsp	lemon juice

TOPPING:

	Flaky Butter Herb Pastry (opposite)
1	egg yolk

DIRECTIONS

FILLING: In Dutch oven or heavy-bottomed saucepan, melt 2 tbsp of the butter over medium-high heat; working in batches, sauté chicken until browned, 4 to 5 minutes per batch. Transfer to bowl.

In same Dutch oven, melt remaining butter over medium heat; cook mushrooms, shallots, thyme and bay leaf, stirring occasionally, until softened and golden, about 6 minutes. Add wine; cook, stirring, until no liquid remains, about 2 minutes.

Stir in rutabaga, potatoes, carrots, salt and pepper; cook, stirring occasionally, for 5 minutes. Stir in broth, chicken and any accumulated juices; bring to boil. Reduce heat, cover and simmer until vegetables are tender-crisp, about 12 minutes.

Whisk flour with ½ cup water; stir into chicken mixture. Bring to boil; reduce heat and simmer, stirring occasionally, until liquid is thickened and vegetables are tender, about 6 minutes. Stir in peas, parsley and cream; cook, stirring, for 1 minute. Remove from heat; stir in lemon juice. Discard thyme and bay leaf.

Scrape mixture into 13- x 9-inch (3 L) baking dish; let cool for 30 minutes. *(Make-ahead: Refrigerate until cold; cover and refrigerate for up to 24 hours. Increase baking time by 15 to 20 minutes.)*

TOPPING: While filling is cooling, on floured work surface, roll out pastry to 15- x 11-inch (38 x 28 cm) rectangle (large enough to fit top of baking dish and leave 1-inch/2.5 cm overhang). Transfer to parchment paper–lined rimless baking sheet; refrigerate until firm, about 30 minutes.

Arrange pastry over top of baking dish, pulling taut over rim. Whisk egg yolk with 1 tsp water; brush over pastry. Using sharp knife, cut steam vents in top. Bake on rimmed baking sheet in 425°F (220°C) oven until pastry is puffed and golden, about 35 minutes. Let cool for 20 minutes before serving.

NUTRITIONAL INFORMATION, PER SERVING: about 465 cal, 25 g pro, 26 g total fat (14 g sat. fat), 33 g carb, 4 g fibre, 149 mg chol, 661 mg sodium, 745 mg potassium. % RDI: 7% calcium, 25% iron, 60% vit A, 37% vit C, 33% folate.

FLAKY BUTTER HERB PASTRY

Cut 1 cup cold butter into cubes. In food processor, pulse 1⅔ cups all-purpose flour with ½ tsp salt. Add ¼ cup of the butter; pulse until combined. Add remaining butter; pulse until mixture forms pea-size pieces, about 5 times. Drizzle ⅓ cup ice water evenly over mixture (not through feed tube). Pulse 6 to 8 times, until loose ragged dough forms (do not let mixture form ball). Transfer to floured 20-inch (50 cm) length of waxed paper; press dough into rectangle. Dust with flour; top with another 20-inch (50 cm) length of waxed paper. Roll out to 15- x 12-inch (38 x 30 cm) rectangle; remove top sheet of waxed paper. Sprinkle with 2 tbsp chopped fresh parsley.

Using bottom sheet of waxed paper to lift pastry, fold 1 long edge over one-third of pastry; fold opposite long edge over top (pastry will form 15- x 4-inch/38 x 10 cm rectangle). Starting from 1 short end, roll up tightly into cylinder; flatten into 5-inch (12 cm) square. Wrap in plastic wrap; refrigerate until firm, about 1 hour. *(Make-ahead: Refrigerate for up to 5 days or freeze in airtight container for up to 2 weeks.)* **MAKES** 1 batch

SLOW COOKER THAI CHICKEN CURRY

This restaurant-style Thai curry is so easy to make in a slow cooker (or on the stove). Serve it over steamed jasmine rice and garnish with lemon or lime wedges to squeeze over top.

HANDS-ON TIME
15 minutes

TOTAL TIME
6½ hours

MAKES
8 servings

INGREDIENTS

900 g	boneless skinless chicken thighs, cut in 1-inch (2.5 cm) chunks
4 cups	cubed seeded peeled butternut squash (1½-inch/4 cm cubes)
1	can (400 mL) coconut milk
2 tbsp	minced fresh ginger
2 tbsp	Thai red curry paste
2 tbsp	tomato paste
3	makrut lime leaves (optional), see tip, below
1 tbsp	packed brown sugar
1 tbsp	each fish sauce and sodium-reduced soy sauce
3	cloves garlic, minced
½ tsp	salt
2 tbsp	all-purpose flour
2	heads Shanghai bok choy (about 150 g), cut lengthwise in ½-inch (1 cm) thick wedges
2 tbsp	lime juice
⅓ cup	finely chopped roasted peanuts

DIRECTIONS

In slow cooker, combine chicken, squash, coconut milk, ginger, curry paste, tomato paste, lime leaves (if using), brown sugar, fish sauce, soy sauce, garlic and salt.

Cover and cook on low until chicken is fall-apart tender, 6 to 8 hours.

Whisk flour with 3 tbsp water until smooth; stir into slow cooker. Stir in bok choy; cover and cook on high until sauce is thickened and bok choy is tender, about 15 minutes. Discard lime leaves. Stir in lime juice; sprinkle with peanuts.

NUTRITIONAL INFORMATION, PER SERVING: about 344 cal, 26 g pro, 21 g total fat (11 g sat. fat), 17 g carb, 3 g fibre, 94 mg chol, 512 mg sodium, 787 mg potassium. % RDI: 8% calcium, 29% iron, 98% vit A, 37% vit C, 22% folate.

VARIATION

STOVE-TOP THAI CHICKEN CURRY

In large Dutch oven, combine chicken, squash, coconut milk, ginger, curry paste, tomato paste, lime leaves (if using), brown sugar, fish sauce, soy sauce, garlic and salt. Bring to boil, stirring often; reduce heat and simmer, stirring occasionally, until juices run clear when chicken is pierced, about 30 minutes. Add flour mixture and bok choy as directed; simmer, stirring occasionally, until sauce is thickened and bok choy is tender, about 10 minutes. Discard lime leaves. Stir in lime juice; sprinkle with peanuts.

TIP FROM THE TEST KITCHEN
Makrut lime leaves give traditional curries a floral-citrus note, but they can be a little hard to find. Look for them in Asian supermarkets—fresh leaves are more fragrant, but dried ones can work in saucy dishes like this curry.

SLOW COOKER BUTTER CHICKEN

This recipe can easily simmer away for eight hours before you add the chicken. It yields a large quantity of sauce, which freezes well—you can use half to feed a smaller group and freeze the rest for later. Serve over hot steamed basmati rice or with warmed naan.

HANDS-ON TIME
15 minutes

TOTAL TIME
5¾ hours

MAKES
8 servings

INGREDIENTS

1	can (796 mL) diced tomatoes
2	onions, diced
3	cloves garlic, minced
3 tbsp	butter
2 tbsp	grated fresh ginger
2 tbsp	packed brown sugar
2 tsp	chili powder
¾ tsp	each ground coriander and turmeric
½ tsp	each cinnamon and ground cumin
½ tsp	each salt and pepper
1 cup	sodium-reduced chicken broth
¼ cup	almond butter or cashew butter
1.35 kg	boneless skinless chicken thighs, quartered
1 cup	sour cream
2 tbsp	chopped fresh cilantro

DIRECTIONS

In slow cooker, combine tomatoes, onions, garlic, butter, ginger, brown sugar, chili powder, coriander, turmeric, cinnamon, cumin, salt and pepper. Whisk broth with almond butter until smooth; pour into slow cooker. Cover and cook on low for 5 to 8 hours.

Turn off heat; using immersion blender, purée mixture until smooth. Add chicken; cover and cook on high until juices run clear when chicken is pierced, 30 to 40 minutes. Stir in sour cream. Sprinkle with cilantro.

NUTRITIONAL INFORMATION, PER SERVING: about 398 cal, 36 g pro, 22 g total fat (8 g sat. fat), 14 g carb, 2 g fibre, 164 mg chol, 580 mg sodium, 766 mg potassium. % RDI: 11% calcium, 26% iron, 13% vit A, 32% vit C, 13% folate.

EXTRA-CRISPY FRIED CHICKEN

The longer the chicken stays in the seasoned buttermilk marinade, the better, so it's worth taking the time to let it soak overnight. Flour and potato starch work in harmony to create a tasty coating—and the double dip is the secret to the chicken's ultra-crispy exterior.

HANDS-ON TIME
1 hour

TOTAL TIME
5 hours

MAKES
12 to 16 pieces

INGREDIENTS

BUTTERMILK MARINADE:

2 cups	buttermilk
1½ tsp	dry mustard
1 tsp	each garlic powder and onion powder
¾ tsp	salt
½ tsp	each sweet paprika and pepper
¼ tsp	poultry seasoning
pinch	cayenne pepper

FRIED CHICKEN:

2 kg	bone-in skin-on chicken thighs, drumsticks, wings and/or breasts
2 cups	all-purpose flour
½ cup	potato starch
2 tbsp	each garlic powder and onion powder
1 tbsp	dry mustard
2 tsp	sweet paprika
1½ tsp	salt
½ tsp	pepper
	vegetable oil for deep-frying

DIRECTIONS

BUTTERMILK MARINADE: In bowl, whisk together buttermilk, mustard, garlic powder, onion powder, salt, paprika, pepper, poultry seasoning and cayenne pepper.

FRIED CHICKEN: Arrange chicken in single layer in large baking dish. Pour marinade over chicken, turning to coat. Cover and refrigerate for 4 hours. *(Make-ahead: Refrigerate for up to 24 hours.)*

In large bowl, whisk together flour, potato starch, garlic powder, onion powder, mustard, paprika, salt and pepper.

Pour enough oil into large deep skillet or Dutch oven to come 3 inches (8 cm) up side. Heat until deep-fryer thermometer reads 300°F (150°C).

While oil is heating, remove chicken from buttermilk mixture, letting excess drip back into bowl; reserve remaining marinade. Pat chicken dry with paper towels. Dredge chicken in flour mixture, tapping off excess. Dip in reserved marinade, letting excess drip off. Dredge again in flour mixture, tapping off excess.

Working in batches, fry chicken, turning occasionally, until instant-read thermometer inserted into thickest part of several pieces reads 165°F (74°C), 10 to 15 minutes per batch. Drain on rack over paper towel–lined baking sheet; let stand for 5 minutes before serving.

NUTRITIONAL INFORMATION, PER EACH OF 16 PIECES: about 264 cal, 15 g pro, 15 g total fat (3 g sat. fat), 18 g carb, 1 g fibre, 45 mg chol, 314 mg sodium, 216 mg potassium. % RDI: 4% calcium, 10% iron, 4% vit A, 2% vit C, 12% folate.

TIP FROM THE TEST KITCHEN

Using a slightly lower than normal frying temperature cooks the meat all the way through without burning the coating. Keep in mind that the temperature of the frying oil will go up and down during the cooking process. Monitor it with your deep-fryer thermometer and adjust the heat as needed to keep it steady.

HERBED CHEESE–STUFFED CHICKEN ③⓪

A disposable piping bag makes stuffing this tender chicken so easy. For a sharper flavour, add 2 tbsp grated Parmesan cheese to the stuffing or use black pepper cream cheese instead of the garlic-and-fine-herb cheese.

HANDS-ON TIME
15 minutes

TOTAL TIME
30 minutes

MAKES
4 servings

INGREDIENTS

75 g	garlic-and-fine-herb fresh soft cheese (such as Boursin)
¼ cup	fresh bread crumbs or panko bread crumbs
2 tbsp	drained oil-packed sun-dried tomatoes, thinly sliced
5	fresh basil leaves, chopped
4	boneless skinless chicken breasts (about 675 g), filets removed (see tip, below)
pinch	each salt and pepper
1 tsp	olive oil

DIRECTIONS

Stir together garlic-and-fine-herb cheese, bread crumbs, sun-dried tomatoes and basil.

Holding paring knife horizontally, insert into thick end of each chicken breast and wiggle back and forth to form pocket. Using disposable piping bag or small spoon, stuff each pocket with one-quarter of the cheese mixture. Sprinkle chicken with salt and pepper.

In ovenproof skillet, heat oil over medium-high heat; brown chicken on both sides, about 6 minutes. Transfer to 400°F (200°C) oven; bake until chicken is no longer pink inside, about 8 minutes.

NUTRITIONAL INFORMATION, PER SERVING: about 256 cal, 34 g pro, 12 g total fat (6 g sat. fat), 3 g carb, trace fibre, 99 mg chol, 209 mg sodium, 454 mg potassium. % RDI: 2% calcium, 5% iron, 7% vit A, 7% vit C, 4% folate.

TIP FROM THE TEST KITCHEN

Chicken breast filets are the small, tender pieces of meat partially attached to the underside of the breasts. They are delicious, but for this recipe it's easier to trim them off so you have a flat piece of meat to work with. Don't discard them, though—cut the filets up and add to soups or stir-fries, or dredge them in panko to make tasty chicken fingers. You can freeze them in a tightly sealed plastic freezer bag for up to 2 months.

GRILLED CHICKEN MOZZARELLA

HANDS-ON TIME
25 minutes

TOTAL TIME
40 minutes

MAKES
8 servings

This ultra-simple chicken is topped with fragrant fresh basil, juicy tomato and melty mozzarella, which echo the flavours of a Caprese salad. It's a tasty treat on the barbecue.

INGREDIENTS

4	large boneless skinless chicken breasts (about 900 g total)
3 tbsp	olive oil
2	cloves garlic, minced
1 tbsp	lemon juice
¾ tsp	dried oregano
½ tsp	each salt and pepper
8	thick slices tomato
8	slices mozzarella cheese (see tip, below)
8	fresh basil leaves

DIRECTIONS

Place 1 chicken breast on cutting board. Holding knife blade parallel to board and starting at thickest long side, slice horizontally to make 2 thin cutlets. Repeat with remaining chicken. If chicken is uneven, sandwich between plastic wrap; using meat mallet or heavy-bottomed saucepan, pound to even thickness.

In bowl, whisk together oil, garlic, lemon juice, oregano, salt and pepper; remove one-quarter and set aside. Add chicken to remaining oil mixture, turning to coat; let stand for 10 minutes.

Discarding marinade, place chicken and tomato on greased grill over medium-high heat; close lid and grill for 4 minutes. Turn chicken and tomato. Top chicken with mozzarella; cook until chicken is no longer pink inside and tomato is softened and slightly charred, about 2 minutes.

To serve, top chicken with tomato; drizzle with reserved oil mixture. Top each with basil leaf.

NUTRITIONAL INFORMATION, PER SERVING: about 221 cal, 31 g pro, 10 g total fat (4 g sat. fat), 2 g carb, trace fibre, 86 mg chol, 220 mg sodium, 402 mg potassium. % RDI: 12% calcium, 4% iron, 7% vit A, 7% vit C, 4% folate.

TIP FROM THE TEST KITCHEN
While moist fresh mozzarella is great for salads, this recipe is best made with yellower pizza-style mozzarella. It has a drier texture than fresh and will melt well over the chicken.

COQ AU VIN

This classic dish is ideal for entertaining because you can sit and sip with guests while it simmers. Serve the same type of wine for drinking as you used in the sauce.

HANDS-ON TIME
45 minutes

TOTAL TIME
1½ hours

MAKES
8 servings

INGREDIENTS

1	whole chicken (1.5 kg)
2 tbsp	butter
1	pkg (284 g) pearl onions, peeled
2 cups	button mushrooms (about 225 g)
1 cup	chopped onions
2 tsp	chopped fresh thyme (or 1 tsp dried)
pinch	each salt and pepper
1	bay leaf
1½ cups	dry red wine
1½ cups	chicken broth
2 tbsp	tomato paste
1 tbsp	cognac or brandy (optional)
2 tbsp	chopped fresh parsley

DIRECTIONS

Remove giblets and neck (if any) from chicken. Using kitchen shears, cut chicken down each side of backbone. **PHOTO A**

Discard backbone. Cut off wing tips; cut chicken in half along breastbone. Cut each half between thigh and breast. **PHOTO B**

Cut each breast in half crosswise. Cut each leg at joint between drumstick and thigh.

In shallow Dutch oven, heat 1 tbsp of the butter over medium-high heat; working in batches, brown chicken, 4 to 5 minutes per batch. Using slotted spoon, transfer to plate.

Drain fat from pan; reduce heat to medium. Add pearl onions and mushrooms; cook, stirring often, until browned, about 5 minutes. Transfer to separate plate. Melt remaining butter in pan; cook chopped onions, thyme, salt, pepper and bay leaf, stirring often, until onions are softened, about 8 minutes.

Add wine, broth, tomato paste, and cognac (if using); bring to boil over high heat, stirring and scraping up any browned bits from bottom of pan. Return chicken and any accumulated juices to pan. Reduce heat to medium; cover and simmer, stirring occasionally, for 20 minutes.

Return mushroom mixture to pan; cover and simmer, stirring occasionally, until reduced to consistency of maple syrup and juices run clear when chicken is pierced, about 25 minutes. Discard bay leaf. Stir in parsley. *(Make-ahead: Let cool for 30 minutes. Scrape into casserole dish; refrigerate until cold. Cover and refrigerate for up to 2 days. Reheat in 350°F/180°C oven, about 30 minutes.)*

NUTRITIONAL INFORMATION, PER SERVING: about 296 cal, 25 g pro, 18 g total fat (6 g sat. fat), 7 g carb, 1 g fibre, 100 mg chol, 287 mg sodium, 490 g potassium. % RDI: 3% calcium, 11% iron, 8% vit A, 8% vit C, 8% folate.

TIP FROM THE TEST KITCHEN
If you prefer a lighter-bodied wine and sauce, use a Pinot Noir or Gamay. For robust flavour, choose a Cabernet Sauvignon, a Meritage (or Bordeaux) blend or a Baco Noir.

CHICKEN AND MOLE POBLANO

A complex sauce of chilies, seeds and chocolate, mole poblano (pronounced moh-lay poh-blah-no) often tops chicken, turkey and cheese enchiladas. This recipe makes more sauce than you need for the chicken—about 7 cups— but the leftovers freeze well.

HANDS-ON TIME
45 minutes

TOTAL TIME
2½ hours

MAKES
6 servings

INGREDIENTS

MOLE POBLANO:

4	ancho chilies
3	mulato chilies
3	pasilla or guajillo chilies
3 tbsp	lard
5 cups	boiling water
⅓ cup	each pepitas and slivered almonds
2 tbsp	sesame seeds
1	onion, diced
2	cloves garlic, minced
½ tsp	cinnamon
¼ tsp	each ground coriander, ground aniseed, ground cloves and pepper
1	small (6-inch/15 cm) corn tortilla (or ⅓ cup crushed tortilla chips)
5	plum tomatoes, chopped
2 tbsp	golden raisins
2 tsp	salt
30 g	Mexican or semisweet chocolate, coarsely chopped

CHICKEN WITH MOLE:

1.8 kg	bone-in chicken pieces
½ tsp	salt
1 tbsp	lard or vegetable oil
1 tbsp	sesame seeds, toasted

DIRECTIONS

MOLE POBLANO: Remove seeds and veins from ancho, mulato and pasilla chilies. In large heavy skillet, melt 1 tsp of the lard over medium-high heat; fry chilies, turning often, until beginning to blister, about 1 minute. Transfer to large heatproof bowl; cover with boiling water and let stand for 30 minutes. Pour into blender; purée. Transfer to bowl. (Do not clean blender.)

In dry skillet, toast pepitas and almonds over medium heat, shaking pan often, until golden, about 4 minutes. Transfer to separate bowl. Repeat with sesame seeds, toasting for 2 minutes; add to pepita mixture.

In shallow Dutch oven, melt remaining lard over medium heat; fry onion, garlic, cinnamon, coriander, aniseed, cloves and pepper, stirring often, until golden, about 5 minutes.

Tear tortilla into pieces; add to Dutch oven along with tomatoes, raisins and pepita mixture. Fry, stirring often, until tomatoes are softened, about 5 minutes.

Stir in chili mixture and salt; bring to boil. Reduce heat and simmer, uncovered and stirring often, until reduced to 7 cups, about 25 minutes.

Stir in chocolate until melted. Let cool slightly. Working in batches, in blender, purée until smooth. Set aside 2 cups of the sauce for chicken; save remainder for another use. *(Make-ahead: Refrigerate in airtight container for up to 3 days or freeze for up to 1 month.)*

CHICKEN WITH MOLE: Sprinkle chicken with salt. In shallow Dutch oven, heat lard over medium-high heat; working in batches, brown chicken, 4 to 5 minutes per batch. Drain off fat.

Pour reserved mole poblano over chicken; bring to boil. Reduce heat, cover and simmer, turning chicken once, until juices run clear when chicken is pierced, about 40 minutes. Sprinkle with sesame seeds.

NUTRITIONAL INFORMATION, PER SERVING (WITHOUT SKIN): about 310 cal, 31 g pro, 17 g total fat (5 g sat. fat), 8 g carb, 3 g fibre, 100 mg chol, 520 mg sodium. % RDI: 3% calcium, 19% iron, 18% vit A, 3% vit C, 9% folate.

TIP FROM THE TEST KITCHEN
Look for the chilies and Mexican chocolate in fine food stores, Latin American grocery stores and the Mexican section of some supermarkets.

SESAME-CRUSTED CHICKEN ③⓪

Instead of the typical bread crumbs, a mixture of flour and sesame seeds creates a crispy coating on these simple chicken cutlets. Serve this quick and easy dinner with sautéed greens, such as spinach or kale.

HANDS-ON TIME
22 minutes

TOTAL TIME
25 minutes

MAKES
4 servings

INGREDIENTS

⅓ cup	sesame seeds
4 tsp	all-purpose flour
½ tsp	each salt and cayenne pepper
¼ tsp	black pepper
4	boneless skinless chicken breasts (about 600 g)
1 tbsp	each butter and olive oil

DIRECTIONS

In blender or food processor, blend together sesame seeds, flour, salt, cayenne pepper and black pepper until fine with some whole seeds remaining. Transfer to shallow dish.

Sandwich chicken between plastic wrap; using meat mallet or heavy-bottomed saucepan, pound chicken to ½-inch (1 cm) thickness. Press into sesame seed mixture, turning and patting to coat.

In large skillet, heat butter and oil over medium heat; cook chicken, turning once, until no longer pink inside, 12 to 14 minutes.

NUTRITIONAL INFORMATION, PER SERVING: about 247 cal, 32 g pro, 12 g total fat (3 g sat. fat), 2 g carb, 1 g fibre, 85 mg chol, 241 mg sodium, 414 mg potassium. % RDI: 1% calcium, 8% iron, 4% vit A, 2% vit C, 5% folate.

TIP FROM THE TEST KITCHEN

Pounding chicken can get a little messy. To keep the chicken from sticking to your work surface and tools, place it between 2 layers of plastic wrap before pounding it. Or use waxed paper; it can break, so pound a little more gently.

EASY BAKED HERBED CHICKEN

Pop this chicken in the oven and make your favourite side dishes while it roasts. Starting the chicken with the skin side down on the baking sheet ensures it will be crispy; use tongs to carefully flip the chicken, making sure not to tear the skin.

HANDS-ON TIME
5 minutes

TOTAL TIME
35 minutes

MAKES
4 servings

INGREDIENTS

2 tbsp	chopped fresh parsley
2 tsp	finely chopped fresh rosemary
2 tsp	finely chopped fresh thyme
2	cloves garlic, pressed or grated
2 tsp	olive oil
½ tsp	each salt and pepper
1	whole chicken (about 1.6 kg), cut in quarters (or 2 each bone-in, skin-on chicken breasts and leg quarters)

DIRECTIONS

Stir together parsley, rosemary, thyme, garlic, oil, salt and pepper. Rub all over chicken.

Arrange, skin side down, on lightly greased foil-lined rimmed baking sheet. Bake in 425°F (220°C) oven, turning once, until juices run clear when chicken is pierced and instant-read thermometer inserted into thickest part of breast reads 165°F (74°C), about 30 minutes.

NUTRITIONAL INFORMATION, PER SERVING: about 427 cal, 47 g pro, 25 g total fat (7 g sat. fat), 1 g carb, trace fibre, 156 mg chol, 424 mg sodium, 476 mg potassium. % RDI: 2% calcium, 15% iron, 8% vit A, 5% vit C, 5% folate.

VARIATION

EASY BAKED SPICED CHICKEN

Replace parsley, rosemary, thyme and garlic with ½ tsp each garlic powder, onion powder and sweet paprika. Proceed with recipe as directed.

CRISPY SALT AND PEPPER CHICKEN WINGS

You won't believe how crispy these oven-baked wings are! Tossing the wings in flour gives them the same texture you would get from frying, without the mess. We love them with a squeeze of lemon, but they're also terrific in our saucy variations (below).

HANDS-ON TIME
5 minutes

TOTAL TIME
50 minutes

MAKES
about 24 pieces

INGREDIENTS

900 g	separated trimmed chicken wings (see tip, below)
¾ tsp	each salt and pepper
3 tbsp	all-purpose flour or cornstarch
	lemon wedges

DIRECTIONS

In bowl, toss together wings, salt and pepper; sprinkle with flour, tossing to coat. Arrange wings on lightly greased foil-lined rimmed baking sheet. Bake in 400°F (200°C) oven, turning once, until crispy and golden, 45 to 50 minutes.

Serve with lemon wedges to squeeze over top.

NUTRITIONAL INFORMATION, PER PIECE: about 61 cal, 5 g pro, 4 g total fat (1 g sat. fat), 1 g carb, 0 g fibre, 20 mg chol, 91 mg sodium, 42 mg potassium. % RDI: 2% iron, 1% vit A, 1% folate.

VARIATIONS

CRISPY BUFFALO CHICKEN WINGS

Omit lemon wedges. In small saucepan, combine ⅓ cup cayenne-based hot pepper sauce (such as Frank's RedHot Original), 2 tbsp butter, 1 tsp Worcestershire sauce and ½ tsp onion powder; bring to boil. Let cool to room temperature. Prepare wings as directed; toss with sauce just before serving.

CRISPY BARBECUE CHICKEN WINGS

Omit lemon wedges. In saucepan, combine 1 cup ketchup, ½ cup water, ⅓ cup fancy molasses, 2 tbsp cider vinegar, 1 tbsp Dijon mustard, 1 tsp onion powder, ½ tsp garlic powder and ¼ tsp salt; bring to boil. Reduce heat and simmer until thickened, about 20 minutes. Prepare wings as directed, brushing with sauce during last 5 minutes of baking time.

TIP FROM THE TEST KITCHEN
Already separated and trimmed chicken wings are a real time-saver. If you can't find them, cut tips off whole chicken wings, and then cut wings at remaining joint.

CLASSIC ROAST CHICKEN
WITH GRAVY

*Our foolproof take on the classic Sunday supper is so good—and so easy—
you might be tempted to make it on weeknights. It has gorgeous, crispy skin flecked
with herbs and garlic, and a rich gravy that is definitely worth the indulgence.*

HANDS-ON TIME
30 minutes

TOTAL TIME
1¾ hours

MAKES
4 servings

INGREDIENTS

GARLIC BUTTER:

4 tsp	butter, softened
2	cloves garlic, pressed or finely grated
2 tsp	chopped fresh thyme
1 tsp	chopped fresh rosemary
¼ tsp	each salt and pepper

ROAST CHICKEN:

1	whole chicken (1.5 kg)
¼ tsp	each salt and pepper
1	small onion, quartered
4	sprigs fresh thyme
1	sprig fresh rosemary

GRAVY:

2 tbsp	all-purpose flour
4 tsp	butter, softened
¼ cup	dry white wine
1 cup	sodium-reduced chicken broth
pinch	pepper
	boiling water (optional)

DIRECTIONS

GARLIC BUTTER: In small bowl, stir together butter, garlic, thyme, rosemary, salt and pepper. Set aside.

ROAST CHICKEN: Remove giblets and neck (if any) from chicken; remove any excess fat and skin. Sprinkle cavity with salt and pepper; place onion, thyme and rosemary in cavity. Rub chicken all over with garlic butter. Place chicken, breast side up, on greased rack in roasting pan; tuck wings under back.

Roast in 375°F (190°C) oven for 45 minutes; baste and continue to roast, basting occasionally, until instant-read thermometer inserted in thickest part of thigh reads 185°F (85°C), about 30 more minutes. Discard contents of cavity. Using tongs, tip chicken to pour juices into pan. Transfer chicken to platter; cover loosely with foil and let rest for 20 minutes before carving.

GRAVY: Meanwhile, tilt pan so juices collect at 1 end. Skim fat from surface, reserving 1 tbsp.

In small bowl, stir together flour, butter and reserved fat; set aside. Place pan over medium heat; whisk in wine. Cook, whisking and scraping up browned bits from bottom of pan, until reduced by half, about 1 minute.

Whisk in broth; bring to boil. Whisk in butter mixture, 2 tsp at a time, until smooth. Cook, whisking constantly, until thickened, about 2 minutes. Strain through fine-mesh sieve; stir in pepper.

If necessary, stir in enough boiling water to loosen and make 1 cup gravy. Serve with chicken.

NUTRITIONAL INFORMATION, PER SERVING: about 435 cal, 37 g pro, 29 g total fat (11 g sat. fat), 4 g carb, trace fibre, 152 mg chol, 601 mg sodium, 431 mg potassium. % RDI: 2% calcium, 11% iron, 13% vit A, 2% vit C, 6% folate.

TIP FROM THE TEST KITCHEN
The trick to rich, lump-free gravy is to whisk the butter and flour mixture into the pan a little at a time. The flour gradually thickens the gravy as the butter melts.

ROASTED STUFFED CORNISH HENS

Cornish hens take less time to bake than a large whole chicken—plus, there is no carving necessary. To serve, cut each hen in half and arrange over mounds of the moist rice-based stuffing.

HANDS-ON TIME
25 minutes

TOTAL TIME
2¼ hours

MAKES
8 servings

INGREDIENTS

RICE STUFFING:

2 tbsp	butter
3	leeks (white parts only), sliced
1	rib celery, thinly sliced
2	cloves garlic, minced
1½ cups	long-grain rice
2½ cups	sodium-reduced chicken broth
1 tbsp	chopped fresh tarragon
1 tsp	grated lemon zest
¼ tsp	each salt and pepper

ROASTED CORNISH HENS:

2 tbsp	butter, melted
½ tsp	grated lemon zest
4	Cornish hens (about 2.7 kg total)
¼ tsp	salt
pinch	pepper

DIRECTIONS

RICE STUFFING: In saucepan, melt butter over medium-high heat; cook leeks, celery and garlic, stirring occasionally, until softened, about 5 minutes.

Add rice, stirring to coat. Add broth, tarragon, lemon zest, salt and pepper; bring to boil. Reduce heat, cover and simmer until rice is tender and no liquid remains, about 18 minutes. Remove from heat and let stand for 10 minutes. *(Make-ahead: Let cool for 30 minutes; refrigerate in airtight container for up to 24 hours, adding 10 minutes to cooking time for baking dish.)*

ROASTED CORNISH HENS: Stir butter with lemon zest; set aside. Remove giblets and neck (if any) from hens. Trim ends of wings; trim off excess fat and skin. Fill each cavity with about ½ cup of the stuffing. Brush hens with butter mixture; sprinkle with salt and pepper. Place remaining stuffing in greased 8-inch (2 L) square baking dish; cover with foil.

Place hens, breast side up, on greased rack in shallow roasting pan. Bake in 400°F (200°C) oven for 45 minutes, basting occasionally. Add stuffing to oven; bake, uncovering halfway through, until stuffing is hot and instant-read thermometer inserted into thickest part of thigh reads 185°F (85°C), about 30 minutes.

Transfer hens to cutting board; let rest for 10 minutes before cutting in half.

NUTRITIONAL INFORMATION, PER SERVING: about 613 cal, 40 g pro, 35 g total fat (12 g sat. fat), 32 g carb, 1 g fibre, 225 mg chol, 505 mg sodium, 583 mg potassium. % RDI: 5% calcium, 17% iron, 10% vit A, 7% vit C, 9% folate.

SWEET-AND-SOUR TURKEY BURGERS ㉚

Ground turkey is a lighter-tasting alternative to beef in grilled burgers. A simple sweet-and-sour barbecue sauce keeps these patties moist and flavourful.

HANDS-ON TIME
20 minutes

TOTAL TIME
30 minutes

MAKES
4 servings

INGREDIENTS

SWEET-AND-SOUR BARBECUE SAUCE:

2 tsp	vegetable oil
1	onion, finely diced
2	cloves garlic, minced
⅔ cup	bottled strained tomatoes (passata)
1	canned chipotle pepper in adobo sauce, chopped
2 tbsp	tomato paste
1 tbsp	red wine vinegar
2 tsp	packed brown sugar
pinch	salt

TURKEY BURGERS:

450 g	lean ground turkey
¼ cup	fresh bread crumbs
1	egg
1 tsp	chili powder
½ tsp	salt
¼ tsp	pepper
1	avocado, pitted, peeled and sliced
½ cup	sliced cucumber
3	radishes, sliced
1 cup	shredded iceberg lettuce
4	onion buns, halved

DIRECTIONS

SWEET-AND-SOUR BARBECUE SAUCE: In small saucepan, heat oil over medium heat; cook onion and garlic, stirring occasionally, until tender and light golden, about 5 minutes.

Stir in strained tomatoes, chipotle pepper, tomato paste, vinegar, brown sugar and salt; bring to boil. Reduce heat and simmer until thickened, 10 to 12 minutes. Let cool slightly. Using immersion blender, purée until smooth; set aside.

TURKEY BURGERS: While barbecue sauce is cooling, stir together turkey, bread crumbs, egg, chili powder, salt and pepper until combined. Shape into four ½-inch (1 cm) thick patties.

Place patties on greased grill over medium-high heat; brush with half of the barbecue sauce. Close lid and grill, turning once and brushing with remaining sauce, until instant-read thermometer inserted sideways into centre of several patties reads 165°F (74°C), 10 to 12 minutes.

Sandwich patties, avocado, cucumber, radishes and lettuce in buns.

NUTRITIONAL INFORMATION, PER SERVING: about 527 cal, 30 g pro, 24 g total fat (5 g sat. fat), 49 g carb, 6 g fibre, 128 mg chol, 872 mg sodium, 829 mg potassium. % RDI: 11% calcium, 38% iron, 8% vit A, 18% vit C, 60% folate.

ROLLED CRANBERRY TURKEY BREAST
WITH CREAMY GRAVY

Sometimes a whole turkey is just too much for a small group at the holidays. Instead, celebrate with slices of this beautiful, easy all-in-one turkey-and-stuffing dinner. Look for a fresh boneless skin-on turkey breast at the butcher's counter.

HANDS-ON TIME
30 minutes

TOTAL TIME
2¼ hours

MAKES
4 to 6 servings

INGREDIENTS

CRANBERRY SAUSAGE STUFFING:

115 g	turkey sausage, casings removed
2 tsp	olive oil
2	cloves garlic, minced
¼ cup	each finely diced onion and celery
1 tbsp	chopped fresh sage
2 tsp	chopped fresh thyme
1 cup	cubed sourdough bread
¼ cup	dried cranberries
¼ cup	sodium-reduced chicken broth
¼ tsp	pepper

TURKEY BREAST:

1	boneless skin-on turkey breast (900 g)
1 tsp	olive oil
pinch	each salt and pepper

CREAMY GRAVY:

1 tbsp	butter
3	cloves garlic, minced
2 tsp	chopped fresh thyme
2 cups	sodium-reduced chicken broth
⅓ cup	whipping cream (35%)
2 tsp	grainy mustard
¼ tsp	pepper
pinch	salt
2 tbsp	cornstarch

DIRECTIONS

CRANBERRY SAUSAGE STUFFING: In skillet, cook sausage over medium heat, breaking up with spoon, until browned, 4 minutes. Transfer to plate.

Add oil to skillet; cook garlic, onion, celery, sage and thyme, stirring often, until onion is softened, about 5 minutes. Stir in sausage, bread, cranberries, broth and pepper until bread is softened. Let cool. *(Make-ahead: Refrigerate in airtight container for up to 24 hours.)*

TURKEY BREAST: Place turkey breast on cutting board. Holding knife blade parallel to board and starting at thickest long side, slice horizontally through breast to within 1 inch (2.5 cm) of opposite side; open. Cover with waxed paper; using meat mallet or heavy-bottomed saucepan, pound to ½-inch (1 cm) thickness.

Leaving 1-inch (2.5 cm) border on all sides, spread stuffing over turkey. Starting at skinless side, roll up. Tie securely with kitchen string at 2-inch (5 cm) intervals.

Brush turkey with oil; sprinkle with salt and pepper. Place on rack in roasting pan; add 1 cup water. Roast in 325°F (160°C) oven until no longer pink inside and instant-read thermometer inserted in thickest part of turkey reads 165°F (74°C), about 1½ hours. Transfer to cutting board; cover loosely with foil and let rest for 10 minutes before slicing. Discard string.

CREAMY GRAVY: While turkey is resting, in saucepan, melt butter over medium-high heat; cook garlic and thyme, stirring, until fragrant, about 1 minute. Add broth; cook until slightly reduced, about 4 minutes. Stir in cream, mustard, pepper and salt. Stir cornstarch with 1 tbsp water; stir into broth mixture and cook until thickened, about 1 minute. Serve with turkey.

NUTRITIONAL INFORMATION, PER EACH OF 6 SERVINGS: about 313 cal, 41 g pro, 16 g total fat (17 g sat. fat), 12 g carb, 1 g fibre, 126 mg chol, 465 mg sodium, 503 mg potassium. % RDI: 4% calcium, 9% iron, 7% vit A, 3% vit C, 8% folate.

VARIATION

ROLLED LEEK AND MUSHROOM TURKEY BREAST
WITH CREAMY GRAVY

STUFFING: Omit sausage. Substitute 1 leek (white and light green parts only), thinly sliced, and 1 cup sliced cremini mushrooms for onion, celery and cranberries. Add ¼ cup grated Parmesan cheese along with bread.

SMOKED BRINED TURKEY

Cooking your turkey on the barbecue keeps your oven free for other dishes. For best results, do not use a bird larger than 6 kg on the barbecue. You'll need about 2½ cups applewood chips; soak them in water for an hour before using.

HANDS-ON TIME
50 minutes

TOTAL TIME
16 hours

MAKES
12 to 15 servings

INGREDIENTS

BRINED TURKEY:

1¼ cups	coarse salt
½ cup	packed brown sugar
5 cups	boiling water
1	orange
1	lemon
6	cloves garlic, crushed
2 tbsp	whole allspice
1 tbsp	black peppercorns
6	bay leaves
11 cups	ice water
1	whole fresh turkey (4.5 to 6 kg)
3 tbsp	olive oil

GRAVY:

	chicken broth (optional)
	unsalted butter (optional), melted
⅓ cup	all-purpose flour
⅓ cup	dry white wine
pinch	pepper

DIRECTIONS

BRINED TURKEY: In large saucepan, dissolve salt and sugar in boiling water. Peel zest from orange and lemon; squeeze juice into bowl. Add orange and lemon juices and zest to pan. Add garlic, allspice, peppercorns and bay leaves. Let cool slightly. In large stockpot placed inside cooler or large bucket, combine brine mixture with ice water. Let cool completely, about 1 hour. *(Make-ahead: Cover and refrigerate for up to 3 days.)*

Remove neck and giblets from turkey; set neck aside for gravy. Discard giblets. Add turkey to brine; cover and refrigerate for 12 to 15 hours.

Heat 1 burner of 2-burner barbecue or 2 outside burners of 3-burner barbecue to medium. Seal soaked applewood chips in heavy-duty foil; poke several holes in top. Place over lit burner(s) or directly on coals. Remove turkey from brine and rinse in cold water. Discard brine. Pat turkey dry inside and out. Place on greased rack in roasting pan; add reserved turkey neck to pan. Brush turkey all over with oil. Place pan on grill over unlit burner with legs facing centre of grill.

Close lid and cook, basting occasionally and covering loosely with foil if browning too quickly, until instant-read thermometer inserted in thickest part of breast reads 170°F (77°C) and juices run clear when meat is pierced, 2½ to 3 hours. Transfer to cutting board; cover loosely with foil and let rest for 30 minutes before carving.

GRAVY: Remove neck from pan; set aside. Pour juices in cavity into heatproof liquid measure. If necessary, add enough chicken broth to make ¾ cup. Drain all but ¼ cup fat from pan, adding butter if not enough fat remains; cook over medium heat for 1 minute, scraping up browned bits from bottom of pan.

Add flour; cook, stirring, until slightly darkened, about 3 minutes. Add wine and reserved turkey juices. Stirring constantly, slowly add 2½ cups water and bring to boil. Add neck and pepper; cook over medium heat, stirring constantly, until thickened, 7 to 10 minutes, adding more water to thin, if desired. Strain and serve with turkey.

NUTRITIONAL INFORMATION, PER EACH OF 15 SERVINGS: about 263 cal, 44 g pro, 12 g total fat (3 g sat. fat), 3 g carb, trace fibre, 152 mg chol, 463 mg sodium, 583 mg potassium. % RDI: 2% calcium, 9% iron, 2% vit C, 9% folate.

VARIATION

OVEN-ROASTED BRINED TURKEY

Roast turkey in 325°F (160°C) oven, basting occasionally and covering loosely with foil if browning too quickly, until instant-read thermometer inserted in thickest part of thigh reads 170°F (77°C), 2½ to 3 hours.

STEAK FLORENTINE
page 157

ULTIMATE BEEF & LAMB | 6

"Growing up, beef was at the centre of most of our family meals, but I still never get tired of it. There are times when, on a very basic level, I require a big-old juicy steak for dinner."

ANNABELLE WAUGH FOOD DIRECTOR

STEAK FRITES

It's hard to find a French bistro that doesn't serve up classic steak and fries. Now it's just as easy to indulge without leaving home.

HANDS-ON TIME
15 minutes

TOTAL TIME
35 minutes

MAKES
4 servings

INGREDIENTS

675 g	yellow-fleshed potatoes, scrubbed
1 tbsp	olive oil
¼ tsp	each salt and pepper
450 g	beef sirloin grilling steak, cut in 4 portions
2 tsp	chopped fresh thyme
⅓ cup	mayonnaise
1 tbsp	chopped fresh chives
2 tsp	Dijon mustard
1 tsp	lemon juice

DIRECTIONS

Cut potatoes into ½-inch (1 cm) thick wedges; toss with half each of the oil, salt and pepper. Spread on parchment paper–lined rimmed baking sheet; bake in 450°F (230°C) oven, turning once, until tender, about 30 minutes. Broil until golden brown, about 3 minutes.

While potatoes are baking, sprinkle steak with thyme and remaining salt and pepper. In skillet, heat remaining oil over medium-high heat; cook steak, turning once, until medium-rare, about 6 minutes. Transfer to cutting board; cover loosely with foil and let rest for 10 minutes.

Stir together mayonnaise, chives, mustard and lemon juice. Serve with steak as dipping sauce for potatoes.

NUTRITIONAL INFORMATION, PER SERVING: about 412 cal, 26 g pro, 23 g total fat (5 g sat. fat), 26 g carb, 2 g fibre, 60 mg chol, 333 mg sodium, 1,047 mg potassium. % RDI: 2% calcium, 25% iron, 2% vit A, 37% vit C, 10% folate.

TIP FROM THE TEST KITCHEN
Letting the steak rest after cooking allows the juices to redistribute throughout the meat. This small but important step will ensure every bite is perfectly juicy.

STEAKHOUSE RIB EYE ③⓪
WITH BÉARNAISE SAUCE

The Test Kitchen cooks rib eyes to medium-rare—enough to render some of the fat but not enough to toughen the meat. The béarnaise sauce won't keep; for a smaller crowd, try our Shallot-and-Herb Compound Butter (below) and refrigerate the leftovers.

HANDS-ON TIME
30 minutes

TOTAL TIME
30 minutes

MAKES
6 servings

INGREDIENTS

BÉARNAISE SAUCE:

1	shallot, finely chopped
2 tbsp	white wine vinegar
pinch	pepper
4	egg yolks
½ cup	butter, melted
1 tbsp	chopped fresh tarragon

STEAKS:

3	beef rib eye grilling steaks (each 340 g and 1 inch/2.5 cm thick)
2 tbsp	olive oil
½ tsp	each salt and pepper

DIRECTIONS

BÉARNAISE SAUCE: In small saucepan, bring shallot, ¼ cup water, vinegar and pepper to simmer over medium heat. Cook until reduced by half, about 3 minutes.

In heatproof bowl, whisk egg yolks until pale; whisk in shallot mixture. Set bowl over saucepan of simmering water; cook, whisking constantly, until sauce is thick enough to coat back of spoon, about 5 minutes. Slowly drizzle in butter, whisking constantly. Whisk in tarragon. Remove saucepan from heat; keep bowl of sauce over top to keep warm.

STEAKS: Brush both sides of steaks with oil; sprinkle with salt and pepper. Place on greased grill over medium-high heat; grill, uncovered and turning at least twice, until instant-read thermometer inserted in centre reads 140°F (60°C), 10 to 12 minutes.

Transfer to rack; let rest, uncovered, until instant-read thermometer inserted in centre reads 145°F (63°C), about 5 minutes. Slice across the grain; serve with Béarnaise Sauce.

NUTRITIONAL INFORMATION, PER SERVING: about 557 cal, 35 g pro, 45 g total fat (21 g sat. fat), trace carb, trace fibre, 251 mg chol, 369 mg sodium, 408 mg potassium. % RDI: 3% calcium, 29% iron, 20% vit A, 12% folate.

VARIATION

STEAKHOUSE RIB EYE
WITH SHALLOT-AND-HERB COMPOUND BUTTER

Omit Béarnaise Sauce. In skillet, melt 1 tbsp butter over medium heat; cook 1 cup chopped shallots and 4 cloves garlic, minced, until shallots are softened, about 6 minutes. Let cool. In bowl, stir together shallot mixture; ½ cup butter, softened; ¼ cup each chopped fresh basil and chopped fresh parsley; and 1 tbsp white wine vinegar. Scrape onto piece of plastic wrap; shape into 1-inch (2.5 cm) thick log and wrap tightly. Refrigerate until firm, about 30 minutes. *(Make-ahead: Refrigerate for up to 3 days or freeze in resealable plastic freezer bag for up to 2 weeks.)* Cook steaks as directed; top with slices of butter mixture.

STEAK FLORENTINE

A thick-cut T-bone or porterhouse works best for this Italian-style steak. Standing it up on the base of the T-bone heats up the bone, which helps cook the meat through to the centre.

HANDS-ON TIME
30 minutes

TOTAL TIME
45 minutes

MAKES
4 to 6 servings

INGREDIENTS

1	beef T-bone grilling steak (1 kg and 1½ inches/4 cm thick)
2 tsp	olive oil
1 tsp	chopped fresh rosemary
¾ tsp	fine sea salt
½ tsp	pepper
	lemon wedges

DIRECTIONS

Brush both sides of steak with oil; sprinkle with rosemary. Let stand for 10 minutes.

Sprinkle both sides of steak with salt and pepper, pressing to adhere. Place on greased grill over medium-high heat; grill, uncovered, rotating in quarter-turns and turning as necessary to prevent overbrowning, until instant-read thermometer inserted in centre reads 125°F (52°C), 18 to 20 minutes. Using tongs, stand steak up on base of T-bone and grill until instant-read thermometer inserted in centre reads 130°F (55°C), about 4 minutes.

Transfer to rack; let rest, uncovered, until instant-read thermometer inserted in centre reads 135°F (57°C), about 5 minutes. Slice across the grain; serve with lemon wedges.

NUTRITIONAL INFORMATION, PER EACH OF 6 SERVINGS: about 273 cal, 28 g pro, 17 g total fat (7 g sat. fat), trace carb, trace fibre, 66 mg chol, 350 mg sodium, 302 mg potassium. % RDI: 2% calcium, 19% iron, 3% folate.

TIP FROM THE TEST KITCHEN
The tenderloin cooks faster than the strip loin portion of the steak, so serve it to people who prefer their meat a bit more done.

CLASSIC MARINATED FLANK STEAK

HANDS-ON TIME
20 minutes

TOTAL TIME
8½ hours

MAKES
6 to 8 servings

Flank steak is excellent for serving to a large crowd because you cook it whole. That means there's only one steak, rather than several, to turn on the grill.

INGREDIENTS

½ cup	balsamic vinegar or dry red wine (see tip, below)
3 tbsp	Dijon mustard
3 tbsp	olive oil
4	cloves garlic, finely grated or pressed
½ tsp	each salt and pepper
1	beef flank marinating steak (900 g)

DIRECTIONS

Whisk together vinegar, mustard, 2 tbsp of the oil, the garlic and ¼ tsp each of the salt and pepper.

Using fork, prick steak all over. Place in large resealable plastic bag or shallow dish; pour in vinegar mixture, massaging or turning steak to coat. Seal bag or cover dish and refrigerate for 8 hours. *(Make-ahead: Refrigerate for up to 24 hours.)*

Remove steak from marinade; discard marinade. Pat steak dry and brush with remaining oil; sprinkle with remaining salt and pepper. Place on greased grill over medium-high heat; grill, uncovered and turning at least twice, until instant-read thermometer inserted in centre reads 140°F (60°C), 10 to 12 minutes.

Transfer to rack; let rest, uncovered, until instant-read thermometer inserted in centre reads 145°F (63°C), about 5 minutes. Slice across the grain.

NUTRITIONAL INFORMATION, PER EACH OF 8 SERVINGS: about 195 cal, 25 g pro, 9 g total fat (3 g sat. fat), 1 g carb, trace fibre, 50 mg chol, 153 mg sodium, 238 mg potassium. % RDI: 1% calcium, 16% iron, 2% folate.

TIP FROM THE TEST KITCHEN
Balsamic vinegar adds bold flavour to the marinade. For a subtler taste, opt for a light- to medium-bodied red wine, such as Pinot Noir or Merlot, instead.

QUICK BEEF BULGOGI ③⓪

Bulgogi, a Korean marinated beef dish, is traditionally served with rice and kimchi, the popular spicy Korean condiment made with cabbage, radish and many other ingredients. It's also yummy with a simple salad or steamed vegetables.

HANDS-ON TIME
15 minutes

TOTAL TIME
30 minutes

MAKES
4 servings

INGREDIENTS

3 tbsp	sodium-reduced soy sauce
2 tbsp	mirin or dry white wine
1 tbsp	granulated sugar
1 tbsp	sesame seeds
1 tbsp	sesame oil
3	cloves garlic, minced
2 tsp	minced fresh ginger
4	green onions, thinly sliced
half	Asian pear (see tip, below), peeled and grated (about ⅓ cup)
450 g	beef sirloin grilling steak, thinly sliced
1 tsp	vegetable oil

DIRECTIONS

In bowl, whisk together soy sauce, mirin, sugar, sesame seeds, sesame oil, garlic, ginger and all but 2 tbsp of the green onions until sugar is dissolved.

Stir in pear and beef; cover and let stand for 15 minutes or refrigerate for up to 2 hours. Drain off marinade.

In wok or large nonstick skillet, heat vegetable oil over high heat; stir-fry beef mixture until beef is browned, about 3 minutes. Garnish with remaining green onions.

NUTRITIONAL INFORMATION, PER SERVING: about 204 cal, 24 g pro, 9 g total fat (3 g sat. fat), 6 g carb, 1 g fibre, 53 mg chol, 293 mg sodium, 361 mg potassium. % RDI: 2% calcium, 19% iron, 1% vit A, 3% vit C, 6% folate.

TIP FROM THE TEST KITCHEN
Asian pears are extraordinarily crisp and tasty, but they're only in season for a short time and can be hard to find in some places. If you can't locate them at your supermarket, substitute any firm ripe pear.

STEAK AND PEPPER STIR-FRY ㉚

This stir-fry comes together in minutes, with little chopping required, so it's great for a busy weeknight. Serve with steamed rice or noodles to soak up the sauce. For a spicy note, add 1 tsp of Asian chili garlic paste.

HANDS-ON TIME
20 minutes

TOTAL TIME
20 minutes

MAKES
4 servings

INGREDIENTS

2 tbsp	oyster sauce
1 tsp	cornstarch
pinch	each salt and pepper
1 tbsp	vegetable oil
450 g	beef flank marinating steak, thinly sliced across the grain
1	onion, sliced
2	sweet peppers (red, orange and/or yellow), sliced

DIRECTIONS

Stir together 3 tbsp water, oyster sauce, cornstarch, salt and pepper. Set aside.

In wok or large nonstick skillet, heat 2 tsp of the oil over high heat; stir-fry beef until browned, about 3 minutes. Transfer to plate.

Add remaining vegetable oil, onion and 2 tbsp water to wok. Stir-fry over medium-high heat, scraping up browned bits from bottom of wok, until softened, about 4 minutes. Add peppers; stir-fry until tender-crisp, about 4 minutes.

Return beef to wok. Add oyster sauce mixture; cook, tossing to coat, until sauce is slightly thickened, about 1 minute.

NUTRITIONAL INFORMATION, PER SERVING: about 249 cal, 26 g pro, 13 g total fat (4 g sat. fat), 8 g carb, 1 g fibre, 53 mg chol, 316 mg sodium, 521 mg potassium. % RDI: 2% calcium, 17% iron, 11% vit A, 157% vit C, 9% folate.

VARIATION
CHICKEN AND PEPPER STIR-FRY
Substitute boneless skinless chicken thighs for beef. Stir-fry until browned and juices run clear when chicken is pierced, about 3 minutes.

MAKE-AHEAD BEEF ENCHILADAS

With a hearty beef filling, gooey cheese and zesty sauce, this enchilada dish is impossible to resist—especially when it's topped with a cool dollop of sour cream. The best part: The filling simmers away untended in the slow cooker, freeing you up for other things.

HANDS-ON TIME
30 minutes

TOTAL TIME
7½ hours

MAKES
5 servings

INGREDIENTS

900 g	stewing beef cubes or cubed beef pot roast (such as inside blade)
1	sweet onion, diced
3	cloves garlic, minced
1	jalapeño pepper, seeded and diced
1½ cups	sodium-reduced beef broth
½ cup	bottled strained tomatoes (passata)
¼ cup	tomato paste
1 tbsp	ancho chili powder
2 tsp	ground cumin
1 tsp	dried oregano
½ tsp	each salt and pepper
¼ cup	all-purpose flour
3 tbsp	cold water
3 tbsp	lime juice
10	small (7-inch/ 18 cm) soft flour tortillas
1½ cups	shredded Monterey Jack cheese
2	green onions, chopped
¼ cup	fresh cilantro leaves

DIRECTIONS

In slow cooker, combine beef, onion, garlic, jalapeño pepper, broth, strained tomatoes, tomato paste, chili powder, cumin, oregano, salt and pepper. Cover and cook on low until beef is tender, 7 to 8 hours.

Using slotted spoon, transfer beef to bowl; using potato masher, break up beef until coarsely shredded.

Meanwhile, whisk together flour, cold water and lime juice. Whisk into liquid in slow cooker; cover and cook on high until slightly thickened, about 15 minutes.

Stir ⅔ cup of the sauce into beef mixture. *(Make-ahead: Let beef mixture and remaining sauce cool separately for 30 minutes. Cover and refrigerate in separate airtight containers for up to 2 days. Reheat separately; continue with recipe.)*

Spread ⅔ cup of the sauce in 13- x 9-inch (3 L) baking dish. Spoon heaping ⅓ cup of the beef mixture onto centre of each tortilla; roll up. Arrange, seam side down, in single layer in baking dish. Pour remaining sauce over top. Sprinkle with Monterey Jack and green onions. Broil until Monterey Jack is melted, about 3 minutes. Garnish with cilantro.

NUTRITIONAL INFORMATION, PER SERVING: about 691 cal, 52 g pro, 33 g total fat (14 g sat. fat), 46 g carb, 4 g fibre, 136 mg chol, 1,238 mg sodium, 1,000 mg potassium. % RDI: 30% calcium, 56% iron, 15% vit A, 17% vit C, 49% folate.

CABBAGE ROLLS ○ ●

Our classic recipe for hearty cabbage rolls is a labour of love that won't disappoint.
Use two smaller cabbages rather than one large head, as the leaves will be more
consistent in size. Serve with sour cream and a little fresh dill.

HANDS-ON TIME
45 minutes

TOTAL TIME
2¾ hours

MAKES
24 rolls

INGREDIENTS

2	small heads Savoy or green cabbage (each about 1.2 kg)
1¼ cups	sodium-reduced chicken broth
½ cup	parboiled rice
8	strips bacon, finely chopped
2 tbsp	butter
3	onions, chopped
½ cup	finely chopped sweet red pepper
2	cloves garlic, minced
1½ tsp	dried marjoram
½ tsp	dried thyme
675 g	lean ground beef
½ cup	chopped fresh parsley
1	egg, whisked
1 tsp	salt
½ tsp	pepper
3 cups	sauerkraut, rinsed, drained and squeezed dry
3 tbsp	packed brown sugar
1	can (1.36 L) tomato juice

DIRECTIONS

Using sharp knife, remove core from each cabbage. In large saucepan of boiling salted water, cook cabbages, 1 at a time, until leaves are softened, about 8 minutes. Transfer to bowl of ice water to chill. Remove outer leaves from each cabbage; set a few of the outer leaves aside to cover rolls while baking.

Working from core end, remove 12 leaves from each cabbage; return cabbages to boiling water for 2 to 3 minutes if leaves become difficult to remove. Drain leaves on paper towels. Trim coarse veins; set aside.

While cabbages are cooking, in saucepan, bring broth to boil; add rice. Reduce heat, cover and simmer until tender, about 20 minutes. Transfer to large bowl.

Meanwhile, in skillet, cook bacon over medium heat, stirring often, until crisp, about 5 minutes; drain off fat.

Add butter to skillet; cook onions, red pepper, garlic, marjoram and thyme, stirring, until onions are softened, about 5 minutes. Add to rice along with beef, parsley, egg, salt and pepper; mix well.

Arrange cabbage leaves on work surface; spoon about ¼ cup of the beef mixture onto each leaf, just above stem. Fold 1 end and both sides over filling; roll up to form cylinders.

In 24-cup (6 L) Dutch oven or roasting pan, spread one-third of the sauerkraut; sprinkle with one-third of the brown sugar. Arrange one-third of the rolls, seam side down, in single layer over top. Spread another one-third each of the sauerkraut and sugar over rolls. Arrange another one-third of the rolls in single layer over top; cover with remaining sauerkraut and sugar. Arrange remaining rolls over top.

Pour tomato juice over rolls. Arrange a few of the reserved outer cabbage leaves over top to prevent scorching. Cover and bake in 350°F (180°C) oven for 1½ hours. Uncover and bake until tender, about 30 more minutes. Discard top leaves.

NUTRITIONAL INFORMATION, PER ROLL: about 138 cal, 8 g pro, 7 g total fat (4 g sat. fat), 12 g carb, 2 g fibre, 31 mg chol, 552 mg sodium, 331 mg potassium. % RDI: 4% calcium, 9% iron, 6% vit A, 37% vit C, 12% folate.

TIP FROM THE TEST KITCHEN
The best leaves for rolling are in the middle of the cabbage, so save the excess ones for coleslaw or soup.

CLASSIC BEEF MEAT LOAF

A touch of horseradish adds zesty flavour to classic meat loaf. Cooking the onion, celery and garlic before adding them to the mixture ensures their tenderness and mellows their flavours.

HANDS-ON TIME
25 minutes

TOTAL TIME
1½ hours

MAKES
4 servings

INGREDIENTS

1 tbsp	vegetable oil
1	onion, finely diced
1	rib celery, finely diced
1	clove garlic, minced
⅔ cup	fresh bread crumbs (see tip, page 27)
1	egg, lightly beaten
1 tbsp	prepared horseradish
1 tsp	Worcestershire sauce
½ tsp	salt
¼ tsp	pepper
450 g	lean ground beef
3 tbsp	ketchup

DIRECTIONS

In skillet, heat oil over medium heat; cook onion, celery and garlic, stirring occasionally, until softened, about 8 minutes. Transfer to large bowl; let stand for 10 minutes.

Stir in bread crumbs, egg, horseradish, Worcestershire sauce, salt and pepper. Add beef; mix just until combined. Shape into 7- x 4-inch (18 x 10 cm) log; place on foil-lined rimmed baking sheet. Brush all over with ketchup.

Bake in 375°F (190°C) oven until instant-read thermometer inserted in centre reads 160°F (71°C), 45 to 50 minutes. Let stand for 10 minutes before slicing.

NUTRITIONAL INFORMATION, PER SERVING: about 304 cal, 24 g pro, 18 g total fat (6 g sat. fat), 10 g carb, 1 g fibre, 110 mg chol, 567 mg sodium, 440 mg potassium. % RDI: 4% calcium, 19% iron, 4% vit A, 8% vit C, 13% folate.

VARIATION

CLASSIC BARBECUE BEEF MEAT LOAF

Omit horseradish. Stir in 1 tsp chili powder and ½ tsp each ground cumin and ground coriander along with bread crumbs. Brush with prepared barbecue sauce instead of ketchup.

STEAK TACOS
WITH PEBRE SALSA

HANDS-ON TIME
20 minutes

TOTAL TIME
25 minutes

MAKES
4 servings

This herbaceous Chilean-style salsa is equally good on chicken tacos.
To make the salsa spicier, add a tablespoon of minced jalapeño peppers.

INGREDIENTS

PEBRE SALSA:

1 cup	packed fresh cilantro leaves
1 cup	packed fresh parsley leaves
1	clove garlic, chopped
¼ cup	chopped red onion
2 tbsp	olive oil
2 tsp	red wine vinegar
¼ tsp	each salt and pepper

STEAK TACOS:

2 tsp	vegetable oil
340 g	beef top sirloin grilling steak
8	small (6-inch/15 cm) whole grain whole wheat tortillas
½ cup	cherry tomatoes, halved
1 cup	shredded Boston or other lettuce

DIRECTIONS

PEBRE SALSA: In food processor, purée together cilantro, parsley, garlic, onion, oil, vinegar, salt and pepper; set aside.

STEAK TACOS: In skillet, heat oil over medium heat; cook steak, turning once, until medium-rare, 6 to 8 minutes. Transfer to cutting board; let rest for 10 minutes before slicing across the grain.

While steak is resting, heat tortillas according to package instructions. Divide steak among tortillas; top with Pebre Salsa, tomatoes and lettuce.

NUTRITIONAL INFORMATION, PER SERVING: about 399 cal, 26 g pro, 18 g total fat (4 g sat. fat), 33 g carb, 5 g fibre, 40 mg chol, 690 mg sodium, 662 mg potassium. % RDI: 3% calcium, 29% iron, 22% vit A, 42% vit C, 32% folate.

VARIATION

STEAK TACOS
WITH PICO DE GALLO

Omit Pebre Salsa. Make Pico de Gallo: In bowl, stir together 3 cups quartered grape or cherry tomatoes, ¾ cup finely diced white or red onion, ¼ cup chopped fresh cilantro, 2 tbsp lime juice, 1 tbsp minced jalapeño pepper and ¼ tsp salt. Let stand for 30 minutes. Proceed with recipe as directed, spooning Pico de Gallo over tacos before serving.

BEEF WELLINGTONS

Wow your guests with this variation on a beloved recipe. These individual Wellingtons are elegant and don't require carving at the table. Cut the steaks to an equal thickness to ensure they're all perfectly cooked through at the same time.

HANDS-ON TIME
40 minutes

TOTAL TIME
2 hours

MAKES
8 servings

INGREDIENTS

340 g	cremini mushrooms
8	beef tenderloin grilling steaks (each 85 g)
½ tsp	each salt and pepper
1 tbsp	unsalted butter
3	shallots, minced
2 tsp	chopped fresh thyme
¼ cup	dry white wine
¼ cup	chopped fresh parsley
2	sheets (450 g pkg) frozen butter puff pastry, thawed
115 g	duck liver pâté or chicken liver pâté
1	egg

DIRECTIONS

In food processor, pulse mushrooms until finely chopped; set aside.

Tie kitchen string around edge of each steak to form tight round. Sprinkle steaks with ¼ tsp each of the salt and pepper.

In large skillet, melt butter over medium-high heat; working in 2 batches, cook steaks, turning once, until browned, about 1 minute per side. Transfer to plate; let cool. Remove string.

In same skillet, cook shallots over medium heat, stirring often, until softened, about 3 minutes. Add mushrooms, thyme and remaining salt and pepper; cook, stirring, until mushrooms are tender and no liquid remains, about 5 minutes.

Add wine; cook, stirring, until no liquid remains, about 2 minutes. Stir in parsley; remove from heat and let cool.

On lightly floured surface, unroll 1 pastry sheet; cut into quarters. On each quarter, spread one-eighth of the liver pâté to same width as steak. Spread rounded 1 tbsp of the mushroom mixture over pâté. Top with steak and another rounded 1 tbsp of the mushroom mixture, spreading evenly. **PHOTO A**

Whisk egg with 2 tsp water; brush lightly over edges of pastry. Gently pulling and stretching, fold pastry over filling, overlapping edges to seal. **PHOTO B**

Repeat with remaining pastry and fillings. Arrange, seam side down, on 2 parchment paper–lined rimmed baking sheets; brush tops with remaining egg mixture. Refrigerate for 1 hour. *(Make-ahead: Refrigerate for up to 4 hours.)*

Bake on top and bottom racks in 425°F (220°C) oven, switching and rotating pans halfway through, until instant-read thermometer inserted in centre of several reads 145°F (63°C) for medium-rare, about 20 minutes.

NUTRITIONAL INFORMATION, PER SERVING: about 401 cal, 25 g pro, 23 g total fat (10 g sat. fat), 23 g carb, 3 g fibre, 149 mg chol, 420 mg sodium, 518 mg potassium. % RDI: 2% calcium, 40% iron, 12% vit A, 3% vit C, 27% folate.

ROAST BEEF
WITH MUSHROOM GRAVY

Sirloin tip, inside round and outside round oven roasts are tasty and less expensive than premium roasts. However, because they are less marbled with fat, they need help to keep them succulent. Here, a tasty garlic-and-herb-infused butter does just that.

HANDS-ON TIME
40 minutes

TOTAL TIME
3 hours

MAKES
12 to 16 servings

INGREDIENTS

½ cup	butter, softened
3	cloves garlic, pressed or pounded into paste
4 tsp	minced fresh thyme (or 1½ tsp dried)
½ tsp	anchovy paste (optional)
¼ tsp	white pepper
pinch	ground cloves
2 tbsp	all-purpose flour
2 kg	beef sirloin tip, or inside or outside round oven roast
1¼ tsp	salt
½ tsp	black pepper
1	onion, thinly sliced
2 tbsp	brandy or whisky (optional)
1 cup	sodium-reduced beef broth
¼ cup	dry sherry, dry white wine or dry white vermouth (or 1 tbsp lemon juice)
375 g	white mushrooms, sliced
¼ cup	finely chopped fresh parsley
2 tsp	Dijon mustard

DIRECTIONS

In bowl and using fork, mash together butter, garlic, thyme, anchovy paste (if using), white pepper and cloves. Transfer 2 tbsp to small bowl; mash with flour. Set aside.

Using long thin knife, make 12 evenly spaced cuts halfway to bottom of roast. Enlarge each hole with handle of wooden spoon; stuff about 1 tsp of the flourless butter mixture into each. Sprinkle roast with 1 tsp of the salt and the black pepper.

Spread onion in roasting pan; place roast on onion. Spread top of roast with remaining flourless butter mixture; sprinkle with brandy (if using).

Roast in 350°F (180°C) oven, basting often with pan juices after first 30 minutes, until instant-read thermometer inserted in centre reads 140°F (60°C) for medium-rare, about 1½ hours. Transfer to cutting board; cover loosely with foil and let rest for 10 to 15 minutes.

While roast is resting, in saucepan, bring broth, ⅓ cup water and sherry to boil over medium heat. Add mushrooms and remaining salt; return to boil. Reduce heat and simmer until mushrooms are tender, 6 to 8 minutes. Reserving cooking liquid, drain; set liquid and mushrooms aside.

Stir cooking liquid into roasting pan; bring to boil over medium heat, stirring and scraping up browned bits from bottom of pan. Strain through fine-mesh sieve into saucepan; bring to boil. Whisk in reserved butter mixture and return to simmer, whisking constantly.

Add mushrooms and any juices from roast; simmer for 2 minutes. Stir in parsley and mustard. Thinly slice roast; serve with sauce.

NUTRITIONAL INFORMATION, PER EACH OF 16 SERVINGS: about 203 cal, 26 g pro, 9 g total fat (5 g sat. fat), 3 g carb, 1 g fibre, 73 mg chol, 335 mg sodium. % RDI: 1% calcium, 21% iron, 6% vit A, 3% vit C, 6% folate.

POT ROAST
WITH PARSNIPS, TURNIPS AND PEARL ONIONS

This not-so-pricey meal cooks to tenderness in its own gravy. The best part: Leftovers heat up well the next day, and open-faced pot roast sandwiches with gravy are divine.

HANDS-ON TIME
40 minutes

TOTAL TIME
4 hours

MAKES
8 to 10 servings

INGREDIENTS

2	each large parsnips and carrots, peeled
2	white turnips, peeled
2 tbsp	all-purpose flour
½ tsp	each salt and pepper
1.5 kg	boneless beef pot roast (such as top or bottom blade, or cross rib)
2 tbsp	vegetable oil
1	large onion, diced
3	cloves garlic, sliced
1 cup	sodium-reduced beef broth
1	can (796 mL) whole tomatoes, drained
½ tsp	dried marjoram or thyme
2	bay leaves
1 tbsp	butter
1	pkg (300 g) pearl onions, peeled

DIRECTIONS

Cut parsnips and carrots in half lengthwise; cut into 2-inch (5 cm) long pieces. Quarter turnips. Set aside.

In large bowl, combine flour, salt and pepper; dredge roast in flour mixture. In Dutch oven, heat 1 tbsp of the oil over medium-high heat; brown roast all over. Transfer to plate.

Add remaining oil to pan; cook onion and garlic over medium heat, stirring occasionally, until softened, about 4 minutes. Add broth, scraping up any browned bits from bottom of pan. Add tomatoes, parsnips, carrots, turnips, marjoram and bay leaves.

Return roast and any accumulated juices to pan; bring to simmer. Cover and braise in 300°F (150°C) oven, basting every 30 minutes and turning once, for 2½ hours.

While roast is braising, in skillet, melt butter over medium heat; cook pearl onions until tender and golden, about 10 minutes. Add to roast; cook, uncovered, until roast is tender, about 30 minutes. Discard bay leaves.

Transfer roast to cutting board; cover loosely with foil and let rest for 10 minutes before thinly slicing across the grain. Serve with vegetables and sauce.

NUTRITIONAL INFORMATION, PER EACH OF 10 SERVINGS: about 354 cal, 30 g pro, 18 g total fat (7 g sat. fat), 19 g carb, 4 g fibre, 83 mg chol, 420 mg sodium. % RDI: 8% calcium, 29% iron, 34% vit A, 38% vit C, 21% folate.

STANDING RIB ROAST
WITH GREEN PEPPERCORN HORSERADISH SAUCE

HANDS-ON TIME	20 minutes
TOTAL TIME	4 hours
MAKES	8 to 10 servings

This foolproof method for cooking a standing rib roast—a.k.a., prime rib— guarantees perfectly medium-rare doneness in the thickest part of the roast, every time. The slices closest to the edges will be more well-done.

INGREDIENTS

STANDING RIB ROAST:

3 kg	beef standing rib premium oven roast
2	cloves garlic, minced
2 tsp	chopped fresh rosemary
½ tsp	pepper
¼ tsp	salt
4 tsp	Dijon mustard

GREEN PEPPERCORN HORSERADISH SAUCE:

1 tbsp	butter
3	shallots, finely chopped
¼ cup	brandy
2¼ cups	sodium-reduced beef broth
2 tbsp	green peppercorns in brine, drained
½ cup	whipping cream (35%)
3 tbsp	prepared horseradish
1 tsp	Worcestershire sauce
¼ tsp	pepper
3 tbsp	cornstarch

DIRECTIONS

STANDING RIB ROAST: Place roast, bone side down, on rack in roasting pan. Mash together garlic, rosemary, pepper and salt. Brush mustard over top and sides of roast; spread garlic mixture over mustard, pressing to adhere. Let stand at room temperature for 45 minutes.

Roast in 500°F (260°C) oven for 11 minutes per kilogram, or 33 minutes. Turn off oven; do not open door. Let stand in oven for 2 hours.

GREEN PEPPERCORN HORSERADISH SAUCE: While roast is standing in oven, in saucepan, melt butter over medium heat; cook shallots, stirring often and reducing heat if browning too quickly, until golden and softened, about 5 minutes.

Add brandy; cook, stirring, until almost no liquid remains, about 1 minute. Stir in broth and peppercorns; simmer over medium-low heat for 5 minutes.

Stir in cream, horseradish, Worcestershire sauce and pepper. Stir cornstarch with 3 tbsp water; whisk into sauce. Cook, whisking, until thickened, about 1 minute. Serve with roast.

NUTRITIONAL INFORMATION, PER EACH OF 10 SERVINGS: about 501 cal, 44 g pro, 31 g total fat (15 g sat. fat), 5 g carb, 1 g fibre, 123 mg chol, 399 mg sodium, 526 mg potassium. % RDI: 4% calcium, 28% iron, 5% vit A, 3% vit C, 6% folate.

TIP FROM THE TEST KITCHEN

This method requires exact timing, so keep an eye on the clock to guarantee the best results. The bonus: This roast doesn't require the usual resting time because it finishes cooking—and cools a bit—in the cooling oven. There's no need to wait to carve after taking it out.

STOUT-GLAZED BEEF RIBS

Beer and ribs are such a good match that this recipe will have everyone asking for more. Pork ribs would make a delicious alternative—just cut them into two-rib portions and add one hour to the braising time.

HANDS-ON TIME
40 minutes

TOTAL TIME
2 hours

MAKES
4 servings

INGREDIENTS

2 kg	beef back ribs, cut in 1-rib portions
½ tsp	each salt and pepper
2	bottles (each 341 mL) stout (see tip, below)
1	onion, sliced
3	cloves garlic, sliced
½ cup	packed brown sugar
¼ cup	tomato paste
3 tbsp	drained prepared horseradish
2 tbsp	Dijon mustard
1 tbsp	Worcestershire sauce

DIRECTIONS

Rub meaty side of ribs with salt and pepper; place, meaty side down, in roasting pan. Add stout, onion and garlic; cover and braise in 325°F (160°C) oven until meat is easy to pierce, 1¼ hours.

Transfer ribs to plate. Skim fat from braising liquid; strain through fine-mesh sieve into heatproof glass measuring cup. Discard onions and any remaining braising liquid. Pour reserved braising liquid into saucepan; whisk in brown sugar, tomato paste, horseradish, mustard and Worcestershire sauce. Bring to boil over medium-high heat, whisking often; cook until thickened and reduced to 1 cup, about 15 minutes.

Place ribs on greased grill over medium-high heat; close lid and grill, basting with sauce every few minutes, until caramelized, 12 to 15 minutes.

NUTRITIONAL INFORMATION, PER SERVING: about 484 cal, 31 g pro, 22 g total fat (10 g sat. fat), 38 g carb, 1 g fibre, 75 mg chol, 473 mg sodium, 728 mg potassium. % RDI: 7% calcium, 27% iron, 2% vit A, 12% vit C, 11% folate.

TIP FROM THE TEST KITCHEN
Check your liquor or beer store for interesting brands of stout. One tasty, widely available option for this dish is Guinness.

WESTERN CHILI

This hearty, pantry-friendly chili is big, bold and tasty. Make it the night before you plan to serve it so the flavours can develop to their full potential. Serve topped with sour cream, shredded cheese and/or chopped fresh cilantro.

HANDS-ON TIME
20 minutes

TOTAL TIME
1¼ hours

MAKES
8 servings

INGREDIENTS

2 tbsp	vegetable oil
2	onions, finely chopped
2	cloves garlic, pressed or grated
2 tsp	ground cumin
900 g	lean ground beef
1	can (796 mL) whole tomatoes
3 tbsp	chili powder
2 tsp	dried oregano
2 tsp	granulated sugar
2 tsp	sweet paprika
1 tsp	cocoa powder
1 tsp	salt
½ tsp	pepper
1	bay leaf
1	can (540 mL) red kidney beans, drained and rinsed

DIRECTIONS

In large saucepan or Dutch oven, heat oil over medium-high heat; cook onions and garlic, stirring often, until onions are softened, about 5 minutes.

Add cumin; cook, stirring, until fragrant, about 1 minute. Add beef; cook, stirring and breaking up with spoon, until no longer pink, about 5 minutes.

Stir in tomatoes, breaking up with spoon. Stir in chili powder, oregano, sugar, paprika, cocoa powder, salt, pepper and bay leaf. Bring to boil; reduce heat, partially cover and simmer, stirring occasionally, for 1 hour. Discard bay leaf.

Stir in kidney beans; cook until heated through, about 3 minutes.

NUTRITIONAL INFORMATION, PER SERVING: about 360 cal, 27 g pro, 20 g total fat (7 g sat. fat), 19 g carb, 6 g fibre, 67 mg chol, 688 mg sodium, 754 mg potassium. % RDI: 8% calcium, 34% iron, 12% vit A, 30% vit C, 20% folate.

VARIATION

SLOW COOKER WESTERN CHILI

Decrease oil to 1 tbsp; heat in saucepan over medium-high heat; cook beef, breaking up with spoon, until no longer pink, about 5 minutes. Drain off fat. In slow cooker, stir together beef, 1 can (156 mL) tomato paste and remaining ingredients. Cover and cook on low for 8 hours.

TIP FROM THE TEST KITCHEN
This chili is easy to take along for a picnic. Just toss it in a flameproof pan and reheat it on the barbecue.

BEST-EVER BEEF BURGERS

Up your grill game with our juiciest, most crave-worthy burger ever. The mix of sirloin and medium ground beef, and the addition of our secret ingredient (beef broth!), makes this sandwich a bite of heaven from the grill.

HANDS-ON TIME
20 minutes

TOTAL TIME
25 minutes

MAKES
6 burgers

INGREDIENTS

1 cup	fresh bread crumbs (see tip, page 27)
⅔ cup	sodium-reduced beef broth
450 g	medium ground beef
450 g	ground sirloin
½ tsp	salt
¼ tsp	pepper
6	buns (hamburger, pretzel or pain au lait), halved and toasted

DIRECTIONS

In bowl, mix bread crumbs with broth; let stand for 5 minutes.

In large baking dish, combine ground beef and ground sirloin; sprinkle with bread crumb mixture, salt and pepper. Mix gently just until combined and no streaks of bread crumb mixture are visible (do not overmix). Shape into six 5- x ½-inch (12 x 1 cm) patties. *(Make-ahead: Layer between parchment paper in airtight container; refrigerate for up to 24 hours.)*

Place on greased grill over medium-high heat; close lid and grill, turning once, until instant-read thermometer inserted sideways into patties reads 160°F (71°C), about 8 minutes. (Alternatively, cook patties in grill pan or skillet with up to 2 tsp olive oil over medium-high heat, turning once.) Serve in buns.

NUTRITIONAL INFORMATION, PER BURGER: about 416 cal, 34 g pro, 18 g total fat (7 g sat. fat), 28 g carb, 1 g fibre, 80 mg chol, 611 mg sodium, 388 mg potassium. % RDI: 8% calcium, 34% iron, 27% folate.

VARIATION

BEST-EVER PUB-STYLE BEEF BURGERS

Shape beef mixture into six 3½- x 1-inch (9 x 2.5 cm) patties. Place on greased grill over medium-high heat; close lid and grill for 7 minutes. Turn patties and reduce heat to medium; close lid and grill until instant-read thermometer inserted sideways into patties reads 160°F (71°C), about 7 minutes. (Use smaller buns for these thicker patties.)

TIP FROM THE TEST KITCHEN
Stirring the beef mixture together in a baking dish rather than a bowl allows you to evenly season the meat without handling it too much. For the most tender burgers, it's best not to overmix.

FALL-APART-TENDER BEEF STEW 🍴

This stew is so delicious because it's made with well-marbled pot roast rather than the usual stewing beef. The fat melts slowly as it cooks, tenderizing the beef into melt-in-your mouth morsels. A slow finish in the oven gives the stew its rich, robust texture.

HANDS-ON TIME
50 minutes

TOTAL TIME
2½ hours

MAKES
6 to 8 servings

INGREDIENTS

¼ cup	all-purpose flour
½ tsp	salt
¼ tsp	pepper
1.5 kg	well-marbled boneless beef blade pot roast, cut in 1-inch (2.5 cm) cubes
3 tbsp	butter
1 tbsp	vegetable oil
2	ribs celery, diced
1	onion, diced
2 tbsp	tomato paste
½ cup	dry red wine
450 g	mini white potatoes, scrubbed and quartered
3	large carrots, cut in 1½-inch (4 cm) thick chunks (halve bigger pieces)
10	sprigs fresh thyme
6	sprigs fresh parsley
2	bay leaves
3 cups	sodium-reduced beef broth
½ tsp	Worcestershire sauce
¾ cup	pickled cocktail onions, drained and rinsed
¾ cup	frozen peas

DIRECTIONS

In large bowl, whisk flour, salt and pepper; toss with beef to coat.

In large Dutch oven, heat 2 tbsp of the butter and the oil over medium heat; working in small batches, cook beef, stirring, until browned, about 20 minutes total. Using slotted spoon, transfer to bowl; set aside.

Add remaining butter to pan; cook celery and onion over medium heat, stirring occasionally, until softened, about 5 minutes. Add tomato paste; cook, stirring, for 2 minutes. Add wine; cook, stirring and scraping up browned bits from bottom of pan, for 2 minutes.

Return beef and any accumulated juices to pan. Add potatoes, carrots, thyme, parsley and bay leaves. Stir in broth and Worcestershire sauce; bring to boil, stirring occasionally and scraping up any remaining browned bits from bottom of pan.

Cover and braise in 350°F (180°C) oven for 45 minutes. Stir in cocktail onions; cover and braise for 15 minutes. Uncover and cook until vegetables are tender and tip of knife pierces beef with no resistance, 30 to 40 minutes. Stir in peas; cook for 5 minutes.

Skim any fat from surface of stew; discard thyme, parsley and bay leaves. Let stand for 10 minutes before serving.

NUTRITIONAL INFORMATION, PER EACH OF 8 SERVINGS: about 498 cal, 40 g pro, 27 g total fat (11 g sat. fat), 21 g carb, 3 g fibre, 122 mg chol, 780 mg sodium, 731 mg potassium. % RDI: 6% calcium, 35% iron, 74% vit A, 18% vit C, 17% folate.

VARIATIONS

FALL-APART-TENDER BEEF AND MUSHROOM STEW

In large Dutch oven, melt 1 tbsp butter over medium heat; cook 1 pkg (227 g) button or cremini mushrooms, trimmed, stirring occasionally, until tender, golden and no liquid remains, about 7 minutes. Using slotted spoon, transfer to bowl; set aside. Continue with recipe as directed, returning mushrooms to Dutch oven along with beef.

SLOW COOKER FALL-APART-TENDER BEEF STEW

Toss beef with salt and pepper only, reserving flour. Brown beef and cook celery mixture as directed. Transfer browned beef cubes, celery mixture, potatoes, carrots, thyme, parsley, bay leaves, broth, Worcestershire sauce and cocktail onions to slow cooker. Cover and cook on low until beef is tender, about 8 hours. Skim any fat from surface; discard thyme, parsley and bay leaves. Whisk reserved flour with ¼ cup water; stir into slow cooker along with peas. Cover; cook on high until thickened, 20 minutes.

OSSO BUCO

Down-to-earth and delicious, this old-school Italian dish is great for entertaining, because it braises away to tenderness while you sit back and enjoy the company of your guests. Serve over creamy polenta or mashed sweet potatoes.

HANDS-ON TIME
35 minutes

TOTAL TIME
2½ hours

MAKES
6 servings

INGREDIENTS

OSSO BUCO:

6	thick (1½-inch/ 4 cm) pieces veal hind shank (about 1.75 kg total)
2 tbsp	all-purpose flour
½ tsp	each salt and pepper
2 tbsp	olive oil (approx)
1 cup	each chopped onion and carrot
⅔ cup	chopped celery
2	cloves garlic, minced
½ tsp	each dried thyme, crumbled dried sage and dried rosemary
¾ cup	dry white wine
1½ cups	drained canned whole tomatoes, coarsely chopped
½ cup	beef broth
2	bay leaves

GREMOLATA:

¼ cup	chopped fresh parsley
1 tbsp	grated lemon zest
1	clove garlic, minced

DIRECTIONS

OSSO BUCO: Cut six 24-inch (60 cm) lengths of kitchen string; wrap each twice around 1 shank and tie firmly. On plate, combine flour and ¼ tsp each of the salt and pepper; press shanks into flour mixture, turning to coat. Reserve any remaining flour mixture.

In large Dutch oven, heat oil over medium-high heat; working in batches if necessary, brown shanks, adding up to 1 tbsp more oil if necessary. Transfer to separate plate.

Drain any fat from pan; add onion, carrot, celery, garlic, thyme, sage and rosemary. Cook over medium heat, stirring often, for 10 minutes. Sprinkle with any reserved flour mixture; cook, stirring, for 1 minute. Add wine, stirring and scraping up browned bits from bottom of pan. Bring to boil; boil until reduced by half, about 2 minutes.

Stir in tomatoes, broth, bay leaves and remaining salt and pepper. Nestle shanks in sauce; bring to boil. Cover and cook in 350°F (180°C) oven, basting every 30 minutes, for 1½ hours. Turn shanks and cook, uncovered and basting twice, until tender, about 30 minutes.

Transfer shanks to serving platter; cut off string and keep warm. Place pan over medium-high heat; boil gently, stirring, until desired thickness, about 5 minutes. Discard bay leaves. Pour sauce over shanks.

GREMOLATA: While sauce is thickening, stir together parsley, lemon zest and garlic; sprinkle over shanks just before serving.

NUTRITIONAL INFORMATION, PER SERVING: about 346 cal, 42 g pro, 16 g total fat (5 g sat. fat), 11 g carb, 2 g fibre, 171 mg chol, 576 mg sodium. % RDI: 9% calcium, 25% iron, 36% vit A, 25% vit C, 21% folate.

DOUBLE-CORIANDER LAMB RACKS

HANDS-ON TIME
15 minutes

TOTAL TIME
45 minutes

MAKES
4 servings

Fresh cilantro also goes by the name of fresh coriander. The combination of the fresh leaves and the dried seeds of this plant gives the lamb a slightly citrusy, herbal taste. Serve the lamb with mashed potatoes and steamed green beans.

INGREDIENTS

¼ cup	chopped fresh cilantro
2 tbsp	vegetable oil
2	cloves garlic, minced
1 tbsp	minced fresh ginger
1½ tsp	ground coriander
½ tsp	each salt and pepper
2	lamb racks (about 800 g total)

DIRECTIONS

Whisk together cilantro, oil, garlic, ginger, coriander, salt and pepper. Rub all over lamb; let stand for 10 minutes. *(Make-ahead: Cover and refrigerate for up to 8 hours.)*

Roast lamb, fat side down, in small roasting pan in 425°F (220°C) oven until instant-read thermometer inserted in centre reads 140°F (60°C) for rare, about 20 minutes, or until desired doneness.

Transfer to cutting board; cover loosely with foil and let stand for 10 minutes before carving.

NUTRITIONAL INFORMATION, PER SERVING: about 256 cal, 22 g pro, 18 g total fat (4 g sat. fat), 2 g carb, trace fibre, 71 mg chol, 354 mg sodium. % RDI: 2% calcium, 12% iron, 1% vit A, 2% vit C, 9% folate.

ROAST LEG OF LAMB
WITH CARAMELIZED ONION GRAVY

Leg of lamb is an impressive meal for a special gathering. The deeply browned onions add richness to the gravy for the ultimate accompaniment to perfectly cooked lamb. We've included a kosher variation (below), which is excellent as a special Passover meal.

HANDS-ON TIME
30 minutes

TOTAL TIME
3½ hours

MAKES
12 servings

INGREDIENTS

ROAST LEG OF LAMB:

2.7 kg	bone-in leg of lamb
2	cloves garlic, thinly sliced lengthwise
2	sprigs fresh rosemary
¼ tsp	each salt and pepper

CARAMELIZED ONION GRAVY:

2 tsp	olive oil
2	cloves garlic, minced
1	onion, thinly sliced
¼ cup	dry red wine
2 cups	sodium-reduced beef broth
¼ tsp	pepper
1 tsp	cornstarch

DIRECTIONS

ROAST LEG OF LAMB: Trim all but thin layer of fat from lamb. With thin sharp knife, poke about twelve 1½-inch (4 cm) deep slits into top. Stuff each slit with 1 slice of the garlic. Remove leaves from rosemary sprigs; stuff 4 or 5 leaves into each slit. Cover and refrigerate for 1 hour. *(Make-ahead: Refrigerate for up to 24 hours.)* Sprinkle with salt and pepper.

Place lamb on greased rack in roasting pan; roast in 350°F (180°C) oven until medium-rare and instant-read thermometer inserted in thickest part of meat reads 145°F (63°C), about 2 hours. Transfer to cutting board; cover loosely with foil and let rest for 15 minutes before carving.

CARAMELIZED ONION GRAVY: While lamb is resting, in saucepan, heat oil over medium heat; cook garlic, stirring, for 1 minute. Add onion; cook, stirring occasionally, until golden, about 8 minutes. Stir in wine; cook, stirring, for 1 minute. Add broth and pepper; bring to boil. Remove from heat.

Drain fat from roasting pan; place pan over medium-high heat. Add onion mixture and bring to boil, scraping up browned bits from bottom of pan. Stir cornstarch with ¼ cup water; whisk into pan. Cook, stirring, until slightly thickened, about 3 minutes. Serve with lamb.

NUTRITIONAL INFORMATION, PER SERVING: about 272 cal, 38 g pro, 11 g total fat (5 g sat. fat), 2 g carb, trace fibre, 128 mg chol, 269 mg sodium, 649 mg potassium. % RDI: 2% calcium, 17% iron, 1% vit A, 2% vit C, 10% folate.

VARIATION
KOSHER ROAST LEG OF LAMB
WITH CARAMELIZED ONION GRAVY

For roast leg of lamb, use kosher bone-in leg of lamb. For gravy, replace sodium-reduced beef broth with 2 tsp kosher-for-Passover beef consommé instant soup mix (such as Lieber's) mixed with 2 cups water, or 2 cups homemade kosher beef stock. Substitute kosher olive oil for olive oil, kosher-for-Passover red wine for dry red wine, and kosher potato starch for cornstarch.

MOROCCAN LAMB TAGINE
WITH APRICOTS AND GOLDEN RAISINS

Tagines are incredibly fragrant and delicious. This one features tender chunks of lamb, exotic spices, sweet dried fruit and a hit of fresh herbs. Serve over couscous.

HANDS-ON TIME
55 minutes

TOTAL TIME
2¼ hours

MAKES
8 servings

INGREDIENTS

1.35 kg	boneless lamb shoulder
2 tsp	ground cumin
1½ tsp	cinnamon
1 tsp	each salt and ground ginger
½ tsp	turmeric and pepper
2 cups	sodium-reduced chicken broth
1 tsp	saffron threads
¼ cup	slivered almonds
3 tbsp	vegetable oil
2	onions, chopped
3	cloves garlic, minced
4	carrots, diagonally sliced
1 cup	sliced dried apricots
½ cup	golden raisins
1 tbsp	liquid honey
1 tbsp	chopped fresh mint

DIRECTIONS

Trim fat from lamb; cut into 1½-inch (4 cm) cubes. Set aside.

In large bowl, combine cumin, cinnamon, salt, ginger, turmeric and pepper; remove 1 tbsp and set aside. Add lamb to bowl; toss to coat. Set aside.

In saucepan, heat broth until hot; add saffron and let stand for 10 minutes.

While broth is heating, in large dry shallow Dutch oven, toast almonds over medium heat until fragrant, about 2 minutes. Remove from pan; set aside.

Add 1 tbsp of the oil to Dutch oven; heat over medium-high heat. Working in batches, brown lamb, adding up to 1 tbsp more oil as necessary, about 6 minutes per batch. Using slotted spoon, transfer to plate.

Add remaining oil to Dutch oven; reduce heat to medium. Cook onions, garlic and reserved spice mixture, stirring occasionally, until garlic is golden, about 5 minutes.

Return lamb and any accumulated juices to Dutch oven. Add broth mixture and bring to boil. Reduce heat to low; cover and simmer, stirring occasionally, until lamb is tender, about 1 hour.

Add carrots, apricots, raisins and honey; cover and simmer, stirring occasionally, until carrots are tender, about 30 minutes.

Uncover and bring to boil; boil over medium heat until sauce is thickened to consistency of gravy, about 5 minutes. *(Make-ahead: Let cool for 30 minutes; transfer to shallow airtight container and refrigerate, uncovered, until cold. Cover and refrigerate for up to 2 days.)*

Sprinkle with almonds and mint just before serving.

NUTRITIONAL INFORMATION, PER SERVING: about 359 cal, 30 g pro, 14 g total fat (3 g sat. fat), 29 g carb, 4 g fibre, 86 mg chol, 554 mg sodium. % RDI: 6% calcium, 32% iron, 103% vit A, 7% vit C, 15% folate.

**PORCHETTA-STYLE
BARBECUE PORK ROAST**
page 204

ULTIMATE PORK | 7

"My three favourite smells:
A brand-new book, crisp autumn leaves
and bacon sizzling away in a pan."

JENNIFER BARTOLI FOOD SPECIALIST

GINGER GARLIC PORK CHOPS

Bone-in chops require some carving, but the superior flavour from the bones makes it more than worth the extra effort. A lemony green salad is a lovely side with the pork.

HANDS-ON TIME
25 minutes

TOTAL TIME
1 hour

MAKES
4 servings

INGREDIENTS

¼ cup	vegetable oil
4	cloves garlic, minced
2 tbsp	grated fresh ginger
2 tbsp	soy sauce
2½ tsp	fish sauce
2 tsp	vinegar
1½ tsp	granulated sugar
¾ tsp	pepper
2	bone-in pork loin chops, about 1 inch (2.5 cm) thick (675 g total)
1	green onion, thinly sliced diagonally

DIRECTIONS

Whisk together oil, garlic, ginger, soy sauce, fish sauce, vinegar, sugar and pepper. Pour all but 2½ tbsp into large dish, reserving remainder in refrigerator. Add pork to dish, turning to coat. Cover and refrigerate for 30 minutes. *(Make-ahead: Refrigerate for up to 24 hours.)*

Place pork on greased grill over medium-high heat; close lid and grill, turning once, until juices run clear when pork is pierced and just a hint of pink remains inside, 12 to 15 minutes.

Transfer to cutting board. Cover loosely with foil; let rest for 5 minutes.

To serve, cut sections off either side of bone; slice thinly across the grain. Spoon reserved marinade over pork; sprinkle with green onion.

NUTRITIONAL INFORMATION, PER SERVING: about 259 cal, 24 g pro, 16 g total fat (3 g sat. fat), 4 g carb, trace fibre, 66 mg chol, 520 mg sodium, 364 mg potassium. % RDI: 3% calcium, 9% iron, 1% vit A, 5% vit C, 4% folate.

BEER-BRINED PORK CHOPS

This brining technique creates juicy, tender, tasty chops. For a more intense flavour, use molasses instead of brown sugar in the brine.

HANDS-ON TIME
15 minutes

TOTAL TIME
12¼ hours

MAKES
4 servings

INGREDIENTS

BEER-BRINED PORK CHOPS:

2 cups	dark lager or bock beer (see tip, below)
2 tbsp	coarse salt
2 tbsp	packed brown sugar
1 cup	ice cubes
1	onion, sliced
4	bone-in pork chops, 1 to 1¼ inches (2.5 to 3 cm) thick (about 1.125 kg total)

SPICE RUB:

1 tbsp	smoked paprika
1 tsp	each pepper, garlic powder and packed brown sugar
½ tsp	each cayenne pepper and dried thyme

DIRECTIONS

BEER-BRINED PORK CHOPS: In large shallow dish, whisk together beer, salt and brown sugar; stir in ice cubes and onion. Submerge pork in brine mixture; cover and refrigerate for 12 hours. *(Make-ahead: Refrigerate for up to 24 hours.)*

SPICE RUB: Stir together paprika, pepper, garlic powder, brown sugar, cayenne pepper and thyme.

Remove pork from brine; pat dry with paper towel. Rub spice mixture all over pork.

Place pork on greased grill over medium-high heat; close lid and grill, turning once, until juices run clear when pork is pierced and just a hint of pink remains inside, about 8 minutes.

NUTRITIONAL INFORMATION, PER SERVING: about 298 cal, 38 g pro, 10 g total fat (3 g sat. fat), 9 g carb, 1 g fibre, 117 mg chol, 446 mg sodium, 604 mg potassium. % RDI: 4% calcium, 14% iron, 9% vit A, 3% vit C, 4% folate.

TIP FROM THE TEST KITCHEN
You can use your favourite beer in place of the dark lager or bock. Choose a brew you enjoy drinking so you can have some with the finished chops.

SLOW COOKER
BLACK BEAN SPARERIBS

Look for bite-size bone-in pork spareribs at Asian grocery stores, or order them at your butcher's counter. They are so tender and scrumptious, especially when paired with this garlic-and-spice-laced sauce.

HANDS-ON TIME
15 minutes

TOTAL TIME
6½ hours

MAKES
6 to 8 servings

INGREDIENTS

1.35 kg	bite-size pork spareribs
1	onion, finely diced
2 tbsp	black bean garlic sauce
4	cloves garlic, minced
1 tbsp	minced fresh ginger
½ tsp	pepper
½ tsp	chili garlic paste
2 tbsp	cornstarch
1	green onion, thinly sliced

DIRECTIONS

In slow cooker, stir together spareribs, 1¼ cups water, onion, black bean garlic sauce, garlic, ginger, pepper and chili garlic paste.

Cover and cook on low until spareribs are tender, about 6 hours. Using slotted spoon, remove spareribs. Skim fat from cooking liquid.

Stir cornstarch with 2 tbsp water; stir into cooking liquid. Cover and cook on high until thickened, about 20 minutes. Return spareribs to slow cooker; stir to coat. Sprinkle with green onion.

NUTRITIONAL INFORMATION, PER EACH OF 8 SERVINGS: about 254 cal, 24 g pro, 15 g total fat (5 g sat. fat), 5 g carb, trace fibre, 78 mg chol, 415 mg sodium, 361 mg potassium. % RDI: 4% calcium, 13% iron, 1% vit A, 2% vit C, 3% folate.

TIP FROM THE TEST KITCHEN

Some of the protein in the ribs congeals in the cooking liquid, which doesn't affect the flavour but can give the sauce a slightly separated appearance. If you're concerned about the look of the sauce, strain the cooking liquid through a fine-mesh sieve lined with a double layer of cheesecloth. Return the cooking liquid to the slow cooker and thicken it as directed.

CANADA'S ULTIMATE BARBECUE SMOKED RIBS ⊕

These saucy spice-rubbed ribs are smoked for an added layer of flavour. Look for wood smoking chips, such as whiskey, apple or hickory, in the barbecue section of your grocery or hardware store, being sure to check that the chips are food safe.

HANDS-ON TIME
45 minutes

TOTAL TIME
4 hours

MAKES
6 to 8 servings

INGREDIENTS

BARBECUE-SMOKED RIBS:

1.8 kg	pork back ribs
4 tsp	chili powder
2 tsp	packed brown sugar
2 tsp	ground cumin
1 tsp	garlic powder
½ tsp	pepper

MOLASSES BARBECUE SAUCE:

1 tsp	vegetable oil
1	small sweet onion, finely diced
2	cloves garlic, minced
1 tsp	smoked paprika
¾ cup	ketchup
2 tbsp	cooking molasses
¼ tsp	pepper

DIRECTIONS

BARBECUE-SMOKED RIBS: Remove membrane from underside of ribs, if attached. Combine chili powder, brown sugar, cumin, garlic powder and pepper; rub all over ribs. Cover and refrigerate for 2 hours. *(Make-ahead: Refrigerate for up to 24 hours.)*

Soak 3 cups wood chips for 1 hour. Place foil drip pan under 1 rack of 2-burner barbecue or under centre rack of 3-burner barbecue. Heat remaining burner(s) to medium.

For gas barbecue, wrap soaked chips in heavy-duty foil to make packet; poke several holes in top. Place over lit burner; close lid. (For charcoal barbecue, place soaked chips directly on coals.)

Place ribs, meaty side down, on greased grill over unlit burner; close lid and grill, turning once, until meat is tender and pulls away from ends of bones, about 1½ hours.

MOLASSES BARBECUE SAUCE: While ribs are smoking, in saucepan, heat oil over medium heat; cook onion, garlic and paprika, stirring, until onion is softened, about 5 minutes. Stir in ketchup, ¼ cup water, molasses and pepper; reduce heat and simmer until slightly thickened, about 3 minutes. *(Make-ahead: Refrigerate in airtight container for up to 3 days.)*

Brush about half of the sauce over both sides of ribs. Close lid and grill over medium-high heat, turning once, until glazed, about 10 minutes. Serve ribs with remaining sauce.

NUTRITIONAL INFORMATION, PER EACH OF 8 SERVINGS: about 399 cal, 27 g pro, 26 g total fat (10 g sat. fat), 15 g carb, 1 g fibre, 103 mg chol, 390 mg sodium, 557 mg potassium. % RDI: 6% calcium, 16% iron, 7% vit A, 10% vit C, 5% folate.

CEMITA-STYLE PORK SANDWICH

This Latin-style street food is traditionally served on a bun called a cemita, which is a sesame-topped egg bread. Here, we use challah, which is more readily available. A marinade of lime juice, chilies and spices gives the meat a hot edge, which is offset by a cool avocado spread.

HANDS-ON TIME
30 minutes

TOTAL TIME
1½ hours

MAKES
4 servings

INGREDIENTS

PORK:

1 tbsp	lime juice
1	canned chipotle pepper in adobo sauce, finely chopped
1 tsp	adobo sauce from canned chipotles
½ tsp	dried oregano
¼ tsp	each ground cumin and ground coriander
¼ tsp	each salt and pepper
1	pork tenderloin (about 450 g), cut in ¼-inch (5 mm) thick slices

AVOCADO SPREAD:

1	avocado
2 tbsp	chopped fresh cilantro
1 tbsp	lime juice

4	round challah buns or sesame hamburger buns
8	leaves Boston lettuce
2	small tomatoes, thinly sliced
½ cup	thinly sliced red onion

DIRECTIONS

PORK: In bowl, combine lime juice, chipotle pepper, adobo sauce, oregano, cumin, coriander, salt and pepper. Add pork, turning to coat. Cover and refrigerate for 1 hour. *(Make-ahead: Refrigerate for up to 24 hours.)*

Weave pork slices onto 4 metal or soaked wooden skewers. Place on greased grill over medium-high heat; close lid and grill, turning occasionally, until juices run clear when pork is pierced and just a hint of pink remains inside, 8 to 10 minutes. Remove from skewers.

AVOCADO SPREAD: While pork is chilling, pit, peel and chop avocado. In bowl, mash avocado with fork; mix in cilantro and lime juice. Set aside.

TO FINISH: Spread avocado spread on cut side of tops of buns; sandwich pork, lettuce, tomatoes and onion in buns.

NUTRITIONAL INFORMATION, PER SERVING: about 453 cal, 34 g pro, 15 g total fat (3 g sat. fat), 46 g carb, 6 g fibre, 101 mg chol, 620 mg sodium, 868 mg potassium. % RDI: 10% calcium, 31% iron, 15% vit A, 25% vit C, 56% folate.

PORK AND CHORIZO BURGERS ⑳

These tender burgers get their punched-up flavour from fresh chorizo sausages. Look for uncooked fresh chorizo in the meat department; the dry-cured chorizo from the deli section isn't the same and can't be substituted for it.

HANDS-ON TIME
15 minutes

TOTAL TIME
30 minutes

MAKES
4 servings

INGREDIENTS

GARLIC MAYONNAISE:

¼ cup	light mayonnaise
1	clove garlic, grated or pressed

PORK AND CHORIZO BURGERS:

1	small Spanish onion, cut in ½-inch (1 cm) thick rounds
1	sweet red pepper, seeded and quartered
340 g	lean ground pork
115 g	fresh chorizo sausages (about 2), casings removed
half	onion, grated
¼ cup	chopped fresh parsley
½ tsp	sweet paprika
¼ tsp	each salt and pepper
½ cup	grated manchego cheese (see tip, right)
4	whole wheat buns, halved

DIRECTIONS

GARLIC MAYONNAISE: Whisk mayonnaise with garlic; set aside.

PORK AND CHORIZO BURGERS: Place Spanish onion and red pepper on greased grill over medium-high heat; close lid and grill, turning once, until tender and grill-marked, about 16 minutes.

While vegetables are grilling, mix together pork, chorizo, grated onion, parsley, paprika, salt and pepper; shape into four ½-inch (1 cm) thick patties. Add to grill; close lid and grill, turning once, until instant-read thermometer inserted sideways into several patties reads 160°F (71°C), 10 to 12 minutes.

Sprinkle manchego on patties; close lid and grill until manchego is melted, about 1 minute.

TO FINISH: Spread garlic mayonnaise on cut sides of buns. Sandwich patties, peppers and onions in buns.

NUTRITIONAL INFORMATION, PER SERVING: about 464 cal, 32 g pro, 23 g total fat (8 g sat. fat), 36 g carb, 5 g fibre, 94 mg chol, 1,248 mg sodium, 555 mg potassium. % RDI: 20% calcium, 23% iron, 16% vit A, 95% vit C, 20% folate.

TIP FROM THE TEST KITCHEN
Can't find manchego cheese? Use Pecorino-Romano instead. Both are dry, crumbly sheep's milk cheeses.

PORK SOUVLAKI

Try this Greek takeout favourite at home! The tzatziki also makes a wonderful, cool dip on its own—pair it with toasted pita wedges and crunchy fresh vegetables.

HANDS-ON TIME
15 minutes

TOTAL TIME
45 minutes

MAKES
4 servings

INGREDIENTS

TZATZIKI:

1 cup	shredded cucumber
½ tsp	salt
¾ cup	Balkan-style plain yogurt
2	cloves garlic, minced
2 tbsp	chopped fresh dill (optional)
1 tbsp	lemon juice

PORK SOUVLAKI:

675 g	pork tenderloin
2 tbsp	lemon juice
1 tbsp	extra-virgin olive oil
1	large clove garlic, minced
½ tsp	dried oregano
½ tsp	salt
¼ tsp	pepper
2	plum tomatoes, halved and sliced
half	red onion, halved and sliced
1 cup	shredded romaine lettuce
4	Greek-style pocketless pitas

DIRECTIONS

TZATZIKI: In small colander, mix cucumber with salt; let stand for 10 minutes. Squeeze out liquid. Mix together cucumber, yogurt, garlic, dill (if using) and lemon juice. Refrigerate until ready to use.

PORK SOUVLAKI: While cucumber is draining, trim and cut pork into 1-inch (2.5 cm) cubes. In large bowl, whisk together lemon juice, oil, garlic, oregano, salt and pepper; add pork and stir to coat. Let stand for 10 minutes. *(Make-ahead: Cover and refrigerate for up to 6 hours.)*

Thread pork onto metal skewers; brush with any remaining marinade. Place on greased grill over medium-high heat; close lid and grill, turning halfway through, until juices run clear when pork is pierced and just a hint of pink remains inside, about 12 minutes. Remove from skewers.

TO FINISH: Serve pork, tomatoes, onion, lettuce and tzatziki on pitas.

NUTRITIONAL INFORMATION, PER SERVING: about 463 cal, 46 g pro, 10 g total fat (4 g sat. fat), 44 g carb, 3 g fibre, 100 mg chol, 863 mg sodium, 910 mg potassium. % RDI: 14% calcium, 28% iron, 12% vit A, 22% vit C, 49% folate.

TIP FROM THE TEST KITCHEN
You can substitute cubed boneless skinless chicken breast or thigh for the pork. Just cook it a little longer, until it's no longer pink inside and the juices run clear when the meat is pierced.

PORK PIE WITH OKA MASH ●

This twist on shepherd's pie features lean ground pork and smoky, spicy dry-cured chorizo in place of ground beef. Oka cheese is made in Quebec; its buttery, mild flavour transforms the mash into a golden, rich topping.

HANDS-ON TIME
20 minutes

TOTAL TIME
1¼ hours

MAKES
8 to 10 servings

INGREDIENTS

PORK PIE FILLING:

1 tbsp	olive oil
2	leeks (white and light green parts only), trimmed and thinly sliced
3	cloves garlic, minced
900 g	lean ground pork
115 g	dry-cured chorizo (see tip, page 124), cubed
2 cups	sodium-reduced beef broth
⅓ cup	all-purpose flour
1	sweet potato, peeled and finely chopped
1 tsp	smoked paprika
¼ tsp	each salt and pepper
pinch	cinnamon
1 cup	frozen peas

OKA MASH:

1.35 kg	russet potatoes, peeled and quartered
2	cloves garlic
1 cup	milk
225 g	Oka cheese, shredded
2 tbsp	butter

DIRECTIONS

PORK PIE FILLING: In large saucepan, heat oil over medium heat; cook leeks and garlic, stirring occasionally, until softened, about 6 minutes. Transfer to bowl.

Add pork and chorizo to pan; increase heat to medium-high. Cook, breaking up pork with spoon, until pork is no longer pink, about 5 minutes. Add ¼ cup of the broth; cook, scraping up browned bits from bottom of pan, until no liquid remains. Stir in flour; cook, stirring, for 2 minutes.

Gradually stir in remaining broth; bring to boil. Stir in leek mixture, sweet potato, paprika, salt, pepper and cinnamon; return to boil. Reduce heat and simmer, stirring often, until slightly thickened, about 15 minutes. Stir in peas; scrape into 13- x 9-inch (3 L) baking dish.

OKA MASH: While pork is browning, in large saucepan of boiling salted water, cook potatoes and garlic until tender, about 20 minutes. Drain and return to pan; mash in milk, Oka and butter. Spread over pork mixture. *(Make-ahead: Let cool. Cover with plastic wrap and overwrap in heavy-duty foil; freeze for up to 2 months. Thaw in refrigerator for 24 hours; remove plastic wrap and re-cover with foil. Bake as directed, adding 10 minutes to baking time. Increase heat to 425°F/ 220°C and bake, uncovered, until topping is golden, about 10 minutes.)*

Bake in 400°F (200°C) oven until filling is bubbly and topping is golden, about 25 minutes.

NUTRITIONAL INFORMATION, PER EACH OF 10 SERVINGS: about 523 cal, 30 g pro, 29 g total fat (13 g sat. fat), 34 g carb, 3 g fibre, 105 mg chol, 549 mg sodium, 841 mg potassium. % RDI: 20% calcium, 17% iron, 47% vit A, 23% vit C, 19% folate.

TIP FROM THE TEST KITCHEN
This is a terrific freeze-ahead dinner. A casserole this large will take several days to thaw in the fridge, so don't worry if it's still a bit firm after 1 day. The partial thawing just allows it to reheat a bit more evenly.

CHOUCROUTE GARNIE 🍴

This French casserole is based on pork shoulder, sausages, sauerkraut and often potatoes as well—and there are many variations on it. The key is to find a butcher who sells a wide selection of cured meats so you can create your unique signature version.

HANDS-ON TIME
45 minutes

TOTAL TIME
3½ hours

MAKES
8 to 10 servings

INGREDIENTS

¼ cup	butter
3	large onions, sliced
375 g	slab smoked bacon
2 cups	dry Riesling
1	large carrot, halved crosswise
1	bay leaf
1 tsp	caraway seeds
8	juniper berries
6	black peppercorns
2	whole cloves
2	cloves garlic
900 g	smoked pork shoulder (or 1.35 kg smoked ham hocks)
3	smoked pork sausages (such as Strasbourg, bratwurst, frankfurter, knackwurst or blutwurst)
6 cups	sauerkraut, rinsed, drained and squeezed dry
3	wieners
3	large white potatoes, peeled and halved

DIRECTIONS

In large Dutch oven, melt butter over medium heat; cook onions, stirring, until golden, about 10 minutes.

Cut bacon into 6 same-size chunks. Add to pan; cook, turning often, until browned and fat is rendered, about 6 minutes.

Add wine, ½ cup water, carrot, bay leaf and caraway seeds.

Place juniper berries, peppercorns and cloves on cheesecloth square; tie with kitchen string to make bundle. Add to pan; stir in garlic. Add pork shoulder and sausages; cover with sauerkraut. Cover and cook until heated through.

Transfer to 325°F (160°C) oven. Cook, turning pork shoulder over halfway through and re-covering with sauerkraut, until pork shoulder is tender, 2½ to 3 hours.

Add wieners; cook until heated through, about 15 minutes. Discard bay leaf and spice bundle. Transfer pork shoulder, sausages and wieners to cutting board; cut into portions.

While wieners are cooking, in saucepan of boiling salted water, cook potatoes until tender, about 15 minutes; drain.

Heap sauerkraut on large platter; surround with vegetables, meat and potatoes.

NUTRITIONAL INFORMATION, PER EACH OF 10 SERVINGS: about 628 cal, 27 g pro, 44 g total fat (20 g sat. fat), 33 g carb, 6 g fibre, 126 mg chol, 1,930 mg sodium. % RDI: 8% calcium, 30% iron, 20% vit A, 43% vit C, 23% folate.

BACON-WRAPPED TENDERLOIN KABOBS ㉚

HANDS-ON TIME
25 minutes

TOTAL TIME
25 minutes

MAKES
6 servings

Pork tenderloin is quite lean, so bacon helps out by basting these kabobs, keeping the meat perfectly juicy. Choose rosemary with thick stems that are easy to poke into the pork.

INGREDIENTS

3	pork tenderloins (each 340 g)
9	strips bacon, halved lengthwise
9	sprigs fresh rosemary, halved crosswise
1 tbsp	Dijon mustard
1½ tsp	balsamic vinegar
1½ tsp	extra-virgin olive oil
¼ tsp	each salt and pepper

DIRECTIONS

Cut each tenderloin into 6 rounds; wrap 1 piece of bacon around side of each round. Poke metal skewer through bacon and pork through to other side; remove skewer. Thread rosemary sprig through hole, extending out opposite side.

Thread 3 pork pieces, perpendicular to rosemary, onto each of 6 metal skewers. *(Make-ahead: Cover and refrigerate for up to 24 hours.)*

Stir together mustard, vinegar, oil, salt and pepper; brush over flat sides of pork. Broil on greased rimmed baking sheet, 8 inches (20 cm) from heat, turning once, until juices run clear when pork is pierced and just a hint of pink remains inside, 10 to 12 minutes. Transfer to platter; pour pan juices over top.

NUTRITIONAL INFORMATION, PER SERVING: about 379 cal, 44 g pro, 21 g total fat (10 g sat. fat), 1 g carb, trace fibre, 123 mg chol, 426 mg sodium. % RDI: 1% calcium, 17% iron, 2% vit C, 4% folate.

TIP FROM THE TEST KITCHEN
To grill the kabobs, place them on a greased grill over medium-high heat; close the lid and grill until the juices run clear when the pork is pierced and just a hint of pink remains inside the meat, 16 to 18 minutes.

ORANGE AND SPICE BARBECUED PORK TENDERLOIN

Pork tenderloin is so quick to cook—no wonder it's one of the most-requested recipe ingredients in the Test Kitchen. Serve this fragrant, well-seasoned meat with couscous and a salad for an easy, complete meal.

HANDS-ON TIME
25 minutes

TOTAL TIME
2¾ hours

MAKES
6 servings

INGREDIENTS

ORANGE AND SPICE MARINADE:

½ cup	orange juice
¼ cup	tomato paste
2 tbsp	grainy mustard
3	cloves garlic, minced
4 tsp	chili powder
1½ tsp	granulated sugar
1 tsp	each ground cumin and coriander
½ tsp	Worcestershire sauce
¼ tsp	salt

BARBECUED PORK TENDERLOIN:

2	pork tenderloins (each 340 g)
1 tbsp	cold water
2 tsp	cornstarch
1	green onion, finely chopped
2 tbsp	finely chopped fresh cilantro

DIRECTIONS

ORANGE AND SPICE MARINADE: In large bowl, whisk together orange juice, tomato paste, mustard, garlic, chili powder, sugar, cumin, coriander, Worcestershire sauce and salt.

BARBECUED PORK TENDERLOIN: Add pork to marinade, turning to coat. Cover and refrigerate for 2 hours. *(Make-ahead: Refrigerate for up to 24 hours.)*

Remove pork from marinade, letting excess drip back into bowl. Pour marinade into small saucepan; set aside. Place pork on greased grill over medium heat; close lid and grill, turning 3 times, until browned and just a hint of pink remains inside, about 20 minutes.

While pork is grilling, add ¾ cup water to reserved marinade; bring to boil. Reduce heat and simmer until reduced to 1 cup, about 7 minutes.

Whisk cold water with cornstarch; whisk into marinade. Simmer until thickened and glossy, about 1 minute. Keep warm.

Transfer pork to cutting board; cover loosely with foil and let rest for 10 minutes before slicing across the grain. Sprinkle with green onion and cilantro. Serve with sauce.

NUTRITIONAL INFORMATION, PER SERVING: about 186 cal, 29 g pro, 4 g total fat (1 g sat. fat), 8 g carb, 1 g fibre, 61 mg chol, 244 mg sodium. % RDI: 3% calcium, 17% iron, 9% vit A, 22% vit C, 7% folate.

VARIATIONS

PEANUT CURRY BARBECUED PORK TENDERLOIN

Omit Orange and Spice Marinade. Make Peanut Curry Marinade: In large bowl, whisk together ⅔ cup coconut milk; 3 tbsp chunky natural peanut butter; 2 tbsp fish sauce; 1 tbsp lime juice; 2 tsp Thai green or red curry paste (or mild Indian curry paste); 2 tsp grated fresh ginger; 2 cloves garlic, minced; ½ tsp packed brown sugar; and pinch turmeric. Proceed with recipe as directed. Replace cilantro with 2 tbsp chopped roasted peanuts.

FIVE-SPICE BARBECUED PORK TENDERLOIN

Omit Orange and Spice Marinade. Make Five-Spice Marinade: In large bowl, whisk ⅓ cup finely chopped onion; ¼ cup sodium-reduced beef broth; 2 tbsp each oyster sauce and sodium-reduced soy sauce; 1 tbsp unseasoned rice vinegar; 1 tbsp sesame oil; 4 cloves garlic, minced; 2 tsp finely grated fresh ginger; and 1 tsp five-spice powder. Proceed with recipe as directed. Replace cilantro with 2 tsp sesame seeds, toasted.

MILK-BRAISED PORK LOIN

Braising in milk may seem unusual, but it's a tradition in Italy. The milk will curdle as it cooks, but don't sweat it: Puréeing the cooking liquid smooths it out, transforming it into a creamy, pale golden sauce.

HANDS-ON TIME
35 minutes

TOTAL TIME
2¾ hours

MAKES
8 servings

INGREDIENTS

1	centre-cut pork loin rib-end roast or pork shoulder butt roast (about 1.35 kg), tied
½ tsp	each salt and pepper
2 tbsp	vegetable oil
1	onion, chopped
3 cups	milk
1 tbsp	lemon juice
2 tbsp	chopped fresh parsley

DIRECTIONS

Trim fat from pork, leaving ⅛-inch (3 mm) thick layer. Sprinkle pork with salt and pepper. In large Dutch oven, heat oil over medium-high heat; brown pork all over. Transfer to plate.

Reduce heat to medium and drain fat from pan; cook onion, stirring often, until golden, about 4 minutes. Add milk, stirring and scraping up any browned bits from bottom of pan.

Return pork and any accumulated juices to pan; bring to simmer. Cover and braise in 300°F (150°C) oven, basting every 30 minutes and turning once with 2 wooden spoons, until pork is very tender, 2 to 2½ hours.

Transfer pork to cutting board; cover loosely with foil and let rest for 10 minutes. Cut strings from pork; slice across the grain.

While pork is resting, skim fat from sauce; bring sauce to boil. Boil until reduced to 2½ cups, about 10 minutes. Transfer to blender or food processor; purée until smooth. Add lemon juice and blend to combine; stir in parsley. Serve sauce with sliced pork.

NUTRITIONAL INFORMATION, PER SERVING: about 309 cal, 24 g pro, 21 g total fat (7 g sat. fat), 6 g carb, trace fibre, 74 mg chol, 237 mg sodium. % RDI: 12% calcium, 9% iron, 5% vit A, 3% vit C, 4% folate.

VARIATIONS

MILK-BRAISED PORK LOIN WITH CIPOLLINI ONIONS

Add 8 small cipollini or 16 pearl onions, peeled, to pan during last hour of braising. Using slotted spoon, transfer to platter with pork before puréeing sauce.

SLOW COOKER MILK-BRAISED PORK LOIN

Follow first 2 paragraphs as directed. Transfer pork and pan juices to slow cooker. Cover and cook on low until pork is very tender, about 8 hours. Proceed with recipe starting at fourth paragraph, transferring sauce to saucepan to reduce.

SAUSAGE-STUFFED PORK TENDERLOIN
WITH CREAMY MUSTARD SAUCE

HANDS-ON TIME	30 minutes
TOTAL TIME	1 hour
MAKES	6 servings

Italian sausage and bread make a flavourful and moist stuffing. After rolling up the pork, your hands will be dirty, so have the kitchen string precut and ready before you start.

INGREDIENTS

SAUSAGE-STUFFED PORK TENDERLOIN:

1 cup	cubed (½ inch/1 cm) day-old white bread
¼ cup	milk
225 g	hot or sweet Italian sausages, casings removed
1	large pork tenderloin (450 g)
1 tbsp	Dijon mustard
pinch	each salt and pepper
2 tsp	olive oil

CREAMY MUSTARD SAUCE:

1 tbsp	olive oil
2	cloves garlic, minced
1	small onion, finely chopped
¼ cup	dry white wine
⅓ cup	apple cider
¼ cup	whipping cream (35%)
1 tbsp	Dijon mustard
pinch	each salt and pepper

DIRECTIONS

SAUSAGE-STUFFED PORK TENDERLOIN: Place bread in large bowl; pour milk over top. Let stand until absorbed, about 5 minutes. Mix in sausage.

Meanwhile, trim any fat from pork. Place on cutting board with narrow end closest to you; holding knife parallel to cutting board and starting at right side, cut in half horizontally almost but not all the way through. **PHOTO A**

Open pork like book. Starting at centre, slice left side in half horizontally almost but not all the way through; open. Turn and repeat on opposite side. **PHOTO B**

Sandwich pork between waxed paper or plastic wrap; using meat mallet or heavy-bottomed saucepan, pound to even ½-inch (1 cm) thickness. Spread top with mustard.

Spread sausage mixture in 2-inch (5 cm) wide strip lengthwise along centre of pork. Starting at 1 long side, roll up; tie at 2-inch (5 cm) intervals with kitchen string. Sprinkle with salt and pepper.

In large skillet, heat oil over medium-high heat; brown pork all over, about 5 minutes. Set skillet aside for sauce.

Transfer pork, seam side down, to rimmed baking sheet. Bake in 375°F (190°C) oven until juices run clear when pork is pierced, just a hint of pink remains inside and instant-read thermometer inserted in centre reads 160°F (71°C), about 25 minutes. Transfer to cutting board; cover loosely with foil and let rest for 5 minutes before slicing.

CREAMY MUSTARD SAUCE: While pork is baking, add oil to skillet; heat over medium heat. Cook garlic and onion, stirring often, until softened and golden, about 4 minutes.

Add wine; cook until reduced by half, about 3 minutes. Stir in cider, cream, mustard, salt and pepper; bring to boil. Reduce heat and simmer until thick enough to coat back of spoon, about 5 minutes. Serve with pork.

NUTRITIONAL INFORMATION, PER SERVING: about 295 cal, 24 g pro, 18 g total fat (6 g sat. fat), 8 g carb, 1 g fibre, 74 mg chol, 392 mg sodium, 413 mg potassium. % RDI: 4% calcium, 11% iron, 4% vit A, 2% vit C, 5% folate.

HERE'S HOW

PORCHETTA-STYLE BARBECUE PORK ROAST

Traditional porchetta is slow-roasted pork seasoned with herbs under a layer of crackling (crispy skin and fat). Prosciutto is a lower-fat alternative to crackling that doesn't sacrifice taste. For best results, refrigerate the raw herbed roast overnight to let the flavours meld.

HANDS-ON TIME
25 minutes

TOTAL TIME
3 hours

MAKES
8 to 10 servings

INGREDIENTS

¼ cup	chopped fresh parsley
1 tbsp	each chopped fresh rosemary and fresh sage
3	cloves garlic, pressed or grated
2 tsp	Dijon mustard
1 tsp	fennel seeds, crushed
1 tsp	grated lemon zest
½ tsp	pepper
pinch	each salt and crushed hot pepper flakes
1 tbsp	olive oil
1	boneless pork loin centre roast (about 1.125 kg)
4	slices prosciutto (55 g)

DIRECTIONS

In bowl, combine parsley, rosemary, sage, garlic, mustard, fennel seeds, lemon zest, pepper, salt and hot pepper flakes; stir in oil. Spread all over pork. Cover and refrigerate for 1 hour. *(Make-ahead: Refrigerate for up to 24 hours.)*

Overlapping slices, arrange prosciutto over top of pork. With kitchen string, tie pork in 5 or 6 places to secure. Transfer to roasting pan.

Place foil drip pan over 1 burner of 2-burner barbecue or centre burner of 3-burner barbecue. Heat remaining burner(s) to medium. Place pork in roasting pan on grill over drip pan; close lid and grill until juices run clear when pork is pierced and instant-read thermometer inserted in centre reads 160°F (71°C), about 1½ hours.

Transfer pork to cutting board; cover loosely with foil and let rest for 10 minutes before cutting into ½-inch (1 cm) thick slices.

NUTRITIONAL INFORMATION, PER EACH OF 10 SERVINGS: about 201 cal, 27 g pro, 9 g total fat (3 g sat. fat), 1 g carb, trace fibre, 66 mg chol, 191 mg sodium, 372 mg potassium. % RDI: 1% calcium, 6% iron, 2% vit A, 5% vit C, 2% folate.

VARIATION

PORCHETTA-STYLE OVEN PORK ROAST

Place pork on rack in roasting pan; pour in ½ cup water. Roast in 350°F (180°C) oven until instant-read thermometer inserted in centre reads 160°F (71°C), 1½ to 1¾ hours.

TIP FROM THE TEST KITCHEN
Porchetta leftovers make a great sandwich filling. Slice and pile on sourdough bread with a smear of Dijon mustard and your favourite sandwich toppers.

SLOW COOKER PULLED PORK

Serve this saucy pulled pork piled high on buns, with bowls of garnishes, such as pickled jalapeño peppers, sour cream, shredded cheese and thinly shredded red cabbage (or better yet, red cabbage slaw), and let each diner build his or her dream sandwich.

HANDS-ON TIME
30 minutes

TOTAL TIME
8½ hours

MAKES
8 servings

INGREDIENTS

1.5 kg	boneless pork shoulder blade roast
½ tsp	each salt and pepper
2 tbsp	vegetable oil
2	onions, diced
4	cloves garlic, minced
2 tbsp	chili powder
2 tsp	ground coriander
2	bay leaves
¼ cup	tomato paste
1	can (398 mL) tomato sauce
2 tbsp	packed brown sugar
2 tbsp	cider vinegar
2 tbsp	Worcestershire sauce
2	green onions, thinly sliced

DIRECTIONS

Sprinkle pork with salt and pepper. In Dutch oven, heat oil over medium-high heat; brown pork all over. Transfer to slow cooker.

Add onions, garlic, chili powder, coriander and bay leaves to Dutch oven; cook, stirring often, until onions are softened, about 5 minutes.

Add tomato paste; cook, stirring, until darkened, about 2 minutes. Add tomato sauce, brown sugar, vinegar and Worcestershire sauce, scraping up any browned bits from bottom of pan. Pour into slow cooker. Cover and cook on low until pork is tender, 8 to 10 hours.

Transfer pork to cutting board; cover loosely with foil and let rest for 10 minutes. Using 2 forks, shred or "pull" pork.

Meanwhile, pour liquid from slow cooker into large saucepan; skim off fat. Bring to boil over high heat; boil vigorously until reduced to 3 cups, 10 to 12 minutes. Discard bay leaves.

Add pork; stir to coat and warm through. Sprinkle with green onions.

NUTRITIONAL INFORMATION, PER SERVING: about 342 cal, 43 g pro, 12 g total fat (3 g sat. fat), 13 g carb, 2 g fibre, 118 mg chol, 735 mg sodium. % RDI: 7% calcium, 27% iron, 14% vit A, 22% vit C, 10% folate.

VARIATION
SLOW-BRAISED PULLED PORK

After browning, set pork aside. Return to pan after scraping up browned bits. Cover and braise in 300°F (150°C) oven, basting every 30 minutes and turning once with 2 wooden spoons, until pork is tender, 3½ to 4 hours. Proceed with recipe, starting at fourth paragraph.

PINEAPPLE-GLAZED HAM

Ham is one of the easiest mains to prepare for a large group—there's no trussing or stuffing, and carving is straightforward. This recipe yields many servings, so freeze any leftovers to toss into pastas, stir-fries and casseroles later on.

HANDS-ON TIME
40 minutes

TOTAL TIME
5 hours

MAKES
24 to 46 servings

INGREDIENTS

3½ cups	pineapple juice
1	piece (3 inches/ 8 cm) fresh ginger, peeled and sliced
6.5 kg	fully cooked smoked bone-in ham (see tip, below)
1½ cups	packed brown sugar

DIRECTIONS

Pour 1½ cups of the pineapple juice and 1 cup water into roasting pan; sprinkle in one-third of the ginger. Place ham, fat side up, on greased rack in roasting pan. Cover tightly with foil; roast on bottom rack in 325°F (160°C) oven until instant-read thermometer inserted in centre reads 130°F (55°C), about 4 hours.

While ham is baking, in saucepan, stir together brown sugar, remaining pineapple juice and remaining ginger; bring to boil over medium-high heat. Cook, stirring, until sugar is dissolved, about 5 minutes. Reduce heat to medium-low; simmer, stirring occasionally, until glaze is reduced by half and thick enough to coat back of spoon, about 35 minutes. Let cool slightly, about 20 minutes.

Uncover ham; peel off and discard outer skin. Trim fat layer to ¼-inch (5 mm) thickness. Using paring knife, diagonally score remaining fat to make diamond pattern on ham. Brush half of the pineapple glaze over ham.

Roast, uncovered, in 375°F (190°C) oven, brushing with remaining glaze several times throughout (reheat glaze to loosen, if necessary), until glaze is caramelized and golden and instant-read thermometer inserted in centre reads 140°F (60°C), about 30 minutes.

Transfer ham to cutting board; cover loosely with foil and let rest for 15 minutes before carving.

NUTRITIONAL INFORMATION, PER EACH OF 46 SERVINGS (100 g): about 248 cal, 19 g pro, 15 g total fat (5 g sat. fat), 8 g carb, trace fibre, 55 mg chol, 1,059 mg sodium, 279 mg potassium. % RDI: 1% calcium, 6% iron, 3% vit C, 2% folate.

TIP FROM THE TEST KITCHEN
It's a good idea to order the ham from your butcher in advance to ensure you get the size you need, especially for a party.

BRAISED PORK, POTATOES AND BEANS IN WHITE WINE SAUCE

This spin on the classic French stew blanquette de veau *is a tad more rustic than the original but still supremely tasty. If you don't want to use wine, substitute 1 cup sodium-reduced chicken broth and 2 tsp lemon juice.*

HANDS-ON TIME
35 minutes

TOTAL TIME
2 hours

MAKES
8 servings

INGREDIENTS

2 tbsp	vegetable oil
1.35 kg	boneless pork shoulder butt roast, trimmed and cut in 1½-inch (4 cm) cubes
1 tbsp	butter or vegetable oil
2	each onions and ribs celery, chopped
¼ cup	all-purpose flour
½ tsp	each salt and white pepper
¼ tsp	nutmeg
1 cup	sodium-reduced chicken broth
1 cup	dry white wine
625 g	baby potatoes, halved (about 5 cups)
2 cups	frozen lima beans or peas
⅓ cup	whipping cream (35%)
1 tbsp	chopped fresh dill

DIRECTIONS

In Dutch oven, heat oil over high heat; working in batches, brown pork, 5 to 6 minutes per batch. Using slotted spoon, transfer to bowl.

Add butter to pan; cook onions and celery over medium heat until softened, about 6 minutes. Return pork and accumulated juices to pan. Add flour, salt, pepper and nutmeg; cook, stirring often, for 2 minutes.

Stir in broth and wine; bring to boil, scraping up browned bits from bottom of pan. Reduce heat, cover and simmer for 45 minutes.

Add potatoes; cover and simmer until potatoes and pork are tender, about 40 minutes.

Stir in lima beans, cream and dill; simmer until lima beans are tender, about 7 minutes.

NUTRITIONAL INFORMATION, PER SERVING: about 399 cal, 36 g pro, 15 g total fat (6 g sat. fat), 28 g carb, 4 g fibre, 112 mg chol, 364 mg sodium. % RDI: 5% calcium, 27% iron, 6% vit A, 20% vit C, 16% folate.

TIP FROM THE TEST KITCHEN
If you can't find baby potatoes at the supermarket, use new or waxy potatoes cut into 2-inch (5 cm) cubes. You can also peel the potatoes, if you prefer them without the skin.

MAPLE, MUSTARD AND RIESLING ROAST PORK

HANDS-ON TIME
10 minutes

TOTAL TIME
3¼ hours

MAKES
8 servings

This pork roast requires just a bit of marinating time and a couple of quick bastes while it's in the oven, so it's a perfect laid-back option for entertaining.

INGREDIENTS

1 cup	dry Riesling
¼ cup	maple syrup
3 tbsp	Dijon mustard
3 tbsp	olive oil
2 tbsp	grainy mustard
2	cloves garlic, minced
¼ tsp	pepper
1.35 kg	boneless pork loin centre roast
225 g	shallots (about 8 large)

DIRECTIONS

In dish large enough to hold pork or in large resealable plastic bag, mix together ¾ cup of the wine, maple syrup, Dijon mustard, oil, grainy mustard, garlic and pepper. Add pork; turn to coat. Cover or seal bag and refrigerate, turning once, for 1 hour. *(Make-ahead: Refrigerate for up to 12 hours.)*

Cut shallots into ½-inch (1 cm) thick pieces; place in roasting pan. Top with pork; drizzle with remaining marinade. Roast in 325°F (160°C) oven, basting 2 or 3 times with pan juices, until juices run clear when pork is pierced and just a hint of pink remains inside, and instant-read thermometer inserted in centre reads 160°F (71°C), about 2 hours.

Reserving pan juices, transfer pork and shallots to serving platter; cover loosely with foil and let rest for 10 minutes before slicing pork thinly.

Place pan over medium heat; bring juices to boil. Add remaining wine; cook, stirring and scraping up any browned bits from bottom of pan, for 2 minutes. Stir carving juices into pan juices; spoon some over pork slices. Serve remainder on the side.

NUTRITIONAL INFORMATION, PER SERVING: about 351 cal, 36 g pro, 16 g total fat (5 g sat. fat), 12 g carb, 1 g fibre, 83 mg chol, 196 mg sodium, 678 mg potassium. % RDI: 4% calcium, 12% iron, 3% vit A, 3% vit C, 6% folate.

**PAN-FRIED HALIBUT
WITH LEMON-DILL PESTO**
page 222

ULTIMATE FISH & SEAFOOD | 8

"In my family, special occasions always mean a big seafood feast. Joyous gatherings and lobster will forever be linked in my mind."

AMANDA BARNIER FOOD SPECIALIST

BEER-BATTERED PICKEREL

While this recipe calls for pickerel, any firm-fleshed white fish, such as halibut, whitefish or cod, is just as delicious. Use a deep bowl for the batter to make dipping and coating the fillets easy. For the ultimate fish and chips, serve with our Best-Ever French Fries (page 88).

HANDS-ON TIME
30 minutes

TOTAL TIME
40 minutes

MAKES
8 servings

INGREDIENTS

3⅓ cups	all-purpose flour
1¾ tsp	salt
½ tsp	cayenne pepper
2	bottles (each 341 mL) beer (see tip, below)
	vegetable oil for deep-frying
900 g	pickerel fillets, skinned
8	lemon wedges

DIRECTIONS

In large bowl, whisk together 3 cups of the flour, salt and cayenne pepper; whisk in beer until smooth. Let stand for 15 minutes.

Pour enough oil into deep fryer or deep large deep saucepan to come no more than halfway up side; heat until deep-fryer thermometer reads 375°F (190°C).

Meanwhile, cut fish into serving-size pieces. Dredge in remaining flour, shaking off excess; dip into batter to coat. Deep-fry fish, turning once, until golden brown, 6 to 8 minutes. Using slotted spoon, transfer to paper towel–lined rimmed baking sheet to drain. Serve with lemon wedges to squeeze over top.

NUTRITIONAL INFORMATION, PER SERVING: about 389 cal, 25 g pro, 20 g total fat (2 g sat. fat), 23 g carb, 1 g fibre, 98 mg chol, 340 mg sodium, 491 mg potassium. % RDI: 12% calcium, 20% iron, 3% vit A, 5% vit C, 29% folate.

TIP FROM THE TEST KITCHEN
A light golden pilsner or pale ale would be terrific in this fish batter. It's also delicious to drink with the finished fish.

GRILLED WHOLE TROUT ㉚
WITH PINK PEPPERCORN AND TARRAGON BUTTER

Herbed butters are great on grilled fish, and the tarragon in this one goes especially well with trout and salmon. Try it with lake trout, arctic char, salmon, whitefish and pickerel too.

HANDS-ON TIME
20 minutes

TOTAL TIME
25 minutes

MAKES
4 servings

INGREDIENTS

2 tsp	pink or mixed peppercorns
¼ cup	butter, softened
2 tbsp	chopped fresh tarragon (or 1 tsp dried)
1 tbsp	lemon juice
½ tsp	salt
2	whole trout (each about 625 g)
¼ tsp	pepper

DIRECTIONS

On cutting board and using side of knife, lightly crush peppercorns; transfer to small bowl. Mash in butter, tarragon, lemon juice and ¼ tsp of the salt until smooth; set aside. *(Make-ahead: Cover and refrigerate for up to 2 weeks. Let soften at room temperature before using.)*

Sprinkle fish inside and out with pepper and remaining salt. Place in greased fish basket or on greased grill over medium-high heat; close lid and grill for 7 minutes. Turn basket (or loosen fish with spatula and, using 1 spatula over fish and 1 underneath, turn over). Grill until fish flakes easily when tested, about 8 minutes. Transfer to platter; dot fish with butter.

NUTRITIONAL INFORMATION, PER SERVING: about 336 cal, 40 g pro, 18 g total fat (8 g sat. fat), 1 g carb, trace fibre, 142 mg chol, 456 mg sodium. % RDI: 13% calcium, 29% iron, 14% vit A, 12% vit C, 8% folate.

TIP FROM THE TEST KITCHEN
Unless otherwise specified, when we call for butter, we mean salted butter. If you have only unsalted on hand, be sure to add a good pinch of salt to the mixture before mashing.

GRILLED MISO-MARINATED SABLEFISH ON BABY GREENS

Sablefish, also known as black cod, comes from the cold waters of the northwest Pacific. Because it may be difficult to buy outside the West Coast, you can easily substitute Atlantic halibut in this recipe.

HANDS-ON TIME
20 minutes

TOTAL TIME
6½ hours

MAKES
4 servings

INGREDIENTS

MISO-MARINATED SABLEFISH:

¼ cup	white miso
¼ cup	apple cider
2 tbsp	sodium-reduced soy sauce
2	cloves garlic, minced
1 tsp	minced fresh ginger
4	skin-on sablefish fillets (each about 175 g)
2 tbsp	vegetable oil

BABY GREENS:

3 tbsp	walnut oil
4 tsp	apple cider
4 tsp	Champagne vinegar or red wine vinegar
2 tsp	minced shallots
2 tsp	chopped fresh lemon thyme or fresh thyme
2 tsp	maple syrup
pinch	salt
8 cups	mixed baby greens

DIRECTIONS

MISO-MARINATED SABLEFISH: In shallow dish, whisk together miso, cider, soy sauce, garlic and ginger. Add fish, skin side up; cover and refrigerate for 6 hours.

Remove fish from marinade, discarding marinade; brush fish with oil. Place on greased grill over medium heat; close lid and grill, turning once, until fish flakes easily when tested, about 10 minutes.

BABY GREENS: While fish is grilling, in large bowl, whisk together oil, cider, vinegar, shallots, thyme, maple syrup and salt. *(Make-ahead: Refrigerate for up to 6 hours.)*

Toss greens with vinaigrette; divide among 4 plates. Top with fish.

NUTRITIONAL INFORMATION, PER SERVING: about 518 cal, 24 g pro, 42 g total fat (7 g sat. fat), 12 g carb, 3 g fibre, 76 mg chol, 737 mg sodium. % RDI: 13% calcium, 25% iron, 36% vit A, 27% vit C, 54% folate.

TIP FROM THE TEST KITCHEN
Walnut oil is full of volatile oils that go rancid quickly at room temperature. To extend the shelf life of this spendy ingredient, store it in the fridge.

GRILLED SALMON FILLETS ☻

A simple combination of oil, lemon and dill makes this salmon so appealing.
Choose thick skin-on fillets, as they'll hold together well on the grill.

HANDS-ON TIME
15 minutes

TOTAL TIME
45 minutes

MAKES
4 servings

INGREDIENTS

⅓ cup	olive oil
1 tsp	grated lemon zest
¼ cup	lemon juice
2 tbsp	chopped fresh dill
¼ tsp	each salt and pepper
4	skin-on salmon fillets (each about 125 g)

DIRECTIONS

Whisk together oil, lemon zest, lemon juice, dill, salt and pepper; pour into shallow dish. Add fish, turning to coat. Cover and refrigerate, turning occasionally, for up to 30 minutes.

Remove fish from marinade, reserving excess. Place fish, skin side down, on greased grill over medium-high heat; close lid and grill, turning once and basting frequently with reserved marinade, just until opaque throughout and fish flakes easily when tested, about 10 minutes per every 1 inch (2.5 cm) of thickness.

NUTRITIONAL INFORMATION, PER SERVING: about 341 cal, 19 g pro, 29 g total fat (5 g sat. fat), 2 g carb, trace fibre, 54 mg chol, 197 mg sodium, 355 mg potassium. % RDI: 1% calcium, 4% iron, 2% vit A, 18% vit C, 15% folate.

TIP FROM THE TEST KITCHEN
Fish has delicate flesh, which doesn't lend itself well to long marinating times. Stick to 30 minutes or less.

PAN-FRIED FISH ③⓪
WITH TARTAR SAUCE

Pickerel and perch are lean, fine-textured fish ideal for frying. If you're into fishing, these varieties are common in cold-water lakes and are especially delicious when freshly caught.

HANDS-ON TIME
25 minutes

TOTAL TIME
25 minutes

MAKES
4 servings

INGREDIENTS

TARTAR SAUCE:

½ cup	light mayonnaise
¼ cup	minced bread-and-butter pickles
3 tbsp	Balkan-style plain yogurt
1 tbsp	chopped fresh parsley
1 tbsp	capers, drained, rinsed and chopped
2 tsp	Dijon mustard
1 tsp	white wine vinegar
dash	hot pepper sauce

PAN-FRIED FISH:

⅓ cup	milk
½ cup	all-purpose flour
2 tbsp	chopped fresh parsley
½ tsp	each salt and pepper
675 g	fish fillets (such as pickerel or perch)
2 tbsp	each butter and extra-virgin olive oil (approx)
4	lemon wedges

DIRECTIONS

TARTAR SAUCE: Stir together mayonnaise, pickles, yogurt, parsley, capers, mustard, vinegar and hot pepper sauce. Cover and set aside in refrigerator. *(Make-ahead: Refrigerate in airtight container for up to 1 week.)*

PAN-FRIED FISH: Pour milk into shallow dish. In separate shallow dish, whisk together flour, parsley, salt and pepper. One piece at a time, dip fish into milk, letting excess drip back into dish. Dredge in flour mixture, gently shaking off any excess.

In skillet, heat half each of the butter and oil over medium-high heat; working in batches, fry fish, turning once and adding more oil and butter as needed, until fish flakes easily when tested, 6 to 8 minutes per batch.

TO FINISH: Serve fish with tartar sauce and lemon wedges.

NUTRITIONAL INFORMATION, PER SERVING: about 403 cal, 36 g pro, 20 g total fat (5 g sat. fat), 19 g carb, 1 g fibre, 168 mg chol, 780 mg sodium. % RDI: 22% calcium, 24% iron, 11% vit A, 12% vit C, 22% folate.

POACHED SALMON ③⓪
WITH SALSA VERDE

Poaching gives salmon a delicate, very moist texture. The tangy salsa dresses the fish up with the bright flavours of garlic, capers and vinegar. Serve with a crisp salad and some crusty bread to soak up the salsa.

HANDS-ON TIME
15 minutes

TOTAL TIME
20 minutes

MAKES
4 servings

INGREDIENTS

POACHED SALMON:

1	onion, thinly sliced
1	rib celery, thinly sliced
3	thin slices lemon
4	sprigs fresh parsley
½ tsp	each salt and black peppercorns
4	skin-on salmon fillets (each 175 g)

SALSA VERDE:

⅓ cup	fresh bread crumbs
3 tbsp	red wine vinegar
1	hard-cooked egg, coarsely chopped
1	bunch fresh parsley, stemmed
2 tbsp	capers, drained
2	anchovy fillets
1	clove garlic
¼ cup	extra-virgin olive oil
4	lemon wedges

DIRECTIONS

POACHED SALMON: In wide shallow pan large enough to hold fish in single layer, bring 3 cups water, onion, celery, lemon, parsley, salt and peppercorns to boil. Cover, reduce heat and simmer for 5 minutes.

Add fish; cover and poach just below simmer just until fish flakes easily when tested, 5 to 7 minutes. Using slotted spatula, transfer fish to plates; remove skin.

SALSA VERDE: While onion mixture is coming to boil, soak bread crumbs in vinegar for 5 minutes; transfer to food processor. Add egg, parsley, capers, anchovies and garlic; pulse until finely chopped. With motor running, drizzle in oil and 3 tbsp of the fish poaching liquid.

TO FINISH: Serve fish with salsa verde and lemon wedges.

NUTRITIONAL INFORMATION, PER SERVING: about 476 cal, 37 g pro, 34 g total fat (6 g sat. fat), 4 g carb, 1 g fibre, 149 mg chol, 562 mg sodium, 702 mg potassium. % RDI: 7% calcium, 19% iron, 25% vit A, 65% vit C, 38% folate.

TIP FROM THE TEST KITCHEN
The skin really helps hold the salmon together as it poaches. If you can only get your hands on skinless salmon fillets, try buying a larger side of salmon with the skin on and cut it into single portions yourself.

MINI FISH AND VEGETABLE PIES ③⓪ ◉

Ramekins filled with bubbling creamy sauce, flaky mild fish and fluffy mashed potatoes are perfect little one-dish meals. For a change of pace, you can substitute sweet potatoes for the russets, following the same cooking instructions.

HANDS-ON TIME
20 minutes

TOTAL TIME
30 minutes

MAKES
4 servings

INGREDIENTS

FILLING:

2 tsp	unsalted butter
2 cups	sliced leeks (white and light green parts only)
½ cup	diced carrot
½ cup	diced celery
3	cloves garlic, minced
2 tbsp	all-purpose flour
¾ cup	sodium-reduced vegetable broth
¼ cup	milk
300 g	cod or other firm white fish fillet, cut in 1-inch (2.5 cm) chunks
½ cup	frozen peas
2 tbsp	chopped fresh dill
4 tsp	lemon juice
2 tsp	Dijon mustard
¼ tsp	each salt and pepper

MASHED POTATO TOPPING:

2	russet potatoes (about 500 g total)
¼ cup	milk
2 tsp	prepared horseradish
pinch	each salt and pepper

DIRECTIONS

FILLING: In Dutch oven, melt butter over medium heat; cook leeks, carrot, celery and garlic, stirring occasionally, until beginning to soften, about 5 minutes.

Add flour; cook, stirring, for 1 minute. Whisk in broth and ¼ cup water; cook, whisking, until slightly thickened, about 2 minutes. Whisk in milk. Remove from heat; stir in fish, peas, dill, lemon juice, mustard, salt and pepper.

MASHED POTATO TOPPING: Meanwhile, prick potatoes all over with fork. Microwave on high until fork-tender, about 7 minutes. Set aside until cool enough to handle. Peel potatoes; mash with milk, horseradish, salt and pepper.

Divide filling among four 8-oz (250 mL) ramekins. Spoon potato mixture over filling, smoothing tops. Bake on rimmed baking sheet in 425°F (220°C) oven until filling is bubbly, about 10 minutes.

NUTRITIONAL INFORMATION, PER SERVING: about 257 cal, 19 g pro, 4 g total fat (2 g sat. fat), 38 g carb, 4 g fibre, 40 mg chol, 392 mg sodium, 1,000 mg potassium. % RDI: 11% calcium, 21% iron, 42% vit A, 47% vit C, 30% folate.

PAN-FRIED HALIBUT ㉚
WITH LEMON-DILL PESTO

HANDS-ON TIME
15 minutes

TOTAL TIME
15 minutes

MAKES
4 servings

*A quick herby sauce transforms ordinary pan-fried fish into a bright, lively dish.
Serve with steamed asparagus and lightly buttered brown rice for a simple, fresh meal.*

INGREDIENTS

LEMON-DILL PESTO:

1 cup	packed fresh parsley leaves
⅓ cup	packed fresh dill
⅓ cup	slivered almonds, toasted (see tip, below)
¼ tsp	each salt and pepper
3 tbsp	olive oil
½ tsp	grated lemon zest
1 tbsp	lemon juice

PAN-FRIED HALIBUT:

1	halibut fillet (about 450 g), skinned and cut in 4 pieces
pinch	each salt and pepper
2 tsp	olive oil

DIRECTIONS

LEMON-DILL PESTO: Using mini blender or immersion blender, pulse parsley, dill, almonds, salt and pepper 5 times. Add oil, 1 tbsp water, lemon zest and lemon juice; purée until smooth thick paste. Set aside.

PAN-FRIED HALIBUT: Sprinkle fish with salt and pepper. In skillet, heat oil over medium-high heat; cook fish, turning once, until golden and fish flakes easily when tested, 6 to 8 minutes. Serve with pesto.

NUTRITIONAL INFORMATION, PER SERVING: about 293 cal, 26 g pro, 20 g total fat (2 g sat. fat), 3 g carb, 2 g fibre, 36 mg chol, 216 mg sodium, 668 mg potassium. % RDI: 9% calcium, 17% iron, 18% vit A, 38% vit C, 18% folate.

TIP FROM THE TEST KITCHEN

Toast the almonds in a dry skillet over medium heat until golden and fragrant, about 5 minutes. Watch them carefully and take them out of the pan as soon as they are golden—they can go from brown to burned very quickly.

CORNMEAL-FRIED TROUT ③⓪

Farm-raised rainbow trout is an environmentally responsible choice. Serve this crusty, crisp fish with either a green salad topped with extra crumbled bacon or our Classic Tangy Coleslaw (page 69).

HANDS-ON TIME
15 minutes

TOTAL TIME
20 minutes

MAKES
4 servings

INGREDIENTS

4	strips thick-cut bacon
½ tsp	each salt and black pepper
¼ tsp	cayenne pepper
4	rainbow trout fillets (each about 170 g)
⅔ cup	buttermilk
⅓ cup	cornmeal
⅓ cup	all-purpose flour
2 tbsp	chopped fresh parsley

DIRECTIONS

In skillet, fry bacon over medium heat until crisp, turning occasionally, about 5 minutes. Transfer bacon to paper towel–lined plate; pour fat into heatproof container. Set aside.

Stir together half each of the salt, black pepper and cayenne pepper; sprinkle over fish.

Pour buttermilk into shallow dish. In separate dish, whisk together cornmeal, flour, parsley and remaining salt, black pepper and cayenne pepper. One piece at a time, dip fish into buttermilk, letting excess drip back into dish; dredge in flour mixture, turning and patting to coat.

In clean skillet, heat 2 tbsp of reserved fat over medium heat; working in batches, cook fish, turning once and adding more fat as needed, until fish flakes easily when tested, 6 to 8 minutes per batch. Serve with bacon.

NUTRITIONAL INFORMATION, PER SERVING: about 445 cal, 40 g pro, 24 g total fat (8 g sat. fat), 14 g carb, 1 g fibre, 117 mg chol, 564 mg sodium, 745 mg potassium. % RDI: 14% calcium, 9% iron, 15% vit A, 12% vit C, 29% folate.

TIP FROM THE TEST KITCHEN
Have a little extra oil on standby, in case the bacon doesn't yield quite as much fat as you need for frying.

HOT-SMOKED SALMON ✪

If your grill has a smoker pan or insert, follow the manufacturer's instructions rather than using the foil packet described below. To give the fish a stronger, more pleasing smoke flavour, we used hickory wood chips.

HANDS-ON TIME
30 minutes

TOTAL TIME
8½ hours

MAKES
8 to 12 servings

INGREDIENTS

4 cups	boiling water
½ cup	sea salt, kosher salt or pickling salt
½ cup	packed brown sugar
¼ cup	granulated sugar
1	onion, sliced
1	piece (2 inches/5 cm long) fresh ginger, grated (or 1 tbsp ground ginger)
4 cups	cold water
8	sprigs fresh dill
1	skin-on side of salmon (about 1.35 kg)
¼ cup	finely chopped fresh dill
1 tbsp	black peppercorns, coarsely ground
1 tsp	ground coriander lemon wedges

DIRECTIONS

In large heatproof glass measuring cup or bowl, combine boiling water, salt, brown sugar, granulated sugar, onion and ginger; stir until salt is dissolved. Add cold water; let cool. Add dill sprigs.

Trim 1 inch (2.5 cm) off thinner long edge of fish; remove any remaining pin bones along centre. Place fish, flesh side down, in large shallow glass or ceramic dish, folding over thin tail end if necessary to fit. Pour in brine mixture to cover; weigh down fish with plate(s) to keep submerged. Cover and refrigerate for 4 hours.

Remove fish from brine; rinse, pat dry and place, skin side down, on rack. Sprinkle with dill, pepper and coriander. Refrigerate until flesh is tacky to the touch, 1 to 2 hours. *(Make-ahead: Wrap and refrigerate for up to 24 hours.)*

Meanwhile, soak 2 cups wood chips in water for 1 hour; drain. Set foil drip pan under 1 rack of 2-burner barbecue or under centre rack of 3-burner barbecue. Heat remaining burner(s) to medium-low. Seal soaked chips in foil to make packet; poke several holes in top. Place over unlit burner. (For charcoal grill, set drip pan under 1 side of grill and arrange hot coals on other side. Place packet directly on coals.) Close lid and let smoke fill barbecue.

Place fish, skin side down, on greased grill over drip pan; cover and smoke until fish flakes easily when tested, about 1¾ hours. (If skin sticks to grill, slide fish off skin onto platter.) Serve with lemon wedges.

NUTRITIONAL INFORMATION, PER EACH OF 12 SERVINGS: about 160 cal, 16 g pro, 9 g total fat (2 g sat. fat), 3 g carb, trace fibre, 46 mg chol, 520 mg sodium, 292 mg potassium. % RDI: 1% calcium, 4% iron, 1% vit A, 5% vit C, 11% folate.

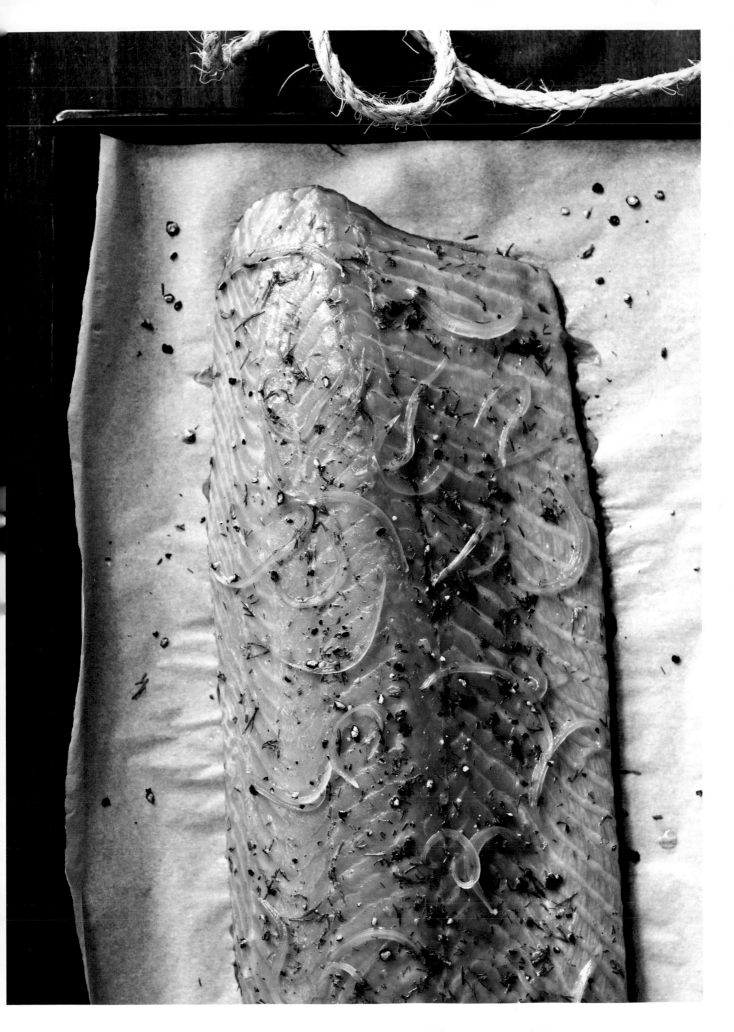

CLASSIC BOUILLABAISSE

This French seafood stew shows off the catch of the day in a delicate homemade stock. Herbed rouille (a thick bread-based garlic sauce) spooned onto the soup or spread over toasted baguette slices adds a rich finishing touch.

HANDS-ON TIME
45 minutes

TOTAL TIME
1¾ hours

MAKES
6 servings

INGREDIENTS

SEAFOOD STOCK:

450 g	raw jumbo shrimp (21 to 25 count)
1 tsp	olive oil
1	leek (white and light green parts), sliced
2	jars (each 240 mL) clam juice
2	bay leaves

HERBED ROUILLE:

3 tbsp	dry white wine
1 cup	chopped baguette
3 tbsp	chopped fresh tarragon
3 tbsp	olive oil
half	red finger hot pepper, seeded
1 tbsp	light mayonnaise
1	clove garlic

BOUILLABAISSE:

half	bulb fennel
1 tbsp	olive oil
2	cloves garlic, minced
1	leek (white and light green parts), sliced
1 tbsp	grated orange zest
1 tbsp	tomato paste
1 cup	dry white wine
½ cup	bottled strained tomatoes (passata)
½ tsp	saffron threads
¼ tsp	each salt and pepper
800 g	littleneck clams (about 12)
250 g	large sea scallops (about 6)
450 g	boneless skinless white fish fillets (such as cod or halibut)
¼ cup	chopped fresh parsley

DIRECTIONS

SEAFOOD STOCK: Reserving shells and leaving tails on, peel and devein shrimp; cover and refrigerate shrimp. In food processor, chop shrimp shells. In large heavy saucepan, heat oil over medium-high heat; sauté shells with leek until shells are pink, about 2 minutes.

Add 6 cups water, clam juice and bay leaves; bring to boil. Reduce heat, cover and simmer for 25 minutes, skimming off any foam. Strain through cheesecloth-lined fine-mesh sieve into large bowl, pressing solids to extract liquid; discard solids. Reserve ¼ cup for rouille; set remainder aside. *(Make-ahead: Let cool for 30 minutes; refrigerate in airtight container for up to 24 hours.)*

HERBED ROUILLE: Drizzle wine over baguette; let stand for 5 minutes. In food processor, purée together reserved seafood stock, baguette mixture, tarragon, oil, hot pepper, mayonnaise and garlic until smooth. Refrigerate until ready to use.

BOUILLABAISSE: While stock is simmering, core and thinly slice fennel. In large heavy saucepan, heat oil over medium heat; cook garlic, stirring, until fragrant, about 1 minute. Add fennel and leek; cook, stirring, until fennel is slightly softened, about 5 minutes.

Stir in orange zest and tomato paste; cook, stirring, over medium-high heat until tomato paste is fragrant, about 1 minute. Stir in wine; cook for 1 minute. Add remaining seafood stock, strained tomatoes, saffron, salt and pepper; bring to boil. Reduce heat, cover and simmer until fennel is just softened, about 30 minutes.

While tomato mixture is simmering, scrub clams; discard any that do not close. Add to tomato mixture; cover and cook over medium-high heat for 3 minutes. Add scallops; cook until tender but firm and clams have opened, about 3 minutes. Discard any clams that do not open. Using slotted spoon, divide scallops and clams among 6 serving bowls.

Cut fish into 1½-inch (4 cm) chunks. Add along with reserved shrimp to tomato mixture; cook until shrimp are pink and fish flakes easily when tested, about 2 minutes. Using slotted spoon, add fish and shrimp to serving bowls; pour tomato mixture over top. Dollop rouille over top; sprinkle with parsley.

NUTRITIONAL INFORMATION, PER SERVING: about 338 cal, 38 g pro, 14 g total fat (2 g sat. fat), 12 g carb, 2 g fibre, 139 mg chol, 583 mg sodium, 1,008 mg potassium. % RDI: 12% calcium, 46% iron, 13% vit A, 32% vit C, 19% folate.

PAN-SEARED SCALLOPS ㉚
WITH TARRAGON WHITE WINE SAUCE

This fancy restaurant-style dish is surprisingly easy—and fast—to make at home. The sauce is also delicious over pan-fried white fish.

HANDS-ON TIME
25 minutes

TOTAL TIME
25 minutes

MAKES
4 servings

INGREDIENTS

PAN-SEARED SCALLOPS:

12	sea scallops (about 250 g total)
2 tbsp	cornstarch
1 tbsp	vegetable oil

TARRAGON WHITE WINE SAUCE:

1 tbsp	butter
1	shallot, minced
¼ tsp	salt
¼ tsp	white or black pepper
⅓ cup	dry white wine
¼ cup	whipping cream (35%)
1 tbsp	each chopped fresh tarragon and fresh chives

DIRECTIONS

PAN-SEARED SCALLOPS: Remove and discard small pink muscle on side of each scallop if present. Pat scallops dry; dredge in cornstarch.

In large nonstick skillet, heat oil over medium-high heat; sear scallops, turning once, until opaque throughout and browned on both sides, about 4 minutes. Transfer to plate. Wash out skillet.

TARRAGON WHITE WINE SAUCE: In same skillet, melt butter over medium heat; cook shallot, salt and pepper until softened, about 3 minutes.

Add wine; cook, stirring, until reduced by half, about 2 minutes. Add cream; cook, stirring, until reduced by half, about 3 minutes. Stir in tarragon and chives.

Return scallops to pan; cook until heated through, about 1 minute.

NUTRITIONAL INFORMATION, PER SERVING: about 182 cal, 10 g pro, 12 g total fat (5 g sat. fat), 6 g carb, trace fibre, 45 mg chol, 434 mg sodium. % RDI: 4% calcium, 5% iron, 9% vit A, 2% vit C, 3% folate.

OYSTERS ON THE HALF SHELL ㉚

Freshly shucked oysters are a classic—and classy—starter to a seafood feast. They should smell briny and fresh; toss out any that don't pass the sniff test. To level the oysters and make sure the juices don't spill out, serve them on a bed of coarse salt.

HANDS-ON TIME
15 minutes

TOTAL TIME
15 minutes

MAKES
8 servings

INGREDIENTS

16	raw oysters
	hot pepper sauce
	lemon wedges
	grated fresh horseradish (see tip, below)

DIRECTIONS

Using stiff brush, scrub oysters under cold running water. Using thick cloth or glove, hold oyster, curved part of shell down; insert oyster knife into small opening near hinge. Twist knife to break hinge; wipe blade clean. Reinsert knife and slide along underside of top shell to sever muscle; discard top shell, removing any grit or broken shell on oyster.

Keeping oyster level to retain juices, slide knife under oyster to sever bottom muscle. Repeat with remaining oysters, wiping knife clean between each.

Serve with hot pepper sauce, lemon wedges and horseradish.

NUTRITIONAL INFORMATION, PER SERVING: about 19 cal, 2 g pro, 1 g total fat (trace sat. fat), 1 g carb, 0 g fibre, 15 mg chol, 59 mg sodium, 44 mg potassium. % RDI: 1% calcium, 14% iron, 1% vit A, 2% vit C, 1% folate.

TIP FROM THE TEST KITCHEN
Grated fresh horseradish is a must for this recipe. If you can't find the fresh root in the produce aisle, skip it and just go with the lemon and hot pepper sauce. Bottled prepared horseradish doesn't have the right pungent tang for these ultra-fresh shellfish.

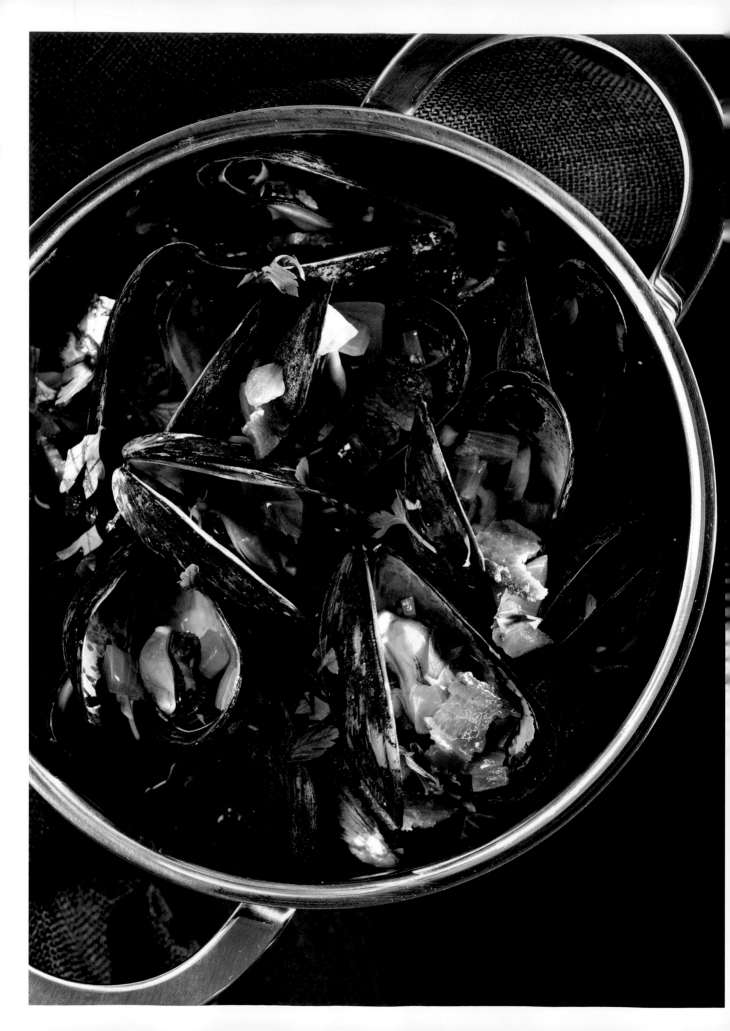

WINE AND BACON–STEAMED MUSSELS ⓧ

*Mussels are readily available year-round in most grocery stores. Prince Edward Island
has an excellent reputation for harvesting these delicious mollusks—you'll see P.E.I. mussels
sold all across North America.*

HANDS-ON TIME
20 minutes

TOTAL TIME
25 minutes

MAKES
8 servings

INGREDIENTS

2 kg	mussels
8	strips bacon, diced
1	large onion, diced
4	cloves garlic, minced
2½ cups	dry white wine
2	bay leaves
2 tbsp	tomato paste
¼ tsp	pepper
2 tbsp	chopped fresh parsley

DIRECTIONS

Scrub mussels; remove any beards (see tip, below). Discard any mussels that do not close when tapped. Set aside. *(Make-ahead: Refrigerate for up to 4 hours.)*

In Dutch oven over medium heat, cook bacon, stirring occasionally, until crisp, about 5 minutes. Using slotted spoon, transfer to paper towel–lined plate; let drain.

Drain all but 1 tbsp fat from pan; cook onion, stirring occasionally, until softened, about 5 minutes. Add garlic; cook until fragrant, about 1 minute.

Add wine and bay leaves; simmer until reduced by half, about 5 minutes. Stir in tomato paste and pepper; return to boil.

Add mussels; cover with tight-fitting lid and steam until mussels open, about 5 minutes. Remove from heat; discard bay leaves and any mussels that do not open. Sprinkle with bacon and parsley.

NUTRITIONAL INFORMATION, PER SERVING: about 151 cal, 12 g pro, 6 g total fat (2 g sat. fat), 7 g carb, 1 g fibre, 29 mg chol, 297 mg sodium, 277 mg potassium. % RDI: 3% calcium, 22% iron, 5% vit A, 13% vit C, 15% folate.

TIP FROM THE TEST KITCHEN
Most mussels are pretty clean, but you will find the odd one that still has a beard—the threadlike bits protruding from the shell that help the mussel cling to surfaces. You can usually pull a beard out with your fingers; if you find a stubborn one, heavy-duty tweezers or needle-nose pliers will do the job.

STEAMED CLAMS
WITH CHORIZO AND TOMATOES

HANDS-ON TIME
20 minutes

TOTAL TIME
50 minutes

MAKES
4 servings

*Dish up these easy, outstanding clams with crusty bread to sop up all the zesty sauce.
To serve this recipe as an appetizer, divide it into six smaller portions.*

INGREDIENTS

2 tbsp	extra-virgin olive oil
1½ cups	sliced dry-cured chorizo (about 170 g), see tip, page 124
1	onion, thinly sliced
1	clove garlic, minced
¼ tsp	each salt and pepper
900 g	plum tomatoes, chopped (about 10)
1 tbsp	sherry vinegar or wine vinegar
2 kg	littleneck clams, scrubbed
½ cup	packed torn fresh basil

DIRECTIONS

In Dutch oven, heat oil over medium heat; cook chorizo, onion, garlic, salt and pepper, stirring occasionally, until onion is softened, about 8 minutes.

Stir in tomatoes and vinegar; cook over medium-high heat, stirring occasionally, until slightly thickened and tomatoes are tender, about 15 minutes.

Add clams; cover with tight-fitting lid and bring to boil over high heat. Cook just until clams open wide, 8 to 10 minutes. Discard any that do not open. Remove from heat; stir in basil.

NUTRITIONAL INFORMATION, PER SERVING: about 365 cal, 22 g pro, 25 g total fat (7 g sat. fat), 15 g carb, 3 g fibre, 61 mg chol, 735 mg sodium. % RDI: 7% calcium, 80% iron, 26% vit A, 60% vit C, 19% folate.

VARIATION
STEAMED MUSSELS
WITH CHORIZO AND TOMATOES
Omit clams. Use 900 g mussels, scrubbed and beards removed; reduce cooking time to 4 to 6 minutes.

BOILED LOBSTER ✿
WITH LEMON-ANCHOVY BUTTER

HANDS-ON TIME
15 minutes

TOTAL TIME
25 minutes

MAKES
4 servings

The best way to enjoy lobster is simply to boil it. Dress it up with our tasty butters (below). Make sure everyone at the table has a lobster pick, a lobster cracker and plenty of napkins.

INGREDIENTS

LEMON-ANCHOVY BUTTER:

⅓ cup	butter, softened
2 tsp	chopped fresh parsley
1	clove garlic, grated
1	anchovy fillet, minced
½ tsp	grated lemon zest
¼ tsp	lemon juice

BOILED LOBSTER:

4	live lobsters (each 565 to 675 g)

DIRECTIONS

LEMON ANCHOVY BUTTER: In bowl, mash together butter, parsley, garlic, anchovy, lemon zest and lemon juice. Set aside. *(Make-ahead: Cover and refrigerate for up to 3 days or freeze in airtight container for up to 2 months.)*

BOILED LOBSTER: Fill stockpot with enough salted water to completely cover lobsters; bring to full rolling boil over high heat. Grasp each lobster around back shell, snip off elastic bands and gently drop headfirst into water. Cover and return to boil, starting timer when water boils.

Reduce heat to slow boil; cook lobsters until bright red and small leg comes away easily when twisted and pulled, 8 to 10 minutes.

TO FINISH: While lobsters are boiling, melt Lemon-Anchovy Butter in saucepan over low heat. Serve with lobster for dipping.

NUTRITIONAL INFORMATION, PER SERVING: about 282 cal, 31 g pro, 16 g total fat (10 g sat. fat), 2 g carb, trace fibre, 147 mg chol, 702 mg sodium, 532 mg potassium. % RDI: 9% calcium, 5% iron, 18% vit A, 2% vit C, 7% folate.

SHERRIED SHALLOT BUTTER

In skillet, heat 1 tsp butter over medium-high heat. Cook 2 shallots, minced; ¼ tsp sweet paprika; and pinch salt until shallots are tender and light golden, about 3 minutes. Stir in 1 tbsp dry sherry; cook until no liquid remains, about 1 minute. Transfer to bowl; let cool for 3 minutes. Mash in ⅓ cup butter, softened, and 1 tsp chopped fresh parsley.

GINGER, HOT PEPPER AND LIME BUTTER

Mash together ⅓ cup butter, softened; 2 tsp grated fresh ginger; 1 tsp minced seeded red or green hot peppers; ¼ tsp grated lime zest; ½ tsp lime juice; and pinch salt.

SPICY GARLIC BUTTER

In small skillet, melt 2 tsp butter over medium heat. Cook 3 cloves garlic, minced, and ½ tsp smoked paprika, stirring, until garlic is softened, about 2 minutes. Transfer to bowl; let cool to room temperature, about 5 minutes. Mash in ⅓ cup butter, softened, and 1 tsp hot pepper sauce.

CURRIED GINGER BUTTER

In small skillet, melt 2 tsp butter over medium heat; cook 2 tbsp minced green onion, 1 tsp minced fresh ginger and ½ tsp curry powder, stirring, until ginger is softened, about 3 minutes. Transfer to bowl; let cool to room temperature, about 5 minutes. Mash in ⅓ cup butter, softened.

ORANGE TARRAGON GARLIC BUTTER

Mash together ⅓ cup butter, softened; 1 clove garlic, grated; 1 tsp each chopped fresh tarragon and fresh parsley; ½ tsp grated orange zest; and pinch salt.

LEMONY DILL BUTTER

Mash together ⅓ cup butter, softened; 2 tbsp chopped fresh dill; and 1 tsp grated lemon zest.

CRISPY CALAMARI

The best calamari are crispy on the outside and tender on the inside. This requires a thin coating of the flour mixture and then quick-frying in oil at the proper temperature. Enjoy it as is, with a squeeze of lemon or with Basil Aïoli Dipping Sauce (below).

HANDS-ON TIME
35 minutes

TOTAL TIME
35 minutes

MAKES
6 servings

INGREDIENTS

675 g	fresh or thawed frozen squid
8 cups	canola, safflower or other vegetable oil
½ cup	all-purpose flour
¼ cup	cornstarch
½ tsp	cayenne pepper
½ tsp	sea salt or salt
1	lemon, cut in wedges

DIRECTIONS

Holding squid tube, pull off head and tentacles; set aside. Rinse tubes under cold water, rubbing off purplish skin. Pull out and discard "pen" (clear long plastic-like skeleton) from centre of each tube. On cutting board, pull off and discard fins from tubes. **PHOTO A**

Cut off and discard eyes and head from tentacles, keeping tentacles attached to ring on top; squeeze hard beak from centre of tentacles and discard. Cut tubes crosswise into ½-inch (1 cm) wide rings; pat dry. Pour oil into wok or deep heavy-bottomed saucepan; heat until deep-fryer thermometer reads 375°F (190°C).

Meanwhile, in large plastic bag, shake together flour, cornstarch and cayenne. All at once, add tentacles and rings to flour mixture; shake to coat. Transfer to sieve; lightly shake off excess flour mixture. **PHOTO B**

Working in batches, fry calamari until golden, 1 to 1½ minutes per batch. Using slotted spoon, transfer to paper towel–lined plate; let drain. Sprinkle with salt just before serving with lemon wedges.

NUTRITIONAL INFORMATION, PER SERVING: about 326 cal, 19 g pro, 20 g total fat (2 g sat. fat), 17 g carb, trace fibre, 265 mg chol, 180 mg sodium. % RDI: 4% calcium, 9% iron, 1% vit C, 12% folate.

BASIL AÏOLI DIPPING SAUCE

In food processor, pulse together ¼ cup lightly packed fresh basil leaves; 1 clove garlic, pressed or minced; 2 tbsp extra-virgin olive oil; 2 tsp lemon juice; and 1 tsp anchovy paste until smooth. Blend in ½ cup mayonnaise. **MAKES** about ½ cup.

TIP FROM THE TEST KITCHEN
No deep-fryer thermometer? If the oil is hot enough, it should bubble vigorously after you drop in 1 piece of floured calamari, and the calamari should turn golden in 1 to 1½ minutes.

DOUBLE-GARLIC BAKED SHRIMP

HANDS-ON TIME 10 minutes

TOTAL TIME 45 minutes

MAKES 4 servings

INGREDIENTS

1	head garlic
2 cups	grape tomatoes or cherry tomatoes
half	lemon, quartered
3 tbsp	olive oil
½ tsp	salt
450 g	peeled deveined large shrimp (31 to 35 count)
2	cloves garlic, pressed or minced
½ tsp	smoked or sweet paprika
¼ tsp	dried marjoram or dried oregano
2 tbsp	finely chopped fresh parsley

DIRECTIONS

Separate garlic into cloves and peel. In shallow 8-cup (2 L) casserole dish, stir together tomatoes, garlic cloves, lemon, oil and salt. Bake in 425°F (220°C) oven, stirring halfway through, for 30 minutes.

Toss together shrimp, pressed garlic, paprika and marjoram; stir into tomato mixture. Bake until shrimp are pink and opaque throughout, about 7 minutes. Stir in parsley.

NUTRITIONAL INFORMATION, PER SERVING: about 243 cal, 24 g pro, 12 g total fat (2 g sat. fat), 9 g carb, 2 g fibre, 173 mg chol, 462 mg sodium, 467 mg potassium. % RDI: 9% calcium, 24% iron, 14% vit A, 42% vit C, 9% folate.

COCONUT SHRIMP ㉚

HANDS-ON TIME 30 minutes

TOTAL TIME 30 minutes

MAKES 4 servings

INGREDIENTS

2	egg whites, whisked
¼ tsp	pepper
pinch	salt
½ cup	panko bread crumbs
¼ cup	unsweetened desiccated coconut (see tip, below)
3 tbsp	all-purpose flour
450 g	raw jumbo shrimp (about 25), peeled (tail-on), deveined and patted dry
4 tsp	vegetable oil
⅓ cup	mango chutney

DIRECTIONS

In shallow bowl, whisk together egg whites, pepper and salt. In separate shallow bowl, stir together panko, coconut and flour. Holding by tail, dip 1 shrimp into egg mixture, shaking off excess. Dip into panko mixture, turning to coat and pressing to adhere. Repeat with remaining shrimp.

In large nonstick skillet, heat half of the oil over medium heat; cook half of the shrimp, turning once, until golden, about 6 minutes. Repeat with remaining oil and shrimp. Serve with mango chutney.

NUTRITIONAL INFORMATION, PER SERVING: about 233 cal, 19 g pro, 8 g total fat (3 g sat. fat), 20 g carb, 1 g fibre, 128 mg chol, 419 mg sodium, 203 mg potassium. % RDI: 4% calcium, 18% iron, 5% vit A, 3% vit C, 5% folate.

TIP FROM THE TEST KITCHEN
Check the label before you buy the coconut. Desiccated coconut comes in both sweetened and unsweetened varieties—you definitely want the one without any added sugar for this recipe.

LEMON HERB SHRIMP BURGERS ③⓪

With a shredded cabbage topping and a simplified homemade tartar sauce, these tender herb-laced burgers taste like a fresh, lighter version of fish and chips.

HANDS-ON TIME
15 minutes

TOTAL TIME
20 minutes

MAKES
4 servings

INGREDIENTS

EASY TARTAR SAUCE:

2 tbsp	each light mayonnaise and plain yogurt
2 tbsp	chopped bread-and-butter pickles
1 tsp	Dijon mustard
1 tsp	lemon juice
pinch	salt
dash	hot pepper sauce

SHRIMP BURGERS:

½ cup	fresh bread crumbs (see tip, page 27)
1	egg
2	cloves garlic, chopped
1 tsp	grated lemon zest
1 tbsp	lemon juice
450 g	raw large shrimp (31 to 35 count), peeled and deveined
1 tbsp	each chopped fresh parsley, fresh chives and fresh dill
pinch	each salt and pepper
1 tbsp	vegetable oil
1 cup	finely shredded green cabbage
4	soft white buns, halved

DIRECTIONS

EASY TARTAR SAUCE: Whisk together mayonnaise, yogurt, pickles, mustard, lemon juice, salt and hot pepper sauce; set aside in refrigerator.

SHRIMP BURGERS: In food processor, pulse together bread crumbs, egg, garlic, lemon zest and lemon juice until combined. Add shrimp; pulse until combined, about 6 times. Stir in parsley, chives, dill, salt and pepper.

In large skillet, heat oil over medium-high heat; divide shrimp mixture into quarters and scoop into skillet, pressing gently to form about ½-inch (1 cm) thick patties. Cook, turning once, until firm and golden and shrimp is pink, 6 to 8 minutes.

TO FINISH: Sandwich patties, cabbage and tartar sauce in buns.

NUTRITIONAL INFORMATION, PER SERVING: about 338 cal, 25 g pro, 12 g total fat (2 g sat. fat), 33 g carb, 2 g fibre, 179 mg chol, 518 mg sodium, 320 mg potassium. % RDI: 14% calcium, 31% iron, 9% vit A, 20% vit C, 39% folate.

TIP FROM THE TEST KITCHEN
When you peel shrimp, freeze the shells. Later, when you have time, simmer them in vegetable stock to extract their flavour. Strain the flavoured stock and use it in fish soups, chowders, stews, pies and pastas.

**BRAISED SHORT RIB RAVIOLI
WITH PORCINI MUSHROOM JUS**
page 248

ULTIMATE PASTA, NOODLES & DUMPLINGS | 9

"I have fond memories of making noodles and dumplings in the kitchen with my mom and grandma. We each have our own way of folding dumplings, but no one seemed to mind, because they all got eaten!"

IRENE FONG SENIOR FOOD SPECIALIST

SPAGHETTI IN ROASTED CHERRY TOMATO SAUCE

HANDS-ON TIME
15 minutes

TOTAL TIME
35 minutes

MAKES
4 servings

Cherry tomatoes seem to ripen all at once in the garden. This delicious sauce is the perfect way to enjoy the bounty. In the off-season, it takes only a couple of boxes from the supermarket, so it's a quick dinner you can make year-round.

INGREDIENTS

ROASTED CHERRY TOMATO SAUCE:

4 cups	cherry tomatoes, halved (about 450 g)
4	cloves garlic, sliced
3 tbsp	extra-virgin olive oil
1 tbsp	balsamic vinegar
2 tsp	minced fresh rosemary
½ tsp	salt
pinch	hot pepper flakes

SPAGHETTI:

340 g	spaghetti
¼ cup	minced fresh basil (approx)
¼ cup	crumbled goat cheese
¼ cup	sliced black olives

DIRECTIONS

ROASTED CHERRY TOMATO SAUCE: In 13- x 9-inch (3.5 L) cake pan, toss together tomatoes, garlic, oil, vinegar, rosemary, salt and hot pepper flakes. Roast in 400°F (200°C) oven until tomatoes are shrivelled, about 25 minutes.

SPAGHETTI: While tomatoes are roasting, in large pot of boiling salted water, cook pasta according to package instructions until al dente. Drain and transfer to large serving bowl.

Add tomato sauce and basil, tossing to combine. Sprinkle with goat cheese, olives, and more basil, if desired.

NUTRITIONAL INFORMATION, PER SERVING: about 474 cal, 14 g pro, 15 g total fat (3 g sat. fat), 72 g carb, 6 g fibre, 4 mg chol, 620 mg sodium. % RDI: 6% calcium, 30% iron, 16% vit A, 32% vit C, 87% folate.

TIP FROM THE TEST KITCHEN
Store fresh tomatoes at room temperature. Refrigerating them can cause them to lose flavour and become mealy.

SPAGHETTI CARBONARA ㉚
WITH PROSCIUTTO

Prosciutto stands in for the traditional pancetta in this egg-based pasta dish.
A spoonful of cream enriches the sauce and helps it coat each strand of spaghetti.

HANDS-ON TIME
10 minutes

TOTAL TIME
15 minutes

MAKES
4 servings

INGREDIENTS

4	eggs
170 g	chopped prosciutto
¼ cup	grated Parmesan cheese (approx)
¼ cup	chopped fresh parsley
1 tbsp	whipping cream (35%)
¼ tsp	pepper
340 g	spaghetti

DIRECTIONS

In large bowl, whisk together eggs, prosciutto, Parmesan, parsley, cream and pepper; set aside.

In large pot of boiling salted water, cook pasta according to package instructions until al dente. Drain pasta; add immediately to egg mixture, tossing to lightly cook eggs and coat pasta in creamy sauce. Serve sprinkled with more Parmesan, if desired.

NUTRITIONAL INFORMATION, PER SERVING: about 498 cal, 27 g pro, 13 g total fat (5 g sat. fat), 65 g carb, 4 g fibre, 219 mg chol, 927 mg sodium, 291 mg potassium. % RDI: 11% calcium, 31% iron, 12% vit A, 7% vit C, 92% folate.

TIP FROM THE TEST KITCHEN
If you are concerned about consuming raw eggs, substitute 1 cup pasteurized whole eggs. Look for them in cartons in the egg section of the grocery store.

GARLIC SHRIMP PASTA 🕥

If you prefer, use some of the pasta cooking liquid instead of wine in the sauce. The starchy water will help thicken it a bit at the same time.

HANDS-ON TIME
20 minutes

TOTAL TIME
20 minutes

MAKES
4 servings

INGREDIENTS

340 g	spaghetti (see tip, below)
3 tbsp	olive oil
2 cups	cherry tomatoes, halved
3	anchovy fillets, chopped
3	cloves garlic, chopped
3	sprigs fresh thyme
¼ tsp	salt
¼ tsp	hot pepper flakes
450 g	thawed peeled deveined large shrimp (31 to 35 count)
⅓ cup	dry white wine
3 tbsp	chopped fresh parsley

DIRECTIONS

In large pot of boiling salted water, cook pasta according to package instructions until al dente. Reserving ½ cup of the cooking liquid, drain pasta; return to pot.

While pasta is cooking, in large skillet, heat oil over medium heat; cook tomatoes, anchovies, garlic, thyme, salt and hot pepper flakes, stirring occasionally, until softened, 3 to 5 minutes.

Stir in shrimp and wine; cook over medium-high heat until shrimp are pink and opaque throughout, about 5 minutes. Sprinkle with parsley. Add to pasta; toss, adding enough of the reserved cooking liquid to coat.

NUTRITIONAL INFORMATION, PER SERVING: about 559 cal, 36 g pro, 14 g total fat (2 g sat. fat), 69 g carb, 5 g fibre, 175 mg chol, 652 mg sodium, 517 mg potassium. % RDI: 9% calcium, 47% iron, 14% vit A, 25% vit C, 88% folate.

TIP FROM THE TEST KITCHEN
Any long pasta will do for this dish. Just follow the package instructions and cook it until al dente.

BEST-EVER LASAGNA 🍴

This classic dish is just as good if you make it ahead, so it's a Monday-night lifesaver. Serve with a simple green salad.

HANDS-ON TIME
45 minutes

TOTAL TIME
3 hours

MAKES
12 servings

INGREDIENTS

TOMATO MEAT SAUCE:

2 tbsp	olive oil
2	onions, diced
1	rib celery, diced
1	carrot, diced
4	cloves garlic, minced
2	cans (each 156 mL) tomato paste
675 g	lean ground beef
2	cans (each 796 mL) diced tomatoes
1 cup	dry red or white wine
2	bay leaves
2 tsp	dried oregano
1 tsp	salt
¾ tsp	pepper

LASAGNA:

12	lasagna noodles
1	pkg (475 g) extra-smooth ricotta cheese
1 cup	grated Parmesan cheese
1	egg
½ cup	chopped fresh basil
1	clove garlic, minced
¼ tsp	each salt and pepper
4½ cups	shredded mozzarella cheese

DIRECTIONS

TOMATO MEAT SAUCE: In Dutch oven, heat oil over medium heat; cook onions, celery, carrot and garlic, stirring occasionally, until softened, about 5 minutes. Stir in tomato paste. Add beef; cook, breaking up with spoon, until no longer pink, about 5 minutes.

Add tomatoes, wine, bay leaves, oregano, salt and pepper; reduce heat and simmer, stirring occasionally, until slightly thickened, about 40 minutes. Discard bay leaves. *(Make-ahead: Let cool for 30 minutes. Refrigerate in airtight container for up to 3 days.)*

LASAGNA: While sauce is simmering, in large pot of boiling salted water, cook noodles for 2 minutes less than package instructions for al dente. Drain; lay noodles, without touching, in single layer on tea towel.

Stir together ricotta, Parmesan, egg, basil, garlic, salt and pepper.

ASSEMBLY: Set aside 1½ cups of the meat sauce. In 13- x 9-inch (3 L) baking dish, spread one-third of the remaining meat sauce. Arrange 3 noodles over top; sprinkle with 1½ cups of the mozzarella. Top with half of the remaining meat sauce, 3 noodles, ricotta mixture, 3 noodles, remaining meat sauce and 3 noodles. Top with reserved meat sauce and remaining mozzarella. *(Make-ahead: Cover with plastic wrap and refrigerate for up to 3 days. Unwrap before baking.)*

Cover with foil. Bake in 375°F (190°C) oven for 45 minutes. Uncover and bake until mozzarella is golden, about 15 minutes. Cover loosely with foil; let stand for 30 minutes before serving.

NUTRITIONAL INFORMATION, PER SERVING: about 551 cal, 35 g pro, 30 g total fat (16 g sat. fat), 36 g carb, 5 g fibre, 92 mg chol, 1,065 mg sodium, 868 mg potassium. % RDI: 47% calcium, 36% iron, 36% vit A, 43% vit C, 33% folate.

SPAGHETTI IN AMATRICIANA SAUCE ㉚

Named for the Italian region of Amatrice, where it originated, this simple sauce is a great example of classic Italian cooking: A few good-quality ingredients yield delicious results.

HANDS-ON TIME
30 minutes

TOTAL TIME
30 minutes

MAKES
4 to 6 servings

INGREDIENTS

4	tomatoes (about 900 g)
115 g	thinly sliced guanciale (see tip, below)
2	cloves garlic, thinly sliced
¼ tsp	hot pepper flakes
6	fresh basil leaves, torn
340 g	spaghetti
⅓ cup	grated Pecorino-Romano cheese

DIRECTIONS

Using sharp knife, score X in bottom of each tomato. In large pot of boiling water, blanch tomatoes until skins begin to split, 20 to 30 seconds. Using slotted spoon, transfer to bowl of ice water; let cool for 1 minute. Drain tomatoes and peel off skins; seed and dice tomatoes. Set aside.

Cut guanciale into narrow strips. In large dry skillet, cook over medium heat until translucent and fat is rendered, about 3 minutes. Add garlic and hot pepper flakes; cook, stirring, for 1 minute.

Stir in tomatoes and three-quarters of the basil; simmer, stirring occasionally, for 10 minutes.

While tomato mixture is simmering, in large pot of boiling salted water, cook pasta according to package instructions until al dente. Reserving 1 cup of the cooking liquid, drain pasta; return to pot.

Stir tomato mixture into pasta; toss, adding enough of the reserved cooking liquid to coat. Cook for 1 minute. Serve sprinkled with Pecorino-Romano and remaining basil.

NUTRITIONAL INFORMATION, PER EACH OF 6 SERVINGS: about 316 cal, 14 g pro, 8 g total fat (3 g sat. fat), 48 g carb, 4 g fibre, 24 mg chol, 524 mg sodium, 348 mg potassium. % RDI: 3% calcium, 18% iron, 11% vit A, 25% vit C, 58% folate.

TIP FROM THE TEST KITCHEN
Guanciale is a salt-cured bacon made from pig's jowl or cheek. Pancetta makes a good substitute; you can also use regular bacon in a pinch.

BROWN BUTTER PASTA ㉚ ◔
WITH TOMATOES AND ASPARAGUS

Brown butter, or beurre noisette, is butter cooked until it becomes a golden hazelnut colour and takes on a nutty flavour. This simple yet elegant technique is a terrific way to spruce up everyday pasta. Choose a cup-shaped pasta that will catch and hold on to the vegetables.

HANDS-ON TIME
15 minutes

TOTAL TIME
20 minutes

MAKES
4 servings

INGREDIENTS

¼ cup	butter
2	cloves garlic, minced
2 cups	grape tomatoes or cherry tomatoes
450 g	asparagus, trimmed and cut in 1-inch (2.5 cm) pieces
½ tsp	each salt and pepper
4 cups	dried gnocchi (see tip, below) orecchiette or shell pasta
½ cup	grated Parmesan cheese
2 tbsp	chopped fresh parsley

DIRECTIONS

In large skillet, melt butter over medium heat until foaming and nutty brown colour, about 2 minutes. Add garlic; cook, stirring, until fragrant, about 30 seconds.

Add tomatoes, asparagus, salt and pepper; cover and cook until tomatoes begin to split and asparagus is tender, about 8 minutes.

Meanwhile, in large pot of boiling salted water, cook pasta according to package instructions until al dente. Drain pasta; return to pot. Add sauce; toss to coat. Stir in Parmesan and parsley.

NUTRITIONAL INFORMATION, PER SERVING: about 435 cal, 15 g pro, 16 g total fat (9 g sat. fat), 60 g carb, 6 g fibre, 38 mg chol, 698 mg sodium. % RDI: 13% calcium, 27% iron, 26% vit A, 30% vit C, 124% folate.

VARIATION
GLUTEN-FREE BROWN BUTTER PASTA
WITH TOMATOES AND ASPARAGUS
Use a short rice-based pasta, such as brown rice fusilli or shells, instead of the gnocchi.

TIP FROM THE TEST KITCHEN
Dried gnocchi are not the same as fresh gnocchi, which are little pillows of pasta dough. Look for dried gnocchi in the pasta aisle rather than the refrigerated section of the supermarket.

BRAISED SHORT RIB RAVIOLI
WITH PORCINI MUSHROOM JUS

Stuffing individual ravioli takes a bit more effort than making ribbon pasta, but the tender beef-and-mushroom filling in this recipe is worth the effort. Pulsing the filling is the secret to creating the best texture and flavour.

HANDS-ON TIME
45 minutes

TOTAL TIME
3¼ hours

MAKES
8 to 10 servings

INGREDIENTS

1	pkg (14 g) dried porcini mushrooms
1 kg	bone-in beef simmering short ribs (see tip, opposite), cut in 2½-inch (6 cm) pieces
½ tsp	each salt and pepper
2 tbsp	olive oil
4	cloves garlic, minced
⅓ cup	dry white or red wine
2⅓ cups	sodium-reduced beef broth
½ cup	fresh bread crumbs (see tip, page 27)
½ cup	grated Pecorino-Romano or Parmesan cheese
6 tbsp	chopped fresh parsley
1 tbsp	red wine vinegar
2 tsp	chopped fresh thyme
1	batch Fresh Pasta Dough (opposite)
½ cup	all-purpose flour (approx)
1	egg
5 cups	lightly packed torn oyster mushrooms

DIRECTIONS

Using spice grinder, grind porcini mushrooms until powdery; set aside. Sprinkle beef with ¼ tsp each of the salt and pepper. In Dutch oven, heat 1 tbsp of the oil over medium-high heat; cook beef, stirring, until browned all over, about 5 minutes. Using slotted spoon, transfer to bowl; set aside.

Drain all but 1 tbsp fat from pan; cook garlic and porcini mushrooms, stirring, until fragrant, about 30 seconds. Stir in wine; cook, stirring, until absorbed, about 30 seconds. Stir in 2 cups of the broth. Add beef; bring to boil. Transfer to 325°F (160°C) oven and cook, covered, until beef is very tender, about 2½ hours.

Using slotted spoon, transfer beef to bowl. Skim and discard fat from juices; set juices aside. *(Make-ahead: Cover and refrigerate for up to 24 hours or freeze in airtight container for up to 3 weeks; let thaw in refrigerator overnight before using.)*

Pull meat from bones; discard bones. In food processor, pulse together beef, remaining broth, bread crumbs, Pecorino-Romano, two-thirds of the parsley, the vinegar, thyme and remaining salt and pepper until beef is shredded and begins to stick together; let cool. *(Make-ahead: Cover and refrigerate for up to 24 hours.)*

While filling is cooling, using pasta machine roller on widest setting, feed 1 sheet of the dough through lightly floured rollers; fold in half, bringing short ends together, and lightly dust with some of the flour. **PHOTO A**

Feed sheet through rollers 3 more times or until edges are smooth, cutting in half if too long to handle. Continue feeding through rollers until sixth-widest setting is reached, about 1 mm. **PHOTO B**

Repeat with remaining sheets. Place sheets on lightly floured surface; brush excess flour off tops. Beat egg with 1 tsp water; brush lengthwise over half of each sheet. Spoon filling by rounded 1 tsp, 1 inch (2.5 cm) apart and ¾ inch (2 cm) from long edge, onto opposite halves. Fold egg-washed halves over filling, pressing around filling to expel air and seal halves together.

TIP FROM THE TEST KITCHEN
Use well-marbled short ribs and add any fat to the food processor along with the meat.

Using sharp knife, pizza cutter or fluted wheel cutter, cut between fillings to make squares, pressing to expel air and pinching edges to reseal as necessary.

Transfer to floured baking sheet; let stand until beginning to dry, about 10 minutes. *(Make-ahead: Freeze until firm, about 1 hour; transfer to airtight container and freeze for up to 2 months. Cook from frozen, adding 1 minute to cooking time.)*

In large saucepan of boiling salted water, cook ravioli, stirring occasionally, until ravioli float to surface, 2 to 3 minutes. Reserving ¾ cup of the cooking liquid, drain.

While ravioli are cooking, in large nonstick skillet, heat remaining oil over medium-high heat; cook oyster mushrooms, stirring, until beginning to soften, about 2 minutes. Add reserved beef juices, ravioli and enough of the pasta cooking liquid to coat generously; cook, stirring, until slightly thickened, about 2 minutes. Garnish with remaining parsley.

NUTRITIONAL INFORMATION, PER EACH OF 10 SERVINGS: about 361 cal, 18 g pro, 22 g total fat (8 g sat. fat), 23 g carb, 2 g fibre, 111 mg chol, 425 mg sodium, 364 mg potassium. % RDI: 7% calcium, 21% iron, 6% vit A, 5% vit C, 28% folate.

FRESH PASTA DOUGH

HANDS-ON TIME 15 minutes
TOTAL TIME 35 minutes
MAKES 1 batch

INGREDIENTS

2 cups	all-purpose flour (approx)
3	eggs
¼ tsp	salt

DIRECTIONS

Mound flour on work surface; make well in centre. Add eggs to well; sprinkle with salt. Using fork, beat eggs. Starting at inside edge and working around well, gradually stir flour into egg mixture until soft dough forms. Sift flour remaining on work surface, discarding bits of dough; set aside.

On lightly floured work surface, knead dough, dusting with some of the remaining flour, until smooth, elastic and no longer sticky, about 10 minutes. Wrap in plastic wrap; let rest for 20 minutes.

Cut dough into thirds; roll or press each into 5-inch (12 cm) wide sheet. Dust with reserved flour. Cover with damp tea towel to prevent drying out.

NUTRITIONAL INFORMATION, PER BATCH: about 1,048 cal, 46 g pro, 21 g total fat (6 g sat. fat), 162 g carb, 6 g fibre, 578 mg chol, 772 mg sodium, 401 mg potassium. % RDI: 9% calcium, 93% iron, 30% vit A, 189% folate.

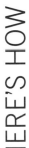

HERE'S HOW

BAKED RIGATONI AND MEATBALLS 🍴

*Making meatballs from scratch is time-consuming, but their beefy,
rich flavour boosts the appeal of this homey baked pasta. A simple salad
is all you need to make it a complete meal.*

HANDS-ON TIME
35 minutes

TOTAL TIME
1½ hours

MAKES
8 to 10 servings

INGREDIENTS

MEATBALLS:

1	egg
¼ cup	dried bread crumbs
¼ cup	grated onion
1	clove garlic, minced
¼ cup	grated Parmesan cheese
½ tsp	dried oregano
¼ tsp	each salt and pepper
450 g	lean ground pork

BAKED RIGATONI:

2 tbsp	extra-virgin olive oil
1	onion, chopped
2	cloves garlic, minced
1	carrot, finely chopped
1	rib celery, finely chopped
3 cups	sliced mushrooms
1	sweet red or yellow pepper, chopped
1½ tsp	each dried basil and dried oregano
½ tsp	each salt and pepper
2	cans (each 796 mL) whole tomatoes
2 tbsp	tomato paste
1 tbsp	balsamic vinegar
4 cups	rigatoni pasta (about 340 g)
2 cups	shredded provolone cheese
½ cup	grated Parmesan cheese

DIRECTIONS

MEATBALLS: In large bowl, combine egg, bread crumbs, onion, garlic, Parmesan, oregano, salt and pepper; mix in pork. Shape by 1 tbsp into balls. Bake on greased rimmed baking sheet in 400°F (200°C) oven until instant-read thermometer inserted into several reads 160°F (71°C), about 15 minutes.

BAKED RIGATONI: While meatballs are baking, in Dutch oven, heat oil over medium-high heat; sauté onion, garlic, carrot, celery, mushrooms, red pepper, basil, oregano, salt and pepper until vegetables are softened, about 10 minutes. Push to 1 side of pan.

Add tomatoes and tomato paste to pan, mashing tomatoes with back of spoon; stir to combine with vegetable mixture. Bring to boil; reduce heat and simmer for 20 minutes.

Stir in meatballs and vinegar; simmer until sauce is thickened, about 5 minutes.

While sauce simmering, in large pot of boiling salted water, cook pasta according to package instructions until al dente. Drain pasta and add to sauce; toss to coat. Scrape into greased 12-cup (3 L) casserole dish. *(Make-ahead: Let cool for 30 minutes; refrigerate until cold. Cover and refrigerate for up to 24 hours. Uncover and add 10 minutes to baking time.)*

Sprinkle with provolone and Parmesan. Bake in 375°F (190°C) oven until bubbly, about 30 minutes.

NUTRITIONAL INFORMATION, PER EACH OF 10 SERVINGS: about 418 cal, 24 g pro, 18 g total fat (8 g sat. fat), 40 g carb, 4 g fibre, 69 mg chol, 842 mg sodium. % RDI: 31% calcium, 31% iron, 27% vit A, 73% vit C, 45% folate.

RICH VEGETABLE LASAGNA 🔘 🍴

*Once you've made this deeply flavourful vegetarian lasagna, you'll
never go back to the frozen version again.*

HANDS-ON TIME
50 minutes

TOTAL TIME
2 hours

MAKES
12 servings

INGREDIENTS

2 tbsp	extra-virgin olive oil
1	onion, diced
4	cloves garlic, minced
¼ tsp	hot pepper flakes
2	zucchini, diced
2	sweet red peppers, diced
1	eggplant, diced
1	bay leaf
½ tsp	each dried thyme and dried oregano
½ tsp	each salt and pepper
1	can (796 mL) whole tomatoes
¼ cup	each chopped fresh basil and fresh parsley (or all parsley)
2	eggs
¼ tsp	nutmeg
1	pkg (475 g) ricotta cheese
3 cups	shredded mozzarella cheese
1 cup	grated Parmesan cheese
15	lasagna noodles

DIRECTIONS

In large Dutch oven, heat oil over medium heat; cook onion, garlic and hot pepper flakes until softened, about 6 minutes.

Add zucchini, red peppers, eggplant, bay leaf, thyme, oregano, salt and pepper; cook, stirring, until edges of eggplant are golden, about 10 minutes.

Stir in tomatoes, mashing with back of spoon; bring to boil. Reduce heat, cover and simmer, stirring occasionally, until thickened, about 30 minutes. Discard bay leaf. Stir in basil and parsley.

In bowl, beat eggs with nutmeg; stir in ricotta, 2 cups of the mozzarella and the Parmesan. Set aside.

In large pot of boiling salted water, cook noodles for 2 minutes less than package instructions for al dente. Drain; lay noodles, without touching, in single layer on tea towel.

In greased 13- x 9-inch (3 L) baking dish, arrange 5 of the noodles in single layer; top with 1 cup of the sauce. Top with 3 of the remaining noodles; spread with one-third of the remaining sauce. Dot with half of the cheese mixture. Starting with 3 noodles, repeat layers once. Top with 4 remaining noodles; spread with remaining sauce. Sprinkle with remaining mozzarella.

Cover loosely with foil; bake in 375°F (190°C) oven for 20 minutes. Uncover and bake until bubbly and knife inserted in centre comes out hot, about 25 minutes.

Let stand for 10 minutes before serving. *(Make-ahead: Let cool for 30 minutes; refrigerate until cold. Cover and refrigerate for up to 24 hours. Reheat, covered, in 375°F/190°C oven for 30 minutes; uncover and reheat for 15 more minutes.)*

NUTRITIONAL INFORMATION, PER SERVING: about 359 cal, 19 g pro, 18 g total fat (10 g sat. fat), 31 g carb, 4 g fibre, 83 mg chol, 537 mg sodium. % RDI: 36% calcium, 18% iron, 26% vit A, 75% vit C, 37% folate.

CRUNCHY-TOPPED MACARONI AND CHEESE

HANDS-ON TIME
25 minutes

TOTAL TIME
1 hour

MAKES
8 servings

If comfort food is what you're after, nothing beats a generous helping of creamy, gooey mac and cheese. This recipe is the yummiest version—and the only one you'll ever need.

INGREDIENTS

MACARONI AND CHEESE:

3 cups	elbow macaroni (about 450 g)
3 tbsp	butter
3	cloves garlic, minced
1 tsp	chopped fresh thyme
⅓ cup	all-purpose flour
4 cups	milk
2 tbsp	Dijon mustard
¼ tsp	grated nutmeg
¼ tsp	each salt and pepper
pinch	cayenne pepper
1½ cups	shredded Gruyère cheese
1½ cups	shredded extra-old Cheddar cheese

TOPPING:

½ cup	panko bread crumbs
¼ cup	grated Parmesan cheese
1 tbsp	butter, diced and softened

DIRECTIONS

MACARONI AND CHEESE: In large saucepan of boiling salted water, cook pasta according to package instructions until al dente. Drain; set aside.

While pasta is cooking, in separate large saucepan, melt butter over medium heat; cook garlic and thyme, stirring occasionally, until fragrant, about 2 minutes.

Whisk in flour; cook, whisking constantly, for 2 minutes. Pour in milk in slow steady stream, whisking constantly until smooth; cook, whisking often, until thickened, about 7 minutes.

Whisk in mustard, nutmeg, salt, pepper and cayenne pepper. Stir in Gruyère and Cheddar until smooth; stir in pasta. Scrape into greased 12-cup (3 L) casserole dish.

TOPPING: In bowl, combine panko with Parmesan; using fingers, rub in butter until mixture resembles coarse sand. Sprinkle over pasta mixture.

Bake in 400°F (200°C) oven until sauce is bubbly and topping is golden, about 25 minutes. Let stand for 10 minutes before serving.

NUTRITIONAL INFORMATION, PER SERVING: about 479 cal, 23 g pro, 24 g total fat (14 g sat. fat), 43 g carb, 2 g fibre, 72 mg chol, 576 mg sodium, 262 mg potassium. % RDI: 51% calcium, 15% iron, 25% vit A, 2% vit C, 45% folate.

TIP FROM THE TEST KITCHEN
The sauce might seem a little runny at first, but it will thicken beautifully when baked with the starchy macaroni.

SINGAPORE NOODLES

These noodles get their signature bright yellow colour from turmeric. We've substituted leaner pork tenderloin for the traditional barbecued pork (though the real thing is definitely worth using, if you can find it).

HANDS-ON TIME
30 minutes

TOTAL TIME
50 minutes

MAKES
4 to 6 servings

INGREDIENTS

225 g	pork tenderloin, trimmed and sliced in thin strips
2 tbsp	sodium-reduced soy sauce
1 tsp	sesame oil
½ tsp	salt
¼ tsp	pepper
280 g	dried rice vermicelli (about ⅟₃₂-inch/ 1 mm thick)
4 tsp	vegetable oil
2	eggs, lightly beaten
225 g	jumbo shrimp (21 to 25 count), peeled and deveined
1	small onion, thinly sliced
half	sweet red pepper, thinly sliced
2	cloves garlic, minced
2	green onions, cut in 1½-inch (4 cm) lengths
2 tsp	curry powder
1 tsp	turmeric
1 tsp	granulated sugar
2 cups	bean sprouts

DIRECTIONS

In bowl, stir together pork, 2 tsp of the soy sauce, the sesame oil, a pinch of the salt and the pepper. Cover and refrigerate for 30 minutes. *(Make-ahead: Refrigerate for up to 24 hours.)*

While pork is marinating, prepare noodles according to package instructions. Drain and rinse under cold water; drain well.

In wok or large nonstick skillet, heat 1 tsp of the vegetable oil over medium-high heat; cook eggs, stirring, just until set, about 1 minute. Scrape onto plate. Wipe out wok. Add 1 tsp of the remaining vegetable oil to wok; sauté shrimp over medium-high heat until pink and opaque, about 2 minutes. Transfer to plate.

Add 1 tsp of the remaining vegetable oil to wok; sauté pork mixture over medium-high heat until just a hint of pink remains inside, about 3 minutes. Transfer to plate.

Add remaining vegetable oil to wok; sauté onion, red pepper and garlic over medium-high heat until pepper is tender-crisp, about 2 minutes. Add noodles, egg, shrimp, pork, green onions, curry powder, turmeric, sugar and remaining soy sauce and salt. Cook, stirring and tossing, until well combined and heated through, about 3 minutes. Add bean sprouts; cook, stirring, until softened, about 1 minute.

NUTRITIONAL INFORMATION, PER EACH OF 6 SERVINGS: about 330 cal, 19 g pro, 7 g total fat (1 g sat. fat), 46 g carb, 3 g fibre, 124 mg chol, 504 mg sodium, 328 mg potassium. % RDI: 4% calcium, 18% iron, 8% vit A, 37% vit C, 18% folate.

VARIATION

VEGETARIAN SINGAPORE NOODLES

Omit shrimp. Substitute 1 pkg (350 g) extra-firm tofu, drained and cut in ½-inch (1 cm) cubes, for the pork; continue with recipe as directed.

TIP FROM THE TEST KITCHEN
This recipe is big, so use a wok or your largest nonstick skillet to make it.

GLUTEN-FREE PAD THAI

Once you've gathered the easy-to-find ingredients for this takeout favourite, it takes less than 10 minutes to cook. As with all gluten-free recipes, make sure you read the label on every prepared ingredient to ensure it was processed in a gluten-free facility.

HANDS-ON TIME
35 minutes

TOTAL TIME
35 minutes

MAKES
4 to 6 servings

INGREDIENTS

half	pkg (454 g pkg) dried rice sticks (about ¼ inch/ 5 mm wide)
⅓ cup	ketchup
⅓ cup	sodium-reduced chicken broth
¼ cup	gluten-free fish sauce
3 tbsp	lime juice
2 tsp	granulated sugar
1 tsp	Asian chili sauce (such as sriracha) or hot pepper sauce
¼ cup	vegetable or peanut oil
2	eggs, lightly beaten
225 g	frozen large shrimp (31 to 35 count), thawed, peeled and deveined
280 g	boneless skinless chicken breasts, thinly sliced
4	shallots or 1 onion, thinly sliced
4	cloves garlic, minced
1	sweet red pepper, thinly sliced
2 tsp	minced fresh ginger
170 g	medium-firm tofu, drained and cubed
3 cups	bean sprouts
3	green onions, sliced
¼ cup	chopped unsalted roasted peanuts
½ cup	fresh cilantro leaves lime wedges

DIRECTIONS

Prepare noodles according to package instructions; drain and set aside.

Meanwhile, whisk together ketchup, broth, fish sauce, lime juice, sugar and chili sauce; set aside.

In wok or large skillet, heat 1 tbsp of the oil over medium-high heat; cook eggs, stirring occasionally, until scrambled and set, about 30 seconds. Transfer to separate bowl.

Wipe out wok. Add 1 tbsp of the remaining oil and heat over high heat; stir-fry shrimp until pink, about 1 minute. Transfer to plate.

Add 1 tbsp of the remaining oil to wok; heat over high heat. Stir-fry chicken until browned and no longer pink inside, about 1 minute. Add to shrimp.

Add remaining oil to wok; heat over high heat. Cook shallots, garlic, red pepper and ginger until softened, about 2 minutes.

Stir in ketchup mixture and noodles. Return shrimp mixture to pan; cook, stirring to coat, until noodles are tender, about 3 minutes.

Return scrambled eggs to pan along with tofu, bean sprouts and green onions; cook just until bean sprouts begin to wilt, about 1 minute. Serve garnished with peanuts, cilantro and lime wedges.

NUTRITIONAL INFORMATION, PER EACH OF 6 SERVINGS: about 453 cal, 28 g pro, 17 g total fat (3 g sat. fat), 47 g carb, 3 g fibre, 133 mg chol, 1,241 mg sodium, 555 mg potassium. % RDI: 11% calcium, 20% iron, 16% vit A, 73% vit C, 31% folate.

TIP FROM THE TEST KITCHEN
The terms for frozen shrimp sizes, such as jumbo or large, aren't standardized, so focus on the number of shrimp in each bag (here, 31 to 35 count) to ensure they're the right size.

SHRIMP LO MEIN ③⓪ 🍴

Golden fresh steamed chow mein noodles are substantial but not overly doughy (like the noodles in some restaurant versions of this dish). Look for them in the refrigerated case at the supermarket near the fresh pasta.

HANDS-ON TIME
20 minutes

TOTAL TIME
20 minutes

MAKES
4 servings

INGREDIENTS

1 cup	sodium-reduced chicken broth
2 tbsp	oyster sauce
1 tbsp	cornstarch
1 tsp	sesame oil
1 tbsp	vegetable oil
450 g	jumbo shrimp (21 to 25 count), peeled and deveined
280 g	fresh steamed chow mein noodles
1	carrot, sliced diagonally
1 cup	snow peas, trimmed and halved diagonally
1 cup	quartered button or cremini mushrooms
3	cloves garlic, minced
3	heads Shanghai bok choy (about 225 g total), quartered

DIRECTIONS

Stir together broth, oyster sauce, cornstarch and sesame oil. Set aside.

In wok or large nonstick skillet, heat 1 tsp of the vegetable oil over medium-high heat; sauté shrimp until pink and opaque, about 2 minutes. Transfer to plate.

In large saucepan of boiling water, cook noodles according to package instructions; drain.

While noodles are cooking, add remaining oil to wok; sauté carrot, snow peas, mushrooms and garlic over medium-high heat until garlic is fragrant, about 1 minute. Add bok choy; sauté just until wilted, about 1 minute. Stir in broth mixture, shrimp and noodles. Cook, tossing, until sauce is thickened and noodles are coated, about 1 minute.

NUTRITIONAL INFORMATION, PER SERVING: about 361 cal, 27 g pro, 7 g total fat (1 g sat. fat), 46 g carb, 3 g fibre, 132 mg chol, 646 mg sodium, 578 mg potassium. % RDI: 11% calcium, 36% iron, 63% vit A, 42% vit C, 19% folate.

VARIATION

TOFU LO MEIN

Omit shrimp. Reduce vegetable oil to 2 tsp; use to cook vegetables only. Add 450 g fried tofu balls along with broth mixture. (Look for tofu balls near the refrigerated wonton wrappers and tofu at the grocery store.)

BACON AND ONION PEROGIES

HANDS-ON TIME
1½ hours

TOTAL TIME
1½ hours

MAKES
36 perogies

Serve these tender, smoky dumplings with a hefty dollop of sour cream (and some fried garlic sausage if you can find it) for an authentic Prairies-style meal.

INGREDIENTS

FILLING:

340 g	russet potatoes, peeled and chopped
¼ tsp	pepper
pinch	salt
3	strips bacon
2	onions, finely diced

DOUGH:

3 cups	all-purpose flour
1 tsp	salt
1	egg
2 tbsp	butter, melted
2 tbsp	butter

DIRECTIONS

FILLING: In large saucepan of boiling salted water, cook potatoes until tender, about 15 minutes. Drain and return to pan; mash well. Stir in pepper and salt.

While potatoes are cooking, in skillet over medium-high heat, cook bacon, turning occasionally, until crisp, about 5 minutes. Transfer to paper towel–lined plate; blot dry. Finely chop bacon; stir into potato mixture.

Drain all but 1 tbsp fat from skillet; cook onions over medium heat, stirring occasionally, until deep golden and very soft, about 12 minutes. Stir into potato mixture. Set aside.

DOUGH: While onions are cooking, in bowl, whisk flour with salt. Whisk together egg, ¾ cup water and butter; stir into flour mixture, adding up to 2 tbsp more water if necessary to make soft but not sticky dough.

Turn out onto lightly floured surface; knead until smooth, about 20 times. Divide dough into 2 balls; cover with plastic wrap or damp tea towel and let rest for 20 minutes.

ASSEMBLY: Working with 1 ball of dough at a time and keeping remainder covered, roll out on lightly floured surface to about ¼-inch (3 mm) thickness. Using 3-inch (8 cm) round cutter, cut into rounds. Place 1 tsp of the filling on each round. Lightly moisten half of edge of round with water; fold over filling, gently stretching as needed to fit. Pinch edges to seal.

Place perogies on flour-dusted tea towel; cover with dry tea towel. Repeat with remaining dough and filling, rerolling scraps, to make 36 perogies. *(Make-ahead: Freeze in single layer on baking sheet. Transfer to airtight container and freeze for up to 1 month. Increase boiling time to 5 to 7 minutes.)*

Working in batches, in large pot of boiling salted water, cook perogies, stirring gently, until floating and tender, about 4 minutes per batch. Using slotted spoon, transfer to colander to drain.

TO FINISH: In skillet, melt butter over medium heat; working in batches, cook perogies, turning once, until golden, about 5 minutes per batch.

NUTRITIONAL INFORMATION, PER PEROGY: about 108 cal, 3 g pro, 2 g total fat (1 g sat. fat), 19 g carb, 1 g fibre, 9 mg chol, 305 mg sodium, 241 mg potassium. % RDI: 1% calcium, 7% iron, 1% vit A, 15% vit C, 14% folate.

POT STICKERS

Traditionally these dumplings are pleated on one side, but we have eliminated this step to simplify the recipe. Enjoy them as is, or with a little soy sauce or Chinese red or black vinegar for dipping. You'll need at least 45 wrappers, and you can freeze any leftovers.

HANDS-ON TIME
55 minutes

TOTAL TIME
1¼ hours

MAKES
about 45 pieces

INGREDIENTS

150 g	bok choy (about 3 leaves), halved crosswise
450 g	lean ground pork
1 tbsp	oyster sauce
1 tsp	cornstarch
1 tsp	soy sauce
¼ tsp	pepper
¼ tsp	sesame oil
pinch	salt
1	egg, lightly beaten
1	pkg (450 g) round dumpling wrappers (see tip, below)
2 tsp	vegetable oil

DIRECTIONS

In saucepan of boiling lightly salted water, cook bok choy until tender, 4 to 5 minutes. Drain and let cool; squeeze out excess liquid. Thinly slice and place in large bowl.

Add pork, oyster sauce, cornstarch, soy sauce, pepper, sesame oil, salt and half of the egg; mix to combine.

Mix 1 tsp water into remaining egg; brush over edge of 1 of the dumpling wrappers. Place rounded 1 tsp of the pork mixture on centre of wrapper. Fold over to match edges, pinching gently to seal and pressing lightly to flatten bottom.

Place, seam side up, on waxed paper–lined rimmed baking sheet; cover with damp tea towel. Repeat with remaining wrappers and filling. *(Make-ahead: Refrigerate, loosely covered with damp tea towel, in airtight container for up to 24 hours. Or freeze in single layer, about 2 hours; transfer to airtight container and freeze for up to 3 weeks. Cook from frozen, adding ½ cup water and 4 minutes to cooking time.)*

In large nonstick skillet, heat 1 tsp of the vegetable oil over medium-high heat; cook half of the pot stickers, seam side up, until bottoms are light golden, about 1 minute. Pour in enough water to come ¼ inch (5 mm) up side of pan. Cover and reduce heat to medium; cook, without turning, until translucent and almost no liquid remains, 5 to 6 minutes.

Uncover and increase heat to medium-high; cook, turning to brown all sides, until no liquid remains, 5 to 6 minutes. Repeat with remaining vegetable oil and pot stickers.

NUTRITIONAL INFORMATION, PER PIECE: about 50 cal, 3 g pro, 2 g total fat (1 g sat. fat), 5 g carb, trace fibre, 11 mg chol, 74 mg sodium, 52 mg potassium. % RDI: 1% calcium, 3% iron, 2% vit A, 2% vit C, 4% folate.

TIP FROM THE TEST KITCHEN
Round dumpling wrappers are thicker than square wonton wrappers, but you can use either.

BUTTERMILK PANCAKES
page 272

ULTIMATE EGGS & BREAKFASTS | 10

"Weekday breakfasts are always a rushed affair in my home, but on weekends we go all out. A plate full of fluffy scrambled eggs, crisp bacon, buttery pancakes and fresh seasonal fruit is the perfect way to ease into a lazy Saturday morning."

GILEAN WATTS ARTICLES EDITOR, FOOD

CLASSIC EGGS BENEDICT ㉚

You can enjoy this popular restaurant brunch dish—complete with crispy back bacon, golden egg yolks and buttery hollandaise—without leaving home.

HANDS-ON TIME
30 minutes

TOTAL TIME
30 minutes

MAKES
6 servings

INGREDIENTS

HOLLANDAISE SAUCE:

½ cup	butter
2	egg yolks
1 tbsp	cold water
1 tbsp	lemon juice
dash	hot pepper sauce
pinch	salt

EGGS BENEDICT:

1 tbsp	vinegar
12	eggs
24	slices back bacon
6	English muffins, halved and toasted

DIRECTIONS

HOLLANDAISE SAUCE: Cut 2 tsp of the butter into tiny pieces; refrigerate. In saucepan, melt remaining butter over medium heat; skim off foam. Reduce heat to low and keep warm.

In heatproof bowl, whisk egg yolks with cold water for 1 minute (mixture should appear pale and foamy). Place bowl over saucepan of barely simmering water; whisk until mixture is thickened, foamy and holds a ribbon for at least 6 seconds when whisk is lifted, about 5 minutes.

Remove from heat; whisk in cubed butter, 1 cube at a time, until melted. Slowly whisk in melted butter. Whisk in lemon juice, hot pepper sauce and salt. If necessary, gently whisk in up to 1 tbsp warm water, 1 tsp at a time, to reach desired consistency. Place bowl over saucepan of hot water (off heat) to keep warm.

EGGS BENEDICT: When hollandaise is done, in large saucepan or deep skillet, pour in enough water to come 2 to 3 inches (5 to 8 cm) up side. Bring to simmer over medium-high heat; add vinegar. Crack 1 egg into small cup; gently slide into simmering water. Working in small batches, repeat with remaining eggs, adding 1 at a time. Reduce heat to low; cook until whites are set but yolks are still soft, about 3 minutes per batch. Using slotted spoon, transfer to paper towel–lined baking sheet to dry.

While eggs are poaching, in large skillet, cook bacon over medium-high heat, turning once, until lightly browned, about 5 minutes.

ASSEMBLY: Top each English muffin half with 2 slices of the bacon and 1 egg. Spoon hollandaise sauce over each.

NUTRITIONAL INFORMATION, PER SERVING: about 563 cal, 35 g pro, 33 g total fat (15 g sat. fat), 30 g carb, 1 g fibre, 509 mg chol, 1,557 mg sodium, 465 mg potassium. % RDI: 15% calcium, 33% iron, 35% vit A, 2% vit C, 59% folate.

TIP FROM THE TEST KITCHEN
To keep poached eggs warm while you're cooking the remaining eggs, place them in a bowl of warm water. Dry them briefly on a paper towel and trim any loose bits off the edges before serving.

SAUSAGE AND EGG BAKE

HANDS-ON TIME 15 minutes

TOTAL TIME 45 minutes

MAKES 4 servings

INGREDIENTS

300 g	pork sausage (such as hot or mild Italian sausage, or breakfast sausage)
1	onion, chopped
⅔ cup	all-purpose flour
¼ tsp	each salt and pepper
3	eggs
⅔ cup	milk
¼ cup	chopped fresh parsley
1 tbsp	butter

DIRECTIONS

Remove casings from sausage. In nonstick skillet over medium heat, cook sausage and onion, breaking up with spoon, until sausage is no longer pink, about 10 minutes.

While sausage is cooking, in large bowl, whisk together flour, salt and pepper. Whisk eggs with milk; whisk into flour mixture until smooth. Stir in sausage mixture and parsley.

Grease 8-inch (2 L) square baking dish with butter; scrape in egg mixture. Bake in 375°F (190°C) oven until golden and toothpick inserted in centre comes out clean, about 25 minutes.

NUTRITIONAL INFORMATION, PER SERVING: about 394 cal, 20 g pro, 26 g total fat (9 g sat. fat), 21 g carb, 1 g fibre, 188 mg chol, 734 mg sodium, 373 mg potassium. % RDI: 9% calcium, 19% iron, 15% vit A, 10% vit C, 29% folate.

SHREDDED HASH BROWNS

HANDS-ON TIME 25 minutes

TOTAL TIME 3¾ hours

MAKES 6 servings

INGREDIENTS

4	russet potatoes (about 900 g total), peeled
¼ cup	butter
1	large onion, thinly sliced
½ tsp	salt
¼ tsp	pepper
¼ cup	whipping cream (35%)

DIRECTIONS

In saucepan of boiling salted water, cook potatoes until slightly softened, about 10 minutes. Drain and refrigerate until cold, about 2 hours. *(Make-ahead: Refrigerate for 24 hours.)*

Coarsely shred potatoes; set aside. In extra-large nonstick skillet, melt butter over medium heat; fry onion until softened, about 5 minutes.

Stir in potatoes, salt and pepper; cook, stirring several times, until crisp and golden, about 12 minutes.

Drizzle in cream; cook until absorbed, about 2 minutes. Remove from heat; let stand for 1 to 3 hours.

Fry over medium heat, turning several times, until crispy and browned, about 2 minutes.

NUTRITIONAL INFORMATION, PER SERVING: about 215 cal, 3 g pro, 11 g total fat (7 g sat. fat), 27 g carb, 2 g fibre, 33 mg chol, 540 mg sodium, 444 mg potassium. % RDI: 2% calcium, 4% iron, 10% vit A, 15% vit C, 7% folate.

NO-FAIL CHEDDAR SOUFFLÉ

Soufflés sound daunting, but this one is so easy to make. Serve it the second it comes out of the oven, when it's puffed and at its most impressive height.

HANDS-ON TIME
20 minutes

TOTAL TIME
1½ hours

MAKES
4 servings

INGREDIENTS

¼ cup	butter
2 tbsp	grated Parmesan cheese
⅓ cup	all-purpose flour
½ tsp	salt
¼ tsp	cayenne pepper
1½ cups	milk
6	egg yolks
1½ cups	shredded old Cheddar cheese
2 tbsp	chopped fresh chives
8	egg whites
¼ tsp	cream of tartar (optional)

DIRECTIONS

Grease 8- x 3¾-inch (2.5 L) soufflé dish with 1 tsp of the butter; sprinkle evenly with Parmesan. Set aside.

In saucepan, melt remaining butter over medium heat. Stir in flour, salt and cayenne pepper; cook, stirring, for 2 minutes. Whisk in milk in 3 additions; cook, whisking, until thick as paste, about 4 minutes. Remove from heat; whisk in egg yolks, Cheddar and chives. Transfer to large bowl; let cool for 10 minutes.

In separate large bowl, beat egg whites with cream of tartar (if using) until stiff peaks form. Fold one-third into cheese mixture; fold in remaining whites. Scrape into prepared soufflé dish.

Bake on rimmed baking sheet in 375°F (190°C) oven until puffed and golden, about 55 minutes. Serve immediately.

NUTRITIONAL INFORMATION, PER SERVING: about 494 cal, 27 g pro, 37 g total fat (20 g sat. fat), 14 g carb, trace fibre, 395 mg chol, 885 mg sodium. % RDI: 46% calcium, 13% iron, 42% vit A, 2% vit C, 30% folate.

TIP FROM THE TEST KITCHEN
Use a large serving spoon to scoop our portions of the soufflé. Start scooping at the edge of the dish, making sure everyone gets a piece of the crispy exterior and some of the soft interior. The soufflé will fall a bit as you start serving it, but that won't affect the taste at all.

TOAD IN THE HOLE

British banger-style sausages are the most authentic choice for this tasty puffed egg dish. If you can't find them, sweet Italian sausages make a nice substitute.

HANDS-ON TIME
15 minutes

TOTAL TIME
45 minutes

MAKES
6 servings

INGREDIENTS

2 tbsp	vegetable oil
6	pork sausages (about 565 g)
3	eggs
1 cup	all-purpose flour
¼ tsp	salt
1 cup	milk
2 tsp	chopped fresh rosemary

DIRECTIONS

In 9-inch (23 cm) cast-iron skillet, heat oil over medium-high heat; brown sausages. Transfer to 425°F (220°C) oven; cook, turning once, until no longer pink inside, 12 to 15 minutes.

Meanwhile, in bowl, whisk together eggs, flour and salt to form thick paste. Gradually whisk in milk until smooth; stir in rosemary. Pour over sausages.

Bake for 25 minutes, without opening oven door (escaping heat could cause puff to collapse). Bake until puffed, golden brown and crisp, about 5 minutes more.

NUTRITIONAL INFORMATION, PER SERVING: about 356 cal, 18 g pro, 30 g total fat (8 g sat. fat), 8 g carb, 0 g fibre, 146 mg chol, 773 mg sodium, 332 mg potassium. % RDI: 7% calcium, 10% iron, 6% vit A, 2% vit C, 7% folate.

TIP FROM THE TEST KITCHEN
If you don't have a cast-iron pan, brown the sausages in a regular skillet, and then transfer them to an 11- x 7-inch (2 L) baking dish before continuing with the recipe, as we did in our photo (opposite).

SMOKED SALMON AND GOAT CHEESE STRATA

HANDS-ON TIME
10 minutes

TOTAL TIME
1½ hours

MAKES
8 to 10 servings

Croissants create a buttery, bready base for this fancied-up strata. It's a wonderful dish to serve for brunch.

INGREDIENTS

10 cups	cubed croissants (6 or 7)
150 g	thinly sliced smoked salmon, torn or cut in pieces
115 g	soft goat cheese, crumbled
⅓ cup	thinly sliced shallots or red onion
2 tbsp	chopped fresh dill
4 tsp	capers, drained and rinsed
10	eggs
4 cups	milk
1 tbsp	Dijon mustard
¼ tsp	each salt and pepper

DIRECTIONS

In greased 13- x 9-inch (3 L) baking dish, toss together croissants, salmon, goat cheese, shallots, dill and capers. Whisk together eggs, milk, mustard, salt and pepper; pour over croissant mixture, pressing to soak. Let stand for 10 minutes.

Bake in 350°F (180°C) oven until puffed, golden and no longer jiggly in centre when gently shaken, about 1 hour. Let cool for 5 minutes before cutting.

NUTRITIONAL INFORMATION, PER EACH OF 10 SERVINGS: about 313 cal, 17 g pro, 17 g total fat (8 g sat. fat), 22 g carb, 1 g fibre, 225 mg chol, 620 mg sodium, 298 mg potassium. % RDI: 16% calcium, 13% iron, 22% vit A, 24% folate.

TIP FROM THE TEST KITCHEN
This dish is perfect for a busy brunch. Just follow the first paragraph as directed, and then cover and refrigerate the baking dish for up to 24 hours. Bake as directed.

GRUYÈRE AND BACON QUICHE

Quiche is always popular because it's versatile—it's welcome at breakfast, brunch, lunch or dinner. This classic version, also known as quiche Lorraine, has a creamy egg custard filling dotted with smoky bacon and nutty Gruyère.

HANDS-ON TIME
30 minutes

TOTAL TIME
3¼ hours

MAKES
8 servings

INGREDIENTS

PASTRY:

1½ cups	all-purpose flour
¼ tsp	salt
¼ cup	each cold butter and lard, cubed
1	egg yolk
1 tsp	vinegar or lemon juice
	ice water

FILLING:

8	strips bacon, chopped
4	eggs
1 cup	each milk and 10% cream
pinch	each salt and pepper
1 cup	shredded Gruyère or Swiss cheese
2	green onions, sliced

DIRECTIONS

PASTRY: In large bowl, whisk flour with salt. Using pastry blender or 2 knives, cut in butter and lard until in coarse crumbs with a few larger pieces.

In liquid measure, whisk egg yolk with vinegar; add enough ice water to make ⅓ cup. Drizzle over dry ingredients, stirring briskly with fork to form ragged dough. Press into disc. Wrap in plastic wrap and refrigerate until chilled, about 30 minutes. *(Make-ahead: Refrigerate for up to 3 days.)*

On lightly floured surface, roll out pastry to generous ⅛-inch (3 mm) thickness; fit into 9-inch (23 cm) pie plate or quiche dish. Trim edge to leave 1-inch (2.5 cm) overhang; fold under pastry rim and flute edge. Prick all over with fork. Refrigerate for 30 minutes.

Line pie shell with foil to cover completely; fill with pie weights or dried beans. Bake on bottom rack in 400°F (200°C) oven for 20 minutes. Remove weights and foil. Bake until light golden, 10 to 15 minutes. Let cool on rack.

FILLING: While pie shell is cooling, in small skillet, cook bacon, stirring often, over medium-high heat until browned and crisp, 6 to 8 minutes. Using slotted spoon, transfer to paper towel–lined plate; let drain.

In bowl, whisk together eggs, milk, cream, salt and pepper. Sprinkle bacon, Gruyère and green onions into pie shell; pour egg mixture over top.

Bake in 375°F (190°C) oven until filling is set and knife inserted in centre comes out clean, 55 to 60 minutes, covering pastry rim with foil if browning too much.

Let cool in pan on rack for 10 minutes before serving.

NUTRITIONAL INFORMATION, PER SERVING: about 356 cal, 14 g pro, 25 g total fat (12 g sat. fat), 19 g carb, 1 g fibre, 168 mg chol, 348 mg sodium, 199 mg potassium. % RDI: 21% calcium, 11% iron, 17% vit A, 2% vit C, 28% folate.

CLASSIC CRÊPES

Master the (very simple!) art of crêpe making, and you'll have endless possibilities, both savoury and sweet. The thin unleavened pancakes are an ideal base for everything from veggies and meat to fruit and chocolate.

HANDS-ON TIME
30 minutes

TOTAL TIME
1½ hours

MAKES
about 8 crêpes

INGREDIENTS

1⅓ cups	all-purpose flour
¼ tsp	salt
4	eggs
1½ cups	milk
¼ cup	butter, melted

DIRECTIONS

In bowl, whisk flour with salt. Whisk together eggs, milk and half of the butter; pour over flour mixture and whisk until smooth. Strain through fine-mesh sieve into clean bowl. Cover and refrigerate for 1 hour. *(Make-ahead: Refrigerate for up to 24 hours.)*

Heat 10-inch (25 cm) nonstick skillet or crêpe pan over medium heat. Brush skillet with some of the remaining butter. Pour scant ⅓ cup of the batter into centre of skillet, tilting and swirling to coat bottom. **PHOTO A**

Cook, flipping when edge begins to curl away from skillet, until set and edge is light golden, about 90 seconds. **PHOTO B**

Transfer to plate; cover and keep warm. Repeat with remaining batter, brushing skillet with some of the remaining butter between crêpes. *(Make-ahead: Layer between parchment paper and wrap in plastic wrap; refrigerate for up to 24 hours or freeze in airtight container for up to 1 month. Reheat in microwave or remove plastic wrap, cover in foil and heat in oven until warm.)*

NUTRITIONAL INFORMATION, PER CRÊPE: about 146 cal, 6 g pro, 6 g total fat (3 g sat. fat), 16 g carb, 1 g fibre, 97 mg chol, 133 mg sodium, 103 mg potassium. % RDI: 6% calcium, 9% iron, 9% vit A, 19% folate.

VARIATION

CLASSIC CHOCOLATE CRÊPES

Reduce flour to 1 cup. Add ¼ cup cocoa powder, sifted, and 3 tbsp granulated sugar to flour mixture. Continue with recipe.

TIP FROM THE TEST KITCHEN
Savoury crêpes are delicious topped with Basic White Sauce (page 328).

BUTTERMILK PANCAKES 🕙 ◔

HANDS-ON TIME 20 minutes

TOTAL TIME 20 minutes

MAKES about 14 pancakes

INGREDIENTS

1½ cups	all-purpose flour
1 tsp	baking powder
1 tsp	baking soda
¼ tsp	salt
1¾ cups	buttermilk
1	egg
2 tbsp	butter, melted
2 tsp	vanilla
1 tbsp	vegetable oil

DIRECTIONS

In large bowl, whisk together flour, baking powder, baking soda and salt. Whisk together buttermilk, egg, butter and vanilla; pour over flour mixture and whisk until combined but still slightly lumpy.

Lightly brush large nonstick skillet or griddle with some of the oil; heat over medium heat. Working in batches and using scant ¼ cup per pancake, pour in batter; spread slightly to form pancakes. Cook until bubbles appear on top, about 3 minutes. Flip and cook until bottom is golden brown, about 1 minute. Transfer to rimmed baking sheet; cover and keep warm in 250°F (120°C) oven.

NUTRITIONAL INFORMATION, PER PANCAKE: about 91 cal, 3 g pro, 4 g total fat (1 g sat. fat), 11 g carb, trace fibre, 19 mg chol, 201 mg sodium, 65 mg potassium. % RDI: 4% calcium, 5% iron, 2% vit A, 10% folate.

VARIATION

MULTIGRAIN BUTTERMILK PANCAKES

Replace all-purpose flour with the same amount of multigrain flour.

JOHNNYCAKES 🕙 ◔

HANDS-ON TIME 30 minutes

TOTAL TIME 30 minutes

MAKES 10 to 12 cakes

INGREDIENTS

¾ cup	all-purpose flour
⅔ cup	cornmeal
2 tsp	baking powder
½ tsp	salt
½ cup	warm milk
2 tbsp	unsalted butter, melted
2	eggs
2 tbsp	vegetable oil

DIRECTIONS

In large bowl, whisk together flour, cornmeal, baking powder and salt. Whisk in milk, butter and eggs just until smooth.

Heat griddle or large cast-iron skillet over medium heat; brush with some of the oil. Working in batches and using 2 tbsp for each, pour batter onto griddle. Cook until bottoms are golden, about 2 minutes. Flip and cook until bottoms are golden, 1 to 2 minutes more. Transfer to rimmed baking sheet; cover and keep warm in 250°F (120°C) oven.

NUTRITIONAL INFORMATION, PER EACH OF 12 CAKES: about 112 cal, 3 g pro, 5 g total fat (2 g sat. fat), 13 g carb, 1 g fibre, 37 mg chol, 161 mg sodium, 49 mg potassium. % RDI: 4% calcium, 4% iron, 4% vit A, 14% folate.

WHOLE GRAIN GLUTEN-FREE BUTTERMILK PANCAKES ③⓪ ◑

Fluffy gluten-free pancakes? They are possible! These wholesome pancakes have a rich, nutty flavour and a light texture that's so appealing.

HANDS-ON TIME
30 minutes

TOTAL TIME
30 minutes

MAKES
12 pancakes

INGREDIENTS

1¼ cups	light buckwheat flour
¼ cup	cornmeal
¼ cup	brown rice flour
¼ cup	tapioca flour
1 tbsp	granulated sugar
1½ tsp	baking soda
1 tsp	baking powder
¼ tsp	salt
pinch	nutmeg
1½ cups	buttermilk
2	eggs
1 tsp	vanilla
2 tbsp	vegetable oil

DIRECTIONS

In large bowl, whisk together buckwheat flour, cornmeal, brown rice flour, tapioca flour, sugar, baking soda, baking powder, salt and nutmeg.

Whisk together buttermilk, eggs and vanilla. Stir into flour mixture just until combined. Let stand for 5 minutes. (Batter will be thick and stretchy.)

In large nonstick skillet, heat 1 tbsp of the oil over medium heat; working in batches and using ⅓ cup per pancake, drop batter into pan. Cook, turning once and adding remaining oil as necessary, until puffed and golden, about 5 minutes. Transfer to rimmed baking sheet; cover and keep warm in 250°F (120°C) oven.

NUTRITIONAL INFORMATION, PER PANCAKE: about 131 cal, 4 g pro, 4 g total fat (1 g sat. fat), 19 g carb, 1 g fibre, 33 mg chol, 270 mg sodium, 152 mg potassium. % RDI: 6% calcium, 6% iron, 2% vit A, 5% folate.

WHOLESOME WHOLE GRAIN WAFFLES ○

Start your day off deliciously with these slightly sweet whole grain waffles. You can find 12-grain flour in most bulk food stores. Freeze leftover waffles and reheat them in the toaster for a quick, satisfying weekday breakfast.

HANDS-ON TIME
15 minutes

TOTAL TIME
1¼ hours

MAKES
about 12 waffles

INGREDIENTS

2¼ cups	12-grain flour
1 tbsp	granulated sugar
2 tsp	baking powder
1 tsp	baking soda
¼ tsp	salt
3	eggs, separated
2¼ cups	buttermilk
¼ cup	unsalted butter, melted
2 tbsp	vegetable oil

DIRECTIONS

In large bowl, whisk together flour, sugar, baking powder, baking soda and salt; set aside.

Beat egg whites until soft peaks form; set aside.

Whisk together egg yolks, buttermilk and butter; pour over flour mixture, stirring to combine. Fold in egg whites just until combined.

Heat waffle iron; brush lightly with some of the oil. Pour in about ⅓ cup of the batter for each waffle, spreading to edge. Close lid and cook until steam stops and waffles are crisp and golden, 4 to 6 minutes. Serve warm. *(Make-ahead: Individually wrap waffles in plastic wrap; freeze for up to 3 months. Reheat in toaster.)*

NUTRITIONAL INFORMATION, PER WAFFLE: about 196 cal, 7 g pro, 10 g total fat (4 g sat. fat), 20 g carb, 3 g fibre, 60 mg chol, 260 mg sodium, 101 mg potassium. % RDI: 11% calcium, 11% iron, 6% vit A, 4% folate.

VARIATION

WHOLESOME WHOLE GRAIN HAM AND CHEESE WAFFLES

Omit salt. Stir 115 g thinly sliced shaved Black Forest ham and 1 cup shredded old Cheddar cheese into batter.

BACON CHEDDAR CORNMEAL WAFFLES

HANDS-ON TIME
15 minutes

TOTAL TIME
50 minutes

MAKES
6 large waffles

Serve these savoury waffles with scrambled eggs for brunch, or enjoy them with our Extra-Crispy Fried Chicken (page 135).

INGREDIENTS

1½ cups	all-purpose flour
¾ cup	cornmeal
1 tbsp	granulated sugar
2½ tsp	baking powder
½ tsp	baking soda
¼ tsp	salt
1 cup	shredded old Cheddar cheese
6	strips bacon, cooked and crumbled
1	green onion, finely chopped
3	eggs
2¼ cups	buttermilk
¼ cup	unsalted butter, melted
2 tbsp	vegetable oil

DIRECTIONS

In large bowl, whisk together flour, cornmeal, sugar, baking powder, baking soda and salt. Stir in Cheddar, bacon and green onion.

In separate bowl, whisk together eggs, buttermilk and butter; pour over flour mixture and stir just until combined. Let stand for 10 minutes.

Heat waffle iron; brush lightly with some of the oil. Pour in about ½ cup of the batter for each waffle, spreading to edge. Close lid and cook until steam stops and waffles are crisp and golden, 4 to 6 minutes. Serve warm.

NUTRITIONAL INFORMATION, PER WAFFLE: about 496 cal, 19 g pro, 26 g total fat (12 g sat. fat), 46 g carb, 2 g fibre, 147 mg chol, 689 mg sodium, 324 mg potassium. % RDI: 31% calcium, 16% iron, 18% vit A, 2% vit C, 53% folate.

VARIATION

BACON CHEDDAR CORNMEAL PANCAKES

Prepare batter as directed. Lightly brush large nonstick skillet or griddle with some of the oil; heat over medium heat. Working in batches and using about ¼ cup per pancake, pour in batter; spread slightly to form pancake. Cook until bubbles break on top but do not fill in, 2 minutes. Flip and cook until bottom is golden brown, 30 to 60 seconds.

TIP FROM THE TEST KITCHEN
A nice side with these waffles is roasted cherry tomatoes. In a small roasting pan, toss cherry tomatoes with a little extra-virgin olive oil, salt and pepper. Roast them in a 425°F (220°C) oven until they are softened, about 30 minutes.

FRENCH TOAST ○
WITH CARAMELIZED BANANAS AND PECANS

*No need to serve extra maple syrup at the table with this sweet French toast—
it's already cooked into the topping.*

HANDS-ON TIME
35 minutes

TOTAL TIME
35 minutes

MAKES
6 to 8 servings

INGREDIENTS

FRENCH TOAST:

6	eggs
1½ cups	5% cream or milk
2 tbsp	maple syrup
1 tsp	cinnamon
1 tsp	vanilla
¼ tsp	salt
1	loaf (450 g) egg bread
2 tbsp	butter

CARAMELIZED BANANAS AND PECANS:

2 tbsp	butter
6	firm ripe bananas, halved crosswise and lengthwise
¾ cup	maple syrup
½ cup	packed brown sugar
¼ cup	corn syrup
¼ cup	dark rum (optional)
⅓ cup	chopped pecans, toasted

DIRECTIONS

FRENCH TOAST: In large bowl, whisk together eggs, cream, maple syrup, cinnamon, vanilla and salt. Cut egg bread into ¾-inch (2 cm) thick slices; dip into egg mixture until soaked.

In large skillet, melt 1 tbsp of the butter over medium heat; working in batches and adding more butter as needed, cook slices, turning once, until golden, about 3 minutes. Transfer to 2 rimmed baking sheets; bake on top and bottom racks in 350°F (180°C) oven until puffed and heated through, about 8 minutes.

CARAMELIZED BANANAS AND PECANS: While French toast is baking, in large nonstick skillet, melt half of the butter over medium-high heat; fry half of the bananas, turning once, until golden and tender, about 3 minutes. Transfer to plate. Repeat with remaining butter and bananas.

In same skillet, bring maple syrup, brown sugar, corn syrup, and rum (if using) to boil over medium-high heat; reduce heat and simmer for 2 minutes. Stir in bananas; simmer for 1 minute. Spoon over French toast; sprinkle with pecans.

NUTRITIONAL INFORMATION, PER EACH OF 8 SERVINGS: about 596 cal, 13 g pro, 19 g total fat (7 g sat. fat), 96 g carb, 3 g fibre, 199 mg chol, 497 mg sodium, 570 mg potassium. % RDI: 17% calcium, 23% iron, 12% vit A, 8% vit C, 34% folate.

BUTTERY POUND CAKE
page 291

ULTIMATE QUICK BREADS | 11

"When I first started baking, quick breads were my way of experimenting in the kitchen without having to test the boundaries of my patience."

IRENE FONG SENIOR FOOD SPECIALIST

OUR FINEST BUTTERMILK SCONES ◉ ◐

Scones, also known as tea biscuits, are a sweet indulgence you can enjoy any time of day. In a hurry? Pat out the dough and cut it into simple squares or triangles. When you're not pressed for time, cut out rounds, rerolling the scraps.

HANDS-ON TIME
15 minutes

TOTAL TIME
40 minutes

MAKES
12 scones

INGREDIENTS

2½ cups	all-purpose flour
2 tbsp	granulated sugar
2½ tsp	baking powder
½ tsp	each baking soda and salt
½ cup	cold butter, cubed
1 cup	buttermilk
1	egg

DIRECTIONS

In large bowl, whisk together flour, sugar, baking powder, baking soda and salt. Using pastry blender or 2 knives, cut in butter until crumbly. Whisk buttermilk with egg; pour over flour mixture. Using fork, stir to make soft ragged dough.

With lightly floured hands, press dough into ball. On floured surface, knead gently 10 times. Pat out into 10- x 7-inch (25 x 18 cm) rectangle; trim edges to straighten.

Cut rectangle into 6 squares; cut each diagonally in half. Place on parchment paper–lined rimless baking sheet.

Bake in 400°F (200°C) oven until golden, 18 to 20 minutes. Transfer to rack; let cool. *(Make-ahead: Store in airtight container at room temperature for up to 1 day or wrap each in plastic wrap and freeze in airtight container for up to 2 weeks.)*

NUTRITIONAL INFORMATION, PER SCONE: about 189 cal, 4 g pro, 9 g total fat (5 g sat. fat), 23 g carb, 1 g fibre, 37 mg chol, 289 mg sodium. % RDI: 6% calcium, 9% iron, 8% vit A, 26% folate.

VARIATIONS

MULTIGRAIN BUTTERMILK SCONES

Replace all-purpose flour with same amount of multigrain flour.

GLAZED APRICOT ALMOND SCONES

Sprinkle ¾ cup chopped dried apricots over ingredients just before stirring together. Shape and bake as directed; let cool completely. Stir together 1 cup icing sugar, 2 tbsp milk, dash of almond extract and up to 1 tsp water, if necessary, to make thin icing; drizzle over scones. Sprinkle with ¼ cup toasted sliced almonds.

DRIED FRUIT AND LEMON SCONES

Add 2 tsp grated lemon zest to flour mixture. Sprinkle ½ cup dried currants, raisins, dried blueberries, dried cranberries, chopped dried cherries or chopped prunes over ingredients just before stirring together. Shape and bake as directed.

GLAZED LEMON POPPY SEED SCONES

Add 1 tbsp grated lemon zest and 4 tsp poppy seeds to flour mixture. Shape and bake as directed; let cool completely. Stir together 1 cup icing sugar, 2 tbsp lemon juice and up to 1 tsp water, if necessary, to make thin icing; drizzle over scones.

CHEESE SCONES

Omit sugar. Add ¼ tsp cayenne pepper to flour mixture. Sprinkle 1 cup shredded old Cheddar or aged Gouda cheese over ingredients just before stirring together. Shape as directed. Brush scones with 1 egg, beaten; sprinkle with ½ cup more shredded old Cheddar or aged Gouda cheese. Bake as directed.

APPLE-CHEDDAR DROP BISCUITS ㉚ ◗

HANDS-ON TIME 15 minutes

TOTAL TIME 30 minutes

MAKES about 12 biscuits

INGREDIENTS

1¾ cups	all-purpose flour
4 tsp	baking powder
1 tbsp	granulated sugar
½ tsp	salt
¼ cup	cold butter, cubed
1 cup	shredded extra-old Cheddar cheese
1 cup	grated peeled Cortland or Spartan apple (about 1)
2	green onions, minced
¾ cup	milk

DIRECTIONS

In large bowl, whisk together flour, baking powder, sugar and salt. Using pastry blender or 2 knives, cut in butter until mixture resembles coarse crumbs. Stir in Cheddar, apple and green onions. Using fork, stir in milk to form ragged dough.

Drop by ¼ cup, 1½ inches (4 cm) apart, onto parchment paper–lined rimmed baking sheet. Bake in 425°F (220°C) oven until browned, 13 to 15 minutes.

NUTRITIONAL INFORMATION, PER BISCUIT: about 157 cal, 5 g pro, 8 g total fat (5 g sat. fat), 17 g carb, 1 g fibre, 21 mg chol, 290 mg sodium, 69 mg potassium. % RDI: 12% calcium, 8% iron, 7% vit A, 2% vit C, 14% folate.

TIP FROM THE TEST KITCHEN
Even if you're a fan of mild Cheddar, you'll want to choose a shaper variety for these biscuits. Mild cheese won't be flavourful enough once it's mixed with the other ingredients.

PERFECT POPOVERS ㉚

HANDS-ON TIME 10 minutes

TOTAL TIME 40 minutes

MAKES 8 servings

INGREDIENTS

2	eggs
1 cup	milk
1 cup	all-purpose flour
½ tsp	salt

DIRECTIONS

In bowl, beat eggs with milk; stir in flour and salt until blended but still lumpy. Pour into 8 greased muffin cups, filling three-quarters full.

Place pan on centre rack in cold oven. Set oven to 450°F (230°C); bake until golden brown, 20 to 25 minutes.

Using skewer, puncture each popover. Turn off oven and let popovers stand in oven until crisp, about 10 minutes.

NUTRITIONAL INFORMATION, PER SERVING: about 90 cal, 4 g pro, 2 g total fat (1 g sat. fat), 13 g carb, 1 g fibre, 49 mg chol, 171 mg sodium, 78 mg potassium. % RDI: 4% calcium, 6% iron, 3% vit A, 18% folate.

APPLE-CHEDDAR DROP BISCUITS opposite, left

YORKSHIRE PUDDING

This traditional partner to roast beef is just as delicious made in one big pan as it is in individual portions. Using roast drippings will give the pudding the richest flavour, but butter is an easy and delicious alternative.

HANDS-ON TIME
10 minutes

TOTAL TIME
1¼ hours

MAKES
6 to 8 servings

INGREDIENTS

1⅓ cups	all-purpose flour
1 cup	homogenized or 2% milk
4	eggs
⅓ cup	roast beef drippings or butter (or a combination)

DIRECTIONS

In large bowl, whisk flour with milk. Whisk eggs until frothy; whisk into milk mixture. Whisk in 1 cup water until bubbly. Let stand for 30 to 60 minutes.

Meanwhile, heat 13- x 9-inch (33 x 23 cm) roasting pan or baking dish in 400°F (200°C) oven until hot. Add drippings; heat until bubbly (if using butter, do not let brown).

Whisk batter again until large bubbles appear. Pour into hot pan; bake for 20 minutes. Reduce heat to 350°F (180°C); bake until pudding is golden brown and firm but springy to the touch in centre, 15 to 20 minutes.

NUTRITIONAL INFORMATION, PER EACH OF 8 SERVINGS: about 163 cal, 8 g pro, 7 g total fat (3 g sat. fat), 18 g carb, 1 g fibre, 104 mg chol, 58 mg sodium. % RDI: 5% calcium, 10% iron, 4% vit A, 26% folate.

TIP FROM THE TEST KITCHEN
If you make your own beef stock (page 45), save the fat you skim off the top and freeze it in an airtight container for up to 3 months. That way, you can make this authentic pudding anytime, without having to make a roast.

SWEET CORN SPOONBREAD ◖

As the name implies, this soft version of corn bread is eaten with a spoon.
Like a soufflé, this spoonbread puffs up in the oven and quickly deflates when
you take it out, so serve it as soon as it's ready.

HANDS-ON TIME
20 minutes

TOTAL TIME
1 hour

MAKES
8 to 10 servings

INGREDIENTS

3 cups	fresh or frozen corn kernels
2½ cups	milk
¾ cup	whipping cream (35%)
¼ cup	butter, cubed
1½ tsp	each salt and granulated sugar
¼ tsp	pepper
1 cup	cornmeal
4	eggs, separated
¼ tsp	cream of tartar

DIRECTIONS

In large saucepan, combine 2 cups of the corn, the milk, cream and butter; bring to boil. Remove from heat; let stand for 15 minutes.

In blender or using immersion blender, purée corn mixture until smooth; strain through fine-mesh sieve into bowl, pressing solids to extract liquid. Discard solids.

Return corn mixture to saucepan; stir in salt, sugar and pepper. Bring to boil. Reduce heat to low; whisking constantly, add cornmeal in slow steady stream. Cook, whisking, until bubbly, 1 to 2 minutes. Scrape into bowl; stir in remaining corn. Let cool to room temperature.

Stir egg yolks into corn mixture until well combined. Beat egg whites with cream of tartar until stiff peaks form; stir one-quarter into cornmeal mixture to loosen. Fold in remaining whites. Scrape into greased 6-cup (1.5 L) round casserole dish.

Bake in 400°F (200°C) oven until puffed and golden, edges are firm and centre barely jiggles when dish is shaken, 40 to 42 minutes. Serve immediately.

NUTRITIONAL INFORMATION, PER EACH OF 10 SERVINGS: about 264 cal, 7 g pro, 15 g total fat (8 g sat. fat), 27 g carb, 2 g fibre, 117 mg chol, 446 mg sodium, 262 mg potassium. % RDI: 9% calcium, 5% iron, 19% vit A, 5% vit C, 16% folate.

JALAPEÑO GREEN ONION ALE CORN BREAD

This sweet-and-spicy corn bread is amazing with barbecued meat and chili. If you love heat, add another jalapeño pepper.

HANDS-ON TIME
10 minutes

TOTAL TIME
1 hour

MAKES
1 loaf, 10 to 12 slices

INGREDIENTS

1 cup	cornmeal
1 cup	all-purpose flour
1 tsp	baking powder
½ tsp	each baking soda and salt
½ cup	buttermilk
½ cup	brown ale or pilsner beer
½ cup	butter, melted
⅓ cup	granulated sugar
2	eggs
1	jalapeño pepper, seeded and diced
4	green onions, chopped

DIRECTIONS

In large bowl, whisk together cornmeal, flour, baking powder, baking soda and salt. Whisk together buttermilk, ale, butter, sugar and eggs; whisk into flour mixture. Fold in jalapeño pepper and green onions; scrape into parchment paper–lined 8- x 4-inch (1.5 L) loaf pan.

Bake in 375°F (190°C) oven until golden and toothpick inserted in centre comes out clean, about 40 minutes.

Turn out onto rack; let cool slightly. Serve warm or at room temperature.

NUTRITIONAL INFORMATION, PER EACH OF 12 SLICES: about 192 cal, 4 g pro, 9 g total fat (5 g sat. fat), 24 g carb, 1 g fibre, 52 mg chol, 248 mg sodium, 81 mg potassium. % RDI: 3% calcium, 6% iron, 9% vit A, 2% vit C, 20% folate.

TIP FROM THE TEST KITCHEN
You can also make an ale-free version of this bread; simply substitute the same amount of buttermilk for the ale.

SIMPLE SODA BREAD

A mix of baking powder, baking soda and buttermilk makes this bread rise.
Bonus: It doesn't require any time-consuming kneading.

HANDS-ON TIME
10 minutes

TOTAL TIME
45 minutes

MAKES
4 servings

INGREDIENTS

1 cup	all-purpose flour
1 cup	whole wheat flour (see tip, below)
1 tbsp	granulated sugar
2 tsp	baking powder
½ tsp	baking soda
¼ tsp	salt
¼ cup	dried currants (optional)
¾ cup	buttermilk
3 tbsp	butter, melted
1	egg

DIRECTIONS

In large bowl, whisk together all-purpose flour, whole wheat flour, sugar, baking powder, baking soda and salt; stir in currants (if using).

Whisk together buttermilk, butter and egg; pour over flour mixture, tossing with fork to form sticky dough.

Scrape onto floured surface; gently knead 10 times. Transfer to parchment paper–lined rimmed baking sheet; press into 7-inch (18 cm) round. Using sharp knife, score top into 8 wedges.

Bake in 350°F (180°C) oven until cake tester inserted in centre comes out clean, about 35 minutes.

NUTRITIONAL INFORMATION, PER SERVING: about 354 cal, 11 g pro, 12 g total fat (6 g sat. fat), 49 g carb, 4 g fibre, 73 mg chol, 579 mg sodium, 211 mg potassium. % RDI: 13% calcium, 20% iron, 10% vit A, 31% folate.

TIP FROM THE TEST KITCHEN
Whole grain flours, such as whole wheat, naturally contain oils that can go rancid when stored at room temperature. To keep your whole grain flour fresh, store it in a tightly sealed airtight container in the freezer.

CHOCOLATE CHUNK CINNAMON SWIRL LOAF ⬭

This indulgent loaf blends semisweet chocolate chunks with a surprising kick of cinnamon. The spiced swirl melts into a gooey interior and the streusel topping adds a satisfying crunch.

HANDS-ON TIME
30 minutes

TOTAL TIME
2½ hours

MAKES
1 loaf, 12 slices

INGREDIENTS

CINNAMON STREUSEL:

⅓ cup	packed brown sugar
⅓ cup	all-purpose flour
¼ tsp	cinnamon
¼ cup	cold butter, cubed

BATTER:

½ cup	butter, softened
1 cup	granulated sugar
2	eggs
2 tsp	vanilla
2¼ cups	all-purpose flour
1 tsp	baking powder
½ tsp	each baking soda, cinnamon and salt
¾ cup	buttermilk
225 g	semisweet chocolate (8 oz), chopped

CINNAMON SWIRL:

3 tbsp	granulated sugar
2 tbsp	butter, melted
2 tsp	cinnamon

DIRECTIONS

CINNAMON STREUSEL: In small bowl, whisk together brown sugar, flour and cinnamon. Using pastry blender or 2 knives, cut in butter until crumbly. Set aside.

BATTER: In large bowl, beat butter with sugar until fluffy. Beat in eggs, 1 at a time. Beat in vanilla.

Whisk together flour, baking powder, baking soda, cinnamon and salt; stir into butter mixture, alternating with buttermilk, making 3 additions of flour mixture and 2 of buttermilk. Fold in chocolate.

CINNAMON SWIRL: Stir together sugar, butter and cinnamon to form paste. Set aside.

ASSEMBLY: Scrape half of the batter into parchment paper–lined 9- x 5-inch (2 L) loaf pan, spreading to edges. Spoon half of the Cinnamon Swirl over top; using butter knife, gently swirl to create marble effect. Scrape remaining batter over top, spreading to edges; gently swirl in remaining Cinnamon Swirl. Top with Cinnamon Streusel.

Bake in 350°F (180°C) oven until cake tester inserted in centre comes out with a few moist crumbs clinging, 65 to 70 minutes.

Let cool in pan for 20 minutes; turn out onto rack and let cool completely. Peel off parchment paper.

NUTRITIONAL INFORMATION, PER SLICE: about 427 cal, 6 g pro, 21 g total fat (12 g sat. fat), 58 g carb, 2 g fibre, 67 mg chol, 299 mg sodium, 144 mg potassium. % RDI: 5% calcium, 16% iron, 13% vit A, 22% folate.

BUTTERY POUND CAKE

*To achieve the fluffiest texture, bring the refrigerated ingredients for this
loaf to room temperature before adding them to the batter. Serve slices of
this quick loaf with jam, berries or a dollop of lemon curd.*

HANDS-ON TIME
25 minutes

TOTAL TIME
2¾ hours

MAKES
1 loaf, 16 slices

INGREDIENTS

1 cup	unsalted butter, softened
1¼ cups	granulated sugar
4	eggs, at room temperature
3 tbsp	milk, at room temperature
1 tbsp	vanilla
½ tsp	salt
1¾ cups	all-purpose flour, sifted

DIRECTIONS

In large bowl, beat butter with sugar until light, fluffy and pale yellow,
about 5 minutes. Add 1 of the eggs; beat for 2 minutes, scraping down
side of bowl. Repeat with remaining eggs, adding 1 at a time. Beat in
milk, vanilla and salt until combined (mixture may appear curdled).

Add half of the flour; stir gently just until combined. Repeat with
remaining flour. Scrape into parchment paper–lined 8- x 4-inch (1.5 L)
loaf pan, smoothing top.

Bake in 325°F (160°C) oven until top is golden and cake tester inserted in
centre comes out clean, about 1¼ hours.

Let cool in pan for 20 minutes. Turn out onto rack; let cool completely.
Peel off parchment paper. *(Make-ahead: Wrap in plastic wrap; store for up
to 2 days.)*

NUTRITIONAL INFORMATION, PER SLICE: about 232 cal, 3 g pro, 13 g total fat (8 g
sat. fat), 26 g carb, trace fibre, 76 mg chol, 90 mg sodium, 35 mg potassium. % RDI:
1% calcium, 6% iron, 13% vit A, 12% folate.

VARIATION

BLUEBERRY LEMON BUTTERY POUND CAKE

Set aside 1 tbsp of the flour before beginning. Add 2 tbsp finely grated
lemon zest when beating in milk, vanilla and salt. Toss 1½ cups fresh
wild blueberries with reserved flour; fold into batter. Bake as directed.

TIP FROM THE TEST KITCHEN

To keep the crust from overbrowning, use a light-coloured
loaf pan. Darker pans tend to impart a deeper colouring
to buttery baked goods.

TENDER BANANA BREAD

Trust us, this is the best banana bread you'll ever make. It uses the surprising (and mysteriously effective) technique of "marinating" the bananas in a buttermilk and baking soda blend to deliver a moist, buttery, sweet loaf that's chock-full of banana flavour.

HANDS-ON TIME
15 minutes

TOTAL TIME
1¼ hours

MAKES
1 loaf, 12 to 16 slices

INGREDIENTS

3	ripe bananas, mashed
½ cup	buttermilk
1½ tsp	baking soda
2¼ cups	all-purpose flour
1½ tsp	baking powder
¼ tsp	salt
¾ cup	unsalted butter, softened
1 cup	packed brown sugar
1	egg
1 tsp	vanilla

DIRECTIONS

Stir together bananas, buttermilk and baking soda. Let stand for 5 minutes.

Meanwhile, whisk together flour, baking powder and salt; set aside.

In large bowl, beat butter with brown sugar until combined; beat in egg, vanilla and banana mixture. Stir in flour mixture until combined; scrape into greased 9- x 5-inch (2 L) loaf pan.

Bake in 350°F (180°C) oven until cake tester inserted in centre comes out clean, 60 to 70 minutes.

Let cool in pan for 15 minutes. Turn out onto rack; let cool completely.

NUTRITIONAL INFORMATION, PER EACH OF 16 SLICES: about 220 cal, 3 g pro, 10 g total fat (6 g sat. fat), 32 g carb, 1 g fibre, 35 mg chol, 200 mg sodium, 133 mg potassium. % RDI: 4% calcium, 8% iron, 8% vit A, 2% vit C, 14% folate.

VARIATIONS

CHOCOLATE CHIP BANANA BREAD

Stir 1 cup semisweet chocolate chips into flour mixture.

CINNAMON BANANA BREAD

Whisk ½ tsp cinnamon into flour mixture.

TIP FROM THE TEST KITCHEN
As much as we love the taste of butter in the Test Kitchen, we don't use it to grease pans. The milk solids cause it to burn quickly. Instead, choose an oil or fat with a higher smoke point for best results.

CHOCOLATE-GLAZED CHOCOLATE CHIP MUFFINS

The velvety chocolate topping makes these muffins simply irresistible. This is a great recipe to make with kids—the steps are easy and will introduce them to baking basics.

HANDS-ON TIME
25 minutes

TOTAL TIME
1 hour

MAKES
12 muffins

INGREDIENTS

MUFFINS:

½ cup	butter, softened
1 cup	granulated sugar
2	eggs
1 cup	milk
1¾ cups	all-purpose flour
2 tsp	baking powder
¼ tsp	salt
1 cup	chocolate chips

GLAZE:

85 g	semisweet chocolate, chopped
3 tbsp	whipping cream (35%)

DIRECTIONS

MUFFINS: In bowl, beat butter with sugar until light and fluffy, about 3 minutes. Beat in eggs, 1 at a time. Gradually stir in milk (mixture may appear curdled).

In large bowl, whisk together flour, baking powder and salt; make well in centre. Pour milk mixture into well and stir just until moistened (mixture will appear separated). Fold in chocolate chips.

Spoon into 12 large paper-lined muffin cups. Bake in 350°F (180°C) oven until tops are firm to the touch, 22 to 25 minutes. Transfer muffins to rack; let cool completely.

GLAZE: In small saucepan, melt semisweet chocolate with cream over medium-low heat until smooth; let cool for 10 minutes. Spread over tops of muffins.

NUTRITIONAL INFORMATION, PER MUFFIN: about 335 cal, 5 g pro, 17 g total fat (10 g sat. fat), 45 g carb, 2 g fibre, 58 mg chol, 175 mg sodium, 145 mg potassium. % RDI: 6% calcium, 11% iron, 10% vit A, 20% folate.

BANANA, DATE AND OAT BRAN MUFFINS ◔

When you spoon the batter for these muffins into the cups, they will be really full but won't overflow. Toasting the oat bran brings out its earthy, warm, nutty flavour. If you don't like dates, substitute dried figs.

HANDS-ON TIME
15 minutes

TOTAL TIME
40 minutes

MAKES
12 muffins

INGREDIENTS

¾ cup	oat bran
1¼ cups	all-purpose flour
2¼ tsp	baking powder
½ tsp	cinnamon
¼ tsp	each baking soda and salt
1⅓ cups	mashed bananas
⅔ cup	finely chopped dates
½ cup	almond butter or natural peanut butter
½ cup	milk
⅓ cup	light-tasting olive oil or safflower oil
⅓ cup	liquid honey
1	egg

DIRECTIONS

In dry skillet, toast oat bran over medium heat until lightly browned, about 3 minutes. Transfer to bowl; let cool. Whisk in flour, baking powder, cinnamon, baking soda and salt.

In large bowl, stir together bananas, dates, almond butter, milk, oil and honey; stir in egg. Stir in flour mixture just until combined. Spoon into 12 paper-lined or greased muffin cups.

Bake in 375°F (190°C) oven until tops are firm to the touch, about 25 minutes. Transfer muffins to rack; let cool. *(Make-ahead: Store in airtight container for up to 3 days.)*

NUTRITIONAL INFORMATION, PER MUFFIN: about 272 cal, 5 g pro, 13 g total fat (2 g sat. fat), 38 g carb, 3 g fibre, 16 mg chol, 143 mg sodium, 308 mg potassium. % RDI: 7% calcium, 12% iron, 1% vit A, 3% vit C, 19% folate.

CRUNCHY-TOP BLUEBERRY MUFFINS

There's no need to stop at the coffee shop for your daily muffin when these are so simple to make and take with you. The combination of orange zest and almonds on top adds crunch and an extra citrusy zing.

HANDS-ON TIME
15 minutes

TOTAL TIME
1¼ hours

MAKES
12 muffins

INGREDIENTS

MUFFINS:

2 cups	all-purpose flour
¾ cup	granulated sugar
1 tbsp	baking powder
1 tsp	baking soda
½ tsp	salt
½ cup	plain yogurt
2 tsp	grated orange zest
¼ cup	orange juice
¼ cup	vegetable oil
2	eggs
1½ cups	fresh blueberries (see tip, below)

CRUNCHY TOPPING:

¼ cup	granulated sugar
1 tbsp	grated orange zest
	sliced almonds (optional)

DIRECTIONS

MUFFINS: In large bowl, whisk together flour, sugar, baking powder, baking soda and salt. Whisk together yogurt, orange zest, orange juice, oil and eggs; pour over flour mixture. Sprinkle with blueberries; stir just until dry ingredients are moistened. Spoon into 12 greased or paper-lined muffin cups.

CRUNCHY TOPPING: Stir together sugar, orange zest, and almonds (if using); sprinkle over batter. Bake in 400°F (200°C) oven until tops are firm to the touch, about 25 minutes.

Let cool in pan for 5 minutes. Transfer muffins to rack; let cool.

NUTRITIONAL INFORMATION, PER MUFFIN: about 214 cal, 4 g pro, 6 g total fat (1 g sat. fat), 37 g carb, 1 g fibre, 32 mg chol, 276 mg sodium. % RDI: 5% calcium, 9% iron, 2% vit A, 8% vit C, 15% folate.

TIP FROM THE TEST KITCHEN
You can use thawed frozen blueberries in place of the fresh blueberries if you like. However, they are juicier and will create purple streaks when you stir them into the batter. The muffins will taste just as good, though!

EASY NO-KNEAD
WHOLE WHEAT SANDWICH BREAD
page 305

ULTIMATE YEAST BREADS | 12

"There are few things I find more satisfying than the feel of soft, supple, handmade dough in my hands. Paired with the aromatherapy of freshly baked bread, that's my Zen place."

ANNABELLE WAUGH FOOD DIRECTOR

MIXED-GRAIN SWISS COUNTRY LOAF ◗

Swiss-style mixed-grain loaves have a texture halfway between that of lighter French or Italian loaves and heavier German loaves. The loaf requires two separate overnight risings, but its rich flavour is worth the time.

HANDS-ON TIME
45 minutes

TOTAL TIME
33 hours

MAKES
1 large loaf,
20 slices

INGREDIENTS

LEVAIN:

1 cup + 2 tbsp	warm water (100°F/38°C)
1 tsp	milk
½ tsp	active dry yeast
⅔ cup	whole (dark) rye flour
⅔ cup	white bread flour
⅓ cup	whole wheat flour

LOAF:

⅔ cup	warm water (100°F/38°C)
1 tbsp	malt syrup (see tip, page 302)
½ tsp	active dry yeast
½ cup	whole spelt flour
2 tsp	salt
2¼ cups	white bread flour (approx)

DIRECTIONS

LEVAIN: In large bowl, combine warm water with milk. Sprinkle in yeast; let stand until frothy, about 10 minutes.

Stir in rye flour, white bread flour and whole wheat flour until smooth. Using wooden spoon, beat 100 strokes in same direction until gluey. Scrape down side of bowl. Cover with plastic wrap; let stand at cool room temperature in draft-free place for 12 hours. *(Make-ahead: Let stand for up to 24 hours.)*

LOAF: In large bowl, stir warm water with malt syrup. Sprinkle in yeast; let stand until frothy, about 10 minutes.

Stir in spelt flour and salt. Scrape in Levain; beat until combined. Stir in white bread flour to form wet, shaggy dough. Knead, adding up to ½ cup more white bread flour as necessary to prevent sticking, until smooth and elastic, 12 to 15 minutes in stand mixer with dough hook on medium-low speed or about 20 minutes by hand. Transfer to greased bowl, turning to grease all over. Cover bowl with plastic wrap; refrigerate overnight.

Bring dough to room temperature, 2 to 3 hours. Punch down dough; on lightly floured surface, knead gently for 1 minute. Shape into smooth ball, pulling down edge and pinching together underneath. Cover with tea towel; let rest for 15 minutes.

Flatten dough into 12- x 8-inch (30 x 20 cm) rectangle; fold long sides in to meet in centre. Pinch seam and ends to seal. Cut 20-inch (50 cm) piece of thin kitchen string; lay string crosswise across centre of parchment paper–lined or rye flour–dusted rimmed baking sheet. Place loaf, seam side down, on baking sheet so that loaf is centred on and perpendicular to string, leaving both ends of string exposed. Cover with tea towel; let rise in warm draft-free place until doubled in bulk, 1 hour.

Using razor blade or sharp serrated knife, score ½-inch (1 cm) deep slash lengthwise down centre of loaf; bring string up around centre of loaf, cutting loaf in half crosswise. Remove string. Bake loaf in 450°F (230°C) oven for 20 minutes, sprinkling bottom of oven with a couple of handfuls of water when putting loaf in oven and again after 3 minutes of baking.

Reduce heat to 400°F (200°C); bake until crust is firm and loaf sounds hollow when tapped on bottom, about 20 minutes. Let cool on rack.

NUTRITIONAL INFORMATION, PER EACH OF 20 SLICES: about 109 cal, 4 g pro, 1 g total fat (trace sat. fat), 22 g carb, 2 g fibre, 0 mg chol, 231 mg sodium, 67 mg potassium. % RDI: 1% calcium, 9% iron, 13% folate.

MALT RYE BREAD

This soft yet fairly dense bread is a relatively quick yeast loaf that doesn't require a starter or a lot of rising time. The tart yogurt balances the sweetness of the rich malt syrup.

HANDS-ON TIME
35 minutes

TOTAL TIME
4 hours

MAKES
1 loaf,
16 to 20 slices

INGREDIENTS

¼ tsp	granulated sugar
¾ cup	warm water (100°F/38°C)
2½ tsp	active dry yeast
1 cup	fat-free plain yogurt
¼ cup	malt syrup (see tip, below)
1½ tsp	salt
2⅓ cups	whole (dark) rye flour
2 cups	white bread flour (approx)
1½ tsp	butter, melted
2 tsp	caraway seeds

DIRECTIONS

In large bowl, dissolve sugar in warm water. Sprinkle in yeast; let stand until frothy, about 10 minutes. Stir in yogurt, malt syrup and salt until combined. Stir in rye flour and bread flour to make shaggy dough.

Turn out onto lightly floured surface; knead, adding up to ½ cup more bread flour as necessary to prevent sticking, until smooth and elastic, about 8 minutes. Place in greased bowl, turning to grease all over; cover and let rise in warm draft-free place until doubled in bulk, 1½ hours.

Punch down dough; on lightly floured surface, knead gently. Shape into smooth ball, pulling down edge and pinching together underneath. Cover with tea towel; let rest for 10 minutes.

Flatten dough into 1-inch (2.5 cm) thick oval, with 1 long side facing you. Fold in top and bottom thirds to meet in centre and form torpedo-shaped loaf; pinch seam to seal. Place, seam side down, on rye flour–dusted or parchment paper–lined rimmed baking sheet. Cover with tea towel; let rise in warm draft-free place until doubled in bulk, ¾ to 1¼ hours.

Brush top with butter; sprinkle with caraway seeds. Using razor blade or sharp serrated knife, cut three or four ½-inch (1 cm) deep slits in top of loaf. Bake in 425°F (220°C) oven for 20 minutes, sprinkling bottom of oven with a few handfuls of water when putting loaf in oven and again after 3 minutes of baking.

Reduce heat to 375°F (190°C); bake until crust is firm and loaf sounds hollow when tapped on bottom, about 25 minutes. Let cool on rack.

NUTRITIONAL INFORMATION, PER EACH OF 20 SLICES: about 115 cal, 5 g pro, 1 g total fat (trace sat. fat), 23 g carb, 3 g fibre, 1 mg chol, 184 mg sodium, 170 mg potassium. % RDI: 3% calcium, 12% iron, 15% folate.

TIP FROM THE TEST KITCHEN
Barley malt syrup is the tastiest malt to use in bread baking; you can substitute wheat malt syrup, which is milder and sweeter. Look for both at health food, bulk food and large grocery stores.

EASY NO-KNEAD WHITE SANDWICH BREAD ○

This simple beginner recipe is a terrific introduction to bread baking. It makes two loaves, so you can serve one right away and freeze the other for later.

HANDS-ON TIME
15 minutes

TOTAL TIME
14¾ hours

MAKES
2 loaves,
each 16 slices

INGREDIENTS

6 cups	white bread flour (approx)
2 tsp	salt
1 tsp	quick-rising (instant) dry yeast
2½ cups	lukewarm water

DIRECTIONS

In large bowl, whisk together 5 cups of the flour, salt and yeast. Stir in lukewarm water until well combined. Cover with plastic wrap; let rise in warm draft-free place until bubbly and doubled in bulk, about 12 hours. *(Make-ahead: Let rise for up to 18 hours.)*

Sprinkle work surface with ⅓ cup of the remaining flour. Scrape dough onto work surface; sprinkle ¼ cup of the remaining flour over top. Cover with tea towel; let stand for 15 minutes.

Using floured hands, gently flatten dough into ½-inch (1 cm) thick rectangle, sprinkling with up to ¼ cup of the remaining flour if dough is too sticky.

Cut in half crosswise. Roll each half into scant 8- x 4-inch (20 x 10 cm) cylinder; place, seam side down, in greased nonstick 8- x 4-inch (1.5 L) loaf pan. Cover loosely with lightly greased plastic wrap; let rise in warm draft-free place until almost doubled in bulk, about 1½ hours.

Bake in 425°F (220°C) oven for 10 minutes. Reduce heat to 375°F (190°C); bake until light golden and loaves sound hollow when tapped, about 30 minutes.

Transfer to racks; serve warm or let cool. *(Make-ahead: Let cool completely. Slice loaves; wrap in plastic wrap and freeze in resealable freezer bag for up to 3 weeks.)*

NUTRITIONAL INFORMATION, PER SLICE: about 93 cal, 4 g pro, 1 g total fat (trace sat. fat), 18 g carb, 1 g fibre, 0 mg chol, 144 mg sodium, 35 mg potassium. % RDI: 9% iron, 18% folate.

TIP FROM THE TEST KITCHEN
In the Test Kitchen, we slice our loaves before we freeze them for convenience—that way, we can pull just a few slices out of the freezer without having to thaw the whole loaf, which can dry out if you do it repeatedly. To keep the slices themselves from drying out, it's important to let the whole loaf cool completely as directed before cutting into it.

EASY NO-KNEAD WHOLE WHEAT SANDWICH BREAD ◐

A combo of whole wheat and white bread flours gives these loaves an airier texture than straight-up whole wheat flour would. When you're dusting the work surface, use white bread flour, not whole wheat, to ensure the perfect balance.

HANDS-ON TIME
15 minutes

TOTAL TIME
14¾ hours

MAKES
2 loaves,
each 16 slices

INGREDIENTS

2 tbsp	sesame seeds
1 tbsp	poppy seeds
¼ tsp	flaxseeds (optional)
3 cups	whole wheat bread flour
3 cups	white bread flour (approx)
2 tsp	salt
1 tsp	quick-rising (instant) dry yeast
2½ cups	lukewarm water

DIRECTIONS

Stir ¼ tsp of the sesame seeds with ¼ tsp of the poppy seeds; stir in flaxseeds (if using). Set aside.

In large bowl, whisk together whole wheat flour, 2 cups of the white flour, remaining sesame seeds and poppy seeds, salt and yeast. Stir in lukewarm water until well combined. Cover with plastic wrap; let rise in warm draft-free place until bubbly and doubled in bulk, about 12 hours. *(Make-ahead: Let rise for up to 18 hours.)*

Sprinkle work surface with ⅓ cup of the remaining white flour. Scrape dough onto work surface; sprinkle ¼ cup of the remaining white flour over top. Cover with tea towel; let stand for 15 minutes.

Using floured hands, gently flatten dough into ½-inch (1 cm) thick rectangle, sprinkling with up to ¼ cup of the remaining white flour if dough is too sticky.

Cut in half crosswise. Roll each half into scant 8- x 4-inch (20 x 10 cm) cylinder; place, seam side down, in greased nonstick 8- x 4-inch (1.5 L) loaf pan. Sprinkle loaves with reserved sesame seed mixture. Cover loosely with lightly greased plastic wrap; let rise in warm draft-free place until almost doubled in bulk, about 1½ hours.

Bake in 425°F (220°C) oven for 10 minutes. Reduce heat to 375°F (190°C); bake until light golden and loaves sound hollow when tapped, about 30 minutes.

Transfer to racks; serve warm or let cool. *(Make-ahead: Let cool completely. Slice loaves; wrap in plastic wrap and freeze in resealable freezer bag for up to 3 weeks.)*

NUTRITIONAL INFORMATION, PER SLICE: about 95 cal, 4 g pro, 1 g total fat (trace sat. fat), 18 g carb, 2 g fibre, 0 mg chol, 146 mg sodium, 23 mg potassium. % RDI: 1% calcium, 8% iron, 10% folate.

WHOLE WHEAT SOURDOUGH BREAD ◐

Although it's not a speedy project—the starter and the bread need time to develop the distinctive tangy taste—this crusty, chewy loaf is actually easy to make and well worth the time spent.

HANDS-ON TIME
25 minutes

TOTAL TIME
17½ hours

MAKES
1 loaf, 12 slices

INGREDIENTS

half	batch Sourdough Starter (opposite)
1 cup	warm water (100°F/38°C)
2 cups	white bread flour (approx)
1¾ cups	whole wheat bread flour
2 tsp	salt
1 tbsp	cornmeal
1	egg

DIRECTIONS

In bowl, stir starter with ¾ cup of the warm water until smooth. Using wooden spoon, beat in 1½ cups of the white bread flour until smooth. Cover with plastic wrap; let rise at room temperature for 12 hours. *(Make-ahead: Let rise for up to 24 hours.)* Stir in remaining warm water.

Stir in whole wheat bread flour and salt; turn out onto floured surface. Knead, dusting with as much of the remaining white flour as necessary to prevent sticking, until smooth and elastic, about 8 minutes. Place in greased bowl, turning to grease all over. Cover with plastic wrap; let rise in warm draft-free place until tripled in bulk, about 2 hours.

Punch down dough; turn out onto floured surface. Knead about 10 times to remove air bubbles. Cover with clean tea towel; let rest for 10 minutes. Press into ½-inch (1 cm) thick circle. Flatten dough into 1-inch (2.5 cm) thick oval, 1 long side facing you. Fold in top and bottom thirds to meet in centre and form torpedo-shaped loaf; pinch seam to seal.

Place loaf, seam side down, on cornmeal-dusted rimless baking sheet. Cover with clean tea towel; let rise in warm draft-free place until doubled in bulk, about 1½ hours.

Whisk egg with 1 tbsp water; brush over loaf. Using razor blade or sharp serrated knife, cut ½-inch (1 cm) deep slashes in top. Bake in 425°F (220°C) oven until golden and loaf sounds hollow when tapped on bottom, 35 to 40 minutes. Transfer to rack; let cool.

NUTRITIONAL INFORMATION, PER SLICE: about 182 cal, 6 g pro, 1 g total fat (0 g sat. fat), 37 g carb, 3 g fibre, 16 mg chol, 390 mg sodium. % RDI: 1% calcium, 14% iron, 1% vit A, 19% folate.

VARIATIONS

WHITE SOURDOUGH BREAD
Omit whole wheat bread flour; increase white bread flour to 3¼ cups.

RYE SOURDOUGH BREAD
Replace whole wheat bread flour with equal amount dark or light rye bread flour.

SOURDOUGH BOULE (ROUND LOAF)
Line 12-cup bowl with clean tea towel. Dust with white bread flour. Shape dough into ball instead of torpedo shape; place, seam side up, in prepared bowl. Let rise as directed. Place, seam side down, on baking sheet; cut crisscross slashes in top.

SOURDOUGH STARTER

Before cake and granular yeasts were commercially available, spongy sourdough starter was the leavener that raised bread. If you feed the starter with fresh flour and water regularly, you can keep the yeast alive and enjoy making sourdough bread for years to come.

HANDS-ON TIME
10 minutes

TOTAL TIME
1 week

MAKES
1 batch

INGREDIENTS

SOURDOUGH STARTER:

2½ cups	all-purpose flour
1 cup	warm water (100°F/38°C)
¼ tsp	active dry yeast
½ cup	water or milk

SOURDOUGH FEED:

1¼ cups	all-purpose flour
¾ cup	water or milk

DIRECTIONS

SOURDOUGH STARTER: In 8-cup container, mix together 2 cups of the flour, warm water and yeast. Cover with plastic wrap; let stand at room temperature until tripled in volume, about 8 hours. *(Make-ahead: Let stand for up to 24 hours.)*

Cover and refrigerate for 3 days. Stir in water and remaining flour. Cover and refrigerate for 3 more days.

Divide starter in half; place 1 half in large bowl to make bread.

SOURDOUGH FEED: To feed remaining starter, stir in flour and water. Refrigerate for 2 days before using. *(Make-ahead: Refrigerate for up to 1 week.)*

NOTE: Starter must be divided and fed once a week in the same manner; if not making bread, dispose of half of the starter and feed remainder.

CLOVERLEAF DINNER ROLLS

HANDS-ON TIME 15 minutes

TOTAL TIME 2¾ hours

MAKES 20 rolls

INGREDIENTS

1   batch Whole Wheat or Soft Dinner Roll Dough (page 310)

1   egg yolk

DIRECTIONS

Punch down dough. Turn out onto lightly floured surface; divide into 20 pieces. Divide each into 3 pieces; shape each into smooth ball, pulling down edge and pinching together underneath.

Place 3 balls in each of 20 greased muffin cups. Cover with tea towel; let rise in warm draft-free place until doubled in bulk, about 1 hour.

Whisk egg yolk with 2 tsp water; brush over rolls. Bake in 375°F (190°C) oven until golden and rolls sound hollow when tapped on bottoms, about 25 minutes. Let cool in pan on rack for 10 minutes; transfer to rack and let cool.

NUTRITIONAL INFORMATION, PER ROLL: about 143 cal, 4 g pro, 3 g total fat (2 g sat. fat), 24 g carb, 1 g fibre, 27 mg chol, 142 mg sodium, 66 mg potassium. % RDI: 2% calcium, 10% iron, 4% vit A, 32% folate.

FANTAN DINNER ROLLS

HANDS-ON TIME 15 minutes

TOTAL TIME 2¾ hours

MAKES 20 rolls

INGREDIENTS

1   batch Whole Wheat or Soft Dinner Roll Dough (page 310)

2 tbsp   butter, softened

1   egg yolk

DIRECTIONS

Punch down dough; divide in half. On lightly floured surface, roll one half into 16- x 10-inch (40 x 25 cm) rectangle. Brush with half of the butter. Cut into forty 2-inch (5 cm) squares. Place, butter side up, in 10 stacks of 4 squares each. Place, cut side up, in 10 greased muffin cups, fanning out. Repeat with remaining dough and butter. Cover with tea towel; let rise in warm draft-free place until doubled in bulk, about 1 hour.

Whisk egg yolk with 2 tsp water; brush over rolls. Bake in 375°F (190°C) oven until golden and rolls sound hollow when tapped on bottoms, 22 to 25 minutes. Let cool in pan on rack for 10 minutes; transfer to rack and let cool.

NUTRITIONAL INFORMATION, PER ROLL: about 153 cal, 4 g pro, 5 g total fat (3 g sat. fat), 24 g carb, 1 g fibre, 30 mg chol, 150 mg sodium, 66 mg potassium. % RDI: 2% calcium, 10% iron, 5% vit A, 32% folate.

TOPKNOT DINNER ROLLS

HANDS-ON TIME 15 minutes

TOTAL TIME 2¾ hours

MAKES 20 rolls

INGREDIENTS

1   batch Whole Wheat or Soft Dinner Roll Dough (page 310)

1   egg yolk

DIRECTIONS

Punch down dough. Turn out onto lightly floured surface; divide into 20 pieces. Remove 1 tsp from each piece; shape each into ball and set aside.

Shape remaining pieces of dough into smooth balls, pulling down edge and pinching together underneath. Place each in greased muffin cup; gently press small ball on centre of each. Cover with tea towel; let rise in warm draft-free place until doubled in bulk, about 1 hour.

Whisk egg yolk with 2 tsp water; brush over rolls. Bake in 375°F (190°C) oven until golden and rolls sound hollow when tapped on bottoms, 22 to 25 minutes. Let cool in pan on rack for 10 minutes; transfer to rack and let cool.

NUTRITIONAL INFORMATION, PER ROLL: about 143 cal, 4 g pro, 3 g total fat (2 g sat. fat), 24 g carb, 1 g fibre, 27 mg chol, 142 mg sodium, 66 mg potassium. % RDI: 2% calcium, 10% iron, 4% vit A, 32% folate.

KNOT DINNER ROLLS

HANDS-ON TIME 15 minutes

TOTAL TIME 2¾ hours

MAKES 20 rolls

INGREDIENTS

1   batch Whole Wheat or Soft Dinner Roll Dough (page 310)

1   egg yolk

DIRECTIONS

Punch down dough. Turn out onto lightly floured surface. Divide into 20 pieces.

Roll each piece into 9-inch (23 cm) rope; tie in knot and place, 2 inches (5 cm) apart, on parchment paper–lined rimmed baking sheet. Cover with tea towel; let rise in warm draft-free place until doubled in bulk, about 1 hour.

Whisk egg yolk with 2 tsp water; brush over rolls. Bake in 375°F (190°C) oven until golden and rolls sound hollow when tapped on bottoms, 22 to 25 minutes. Let cool in pan on rack for 10 minutes; transfer to rack and let cool.

NUTRITIONAL INFORMATION, PER ROLL: about 143 cal, 4 g pro, 3 g total fat (2 g sat. fat), 24 g carb, 1 g fibre, 27 mg chol, 142 mg sodium, 66 mg potassium. % RDI: 2% calcium, 10% iron, 4% vit A, 32% folate.

SOFT DINNER ROLL DOUGH

HANDS-ON TIME 20 minutes

TOTAL TIME 2 hours

MAKES 1 batch, enough for 20 rolls

INGREDIENTS

2 tbsp	granulated sugar
1¼ cups	milk
¼ cup	butter
1 tsp	salt
¼ cup	warm water (100°F/38°C)
1	pkg (8 g) active dry yeast (or 2¼ tsp)
1	egg
4½ cups	all-purpose flour (approx)

DIRECTIONS

Remove 1 tsp of the sugar; set aside. In saucepan, heat together milk, butter, salt and remaining sugar until butter is melted; let cool to lukewarm.

In large bowl, dissolve reserved sugar in warm water. Sprinkle yeast over top; let stand until frothy, about 10 minutes. Whisk in milk mixture and egg.

Stir in 4 cups of the flour, 1 cup at a time, to make soft shaggy dough. Turn out onto lightly floured surface; knead, adding as much of the remaining flour as necessary to prevent sticking, until smooth, elastic and quite soft, about 10 minutes.

Place dough in large greased bowl, turning to grease all over. Cover with plastic wrap or tea towel; let rise in warm draft-free place until doubled in bulk, about 1½ hours. To shape rolls, see pages 308 and 309.

VARIATION

WHOLE WHEAT SOFT DINNER ROLL DOUGH

Replace 1½ cups of the all-purpose flour with whole wheat flour.

GLUTEN-FREE SANDWICH BREAD

HANDS-ON TIME 15 minutes

TOTAL TIME 1¾ hours

MAKES 2 loaves, each 16 slices

INGREDIENTS

2 cups	each tapioca flour and brown rice flour
1½ cups	potato starch
6 tbsp	ground flaxseed
4 tsp	each quick-rising (instant) dry yeast and xanthan gum
1½ tsp	salt
2⅔ cups	warm milk (100°F/38°C)
4	eggs
2 tbsp	liquid honey
4 tsp	light-tasting olive oil
2 tsp	cider vinegar

DIRECTIONS

In large bowl, whisk together tapioca flour, brown rice flour, potato starch, flax meal, yeast, xanthan gum and salt.

Whisk together milk, eggs, honey, oil and vinegar. Pour over tapioca flour mixture; stir until well combined. Divide between 2 greased nonstick 8- x 4-inch (1.5 L) loaf pans; smooth tops. Cover loosely with lightly greased plastic wrap; let rise in warm draft-free place until tops of loaves are just above rims of pans, 25 to 35 minutes.

Bake in 350°F (180°C) oven until light golden and cake tester inserted in centre comes out clean, about 1 hour.

Transfer to racks; serve warm or let cool. *(Make-ahead: Let cool completely. Slice loaves; wrap in plastic wrap and freeze in resealable freezer bag for up to 1 month.)*

NUTRITIONAL INFORMATION, PER SLICE: about 125 cal, 3 g pro, 3 g total fat (1 g sat. fat), 22 g carb, 1 g fibre, 24 mg chol, 137 mg sodium, 86 mg potassium. % RDI: 4% calcium, 4% iron, 3% vit A, 6% folate.

OAT AND MOLASSES BREAD ⬤

Baking bread from scratch is one of the most satisfying endeavours: Kneading the dough, watching it rise, smelling it bake and then slathering a warm slice with butter. This one gets a sweet taste from molasses and a nice chewiness from oats.

HANDS-ON TIME
15 minutes

TOTAL TIME
4 hours

MAKES
2 loaves,
each 12 slices

INGREDIENTS

LOAVES:

1¼ cups	boiling water
¾ cup	large-flake rolled oats
⅓ cup	fancy molasses
2 tbsp	butter, softened
1	egg, beaten
1 tsp	granulated sugar
½ cup	warm water (100°F/38°C)
1 tbsp	active dry yeast
3 cups	all-purpose flour (approx)
1 cup	whole wheat flour
1¾ tsp	salt

TOPPING:

1	egg, lightly beaten
2 tbsp	large-flake rolled oats

DIRECTIONS

LOAVES: In heatproof bowl, stir boiling water with oats; let stand until absorbed, about 15 minutes. Stir in molasses, butter and egg.

Meanwhile, in large bowl, dissolve sugar in warm water. Sprinkle in yeast; let stand until frothy, about 10 minutes. Stir in oatmeal mixture. Stir in 2½ cups of the all-purpose flour, the whole wheat flour and salt to form sticky dough.

Turn out onto floured surface. Knead, adding as much of the remaining all-purpose flour as necessary to prevent sticking, until smooth and elastic, about 5 minutes. Place in greased bowl, turning to grease all over. Cover with plastic wrap; let rise in warm draft-free place until doubled in bulk, about 1 hour.

Punch down dough; divide in half. On floured surface, pat each half into 11- x 8-inch (28 x 20 cm) rectangle. Starting at narrow end, roll up into cylinder; pinch seam and ends to seal. Fit into 2 greased 8- x 4-inch (1.5 L) loaf pans. (Or shape each into round, stretching and pinching dough underneath to smooth top.) Cover with tea towel; let rise in warm draft-free place until doubled in bulk, about 1 hour.

TOPPING: Brush loaves with egg; sprinkle with oats. Bake in 375°F (190°C) oven until loaves sound hollow when tapped on bottoms, about 40 minutes. Let cool on racks.

NUTRITIONAL INFORMATION, PER SLICE: about 114 cal, 3 g pro, 2 g total fat (1 g sat. fat), 21 g carb, 1 g fibre, 19 mg chol, 185 mg sodium. % RDI: 2% calcium, 10% iron, 2% vit A, 16% folate.

VARIATION

BREAD MACHINE OAT AND MOLASSES BREAD (DOUGH ONLY)

Into pan of 2-lb (1 kg) bread machine, place (in order) oat mixture, ¼ cup water, sugar, salt, all of the all-purpose flour, whole wheat flour and 1¼ tsp bread machine yeast. Select dough setting. Shape and bake as directed.

TRADITIONAL CHALLAH

Whether you're enjoying a slice as part of a Jewish Sabbath dinner or a holiday meal, or just because it's totally delicious, this challah is a must-bake recipe. Leftover slices make scrumptious French toast.

HANDS-ON TIME
35 minutes

TOTAL TIME
3¾ hours

MAKES
1 loaf, 16 slices

INGREDIENTS

CHALLAH:

2 tsp	granulated sugar
½ cup	warm water (100°F/38°C)
1	pkg (8 g) active dry yeast (or 2¼ tsp)
3½ cups	all-purpose flour (approx)
1 tsp	salt
¼ cup	liquid honey
2	eggs, lightly beaten
2	egg yolks
¼ cup	butter, melted, or vegetable oil
¾ cup	golden raisins

TOPPING:

1	egg yolk, lightly beaten
1 tbsp	sesame seeds

DIRECTIONS

CHALLAH: In large bowl, dissolve sugar in warm water. Sprinkle in yeast; let stand until frothy, about 10 minutes. Using wooden spoon, stir in 3 cups of the flour and salt; stir in honey, eggs, egg yolks and butter until soft sticky dough forms.

Turn out onto lightly floured surface; knead, adding as much of the remaining flour as necessary to prevent sticking, until smooth and elastic, about 10 minutes. Place in greased bowl, turning to grease all over. Cover and let rise in warm draft-free place until doubled in bulk, about 1 hour.

Punch down dough; knead in raisins. Cover and let rest for 5 minutes.

Divide dough into quarters; roll each into 18-inch (45 cm) rope. Place ropes side by side on parchment paper–lined large baking sheet; pinch together at 1 end. **PHOTO A**

With pinched end opposite you and starting at pinched end, *move second rope from left over second rope from right. Move far right rope over 2 centre ropes so it's now second from left. Move far left rope over 2 centre ropes so its now second from right. Repeat from * until braid is complete. **PHOTO B**

Tuck ends under braid and pinch to seal. Cover braid with damp clean tea towel; let rise in warm draft-free place until doubled in bulk, about 1 hour.

TOPPING: Stir egg yolk with 1 tsp water; brush lightly over dough. Sprinkle with sesame seeds. Bake in 350°F (180°C) oven until golden and loaf sounds hollow when tapped on bottom, 35 to 45 minutes. Transfer to rack; let cool.

NUTRITIONAL INFORMATION, PER SLICE: about 189 cal, 5 g pro, 5 g total fat (2 g sat. fat), 31 g carb, 1 g fibre, 69 mg chol, 175 mg sodium. % RDI: 2% calcium, 12% iron, 5% vit A, 35% folate.

TIP FROM THE TEST KITCHEN

You can also make challah in the shape of a crown: Roll out risen dough into single 30-inch (75 cm) long rope. Holding one end in place, wind remaining rope around end to form fairly tight spiral that is slightly higher in centre. Transfer to prepared pan and continue with second rise.

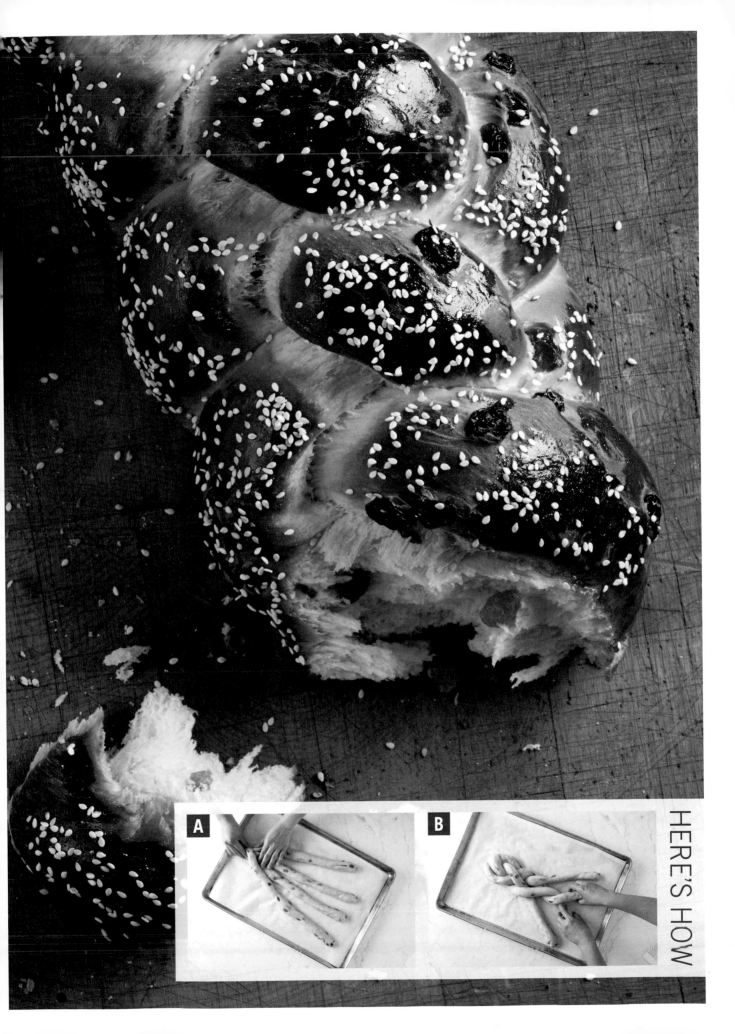

CLASSIC PIZZA DOUGH ●

Our foolproof dough delivers the most amazing pizza crust you'll ever taste. The long rising time results in a lovely texture and extra-rich flavour. It's really easy to make and can be stretched into either a regular or a thin crust.

HANDS-ON TIME
15 minutes

TOTAL TIME
24¼ hours

MAKES
1 crust,
about 8 slices

INGREDIENTS

2 cups	all-purpose flour (approx)
1 tsp	quick-rising (instant) dry yeast
½ tsp	salt
⅔ cup	warm water (100°F/38°C)
2 tsp	olive oil

DIRECTIONS

In large bowl, whisk together 1½ cups of the flour, yeast and salt. Using wooden spoon, stir in warm water and olive oil until ragged dough forms.

Turn dough out onto lightly floured surface; knead, adding as much of the remaining flour, a little at a time, as needed to prevent sticking, until smooth and elastic, about 8 minutes. (Dough will still be slightly tacky but won't stick to hands or work surface.)

Transfer to greased bowl, turning to grease all over. Cover with plastic wrap. Refrigerate for 24 hours. (Or let rise in warm draft-free place until doubled in bulk, about 1½ hours.)

TO MAKE 12-INCH (30 CM) REGULAR PIZZA: On lightly floured surface, roll out dough into 12-inch (30 cm) circle; transfer to greased pizza pan. Add desired toppings. Bake on bottom rack in 500°F (260°C) oven until crust is golden, 12 to 15 minutes.

TO MAKE 14-INCH (35 CM) THIN-CRUST PIZZA: On lightly floured surface, roll out dough into 14-inch (35 cm) circle; transfer to greased pizza pan. Add desired toppings. Bake on bottom rack in 500°F (260°C) oven until crust is golden, 12 to 15 minutes.

NUTRITIONAL INFORMATION, PER EACH OF 8 SLICES OF 12-INCH (30 CM) REGULAR CRUST (WITHOUT TOPPINGS): about 125 cal, 4 g pro, 2 g total fat (trace sat. fat), 23 g carb, 1 g fibre, 0 mg chol, 144 mg sodium, 40 mg potassium. % RDI: 1% calcium, 11% iron, 23% folate.

VARIATION

HERB AND GARLIC PIZZA DOUGH

Stir 1 tsp Italian herb seasoning and 2 cloves garlic, pressed, into flour mixture before continuing with recipe.

CRUMPETS ◔

HANDS-ON TIME 30 minutes

TOTAL TIME 1½ hours

MAKES 18 to 20 crumpets

INGREDIENTS

2½ cups	all-purpose flour
2 tsp	quick-rising (instant) dry yeast
1 tsp	granulated sugar
½ tsp	salt
1½ cups	warm water (100°F/38°C)
1 cup	warm milk (100°F/38°C)
2 tbsp	vegetable oil

DIRECTIONS

In large bowl, stir together flour, yeast, sugar and salt. Stir in water and milk, scraping down side of bowl and mixing well. Cover with plastic wrap; let stand in warm draft-free place until bubbly and doubled in bulk, about 1 hour.

Heat griddle or large cast-iron skillet over medium heat; brush lightly with some of the oil. Grease 3-inch (8 cm) ring moulds; place, 2 inches (5 cm) apart, on griddle. Scoop batter by scant ¼ cup into moulds, filling halfway. Cook until tops are dry, 7 to 10 minutes.

Using tongs or wearing oven mitts, remove moulds. Flip crumpets and cook just until light golden, about 2 minutes. Let cool on rack for 5 minutes. Repeat with remaining batter. *(Make-ahead: Store in airtight container for up to 2 days or freeze for up to 2 weeks.)*

NUTRITIONAL INFORMATION, PER EACH OF 20 CRUMPETS: about 77 cal, 2 g pro, 2 g total fat (trace sat. fat), 13 g carb, 1 g fibre, 1 mg chol, 63 mg sodium, 43 mg potassium. % RDI: 2% calcium, 6% iron, 1% vit A, 19% folate.

ENGLISH MUFFINS ◔

HANDS-ON TIME 30 minutes

TOTAL TIME 2 hours

MAKES 16 muffins

INGREDIENTS

2 cups	warm milk (100°F/38°C)
1½ tsp	active dry yeast
¼ cup	butter, melted
1 tbsp	granulated sugar
1	egg
3¼ cups	all-purpose flour
¾ tsp	salt
2 tsp	baking powder
2 tbsp	vegetable oil
⅓ cup	cornmeal (approx)

DIRECTIONS

Pour ¼ cup of the milk into bowl. Sprinkle in yeast; let stand until frothy, about 10 minutes. Whisk in remaining milk, butter, sugar and egg.

In large bowl, combine flour with salt; stir in milk mixture until smooth. Cover with plastic wrap; let rise in warm draft-free place until doubled in bulk, about 1½ hours.

Mix baking powder with 1 tbsp water; stir into dough. Heat griddle or cast-iron skillet over medium heat; brush with some of the oil. Sprinkle with some of the cornmeal. Using scant ¼ cup per muffin, drop dough onto griddle, leaving 1 inch (2.5 cm) between muffins. Cook until bottoms are browned, 7 to 8 minutes.

Brush each top with some of the remaining oil and sprinkle with ½ tsp of the cornmeal. Flip and cook until bottoms are browned, 7 to 8 minutes. Repeat with remaining dough.

Transfer to parchment paper–lined rimmed baking sheets; bake in 350°F (180°C) oven until firm to the touch, about 7 minutes. Transfer to rack; let cool. *(Make-ahead: Store in airtight container for up to 2 days or freeze for up to 2 weeks.)*

NUTRITIONAL INFORMATION, PER MUFFIN: about 169 cal, 5 g pro, 6 g total fat (2 g sat. fat), 25 g carb, 1 g fibre, 22 mg chol, 183 mg sodium, 92 mg potassium. % RDI: 5% calcium, 9% iron, 4% vit A, 30% folate.

NAAN

*Just right for serving with curries, this flatbread goes well with stew and chili, too.
If you prefer a plain version, simply omit the garlic and sesame seeds.*

HANDS-ON TIME
35 minutes

TOTAL TIME
2 hours

MAKES
8 pieces

INGREDIENTS

NAAN:

1 tsp	granulated sugar
1 cup	warm water (100°F/38°C)
1	pkg (8 g) active dry yeast (or 2¼ tsp)
3¾ cups	all-purpose flour (approx)
1 tsp	salt
½ tsp	baking powder
¼ cup	plain yogurt
¼ cup	butter, melted

TOPPING:

1 tbsp	minced garlic
1 tbsp	sesame seeds
2 tbsp	butter, melted

DIRECTIONS

NAAN: In small bowl, dissolve sugar in warm water. Sprinkle in yeast; let stand until frothy, about 10 minutes.

In large bowl, whisk together 3¼ cups of the flour, salt and baking powder; make well in centre. Pour yeast mixture, yogurt and butter into well; stir, gradually incorporating flour mixture, to form soft, slightly sticky dough.

Turn out onto lightly floured surface; knead, adding as much of the remaining flour as necessary to prevent sticking, until smooth and elastic, about 8 minutes. Place in greased bowl, turning to grease all over. Cover with plastic wrap; let rise in warm draft-free place until doubled in bulk, about 1 hour.

Turn out onto lightly floured surface; form into log. Divide into 8 pieces. Gently stretch each into scant ¼-inch (5 mm) thick teardrop shape. Cover with clean tea towel; let rest for 10 minutes.

TOPPING: Sprinkle naan with garlic and sesame seeds. Place on griddle or in cast-iron skillet over medium-high heat. Bake, turning once, until puffed and golden, about 5 minutes. Brush tops with butter. Wrap in tea towel to keep soft; serve warm.

NUTRITIONAL INFORMATION, PER PIECE: about 309 cal, 7 g pro, 10 g total fat (6 g sat. fat), 47 g carb, 2 g fibre, 24 mg chol, 374 mg sodium. % RDI: 3% calcium, 21% iron, 8% vit A, 66% folate.

TIP FROM THE TEST KITCHEN
If the dough becomes too stretchy when you're shaping it, cover it lightly and let it rest for a few minutes.

MONKEY BREAD ◐
WITH CINNAMON GLAZE

The origin of its name may be a mystery, but what makes monkey bread so delicious and fun is no secret: Balls of sweet yeast dough are dipped in butter and coated with cinnamon sugar, then piled high in a tube pan and baked into a tender pull-apart loaf.

HANDS-ON TIME
30 minutes

TOTAL TIME
3 hours

MAKES
24 pieces

INGREDIENTS

DOUGH:

⅓ cup	granulated sugar
¼ cup	warm water (100°F/38°C)
2 tsp	active dry yeast
¾ cup	milk
¼ cup	butter, melted
2	eggs
2 tsp	vanilla
¾ tsp	salt
4½ cups	all-purpose flour (approx)
1 tsp	cinnamon
½ cup	dried cranberries
½ cup	golden raisins

CINNAMON COATING:

3 tbsp	butter, melted
½ cup	granulated sugar
2 tsp	cinnamon

CINNAMON DRIZZLE:

½ cup	icing sugar
1 tsp	cinnamon

DIRECTIONS

DOUGH: In large bowl, dissolve 1 tsp of the sugar in warm water. Sprinkle in yeast; let stand until frothy, about 10 minutes.

Whisk in remaining sugar, milk, butter, eggs, vanilla and salt. Whisk in 2 cups of the flour and cinnamon. Using wooden spoon, stir in enough of the remaining flour, ½ cup at a time, to make soft, slightly sticky dough.

Turn out onto lightly floured surface; knead, adding as much of the remaining flour as necessary to prevent sticking, until smooth and elastic, about 10 minutes. Knead in cranberries and raisins.

Place in large greased bowl, turning to grease all over. Cover and let rise in warm draft-free place until doubled in bulk, 1 to 1½ hours.

CINNAMON COATING: Punch down dough. Divide into 24 pieces; shape each into ball. Place in large bowl; pour butter over top. Stir gently to coat. In separate bowl, stir sugar with cinnamon; roll balls in mixture.

Arrange in greased 10-inch (4 L) tube pan. Cover with plastic wrap; let rise in warm draft-free place until doubled in bulk, about 45 minutes.

Bake in 350°F (180°C) oven until golden, about 45 minutes. Let cool in pan on rack for 10 minutes. Remove side of pan; let cool completely.

CINNAMON DRIZZLE: Whisk together icing sugar, 2 tbsp water and cinnamon until smooth; using fork, drizzle over bread.

NUTRITIONAL INFORMATION, PER PIECE: about 176 cal, 3 g pro, 4 g total fat (2 g sat. fat), 32 g carb, 1 g fibre, 25 mg chol, 105 mg sodium, 74 mg potassium. % RDI: 2% calcium, 10% iron, 4% vit A, 25% folate.

HERE'S HOW

A

B

KOUIGN AMANN ◐

This impressive treat from the Breton region of France is made by folding together layers of pastry that have been spread with butter and sprinkled with sugar. As they bake, the butter and sugar create a crispy, caramelized crust outside and a gooey sauce inside.

HANDS-ON TIME
20 minutes

TOTAL TIME
3¼ hours

MAKES
12 servings

INGREDIENTS

1	pkg (8 g) active dry yeast (or 2½ tsp)
1 cup	warm water (100°F/38°C)
2½ cups	all-purpose flour (approx)
pinch	salt
⅔ cup	butter, softened
1 cup	granulated sugar

DIRECTIONS

In large bowl, sprinkle yeast over warm water; let stand until frothy, about 10 minutes. Using wooden spoon, stir in 2¼ cups of the flour and salt until ragged dough forms.

Turn out onto lightly floured surface; knead, adding as much of the remaining flour, a little at a time, as necessary to prevent sticking until smooth and elastic, about 8 minutes. (Dough will still be slightly tacky but won't stick to hands or work surface.) Transfer dough to greased bowl; turn to grease all over. Cover with plastic wrap; let rise in warm draft-free place until doubled in bulk, about 1½ hours.

Punch down dough. On lightly floured surface, roll out dough into 10-inch (25 cm) square, about ½ inch (1 cm) thick. Using small offset palette knife, spread 3 tbsp of the butter over dough, right to edges.

Set aside 1 tbsp of the sugar for topping. Sprinkle one-third of the remaining sugar over butter. Fold in each of the 4 corners of square so that points meet in centre. PHOTO A

Roll folded dough out into 10-inch (25 cm) square. PHOTO B

Repeat spreading with butter, sprinkling with sugar and folding in corners. Transfer to lightly floured rimmed baking sheet; cover and refrigerate for 30 minutes.

Flip chilled dough out onto lightly floured surface, folded side down. Roll out into 10-inch (25 cm) square; spread with 3 tbsp of the remaining butter. Sprinkle with remaining sugar. Repeat folding in corners.

Transfer dough, folded side up, to 9-inch (1.5 L) round cake pan; tuck corners under and press dough with palm of hand to fill bottom of pan. *(Make-ahead: Cover with plastic wrap and refrigerate for up to 4 hours.)*

Spread top with remaining butter; sprinkle with reserved sugar. Bake in 425°F (220°C) oven until puffed and golden brown, top sounds hollow when tapped and syrup is thick and bubbly, about 30 minutes.

Let cool in pan on rack for 10 minutes; invert onto serving platter. Let cool completely before cutting into wedges with serrated knife.

NUTRITIONAL INFORMATION, PER SERVING: about 252 cal, 4 g pro, 11 g total fat (7 g sat. fat), 36 g carb, 1 g fibre, 27 mg chol, 74 mg sodium, 43 mg potassium. % RDI: 1% calcium, 10% iron, 9% vit A, 25% folate.

VARIATION
CHOCOLATE KOUIGN AMANN

Finely chop 85 g dark chocolate; sprinkle one-third over each layer of butter and sugar before folding over dough. Continue with recipe.

CINNAMON BUNS ⟳

Enjoy these buns straight out of the oven for a gooey, sweet treat. Remove them from the baking dish while they're still hot; otherwise, the sugar will cool and harden, making them difficult to release.

HANDS-ON TIME
30 minutes

TOTAL TIME
3½ hours

MAKES
16 buns

INGREDIENTS

1¼ cups	butter
¼ cup	granulated sugar
½ cup	warm water (100°F/38°C)
1	pkg (8 g) active dry yeast (or 2¼ tsp)
½ cup	milk
1 tsp	salt
1	egg, lightly beaten
4 cups	all-purpose flour (approx)
1½ cups	packed brown sugar
2 tsp	cinnamon

DIRECTIONS

Bring ½ cup of the butter to room temperature to soften; set aside.

In large bowl, dissolve 1 tsp of the granulated sugar in warm water. Sprinkle in yeast; let stand until frothy, about 10 minutes.

While yeast is dissolving, in small heavy-bottomed saucepan, heat milk over medium heat until bubbles form around edge. Remove from heat; stir in ¼ cup of the remaining butter, the remaining granulated sugar and salt until butter is melted. Let cool until lukewarm; stir into yeast mixture. Stir in egg. Add 2 cups of the flour; stir until smooth and elastic, about 2 minutes. Gradually stir in enough of the remaining flour to make soft dough.

Turn out onto lightly floured work surface; knead until smooth and springy, about 5 minutes. Transfer to greased bowl, turning to grease all over. Cover bowl with plastic wrap; let rise in warm draft-free place until doubled in bulk, about 1½ hours.

While dough is rising, melt remaining butter; pour into 13- x 9-inch (3 L) baking dish. Sprinkle with ½ cup of the brown sugar. Set aside.

On lightly floured work surface, roll out dough into 16- x 14-inch (40 x 35 cm) rectangle. Spread reserved softened butter over top of dough. Mix remaining brown sugar with cinnamon; sprinkle evenly over dough. Starting at 1 long side, tightly roll up; pinch seam to seal. Cut crosswise into 16 buns.

Arrange buns, cut sides up, in prepared baking dish. Cover dish with plastic wrap; let rise in warm draft-free place until doubled in bulk, about 1 hour. *(Make-ahead: Cover and refrigerate for up to 12 hours. Let stand at room temperature for 1 hour before baking.)*

Bake in 375°F (190°C) oven until golden and buns sound hollow when gently tapped, 25 to 30 minutes. Let stand in baking dish for 2 minutes; invert onto serving platter.

NUTRITIONAL INFORMATION, PER BUN: about 341 cal, 5 g pro, 16 g total fat (9 g sat. fat), 46 g carb, 1 g fibre, 50 mg chol, 259 mg sodium, 88 mg potassium. % RDI: 4% calcium, 14% iron, 14% vit A, 27% folate.

VARIATION
CHELSEA BUNS

Sprinkle ⅔ cup chopped pecans into bottom of baking dish after adding butter and brown sugar. Sprinkle ⅔ cup raisins over dough before rolling up. Continue with recipe.

CANOE PADDLE DOUGHNUTS ✦ ◗

This is our Test Kitchen's take on BeaverTails, the signature pastry of the ByWard Market in Ottawa. Stretch the dough as thinly as possible to make the flat canoe paddle shape. The squeeze of fresh lemon on top gives it the most authentic taste.

HANDS-ON TIME
45 minutes

TOTAL TIME
3½ hours

MAKES
12 doughnuts

INGREDIENTS

CANOE PADDLES:

½ cup	granulated sugar
1¼ cups	warm milk (100°F/38°C)
2	pkg (each 8 g) active dry yeast (or 4½ tsp total)
2½ cups	all-purpose flour
1½ cups	whole wheat flour
1 tsp	salt
2	eggs, lightly beaten
¼ cup	vegetable oil vegetable oil for deep-frying

CINNAMON SUGAR TOPPING:

1 cup	granulated sugar
3 tbsp	cinnamon
⅓ cup	butter, melted lemon wedges

DIRECTIONS

CANOE PADDLES: In large bowl, dissolve 1 tbsp of the sugar in milk. Sprinkle in yeast; let stand until frothy, about 10 minutes.

In separate bowl, whisk together 2¼ cups of the all-purpose flour, the whole wheat flour and salt.

Whisk eggs, ¼ cup oil and remaining sugar into yeast mixture. Using wooden spoon, stir in flour mixture until combined. Cover with plastic wrap; let rise in warm draft-free place until doubled in bulk, about 2 hours.

Scrape dough onto lightly floured surface. Knead in remaining all-purpose flour just until dough comes together but is still very sticky, 15 to 20 kneads. Divide dough into 12 pieces; using hands, shape into flat ovals. Place on lightly floured surface; cover with tea towel and let rest for 30 minutes.

In deep fryer, wok or deep saucepan, pour in enough oil to come about 2 inches (5 cm) up side; heat until deep-fryer thermometer reads 375°F (190°C). Working with 1 piece of dough at a time and using hands, gently stretch out dough to scant ⅛-inch (3 mm) thickness to make canoe paddle shape. Deep-fry, gently pressing down with tongs to submerge and turning once, until golden, about 1 minute. Using tongs, transfer to paper towel–lined rimmed baking sheet to drain, about 2 minutes. Repeat with remaining dough.

CINNAMON SUGAR TOPPING: While dough is resting, in large shallow dish, whisk sugar with cinnamon; set aside.

TO FINISH: Brush tops of canoe paddles with butter; press, buttered side down, into Cinnamon Sugar Topping. Turn over and sprinkle with remaining topping to cover completely. Serve with lemon wedges to squeeze over top.

NUTRITIONAL INFORMATION, PER DOUGHNUT: about 542 cal, 8 g pro, 33 g total fat (6 g sat. fat), 57 g carb, 4 g fibre, 46 mg chol, 252 mg sodium, 168 mg potassium. % RDI: 6% calcium, 20% iron, 8% vit A, 2% vit C, 36% folate.

CANADIAN MAPLE-GLAZED DOUGHNUTS ♦ ◗

HANDS-ON TIME
1¼ hours

TOTAL TIME
4¼ hours

MAKES
20 doughnuts and
20 doughnut holes

A sponge is a batterlike mixture that becomes foamy. Here, it creates lightweight (but not airy) doughnuts coated in a simple maple glaze.

INGREDIENTS

SPONGE:

1 tsp	granulated sugar
1 cup	warm water (100°F/38°C)
1	pkg (8 g) active dry yeast (or 2¼ tsp)
1 cup	all-purpose flour

DOUGHNUTS:

¼ cup	butter, softened
⅓ cup	granulated sugar
2	eggs, lightly beaten
1 tsp	vanilla
½ tsp	salt
2¾ cups	all-purpose flour
	oil for deep-frying (canola, safflower or vegetable)

MAPLE GLAZE:

2 cups	icing sugar
¼ cup	maple syrup
1 tsp	maple extract
	granulated or icing sugar (optional)

DIRECTIONS

SPONGE: In large bowl, dissolve sugar in warm water. Sprinkle in yeast; let stand until frothy, about 10 minutes. Stir in flour to form smooth paste. Cover with plastic wrap; let stand until bubbly and stretchy, about 30 minutes.

DOUGHNUTS: In large bowl, beat butter with sugar until fluffy. Beat in eggs, vanilla and salt; beat in sponge. Using wooden spoon, stir in flour to form sticky dough.

Transfer to floured surface; knead until smooth and elastic, about 8 minutes. Place in greased bowl, turning to grease all over. Cover with plastic wrap; let rise in warm draft-free place until tripled in bulk, about 1½ hours.

Punch down dough. On floured surface, roll out to scant ½-inch (1 cm) thickness. Using 3-inch (8 cm) doughnut cutter or round cutter with 1-inch (2.5 cm) hole, cut out doughnuts. Transfer doughnuts and doughnut holes to floured rimmed baking sheet. Cover and let rise until doubled in bulk, about 1 hour.

Pour enough oil into deep fryer, wok or deep saucepan to come 2 inches (5 cm) up side; heat until deep-fryer thermometer reads 350°F (180°C).

Deep-fry 3 doughnuts (or 6 doughnut holes) at a time, turning once, until golden and puffed, about 4 minutes. Using slotted spoon, transfer to paper towel–lined tray to absorb excess oil. Transfer to rack; let cool.

MAPLE GLAZE: Stir together icing sugar, maple syrup, maple extract and 4 tsp water, adding up to 1 tsp more water if necessary to make thick spreadable glaze; spread over tops of doughnuts.

TO FINISH: Dust doughnut holes with sugar, if desired.

NUTRITIONAL INFORMATION, PER DOUGHNUT: about 223 cal, 3 g pro, 9 g total fat (2 g sat. fat), 34 g carb, 1 g fibre, 22 mg chol, 72 mg sodium. % RDI: 1% calcium, 8% iron, 2% vit A, 24% folate.

NUTRITIONAL INFORMATION, PER DOUGHNUT HOLE (WITHOUT SUGAR): about 21 cal, trace pro, 1 g total fat (trace sat. fat), 2 g carb, 0 g fibre, 3 mg chol, 9 mg sodium. % RDI: 1% iron, 3% folate.

BOLOGNESE SAUCE
page 326

ULTIMATE SAUCES, SEASONINGS & PRESERVES | **13**

"Sometimes the thing that dresses up a dish is the best part. I love getting that first bite of the perfect sauce, the crispiest pickle or the ripest jam. It tastes like home."

AMANDA BARNIER FOOD SPECIALIST

BOLOGNESE SAUCE

Serve this rich meat sauce on spaghetti or other long pasta.
The sauce tastes even better if you make it a day ahead and refrigerate
it overnight because the flavour has time to ripen.

HANDS-ON TIME
30 minutes

TOTAL TIME
1¼ hours

MAKES
about 5 cups

INGREDIENTS

450 g	lean ground beef
1 tsp	fennel seeds
1 tbsp	extra-virgin olive oil
¼ cup	chopped pancetta or bacon
1	large onion, chopped
3	cloves garlic, minced
2	carrots, finely diced
2	ribs celery, finely diced
1 tsp	dried oregano
½ tsp	each salt and pepper
1 cup	milk
1	can (796 mL) whole tomatoes
1 cup	dry red wine
2 tbsp	tomato paste
1	bay leaf
pinch	each granulated sugar and hot pepper flakes
¼ cup	minced fresh parsley

DIRECTIONS

In large Dutch oven, cook beef over medium-high heat, breaking up with spoon, until no longer pink, about 5 minutes. Using slotted spoon, transfer to bowl; set aside. Drain fat from pan.

While beef is cooking, using mortar and pestle or bottom of small saucepan, crush fennel seeds; add to beef.

Add oil to pan; heat over medium heat. Cook pancetta, onion, garlic, carrots, celery, oregano, salt and pepper, stirring occasionally, until vegetables are softened, about 8 minutes.

Add milk; simmer until almost no liquid remains. Add tomatoes, mashing with back of spoon. Return beef mixture to pan.

Add wine, tomato paste, bay leaf, sugar and hot pepper flakes; bring to boil. Reduce heat and simmer until thick enough to mound on spoon, about 45 minutes. Discard bay leaf.

Stir in parsley; cook for 2 minutes. *(Make-ahead: Let cool for 30 minutes; refrigerate, uncovered, in airtight container until cold. Cover and refrigerate for up to 2 days or freeze for up to 1 month.)*

NUTRITIONAL INFORMATION, PER ¼ CUP: about 92 cal, 6 g pro, 6 g total fat (3 g sat. fat), 5 g carb, 1 g fibre, 16 mg chol, 160 mg sodium. % RDI: 4% calcium, 8% iron, 15% vit A, 13% vit C, 3% folate.

VARIATION
SLOW COOKER BOLOGNESE SAUCE

Cook as directed through point of adding milk; scrape into slow cooker. Add tomatoes to slow cooker, mashing with back of spoon; add wine, bay leaf, sugar and hot pepper flakes. Cover and cook on low until vegetables are tender, about 6 hours. Stir in tomato paste and parsley; cover and cook on high until thickened and bubbly, about 20 minutes. Discard bay leaf.

SIMPLE TOMATO SAUCE ○

HANDS-ON TIME 10 minutes

TOTAL TIME 40 minutes

MAKES about 8 cups

INGREDIENTS

¼ cup	olive oil
½ cup	chopped onion
2	cloves garlic, minced
2	cans (each 796 mL) whole tomatoes
2	cans (each 156 mL) tomato paste
2	sprigs fresh basil and parsley
2	bay leaves
1 tsp	salt

DIRECTIONS

In large saucepan, heat oil over medium-high heat; sauté onion and garlic until softened and translucent, about 3 minutes.

Stir in tomatoes, mashing with back of spoon. Stir in tomato paste, 2 cups water, basil, parsley, bay leaves and salt; bring to boil. Reduce heat to medium-low, cover and simmer, stirring often to prevent scorching, for 30 minutes.

Discard bay leaves, basil and parsley.

NUTRITIONAL INFORMATION, PER ¼ CUP: about 34 cal, 1 g pro, 2 g total fat (trace sat. fat), 4 g carb, 1 g fibre, 0 mg chol, 148 mg sodium, 213 mg potassium. % RDI: 2% calcium, 6% iron, 2% vit A, 15% vit C, 2% folate.

VARIATION
PURÉED TOMATO SAUCE

Remove bay leaves from cooked sauce. Working in batches, in food processor or blender, purée sauce until smooth. Press through fine-mesh sieve, discarding solids.

SUN-DRIED TOMATO AND ROASTED RED PEPPER CREAM SAUCE ○

HANDS-ON TIME 15 minutes

TOTAL TIME 15 minutes

MAKES about 1 cup

INGREDIENTS

1 tbsp	olive oil
3	cloves garlic, minced
¼ cup	chopped drained oil-packed sun-dried tomatoes
¼ cup	chopped roasted red pepper
¼ tsp	hot pepper flakes
1 cup	whipping cream (35%)
2 tbsp	sliced fresh basil

DIRECTIONS

In saucepan, heat oil over medium heat; cook garlic until light golden, about 1 minute. Add sun-dried tomatoes, roasted red pepper and hot pepper flakes; cook, stirring occasionally, until fragrant, about 2 minutes.

Stir in cream; simmer until thick enough to coat back of spoon, about 5 minutes. Stir in basil.

NUTRITIONAL INFORMATION, PER ¼ CUP: about 246 cal, 2 g pro, 25 g total fat (14 g sat. fat), 5 g carb, 1 g fibre, 76 mg chol, 86 mg sodium, 193 mg potassium. % RDI: 5% calcium, 3% iron, 25% vit A, 47% vit C, 3% folate.

BASIC WHITE SAUCE ⊙

HANDS-ON TIME 10 minutes

TOTAL TIME 25 minutes

MAKES 3⅔ cups

INGREDIENTS

2 tbsp	butter
2 tbsp	all-purpose flour
3½ cups	2% milk
½ cup	whipping cream (35%)
2	cloves garlic
1	fresh bay leaf
½ tsp	salt
⅛ tsp	pepper

DIRECTIONS

In saucepan, melt butter over medium heat; cook flour, stirring constantly, for 2 minutes, without browning. Whisk in milk, cream, garlic, bay leaf, salt and pepper; bring to boil, whisking often.

Reduce heat to low; simmer for 15 minutes (sauce will thicken slightly). Strain through fine-mesh sieve.

NUTRITIONAL INFORMATION, PER ¼ CUP: about 74 cal, 2 g pro, 6 g total fat (4 g sat. fat), 4 g carb, 0 g fibre, 19 mg chol, 116 mg sodium, 97 mg potassium. % RDI: 7% calcium, 1% iron, 7% vit A, 2% folate.

MUSHROOM CREAM SAUCE ⊙

HANDS-ON TIME 15 minutes

TOTAL TIME 15 minutes

MAKES 1¼ cups

INGREDIENTS

1 tbsp	butter
1	shallot, diced
2	cloves garlic, minced
2 cups	mixed sliced exotic mushrooms (cremini, shiitake and oyster)
½ cup	dry white wine
½ cup	whipping cream (35%)
pinch	each salt and pepper
1 tbsp	chopped fresh parsley

DIRECTIONS

In skillet, melt butter over medium heat; cook shallot until softened, about 2 minutes. Add garlic; cook for 1 minute.

Add mushrooms; cook over medium-high heat until softened and no liquid remains, about 5 minutes. Add wine; reduce heat and simmer for 4 minutes.

Add cream, salt and pepper; simmer until thick enough to coat back of spoon, about 2 minutes. Stir in parsley.

NUTRITIONAL INFORMATION, PER ¼ CUP: about 94 cal, 1 g pro, 8 g total fat (5 g sat. fat), 3 g carb, 1 g fibre, 26 mg chol, 27 mg sodium, 159 mg potassium. % RDI: 2% calcium, 3% iron, 8% vit A, 2% vit C, 3% folate.

CREAMY MAPLE MUSTARD BASTING SAUCE ⊙

HANDS-ON TIME 10 minutes

TOTAL TIME 10 minutes

MAKES about 2 cups

INGREDIENTS

2 tbsp	vegetable oil
2	small onions, chopped
4	cloves garlic, minced
⅔ cup	dry white wine
½ cup	maple syrup
¼ cup	cider vinegar
2 tsp	dry mustard
½ tsp	each salt and pepper
⅓ cup	Dijon mustard
3 tbsp	unsalted butter

DIRECTIONS

In saucepan, heat oil over medium heat; cook onions and garlic, stirring often, until fragrant and golden, about 2 minutes.

Stir in wine and bring to boil; boil for 1 minute. Add maple syrup, vinegar, dry mustard, salt and pepper; return to boil and boil until slightly syrupy, about 3 minutes.

Stir in Dijon mustard and butter until melted. Let cool. In blender, purée until smooth. To use, see Using Basting Sauces, opposite. *(Make-ahead: Refrigerate in airtight container for up to 2 weeks.)*

NUTRITIONAL INFORMATION, PER ¼ CUP: about 153 cal, 1 g pro, 9 g total fat (3 g sat. fat), 17 g carb, 1 g fibre, 11 mg chol, 282 mg sodium, 115 mg potassium. % RDI: 4% calcium, 5% iron, 4% vit A, 2% vit C, 2% folate.

HONEY GINGER BASTING SAUCE

HANDS-ON TIME 15 minutes

TOTAL TIME 15 minutes

MAKES about 2 cups

INGREDIENTS

2 tbsp	vegetable oil
6	shallots, minced
6	cloves garlic, minced
6 tbsp	grated fresh ginger
½ cup	hoisin sauce
½ cup	liquid honey
2 tbsp	unseasoned rice vinegar
2 tsp	sesame oil
½ tsp	hot pepper flakes
2 tsp	cornstarch

DIRECTIONS

In saucepan, heat oil over medium heat; cook shallots, garlic and ginger, stirring occasionally, until fragrant and golden, about 2 minutes.

Stir in hoisin sauce, honey, ¼ cup water, vinegar, sesame oil and hot pepper flakes; bring to boil. Boil until thickened slightly, 2 to 3 minutes.

Whisk ¼ cup water with cornstarch; whisk into sauce and simmer until thickened, about 1 minute. To use, see Using Basting Sauces, below. *(Make-ahead: Let cool for 30 minutes; refrigerate in airtight container for up to 2 weeks.)*

NUTRITIONAL INFORMATION, PER ¼ CUP: about 159 cal, 1 g pro, 5 g total fat (1 g sat. fat), 29 g carb, 1 g fibre, 0 mg chol, 262 mg sodium, 103 mg potassium. % RDI: 1% calcium, 3% iron, 1% vit A, 2% vit C, 3% folate.

SWEET SMOKY TOMATO BASTING SAUCE

HANDS-ON TIME 25 minutes

TOTAL TIME 25 minutes

MAKES 2 cups

INGREDIENTS

1 tbsp	vegetable oil
1	small onion, diced
2	cloves garlic, minced
1 cup	bottled strained tomatoes (passata)
¼ cup	tomato paste
3 tbsp	each apple cider, cider vinegar and fancy molasses
2	canned chipotle peppers in adobo sauce, minced
2 tbsp	packed brown sugar
1 tbsp	adobo sauce from canned chipotles
1 tsp	Dijon mustard
½ tsp	liquid smoke

DIRECTIONS

In small saucepan, heat oil over medium heat; cook onion and garlic, stirring occasionally, until light golden, about 3 minutes.

Add strained tomatoes, tomato paste, apple cider, vinegar, molasses, chipotle peppers, brown sugar, adobo sauce, mustard and liquid smoke; bring to boil. Reduce heat and simmer, stirring often, until thickened, about 15 minutes.

Let cool slightly. Transfer to food processor; purée until smooth. To use, see Using Basting Sauces, below. *(Make-ahead: Let cool for 30 minutes; refrigerate in airtight container for up to 2 weeks.)*

NUTRITIONAL INFORMATION, PER ¼ CUP: about 79 cal, 1 g pro, 2 g total fat (trace sat. fat), 15 g carb, 1 g fibre, 0 mg chol, 119 mg sodium, 296 mg potassium. % RDI: 3% calcium, 10% iron, 4% vit A, 5% vit C, 2% folate.

USING BASTING SAUCES

The basting sauces on these two pages are perfect for dressing up grilled meats and fish. Use ¼ to ½ cup sauce for every 4 servings (450 g boneless or 900 g bone-in) of meat, poultry or fish. Baste with the sauce during the last few minutes of grilling. Serve extra sauce on the side, if desired.

CLASSIC PESTO ◔

HANDS-ON TIME 5 minutes

TOTAL TIME 5 minutes

MAKES ¾ cup

INGREDIENTS

½ cup	grated Parmesan cheese
⅓ cup	pine nuts
2	cloves garlic
2½ cups	packed fresh basil
¼ tsp	each salt and pepper
⅓ cup	extra-virgin olive oil

DIRECTIONS

In food processor, pulse together Parmesan, pine nuts and garlic until coarsely ground. Add basil, salt and pepper; pulse 6 times.

With motor running, add oil in thin steady stream until smooth. *(Make-ahead: Refrigerate in airtight container for up to 3 days or freeze for up to 6 months.)*

NUTRITIONAL INFORMATION, PER 1 TBSP: about 99 cal, 2 g pro, 10 g total fat (2 g sat. fat), 1 g carb, trace fibre, 4 mg chol, 112 mg sodium, 60 mg potassium. % RDI: 5% calcium, 4% iron, 4% vit A, 2% vit C, 3% folate.

SUN-DRIED TOMATO AND ALMOND PESTO ◔

HANDS-ON TIME 5 minutes

TOTAL TIME 5 minutes

MAKES 1 cup

INGREDIENTS

½ cup	slivered almonds
2	cloves garlic
1 cup	drained oil-packed sun-dried tomatoes
¼ tsp	each salt and pepper
⅓ cup	extra-virgin olive oil

DIRECTIONS

In food processor, pulse almonds with garlic until coarsely ground. Add sun-dried tomatoes, salt and pepper; pulse until finely chopped.

With motor running, add oil in thin steady stream until smooth. *(Make-ahead: Refrigerate in airtight container for up to 3 days or freeze for up to 6 months.)*

NUTRITIONAL INFORMATION, PER 1 TBSP: about 75 cal, 1 g pro, 7 g total fat (1 g sat. fat), 2 g carb, 1 g fibre, 0 mg chol, 55 mg sodium, 133 mg potassium. % RDI: 1% calcium, 3% iron, 1% vit A, 12% vit C, 1% folate.

CILANTRO, CHILI AND SUNFLOWER SEED PESTO ◔

HANDS-ON TIME 5 minutes

TOTAL TIME 5 minutes

MAKES 1 cup

INGREDIENTS

1	red hot pepper, seeded and chopped
½ cup	unsalted roasted sunflower seeds
3	cloves garlic
1 cup	fresh cilantro leaves
½ tsp	grated lime zest
pinch	salt
⅓ cup	light-tasting olive oil

DIRECTIONS

In food processor, pulse together hot pepper, sunflower seeds and garlic until coarsely ground. Add cilantro, lime zest and salt; pulse 6 times.

With motor running, add oil in thin steady stream until smooth. *(Make-ahead: Refrigerate in airtight container for up to 3 days or freeze for up to 6 months.)*

NUTRITIONAL INFORMATION, PER 1 TBSP: about 66 cal, 1 g pro, 7 g total fat (1 g sat. fat), 1 g carb, trace fibre, 0 mg chol, 1 mg sodium, 30 mg potassium. % RDI: 1% calcium, 1% iron, 1% vit A, 3% vit C, 5% folate.

WATERCRESS AND WALNUT PESTO 🌀

HANDS-ON TIME 5 minutes

TOTAL TIME 5 minutes

MAKES ¾ cup

INGREDIENTS

½ cup	walnuts, toasted
1	clove garlic, chopped
2 cups	loosely packed trimmed watercress
½ cup	tightly packed fresh flatleaf parsley leaves
¼ tsp	each salt and pepper
⅓ cup	olive oil

DIRECTIONS

In food processor, pulse walnuts with garlic until coarsely ground. Add watercress, parsley, salt and pepper; pulse 6 times.

With motor running, add oil in thin steady stream until smooth. *(Make-ahead: Refrigerate in airtight container for up to 3 days or freeze for up to 6 months.)*

NUTRITIONAL INFORMATION, PER 1 TBSP: about 87 cal, 1 g pro, 9 g total fat (1 g sat. fat), 1 g carb, 1 g fibre, 0 mg chol, 52 mg sodium, 56 mg potassium. % RDI: 1% calcium, 3% iron, 4% vit A, 10% vit C, 4% folate.

MINT AND PISTACHIO PESTO 🌀

HANDS-ON TIME 5 minutes

TOTAL TIME 5 minutes

MAKES 1 cup

INGREDIENTS

½ cup	unsalted shelled pistachios
1	clove garlic
1 cup	each packed fresh mint leaves and fresh flatleaf parsley leaves
pinch	each salt and pepper
⅓ cup	extra-virgin olive oil

DIRECTIONS

In food processor, pulse pistachios with garlic until coarsely ground. Add mint, parsley, salt and pepper; pulse 6 times.

With motor running, add oil in thin steady stream until smooth. *(Make-ahead: Refrigerate in airtight container for up to 3 days or freeze for up to 6 months.)*

NUTRITIONAL INFORMATION, PER 1 TBSP: about 64 cal, 1 g pro, 6 g total fat (1 g sat. fat), 2 g carb, 1 g fibre, 0 mg chol, 3 mg sodium, 78 mg potassium. % RDI: 2% calcium, 6% iron, 5% vit A, 10% vit C, 5% folate.

ARUGULA AND PEPITA PESTO 🌀

HANDS-ON TIME 5 minutes

TOTAL TIME 5 minutes

MAKES 1 cup

INGREDIENTS

¾ cup	unsalted roasted pepitas
1	clove garlic
2 cups	packed trimmed arugula
1 tbsp	lemon juice
¼ tsp	salt
pinch	each grated nutmeg and pepper
⅓ cup	extra-virgin olive oil

DIRECTIONS

In food processor, pulse pepitas with garlic until coarsely ground. Add arugula, lemon juice, salt, nutmeg and pepper; pulse 6 times.

With motor running, add oil in thin steady stream until smooth. *(Make-ahead: Refrigerate in airtight container for up to 3 days or freeze for up to 6 months.)*

NUTRITIONAL INFORMATION, PER 1 TBSP: about 97 cal, 4 g pro, 9 g total fat (2 g sat. fat), 2 g carb, 2 g fibre, 0 mg chol, 39 mg sodium, 97 mg potassium. % RDI: 1% calcium, 12% iron, 1% vit A, 2% vit C, 4% folate.

TANDOORI YOGURT MARINADE

HANDS-ON TIME 10 minutes

TOTAL TIME 10 minutes

MAKES about 1 cup

INGREDIENTS

¾ cup	2% plain yogurt
2 tbsp	chopped fresh cilantro
2 tbsp	lemon juice
1	clove garlic, minced
1 tbsp	grated fresh ginger
1 tbsp	garam masala
1 tsp	each sweet paprika, salt and cracked black pepper

DIRECTIONS

Whisk together yogurt, cilantro, lemon juice, garlic, ginger, garam masala, paprika, salt and pepper. To use, see Using Marinades, opposite.

NUTRITIONAL INFORMATION, PER 2 TBSP: about 21 cal, 1 g pro, 1 g total fat (trace sat. fat), 3 g carb, trace fibre, 2 mg chol, 304 mg sodium, 83 mg potassium. % RDI: 4% calcium, 3% iron, 2% vit A, 3% vit C.

LEMON HERB GARLIC MARINADE

HANDS-ON TIME 10 minutes

TOTAL TIME 10 minutes

MAKES about ¾ cup

INGREDIENTS

⅓ cup	olive oil
¼ cup	white wine vinegar
2 tbsp	each chopped fresh thyme and fresh oregano
4 tsp	grated lemon zest
2 tbsp	lemon juice
4	cloves garlic, minced
1 tsp	each salt and pepper

DIRECTIONS

Whisk together oil, vinegar, thyme, oregano, lemon zest, lemon juice, garlic, salt and pepper. To use, see Using Marinades, opposite.

NUTRITIONAL INFORMATION, PER 2 TBSP: about 116 cal, trace pro, 12 g total fat (2 g sat. fat), 2 g carb, 1 g fibre, 0 mg chol, 384 mg sodium, 38 mg potassium. % RDI: 2% calcium, 4% iron, 1% vit A, 10% vit C, 1% folate.

APPLE CIDER SHALLOT MARINADE

HANDS-ON TIME 10 minutes

TOTAL TIME 10 minutes

MAKES about 1 cup

INGREDIENTS

¾ cup	apple cider
2 tbsp	cider vinegar
4	shallots, sliced
3	sprigs fresh thyme
1 tsp	whole allspice
1 tsp	Dijon mustard
½ tsp	Worcestershire sauce

DIRECTIONS

Whisk together cider, vinegar, shallots, thyme, allspice, mustard and Worcestershire sauce. To use, see Using Marinades, opposite.

NUTRITIONAL INFORMATION, PER 2 TBSP: about 17 cal, trace pro, trace total fat (0 g sat. fat), 5 g carb, trace fibre, 0 mg chol, 13 mg sodium, 55 mg potassium. % RDI: 1% calcium, 2% iron, 1% vit A, 2% vit C, 1% folate.

BANGKOK MARINADE

HANDS-ON TIME 10 minutes

TOTAL TIME 10 minutes

MAKES about ⅔ cup

INGREDIENTS

¼ cup	minced fresh cilantro
2 tbsp	each vegetable oil and lime juice
1 tbsp	fish sauce or soy sauce
2	cloves garlic, minced
1	green onion, minced
1 tsp	granulated sugar
1 tsp	minced hot pepper

DIRECTIONS

Whisk together cilantro, 3 tbsp water, oil, lime juice, fish sauce, garlic, green onion, sugar and hot pepper. To use, see Using Marinades, below.

NUTRITIONAL INFORMATION, PER 2 TBSP: about 54 cal, trace pro, 5 g total fat (trace sat. fat), 2 g carb, trace fibre, 0 mg chol, 263 mg sodium, 32 mg potassium. % RDI: 1% calcium, 1% iron, 1% vit A, 3% vit C, 2% folate.

PROVENÇAL MARINADE ◓

HANDS-ON TIME 10 minutes

TOTAL TIME 10 minutes

MAKES about ⅔ cup

INGREDIENTS

¼ cup	dry red wine
2 tbsp	extra-virgin olive oil
1 tbsp	herbes de Provence
1 tbsp	red wine vinegar
2	cloves garlic, minced
1	shallot, minced
¼ tsp	each salt and pepper

DIRECTIONS

Whisk together wine, oil, herbes de Provence, vinegar, garlic, shallot, salt and pepper. To use, see Using Marinades, below.

NUTRITIONAL INFORMATION, PER 2 TBSP: about 54 cal, trace pro, 5 g total fat (1 g sat. fat), 1 g carb, trace fibre, 0 mg chol, 109 mg sodium, 34 mg potassium. % RDI: 2% calcium, 4% iron, 1% vit A, 2% vit C, 1% folate.

CHIMICHURRI MARINADE ◓

HANDS-ON TIME 10 minutes

TOTAL TIME 10 minutes

MAKES about ⅔ cup

INGREDIENTS

¼ cup	minced fresh parsley
2 tbsp	extra-virgin olive oil
2 tbsp	sherry vinegar or red wine vinegar
1 tbsp	minced onion
2	cloves garlic, minced
1	jalapeño pepper, seeded and minced
½ tsp	salt

DIRECTIONS

Whisk together parsley, oil, vinegar, 2 tbsp water, onion, garlic, jalapeño pepper and salt. To use, see Using Marinades, below.

NUTRITIONAL INFORMATION, PER 2 TBSP: about 50 cal, trace pro, 5 g total fat (1 g sat. fat), 1 g carb, trace fibre, 0 mg chol, 217 mg sodium, 31 mg potassium. % RDI: 1% calcium, 2% iron, 2% vit A, 8% vit C, 2% folate.

USING MARINADES

The marinades on the opposite page work on just about anything. Use ½ cup Tandoori Yogurt, Lemon Herb Garlic or Apple Cider Shallot marinade (opposite) for every 4 servings (450 g boneless or 675 g bone-in) of meat, poultry or fish. Cover and marinate fish in the refrigerator for no more than 30 minutes. Cover and marinate meat or poultry in the refrigerator for 6 to 24 hours.

The marinades on this page are especially well-suited to salmon, chicken and pork. Use ⅓ cup Bangkok, Provençal or Chimichurri marinade (above) for every 4 to 6 servings (750 g) of boneless skinless chicken breasts or thighs, pork tenderloin or salmon fillets. Cover and marinate salmon in the refrigerator for 30 minutes; cover and marinate chicken or pork in the refrigerator for up to 4 hours.

Always keep sauces and marinades that have come into contact with raw food separate from cooked food. If you plan to serve some of the sauce or marinade at the table, remove it before basting or marinating meat with the remainder.

UNIVERSAL SPICE RUB

HANDS-ON TIME 5 minutes

TOTAL TIME 5 minutes

MAKES about ½ cup

INGREDIENTS

3 tbsp	sweet paprika
1 tbsp	packed brown sugar
2 tsp	garlic powder
2 tsp	ground cumin
1 tsp	salt
1 tsp	dried oregano
1 tsp	onion powder
1 tsp	black pepper
½ tsp	dry mustard
¼ tsp	cayenne pepper

DIRECTIONS

Stir together paprika, brown sugar, garlic powder, cumin, salt, oregano, onion powder, black pepper, dry mustard and cayenne pepper. To use, see Using Rubs, below. *(Make-ahead: Store in airtight container for up to 3 months.)*

NUTRITIONAL INFORMATION, PER 2 TBSP: about 42 cal, 1 g pro, 1 g total fat (trace sat. fat), 9 g carb, 3 g fibre, 0 mg chol, 579 mg sodium, 190 mg potassium. % RDI: 3% calcium, 17% iron, 25% vit A, 8% vit C, 4% folate.

SALT AND PEPPER STEAK RUB

HANDS-ON TIME 7 minutes

TOTAL TIME 7 minutes

MAKES about ⅓ cup

INGREDIENTS

2 tbsp	coriander seeds
2 tbsp	black peppercorns
2 tsp	coarse salt
2 tsp	dehydrated minced garlic

DIRECTIONS

In dry skillet, toast coriander seeds and peppercorns over medium heat, shaking pan often, until fragrant, about 4 minutes. Let cool.

In spice mill or clean coffee grinder, coarsely grind together coriander seeds, peppercorns and salt. Transfer to small bowl; stir in garlic. To use, see Using Rubs, below. *(Make-ahead: Store in airtight container for up to 3 months.)*

NUTRITIONAL INFORMATION, PER 2 TBSP: about 31 cal, 1 g pro, 1 g total fat (trace sat. fat), 7 g carb, 3 g fibre, 0 mg chol, 1,164 mg sodium, 112 mg potassium. % RDI: 5% calcium, 16% iron, 3% vit C.

CARIBBEAN SEASONING

HANDS-ON TIME 5 minutes

TOTAL TIME 5 minutes

MAKES about ⅓ cup

INGREDIENTS

2 tbsp	dried thyme
2 tsp	salt
2 tsp	black pepper
2 tsp	garlic powder
1 tsp	cinnamon
1 tsp	ground coriander
1 tsp	ground ginger
¾ tsp	cayenne pepper
½ tsp	ground allspice
½ tsp	nutmeg

DIRECTIONS

Stir together thyme, salt, black pepper, garlic powder, cinnamon, coriander, ginger, cayenne pepper, allspice and nutmeg. To use, see Using Rubs, below. *(Make-ahead: Store in airtight container for up to 3 months.)*

NUTRITIONAL INFORMATION, PER 2 TBSP: about 31 cal, 1 g pro, 1 g total fat (trace sat. fat), 7 g carb, 3 g fibre, 0 mg chol, 1,724 mg sodium, 106 mg potassium. % RDI: 8% calcium, 36% iron, 3% vit A, 5% vit C, 5% folate.

USING RUBS

Our rubs on these pages are marvellous on meat, poultry and fish.
Use 2 tbsp rub for every 4 to 6 servings (450 g boneless or 675 g bone-in) of meat, poultry or fish. Rub over meat, poultry or fish and refrigerate for 15 minutes. Or refrigerate meat or poultry (but not fish) in an airtight container for up to 24 hours before grilling.

TIKKA MASALA RUB

HANDS-ON TIME 5 minutes

TOTAL TIME 5 minutes

MAKES ½ cup

INGREDIENTS

3 tbsp	ground coriander
2 tbsp	ground cumin
2 tsp	cinnamon
1 tsp	ground cardamom
½ tsp	ground ginger
½ tsp	each salt and pepper

DIRECTIONS

Stir together coriander, cumin, cinnamon, cardamom, ginger, salt and pepper. To use, see Using Rubs, opposite. *(Make-ahead: Store in airtight container for up to 3 months.)*

NUTRITIONAL INFORMATION, PER 2 TBSP: about 30 cal, 1 g pro, 2 g total fat (trace sat. fat), 5 g carb, 3 g fibre, 0 mg chol, 294 mg sodium, 126 mg potassium. % RDI: 7% calcium, 24% iron, 1% vit A, 3% vit C.

FIRE AND BRIMSTONE RUB

HANDS-ON TIME 5 minutes

TOTAL TIME 5 minutes

MAKES ½ cup

INGREDIENTS

¼ cup	chili powder
2 tbsp	smoked or sweet paprika
1 tsp	cracked black pepper
½ tsp	salt
½ tsp	cayenne pepper

DIRECTIONS

Mix together chili powder, paprika, black pepper, salt and cayenne pepper. To use, see Using Rubs, opposite. *(Make-ahead: Store in airtight container for up to 3 months.)*

NUTRITIONAL INFORMATION, PER 2 TBSP: about 36 cal, 2 g pro, 2 g total fat (trace sat. fat), 6 g carb, 4 g fibre, 0 mg chol, 364 mg sodium, 236 mg potassium. % RDI: 3% calcium, 15% iron, 40% vit A, 13% vit C, 5% folate.

SCARBOROUGH FAIR RUB

HANDS-ON TIME 5 minutes

TOTAL TIME 5 minutes

MAKES ½ cup

INGREDIENTS

⅓ cup	dried parsley
2 tbsp	crumbled dried sage
2 tbsp	dried rosemary
2 tbsp	dried thyme
½ tsp	salt
¼ tsp	pepper

DIRECTIONS

In clean coffee grinder, combine parsley, sage, rosemary, thyme, salt and pepper. Pulse until powdery with some small bits still remaining. To use, see Using Rubs, opposite. *(Make-ahead: Store in airtight container for up to 3 months.)*

NUTRITIONAL INFORMATION, PER 2 TBSP: about 17 cal, 1 g pro, 1 g total fat (trace sat. fat), 3 g carb, 2 g fibre, 0 mg chol, 296 mg sodium, 103 mg potassium. % RDI: 8% calcium, 31% iron, 3% vit A, 7% vit C, 6% folate.

ZESTY TOMATO JAM

HANDS-ON TIME 40 minutes

TOTAL TIME 2¾ hours

MAKES 2 cups

INGREDIENTS

1.125 kg	ripe tomatoes (about 8 medium)
1 tbsp	olive oil
1	onion, finely diced
3	cloves garlic, minced
1½ tsp	mixed pickling spice
¼ cup	balsamic vinegar
3 tbsp	packed brown sugar
½ tsp	each salt and pepper

DIRECTIONS

Using sharp knife, score X in bottom of each tomato. In large pot of boiling water, blanch tomatoes until skins begin to loosen, 12 seconds. Using slotted spoon, transfer to bowl of ice water; let cool for 20 seconds. Drain tomatoes and peel off skins; core and chop to make 4½ cups. Set aside.

In large shallow saucepan, heat oil over medium heat; cook onion, garlic and mixed pickling spice, stirring often, until onion is tender, 3 minutes.

Add tomatoes, vinegar, brown sugar, salt and pepper; cook, stirring occasionally, until thickened and reduced to about 2 cups, about 30 minutes. Let cool. *(Make-ahead: Refrigerate in airtight containers for up to 3 weeks or freeze for up to 3 months.)*

NUTRITIONAL INFORMATION, PER 1 TBSP: about 17 cal, trace pro, 1 g total fat (trace sat. fat), 3 g carb, trace fibre, 0 mg chol, 38 mg sodium, 70 mg potassium. % RDI: 1% calcium, 1% iron, 2% vit A, 5% vit C, 1% folate.

QUICK PICKLED GREEN BEANS

HANDS-ON TIME 20 minutes

TOTAL TIME 2 hours

MAKES 4 servings

INGREDIENTS

450 g	green beans
1¼ cups	vinegar
3 tbsp	granulated sugar
1 tbsp	pickling salt (see tip, below)
2 tsp	mustard seeds
1	hot pepper, halved lengthwise and seeded

DIRECTIONS

Cut beans into 3½-inch (9 cm) lengths, discarding stem ends.

In saucepan, bring 1½ cups water, vinegar, sugar, salt and mustard seeds to boil, stirring until sugar and salt are dissolved. Add beans; cook, stirring occasionally, just until tender, about 8 minutes. Add hot pepper. Let cool completely.

Stand beans in two 2-cup (500 mL) canning jars; add pepper half to each jar. Fill with vinegar mixture; cover with lid. Let stand for at least 1 hour before serving. *(Make-ahead: Refrigerate for up to 3 weeks.)*

NUTRITIONAL INFORMATION, PER SERVING: about 56 cal, 2 g pro, 1 g total fat (trace sat. fat), 13 g carb, 2 g fibre, 0 mg chol, 424 mg sodium, 177 mg potassium. % RDI: 4% calcium, 6% iron, 7% vit A, 38% vit C, 15% folate.

TIP FROM THE TEST KITCHEN
Pickling salt is also called preserving salt or canning salt. It is pure sodium chloride and does not contain additives, such as iodine or anti-caking agents. It keeps brine crystal clear and ensures pickles stay brightly coloured and don't darken.

TOMATILLO SALSA ◐

Tomatillos are relatives of the Cape gooseberry. Look for fresh tomatillos in farmer's markets from late summer to early fall.

HANDS-ON TIME
1½ hours

TOTAL TIME
26 hours

MAKES
8 cups

INGREDIENTS

4	sweet green peppers
6	jalapeño peppers
6 cups	chopped fresh tomatillos (about 900 g)
2 cups	chopped white onions
4	cloves garlic, minced
⅔ cup	white wine vinegar
3½ tsp	salt
1 tbsp	granulated sugar
1 tsp	ground coriander
1 tsp	ground cumin
¼ tsp	pepper
¾ cup	finely chopped fresh cilantro
½ cup	finely chopped fresh parsley
¼ cup	lime juice

DIRECTIONS

Arrange green peppers and jalapeño peppers on rimmed baking sheet; roast in 475°F (240°C) oven, turning once, until charred, about 30 minutes. Let cool. Peel, seed and chop.

In large saucepan, combine green peppers, jalapeño peppers, tomatillos, onions, garlic, vinegar, salt, sugar, coriander, cumin and pepper; bring to boil, stirring.

Reduce heat to medium; cover and simmer for 5 minutes. Uncover and simmer, stirring occasionally, until no longer watery, about 30 minutes.

Stir in cilantro, parsley and lime juice; simmer for 3 minutes.

Pack into 8 hot (sterilized) 1-cup (250 mL) canning jars with tight-fitting lids, leaving ½-inch (1 cm) headspace, and scrape down sides of jars with non-metallic utensil to remove any air bubbles. Cover with lids. Screw on bands until resistance is met; increase to fingertip tight.

Transfer to boiling water canner; boil for 20 minutes. Turn off heat. Uncover and let jars stand in canner for 5 minutes. Lift up rack. Using canning tongs, transfer jars to cooling rack; let cool for 24 hours.

NUTRITIONAL INFORMATION, PER 1 TBSP: about 5 cal, trace pro, trace total fat (0 g sat. fat), 1 g carb, trace fibre, 0 mg chol, 63 mg sodium, 31 mg potassium. % RDI: 1% iron, 1% vit A, 7% vit C, 1% folate.

CLASSIC CHILI SAUCE

In the Test Kitchen, we used to make chili sauce with canned tomatoes, but this recipe has been updated with fresh tomatoes for a more intense taste.

HANDS-ON TIME
1 hour

TOTAL TIME
25¾ hours

MAKES
about 6 cups

INGREDIENTS

8 cups	chopped peeled tomatoes (about 1.5 kg)
1½ cups	chopped onions
1½ cups	chopped sweet red peppers
1½ cups	vinegar
1 cup	chopped sweet green peppers
1 cup	chopped celery
¾ cup	granulated sugar (approx)
1 tbsp	finely chopped red finger hot pepper
1	clove garlic, minced
1 tsp	salt
1 tsp	mustard seeds
½ tsp	each celery seeds, ground cloves and cinnamon
¼ tsp	each ground ginger and black pepper
pinch	cayenne pepper (approx)

DIRECTIONS

In large heavy-bottomed saucepan, combine tomatoes, onions, red peppers, vinegar, green peppers, celery, sugar, hot pepper, garlic, salt, mustard seeds, celery seeds, cloves, cinnamon, ginger, black pepper and cayenne pepper. Bring to boil, stirring often. Reduce heat and simmer briskly, stirring often, until thickened and saucy, and reduced to just over 6 cups, about 1 hour. Add up to ¼ cup more sugar and increase cayenne pepper to taste, if desired.

Pack into 6 hot (sterilized) 1-cup (250 mL) canning jars with tight-fitting lids, leaving ½-inch (1 cm) headspace, and scrape down sides of jars with non-metallic utensil to remove any air bubbles. Cover with lids. Screw on bands until resistance is met; increase to fingertip tight.

Transfer to boiling water canner; boil for 10 minutes. Turn off heat. Uncover and let jars stand in canner for 5 minutes. Lift up rack. Using canning tongs, transfer jars to cooling rack; let cool for 24 hours.

NUTRITIONAL INFORMATION, PER 1 TBSP: about 12 cal, trace pro, trace total fat (trace sat. fat), 3 g carb, trace fibre, 0 mg chol, 26 mg sodium, 50 mg potassium. % RDI: 1% iron, 2% vit A, 12% vit C, 1% folate.

TIP FROM THE TEST KITCHEN

To strike the perfect balance between sweet and heat, you may want to add more sugar if your tomatoes are a bit tart. Just don't use less sugar that what's called for— the food safety of the final product depends on a specific amount of sugar.

SPICED PEACH CHUTNEY ⌀

HANDS-ON TIME 25 minutes

TOTAL TIME 2 hours

MAKES 3 cups

INGREDIENTS

4	firm ripe peaches
2 tsp	vegetable oil
1	onion, chopped
1 tbsp	minced seeded jalapeño pepper
2 tsp	minced fresh ginger
¼ tsp	ground coriander
pinch	cinnamon
6 tbsp	granulated sugar
3 tbsp	cider vinegar
½ tsp	each salt and pepper
1 tsp	cornstarch

DIRECTIONS

Using sharp knife, score X in bottom of each peach. In pot of boiling water, blanch peaches until skins begin to loosen, about 30 seconds. Using slotted spoon, transfer to bowl of ice water; let cool for 20 seconds. Drain peaches and peel off skins; halve and remove pits. Cut into ½-inch (1 cm) chunks to make about 3 cups; set aside.

In saucepan, heat oil over medium heat; cook onion, jalapeño pepper, ginger, coriander and cinnamon, stirring often, until onion is golden, about 10 minutes.

Stir in peaches, sugar, vinegar, 2 tbsp water, salt and pepper; cook, stirring, until peaches are tender but still hold their shape, about 5 minutes.

Stir 1 tbsp water with cornstarch; stir into peach mixture and cook, stirring, until thickened, about 1 minute. Let cool. *(Make-ahead: Refrigerate in airtight containers for up to 3 weeks or freeze for up to 2 months.)*

NUTRITIONAL INFORMATION, PER 1 TBSP: about 13 cal, trace pro, trace total fat (0 g sat. fat), 3 g carb, trace fibre, 0 mg chol, 24 mg sodium, 25 mg potassium. % RDI: 2% vit C.

RHUBARB TOMATO CHUTNEY ⌀

HANDS-ON TIME 45 minutes

TOTAL TIME 26 hours

MAKES 4 cups

INGREDIENTS

4 cups	chopped rhubarb
2 cups	packed brown sugar
2 cups	chopped seeded peeled tomatoes
1 cup	cider vinegar
½ cup	golden raisins
1 tbsp	mustard seeds
1 tbsp	grated fresh ginger
2	cloves garlic, minced
½ tsp	salt
½ tsp	hot pepper sauce

DIRECTIONS

In large shallow Dutch oven, combine rhubarb, brown sugar, tomatoes, vinegar, raisins, mustard seeds, ginger, garlic, salt and hot pepper sauce; bring to boil. Reduce heat and simmer, stirring occasionally, until mixture is reduced to 4 cups and is thick enough to mound on spoon, 1½ to 2 hours.

Pack into 4 hot (sterilized) 1-cup (250 mL) canning jars with tight-fitting lids, leaving ½-inch (1 cm) headspace, and scrape down sides of jars with non-metallic utensil to remove any air bubbles. Cover with lids. Screw on bands until resistance is met; increase to fingertip tight.

Transfer to boiling water canner; boil for 15 minutes. Turn off heat. Uncover and let jars stand in canner for 5 minutes. Lift up rack. Using canning tongs, transfer jars to cooling rack; let cool for 24 hours.

NUTRITIONAL INFORMATION, PER 1 TBSP: about 34 cal, trace pro, 0 g total fat (0 g sat. fat), 9 g carb, trace fibre, 0 mg chol, 21 mg sodium. % RDI: 1% calcium, 2% iron, 1% vit A, 2% vit C.

STRAWBERRY VANILLA JAM ⟳

Make strawberry season last much longer by preserving jars of this classic ruby-red jam. The vanilla bean gives it a sophisticated flavour and fragrance.

HANDS-ON TIME
35 minutes

TOTAL TIME
25 hours

MAKES
about 8 cups

INGREDIENTS

12 cups	strawberries, hulled
1	pkg (49 g) light pectin
4½ cups	granulated sugar
1	vanilla bean

DIRECTIONS

In large Dutch oven and using potato masher, mash strawberries, 1 cup at a time, to make 6 cups fruit.

Mix pectin with ¼ cup of the sugar; stir into strawberries. Halve vanilla bean lengthwise; using tip of sharp knife, scrape out seeds. Stir seeds and pod into strawberries. Bring to full rolling boil over high heat, stirring constantly with wooden spoon. Stir in remaining sugar and return to full rolling boil; boil hard, stirring constantly, for 1 minute. Remove from heat. Stir, skimming off foam, for 5 minutes. Discard vanilla pod.

Pack into 8 hot (sterilized) 1-cup (250 mL) canning jars with tight-fitting lids, leaving ¼-inch (5 mm) headspace, and scrape down sides of jars with non-metallic utensil to remove any air bubbles. Cover with lids. Screw on bands until resistance is met; increase to fingertip tight.

Transfer to boiling water canner; boil for 10 minutes. Turn off heat. Uncover and let jars stand in canner for 5 minutes. Lift up rack. Using canning tongs, transfer jars to cooling rack; let cool for 24 hours.

NUTRITIONAL INFORMATION, PER 1 TBSP: about 32 cal, trace pro, 0 g total fat (0 g sat. fat), 8 g carb, trace fibre, 0 mg chol, 1 mg sodium, 17 mg potassium. % RDI: 1% iron, 7% vit C.

VARIATION
STRAIGHT-UP STRAWBERRY JAM
Omit vanilla bean. Continue with recipe as directed.

ONE-PINT RASPBERRY JAM ◐

HANDS-ON TIME 10 minutes

TOTAL TIME 1¼ hours

MAKES 1 cup

INGREDIENTS

1 pint	raspberries (about 340 g)
1 cup	granulated sugar
1 tsp	lemon juice
1½ tsp	vanilla
pinch	salt

DIRECTIONS

Place 2 small plates in freezer.

In saucepan over medium-high heat, bring raspberries, sugar, lemon juice, vanilla and salt to boil, stirring constantly and mashing raspberries with back of spoon, until sugar is dissolved. Boil hard, skimming off foam and stirring often, until thickened to consistency of soft jelly, 6 to 7 minutes. Remove from heat.

Drop ½ tsp of the hot jam onto 1 of the chilled plates; let cool. Return to freezer for 1 minute. Tilt plate; mixture should be firm and wrinkle when edge is pushed with finger. If mixture is too soft, return to boil, checking at 1-minute intervals until proper consistency is achieved. Let cool completely before serving or storing. *(Make-ahead: Refrigerate in airtight container for up to 3 weeks.)*

NUTRITIONAL INFORMATION, PER 1 TBSP: about 58 cal, trace pro, trace total fat (0 g sat. fat), 15 g carb, 1 g fibre, 0 mg chol, 1 mg sodium, 28 mg potassium. % RDI: 1% iron, 5% vit C, 1% folate.

EASY BLUEBERRY LEMON SPREAD ◐

HANDS-ON TIME 20 minutes

TOTAL TIME 2 hours

MAKES 1½ cups

INGREDIENTS

1	lemon
2 cups	wild blueberries
2 cups	granulated sugar
pinch	salt

DIRECTIONS

Finely grate lemon zest and juice lemon. Place lemon seeds on 1-inch (2.5 cm) square of cheesecloth; tie with kitchen string to make bundle (see tip, below). Set aside.

In saucepan and using potato masher, lightly crush blueberries. Add sugar, 2 tbsp of the lemon juice, 2 tsp of the lemon zest and salt. Cook over medium heat, stirring constantly, until sugar is dissolved.

Add lemon seed bundle. Boil hard for 4 minutes, skimming off foam from surface and stirring often (mixture will be thin). Let cool. *(Make-ahead: Refrigerate in airtight container for up to 3 weeks or freeze for up to 2 months.)*

NUTRITIONAL INFORMATION, PER 1 TBSP: about 72 cal, trace pro, 0 g total fat (0 g sat. fat), 19 g carb, trace fibre, 0 mg chol, 0 mg sodium, 12 mg potassium. % RDI: 2% vit C.

TIP FROM THE TEST KITCHEN
The bundle of lemon seeds helps this spread jell. The seeds are a natural source of pectin, which makes jams, jellies and spreads set.

SOUR CHERRY AND VODKA SAUCE ◯

A fancy sauce is a terrific way to dress up all sorts of desserts. Serve this cherry-vodka blend warm over crêpes with a bit of mascarpone cheese or cold over ice cream.

HANDS-ON TIME
5 minutes

TOTAL TIME
20 minutes

MAKES
about 2 cups

INGREDIENTS

2¼ cups	thawed frozen or canned sour cherries in juice
½ cup	granulated sugar
2 tbsp	lemon juice
¼ cup	vodka
1 tsp	vanilla

DIRECTIONS

Reserving juice, drain cherries. In saucepan, bring cherries, ¼ cup of the cherry juice, sugar and lemon juice to boil. Reduce heat and simmer until reduced to 1¾ cups, 12 to 15 minutes.

Stir in vodka and vanilla. Let cool slightly before serving. *(Make-ahead: Refrigerate in airtight container for up to 5 days. Reheat before using, if desired.)*

NUTRITIONAL INFORMATION, PER 2 TBSP: about 43 cal, trace pro, trace total fat (trace sat. fat), 9 g carb, trace fibre, 0 mg chol, 1 mg sodium. % RDI: 1% iron, 2% vit A, 2% vit C.

CLASSIC CRÈME ANGLAISE ◐

This velvety custard is fantastic drizzled over pudding, apple crisp, bread pudding, crêpes, fruit or sponge cake. We've created four different flavour variations that will complement all sorts of desserts.

HANDS-ON TIME
10 minutes

TOTAL TIME
1½ hours

MAKES
about 2 cups

INGREDIENTS

1 cup	whipping cream (35%) or 18% cream
1 cup	milk
¼ cup	granulated sugar
6	egg yolks
1 tsp	vanilla

DIRECTIONS

In small saucepan over medium heat, heat cream, milk and 2 tbsp of the sugar until steaming and bubbles form around edge.

Meanwhile, in bowl, whisk egg yolks with remaining sugar. Whisk in hot cream mixture in thin steady stream; stir back into pan. Cook, stirring constantly, until thick enough to coat back of spoon, about 5 minutes.

Strain into clean bowl; stir in vanilla. Place plastic wrap directly on surface; let cool. Refrigerate until cold, about 1 hour. *(Make-ahead: Refrigerate in airtight container for up to 3 days.)*

NUTRITIONAL INFORMATION, PER 2 TBSP: about 91 cal, 2 g pro, 8 g total fat (4 g sat. fat), 4 g carb, 0 g fibre, 97 mg chol, 16 mg sodium. % RDI: 3% calcium, 1% iron, 9% vit A, 5% folate.

VARIATIONS

VANILLA BEAN CRÈME ANGLAISE

Omit vanilla. Halve 1 vanilla bean lengthwise; using tip of sharp knife, scrape out seeds. Add seeds and pod to cream mixture before heating. Remove pod before serving.

ORANGE WHISKY CRÈME ANGLAISE

Omit vanilla. Add 1 tsp grated orange zest to cream mixture before heating. Stir 2 tbsp whisky into finished sauce.

TEA CRÈME ANGLAISE

Omit vanilla. Add 4 bags Ceylon tea or heaping 1 tbsp loose rooibos tea to cream mixture before heating. Strain if using rooibos tea.

EGGNOG CRÈME ANGLAISE

Omit vanilla. Stir 2 tbsp dark rum and ¼ tsp grated nutmeg into finished sauce.

SILKY BITTERSWEET CHOCOLATE SAUCE ㉚ ◓

This sauce is an all-time favourite—so rich and luscious poured over ice cream or cake. It's wonderful cold or at room temperature. If you want to turn it into hot fudge, try the variation (below).

HANDS-ON TIME
5 minutes

TOTAL TIME
20 minutes

MAKES
about 2 cups

INGREDIENTS

1¼ cups	whipping cream (35%)
3 tbsp	corn syrup
175 g	bittersweet chocolate, chopped

DIRECTIONS

In saucepan, bring cream and corn syrup to boil; remove from heat. Whisk in chocolate until smooth. Let stand until thickened, about 15 minutes. Serve at room temperature or refrigerate until ready to use. *(Make-ahead: Refrigerate in airtight container for up to 5 days.)*

NUTRITIONAL INFORMATION, PER 2 TBSP: about 127 cal, 1 g pro, 12 g total fat (8 g sat. fat), 6 g carb, 2 g fibre, 24 mg chol, 13 mg sodium. % RDI: 2% calcium, 5% iron, 6% vit A.

VARIATIONS

HOT SILKY BITTERSWEET CHOCOLATE SAUCE

Increase chocolate to 250 g. Serve hot.

SILKY MOCHA SAUCE

Add 2 tsp instant coffee granules along with chopped chocolate.

LEMON MERINGUE PIE
page 357

"Homemade fruit tarts are a sweet reminder of the summers I spend at home in France. Ending dinner with a generous slice of fruit-topped flaky pastry is one of my favourite ways to enjoy summer's fresh bounty."

JENNIFER BARTOLI FOOD SPECIALIST

APPLE AND CRANBERRY LATTICE PIE

If you like, flute the edge of the crust for a little extra flourish. If you want to make a half-batch of the pastry (below) for a single-crust pie, use 1 egg yolk instead of a whole egg and halve the remaining ingredients.

HANDS-ON TIME
45 minutes

TOTAL TIME
3½ hours

MAKES
8 servings

INGREDIENTS

1 cup	packed brown sugar
2 tsp	cornstarch
2 tsp	vanilla
pinch	each cinnamon and ground ginger
pinch	salt
3	firm cooking apples (such as Golden Delicious), peeled and chopped
1½ cups	fresh cranberries, coarsely chopped
1	batch Easy-Roll Pie Pastry (below)
1	egg yolk, lightly beaten
1 tbsp	coarse sugar

DIRECTIONS

In large bowl, stir together brown sugar, cornstarch, vanilla, cinnamon, ginger and salt; add apples and cranberries, tossing to coat. Set aside.

On lightly floured surface, roll out half of the pastry to generous ⅛-inch (3 mm) thickness; fit into 9-inch (23 cm) pie plate. Trim edge to leave ¾-inch (2 cm) overhang. Scrape filling into pie shell, packing firmly. Roll out remaining pastry to generous ⅛-inch (3 mm) thickness; using fluted pastry wheel, cut into six scalloped 2-inch (5 cm) wide strips. Lay 3 of the strips, about 1 inch (2.5 cm) apart, over filling. Across centre of pie, weave 1 of the remaining strips over and under previous strips. PHOTO A

On either side of centre strip, weave remaining strips over and under pastry strips to form lattice top. PHOTO B

Trim pastry, leaving ½-inch (1 cm) overhang. Brush some of the egg yolk over bottom pastry rim under each strip; press to seal. Fold both edges under and press to seal. Brush lattice with remaining egg yolk; sprinkle pie with coarse sugar.

Bake on rimmed baking sheet on bottom rack in 425°F (220°C) oven for 20 minutes. Reduce heat to 350°F (180°C); bake, shielding top with foil if browning too much, until bottom is golden and filling is bubbly, 55 to 60 minutes. Let cool in pan on rack.

NUTRITIONAL INFORMATION, PER SERVING: about 494 cal, 6 g pro, 25 g total fat (12 g sat. fat), 63 g carb, 2 g fibre, 85 mg chol, 216 mg sodium, 152 mg potassium. % RDI: 4% calcium, 15% iron, 12% vit A, 5% vit C, 27% folate.

EASY-ROLL PIE PASTRY

In bowl, whisk 2½ cups all-purpose flour with ¾ tsp salt. Using pastry blender or 2 knives, cut in ½ cup each cold unsalted butter and cold lard or vegetable shortening, cubed, until mixture resembles coarse crumbs with a few larger pieces. Whisk ¼ cup cold water, 3 tbsp sour cream and 1 egg; drizzle over flour mixture, tossing with fork and adding up to 1 tsp more cold water if necessary until ragged dough forms. Divide in half; shape into discs. Wrap each; refrigerate until chilled, 30 minutes. *(Make-ahead: Refrigerate for up to 3 days or freeze for up to 1 month.)*
MAKES 1 batch, enough for one 9-inch (23 cm) double-crust pie, or 8 servings

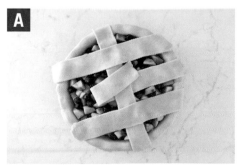

CLASSIC TARTE TATIN

Juicy apples covered in a caramel pan sauce make this French upside-down tart gorgeous and luscious at the same time. Real vanilla bean accentuates the apples' natural sweetness and adds a warm, inviting aroma.

HANDS-ON TIME
1 hour

TOTAL TIME
2 hours

MAKES
8 servings

INGREDIENTS

PASTRY:

1 cup	all-purpose flour
1 tbsp	granulated sugar
pinch	salt
½ cup	cold butter, cubed
1	egg yolk
2 tbsp	ice water (approx)

APPLE TOPPING:

4	Pink Lady apples (see tip, below)
2	Granny Smith apples
⅓ cup	butter
1 cup	granulated sugar
half	vanilla bean, halved lengthwise
pinch	salt

DIRECTIONS

PASTRY: In large bowl, whisk flour, sugar and salt. Using pastry blender or 2 knives, cut in butter until mixture resembles coarse crumbs. Whisk egg yolk with ice water; drizzle over flour mixture, tossing with fork and adding up to 2 tsp more ice water if necessary until mixture clumps.

With floured hands, quickly press into 1-inch (2.5 cm) thick disc. Wrap pastry in plastic wrap; refrigerate for 30 minutes. *(Make-ahead: Refrigerate for up to 24 hours.)*

APPLE TOPPING: While pastry is chilling, peel and quarter Pink Lady and Granny Smith apples; halve each quarter lengthwise. Set aside. In 10-inch (25 cm) cast-iron skillet, melt butter over medium heat.

Stir in sugar and vanilla bean; cook, stirring, for 2 minutes. Spread sugar mixture evenly over bottom of pan; arrange apples over top, overlapping and wedging tightly to fill pan. Cook, gently stirring and turning apples, tipping and rotating pan to baste with liquid, until apples are tender and syrup is thick and golden caramel in colour, about 30 minutes.

Remove from heat; sprinkle with salt. Refrigerate in pan on rack for 20 minutes. Discard vanilla bean; carefully rearrange apples in pan into overlapping concentric circles.

ASSEMBLY: On lightly floured surface, roll out pastry into 11-inch (28 cm) circle. Drape loosely over rolling pin; unroll over apple mixture, tucking edge in between pan and apples. Cut 4 steam vents in centre of pastry.

Bake in 425°F (220°C) oven for 10 minutes. Reduce heat to 375°F (190°C); bake until crust is golden, 20 to 25 minutes. Let cool in pan on rack for 5 minutes.

Invert heatproof platter over pan. Wearing oven mitts, turn pan upside down onto platter; carefully lift away pan. Using spatula, remove any apples stuck to pan and arrange over tarte. Spoon any pan syrup over top; let cool for 5 minutes before serving.

NUTRITIONAL INFORMATION, PER SERVING: about 418 cal, 3 g pro, 24 g total fat (15 g sat. fat), 50 g carb, 2 g fibre, 85 mg chol, 165 mg sodium, 112 mg potassium. % RDI: 2% calcium, 6% iron, 21% vit A, 5% vit C, 12% folate.

TIP FROM THE TEST KITCHEN
Pink Lady apples are crisp, sweet-tart and great for eating out of hand. They are also terrific for cooking because they hold their shape well. If they aren't available, try Golden Delicious.

GLUTEN-FREE STRAWBERRY RHUBARB PIE

This tasty gluten-free pastry requires gentle handling to keep it from crumbling—rolling it out between sheets of parchment paper makes it much easier to transfer to the pie plate.

HANDS-ON TIME
30 minutes

TOTAL TIME
2¼ hours

MAKES
8 servings

INGREDIENTS

GLUTEN-FREE PASTRY:

⅔ cup	each brown rice flour and white rice flour
½ cup	each sweet rice flour and tapioca flour
1 tbsp	granulated sugar
1 tsp	xanthan gum
¼ tsp	salt
1 cup	cold butter, cubed
1 tbsp	vinegar
¼ cup	ice water (approx)

FILLING:

4 cups	chopped (1-inch/ 2.5 cm pieces) rhubarb
2 cups	quartered hulled strawberries
1 cup	granulated sugar
½ cup	tapioca flour
1 tsp	vanilla
pinch	ground ginger
2 tbsp	butter
1	egg yolk
1 tbsp	coarse sugar

DIRECTIONS

GLUTEN-FREE PASTRY: In large bowl, whisk together brown rice, white rice, sweet rice and tapioca flours; sugar; xanthan gum; and salt. Using pastry blender or 2 knives, cut in butter until mixture resembles coarse crumbs with a few larger pieces.

Combine vinegar with ice water; drizzle over flour mixture, tossing with fork and adding up to 2 tbsp more ice water if necessary until ragged dough forms.

Divide in half; shape into discs. Wrap each and refrigerate until chilled, about 30 minutes. *(Make-ahead: Refrigerate for up to 1 day.)*

FILLING: In large bowl, combine rhubarb, strawberries, sugar, tapioca flour, vanilla and ginger.

ASSEMBLY: Cube butter; set aside. Between 2 sheets of parchment paper, slowly roll out 1 piece of the pastry (pressing edges together if cracks form) into circle large enough to fit into 9-inch (23 cm) glass pie plate. Peel off top sheet of paper; place back onto pastry. Carefully turn over; peel off top sheet of paper. Transfer, pastry side down, to pie plate; peel off remaining paper. Trim edge to leave ¾-inch (2 cm) overhang. Scrape filling into pie shell; dot with butter.

Roll out remaining pastry between 2 sheets of parchment paper to 9-inch (23 cm) circle; peel off top sheet of paper. Whisk egg yolk with 2 tsp water; brush some over bottom pastry rim. Centre pastry over filling; peel off remaining paper. Trim edge to leave ¾-inch (2 cm) overhang. Fold overhang under bottom pastry rim; crimp with fork. Brush top with remaining egg wash; sprinkle with coarse sugar. Cut steam vents in top.

Bake on rimmed baking sheet on bottom rack in 425°F (220°C) oven for 10 minutes. Reduce heat to 350°F (180°C); bake until bubbly and bottom is golden, 60 to 65 minutes. Let cool in pan on rack.

NUTRITIONAL INFORMATION, PER SERVING: about 577 cal, 4 g pro, 28 g total fat (17 g sat. fat), 79 g carb, 4 g fibre, 94 mg chol, 274 mg sodium, 291 mg potassium. % RDI: 7% calcium, 8% iron, 24% vit A, 37% vit C, 7% folate.

TIP FROM THE TEST KITCHEN
Use tapioca flour to lightly dust the parchment paper if you find the pastry sticking to it.

EASY FRESH FRUIT PIES

It's as simple as, well, pie to put together one of these fantastic fruit desserts. The pastry works with many different fillings, so this is a pie you can make no matter what fruit is available or in season. Serve with whipped cream or a scoop of vanilla ice cream.

HANDS-ON TIME
45 minutes

TOTAL TIME
3½ hours

MAKES
8 servings

INGREDIENTS

1	batch Easy-Roll Pie Pastry (page 348)
	fruit filling (variations, below)
2 tbsp	milk or cream (or 1 egg yolk mixed with 1 tbsp water)
1 tbsp	coarse sugar

DIRECTIONS

On lightly floured surface, roll out half of the pastry to generous ⅛-inch (3 mm) thickness; fit into 9-inch (23 cm) pie plate. Trim edge even with rim of pie plate; scrape filling into pie shell.

Roll out remaining pastry to generous ⅛-inch (3 mm) thickness. Lightly brush milk over bottom pastry rim. Centre pastry over filling; trim to leave ¾-inch (2 cm) overhang. Fold overhang under pastry at rim; flute edge to seal. Brush remaining milk over pastry. Cut steam vents in top; sprinkle with coarse sugar.

Bake on rimmed baking sheet on bottom rack in 425°F (220°C) oven for 15 minutes. Reduce heat to 350°F (180°C); bake until bottom is golden and filling is bubbly, 60 to 75 minutes. Let cool in pan on rack. *(Make-ahead: Set aside at room temperature for up to 8 hours.)*

NUTRITIONAL INFORMATION, PER SERVING (WITH APPLE FILLING): about 468 cal, 6 g pro, 23 g total fat (12 g sat. fat), 61 g carb, 3 g fibre, 60 mg chol, 200 mg sodium, 161 mg potassium. % RDI: 3% calcium, 14% iron, 11% vit A, 7% vit C, 25% folate.

VARIATIONS

APPLE FILLING

Toss together 8 cups sliced peeled apples, ¾ cup granulated sugar, 2 tbsp cornstarch, 1 tbsp lemon juice, 1 tsp cinnamon, and pinch each nutmeg and salt.

APPLE BERRY FILLING

Toss together 6 cups sliced peeled apples, 1 cup blackberries or raspberries, ¾ cup granulated sugar, 3 tbsp all-purpose flour and 1 tbsp lemon juice.

BLUEBERRY FILLING

Toss together 5 cups fresh or drained thawed frozen wild blueberries, ¾ cup granulated sugar and ¼ cup all-purpose flour.

NECTARINE FILLING

Toss together 5 cups sliced peeled nectarines, ¾ cup granulated sugar, ¼ cup all-purpose flour, 2 tbsp chopped crystallized ginger and 1 tbsp lemon juice.

RASPBERRY FILLING

Toss together 4 cups raspberries, 1 cup granulated sugar, 3 tbsp all-purpose flour and 1 tbsp lemon juice.

RASPBERRY NECTARINE FILLING

Toss together 5 cups sliced nectarines, 1½ cups raspberries, ¾ cup granulated sugar, ¼ cup all-purpose flour and 1 tbsp lemon juice.

SASKATOON BERRY FILLING

Toss together 5 cups fresh or drained thawed frozen saskatoon berries, ¾ cup granulated sugar, ¼ cup all-purpose flour, ½ tsp grated lemon zest and ½ tsp cinnamon.

SUGAR PIE ○ ○

Tarte au sucre is a traditional French-Canadian recipe that's practically an obsession. It's also incredibly easy to make and enjoyable to eat, especially with a drizzle of Classic Crème Anglaise (page 344).

HANDS-ON TIME
25 minutes

TOTAL TIME
4½ hours

MAKES
12 servings

INGREDIENTS

PASTRY:

1¾ cups	all-purpose flour
¼ cup	granulated sugar
pinch	salt
½ cup	cold unsalted butter, cubed
1	egg yolk
⅓ cup	milk

FILLING:

1 cup	packed brown sugar
2 tbsp	all-purpose flour
1	egg
1	egg yolk
1 cup	whipping cream (35%)

DIRECTIONS

PASTRY: In large bowl, whisk together flour, sugar and salt. Using pastry blender or 2 knives, cut in butter until mixture resembles coarse crumbs. Whisk egg yolk with milk; drizzle over flour mixture, tossing with fork until loose shaggy dough forms. Shape into disc. Wrap and refrigerate for 1 hour. *(Make-ahead: Refrigerate for up to 1 day.)*

Let pastry stand at room temperature for 20 minutes. On lightly floured surface, roll out pastry into 12-inch (30 cm) circle; fit into 11-inch (28 cm) tart pan with removable bottom, pressing up side; fold any excess pastry inside rim and press together. Refrigerate for 30 minutes. *(Make-ahead: Cover and refrigerate for up to 12 hours.)*

Using fork, prick bottom at ½-inch (1 cm) intervals all over. Line with foil; fill with pie weights or dried beans. Bake on bottom rack in 375°F (190°C) oven until light golden and firm, about 15 minutes. Remove weights and foil; let cool in pan on rack.

FILLING: In large bowl and using fingertips, blend brown sugar with flour. Add egg and egg yolk; whisk until smooth.

Meanwhile, in small saucepan, bring whipping cream to boil; whisk into egg mixture until blended.

ASSEMBLY: Strain filling through fine-mesh sieve into pastry shell. Bake in 350°F (180°C) oven until centre is just firm, about 30 minutes. Let cool in pan on rack. *(Make-ahead: Set aside at room temperature for up to 4 hours.)*

NUTRITIONAL INFORMATION, PER SERVING: about 315 cal, 4 g pro, 17 g total fat (10 g sat. fat), 37 g carb, 1 g fibre, 138 mg chol, 22 mg sodium. % RDI: 4% calcium, 11% iron, 18% vit A, 13% folate.

HONEY PECAN PIE ◐

This classic pie ditches highly processed corn syrup in favour of natural honey for a richer, more complex flavour. Letting the pie cool to room temperature before slicing it guarantees the filling will be completely set.

HANDS-ON TIME
20 minutes

TOTAL TIME
4½ hours

MAKES
12 servings

INGREDIENTS

PASTRY:

1¼ cups	all-purpose flour
1 tbsp	granulated sugar
¼ tsp	salt
½ cup	cold unsalted butter, cubed
¼ cup	cold water (approx)

FILLING:

½ cup	unsalted butter
1 cup	packed brown sugar
½ cup	liquid honey
1 tbsp	cider vinegar
2 tsp	vanilla
¼ tsp	salt
3	eggs, lightly beaten
2 cups	pecan halves

DIRECTIONS

PASTRY: In large bowl, whisk together flour, sugar and salt. Using pastry blender or 2 knives, cut in butter until mixture resembles coarse crumbs with a few larger pieces.

Drizzle cold water over flour mixture, tossing with fork and adding up to 1 tsp more cold water if necessary until ragged dough forms.

Shape into disc; wrap and refrigerate until chilled, about 1 hour. *(Make-ahead: Refrigerate for up to 3 days or freeze in airtight container for up to 1 month.)*

Let pastry stand at room temperature until slightly softened, about 5 minutes. On lightly floured surface, roll out pastry into 12-inch (30 cm) circle; fit into 9-inch (23 cm) pie plate. Trim edge to leave 1-inch (2.5 cm) overhang; fold overhang under pastry at rim and flute edge. Prick bottom all over with fork. Refrigerate until firm, about 30 minutes.

FILLING: In small saucepan, melt butter over medium heat; whisk in brown sugar until smooth. Remove from heat; whisk in honey, vinegar, vanilla and salt. Whisk in eggs. Sprinkle pecans in pie shell; pour egg mixture over top.

Bake on rimmed baking sheet on bottom rack in 350°F (180°C) oven until filling is set, 50 to 60 minutes. Let cool completely in pan on rack.

NUTRITIONAL INFORMATION, PER SERVING: about 434 cal, 5 g pro, 29 g total fat (11 g sat. fat), 43 g carb, 2 g fibre, 87 mg chol, 121 mg sodium, 175 mg potassium. % RDI: 4% calcium, 11% iron, 15% vit A, 17% folate.

VARIATION

HONEY WALNUT PIE

Replace pecans with walnut halves.

TIP FROM THE TEST KITCHEN
Put the baking sheet in the oven during preheating—the hot pan underneath the pie plate will help the bottom crust cook to the perfect golden brown.

FRESH PUMPKIN PIE

This classic pie uses sugar (or pie) pumpkins, which are abundant in the fall. They are much smaller than jack-o'-lantern pumpkins; one average-size sugar pumpkin will yield enough purée for just a single pie.

HANDS-ON TIME
45 minutes

TOTAL TIME
4 hours

MAKES
8 servings

INGREDIENTS

PUMPKIN PIE:

1	sugar pumpkin (about 1.2 kg)
half	batch Easy-Roll Pie Pastry (page 348)
2	eggs
½ cup	whipping cream (35%)
⅓ cup	packed brown sugar
⅓ cup	granulated sugar
¾ tsp	cinnamon
½ tsp	ground ginger
½ tsp	vanilla
¼ tsp	each ground cloves and nutmeg
pinch	salt

GARNISH:

⅔ cup	whipping cream (35%)
2 tsp	granulated sugar

DIRECTIONS

PUMPKIN PIE: Halve and seed pumpkin; prick skin all over with fork. Roast, cut side down, on foil-lined rimmed baking sheet in 350°F (180°C) oven until flesh is tender, about 1 hour. Let cool.

Scoop pumpkin flesh into food processor; purée until smooth to make 2 cups. Drain in cheesecloth-lined fine-mesh sieve for 30 minutes; discard liquid.

Meanwhile, on lightly floured surface, roll out pastry into 12-inch (30 cm) circle; fit into 9-inch (23 cm) pie plate. Trim edge to leave 1-inch (2.5 cm) overhang; fold overhang under pastry at rim and flute edge.

Line with foil; fill with pie weights or dried beans. Bake on bottom rack in 375°F (190°C) oven until rim is light golden, about 30 minutes. Remove weights and foil; bake until golden, about 10 minutes.

Whisk together pumpkin purée, eggs, cream, brown sugar, granulated sugar, cinnamon, ginger, vanilla, cloves, nutmeg and salt. Scrape into crust; smooth top.

Bake in 350°F (180°C) oven until filling is set, 30 to 45 minutes. Let cool in pan on rack. Refrigerate until chilled, about 1 hour. *(Make-ahead: Cover and refrigerate for up to 12 hours.)*

GARNISH: Whip cream with sugar. Spoon into pastry bag fitted with ½-inch (1 cm) star tip; pipe rosettes around edge of pie.

NUTRITIONAL INFORMATION, PER SERVING: about 406 cal, 6 g pro, 27 g total fat (15 g sat. fat), 37 g carb, 1 g fibre, 124 mg chol, 146 mg sodium, 230 mg potassium. % RDI: 5% calcium, 12% iron, 27% vit A, 5% vit C, 20% folate.

LEMON MERINGUE PIE ◗

The Test Kitchen's take on this indulgent diner dessert—with its fluffy meringue and ultra-flaky crust—is a brilliant mix of sweet and tart. Let the pie rest for the full five hours before slicing it so the filling will be completely set and the wedges will look beautiful.

HANDS-ON TIME
40 minutes

TOTAL TIME
7 hours

MAKES
10 to 12 servings

INGREDIENTS

PASTRY:

1½ cups	all-purpose flour
¼ tsp	salt
¼ cup	cold butter, cubed
¼ cup	cold vegetable shortening or lard, cubed
1	egg yolk
1 tsp	lemon juice
	ice water (approx)

LEMON FILLING:

1¼ cups	granulated sugar
6 tbsp	cornstarch
½ tsp	salt
4	egg yolks, lightly beaten
1 tbsp	grated lemon zest
½ cup	lemon juice
3 tbsp	butter, cubed

MERINGUE:

5	egg whites
¼ tsp	cream of tartar
⅓ cup	instant dissolving (fruit/berry) sugar

DIRECTIONS

PASTRY: In bowl, whisk flour with salt. Using pastry blender or 2 knives, cut in butter and shortening until mixture resembles coarse crumbs with a few larger pieces. In glass measure, whisk egg yolk with lemon juice; add enough ice water to make ⅓ cup. Whisk to combine; drizzle over flour mixture, tossing with fork and adding up to 1 tsp more ice water if necessary until ragged dough forms. Shape into disc; wrap and refrigerate until chilled, 30 minutes. *(Make-ahead: Refrigerate for up to 3 days.)*

On lightly floured surface, roll out pastry to ⅛-inch (3 mm) thickness. Fit into 9-inch (23 cm) pie plate. Trim edge to leave 1-inch (2.5 cm) overhang; fold overhang under pastry at rim and flute edge.

Line with foil; fill with pie weights or dried beans. Bake on bottom rack in 400°F (200°C) oven for 15 minutes. Remove weights and foil; using fork, prick pastry all over. Bake until golden, 10 to 12 minutes. Let cool in pan on rack.

LEMON FILLING: While pie shell is cooling, in heavy-bottomed saucepan, whisk together sugar, cornstarch and salt; whisk in 2 cups water. Bring to boil over medium-high heat, whisking constantly.

Reduce heat to medium-low; simmer, whisking constantly, for 3 minutes. Remove from heat. Gradually whisk one-quarter of the sugar mixture into egg yolks; whisk back into pan. Cook over medium heat, whisking constantly, for 2 minutes. Remove from heat; whisk in lemon zest, lemon juice and butter until butter is melted. Scrape into bowl; let cool for 30 minutes. Scrape into pie shell; smooth top.

MERINGUE: In bowl, beat egg whites with cream of tartar until soft peaks form. Beat in sugar, 1 tbsp at a time, until stiff peaks form. Starting at edge and using spatula, spread some of the meringue around outer edge of filling, sealing meringue to crust. Pipe remaining meringue evenly over remaining filling. (Or, using spoon, spread meringue over remaining filling, making peaks with back of spoon.)

TO FINISH: Bake in 400°F (200°C) oven until meringue is golden, 5 to 6 minutes. Let cool in pan on rack until completely set, about 5 hours.

NUTRITIONAL INFORMATION, PER EACH OF 12 SERVINGS: about 315 cal, 5 g pro, 13 g total fat (6 g sat. fat), 45 g carb, 1 g fibre, 98 mg chol, 218 mg sodium, 68 mg potassium. % RDI: 2% calcium, 8% iron, 10% vit A, 8% vit C, 16% folate.

CHOCOLATE BANANA CREAM PIE

Banana cream pie is another old-fashioned favourite. We've updated it and made it even more exquisite with a surprise semisweet chocolate layer, chocolate-hazelnut custard filling and bourbon whipped cream.

HANDS-ON TIME
45 minutes

TOTAL TIME
6½ hours

MAKES
8 servings

INGREDIENTS

BANANA CREAM PIE:

half	batch Easy-Roll Pie Pastry (page 348)
4	egg yolks
2 cups	milk
⅓ cup	granulated sugar
¼ cup	cornstarch
¼ cup	chocolate hazelnut spread (such as Nutella)
1 tsp	vanilla
45 g	semisweet chocolate (1½ oz), chopped and melted
4	bananas, thinly sliced crosswise

GARNISH:

½ cup	whipping cream (35%)
2 tsp	granulated sugar
2 tsp	bourbon
1 tsp	vanilla
30 g	semisweet chocolate (1 oz), shaved

DIRECTIONS

BANANA CREAM PIE: On lightly floured surface, roll out pastry to generous ⅛-inch (3 mm) thickness; fit into 9-inch (23 cm) pie plate. Trim edge to leave ¾-inch (2 cm) overhang; fold overhang under pastry at rim and flute edge. Refrigerate for 30 minutes.

Using fork, prick bottom of pie shell. Line with foil; fill with pie weights or dried beans. Bake on bottom rack in 400°F (200°C) oven until rim is light golden, about 20 minutes. Remove weights and foil; bake until side is golden, about 10 minutes. Let cool in pan on rack.

While pie shell is cooling, in large bowl, whisk together egg yolks, ½ cup of the milk, sugar and cornstarch. In heavy saucepan, heat remaining milk over medium heat just until bubbles form around edge; gradually whisk into yolk mixture. Return to pan and cook, whisking, until thick enough to mound on spoon, about 3 minutes.

Strain through fine-mesh sieve into bowl; stir in chocolate hazelnut spread and vanilla. Place plastic wrap directly on surface. Refrigerate until cold, about 1 hour. *(Make-ahead: Refrigerate for up to 24 hours.)*

Meanwhile, using pastry brush, paint melted chocolate on bottom and side of pie shell. Refrigerate until chocolate is hard, about 10 minutes.

Layer bananas in pie shell. Top with custard; smooth top. Refrigerate for 4 hours.

GARNISH: In bowl, whip cream; whisk in sugar, bourbon and vanilla. Leaving 2-inch (5 cm) border, spread over filling. Sprinkle shaved chocolate over whipped cream.

NUTRITIONAL INFORMATION, PER SERVING: about 498 cal, 8 g pro, 28 g total fat (13 g sat. fat), 56 g carb, 3 g fibre, 153 mg chol, 155 mg sodium, 427 mg potassium. % RDI: 11% calcium, 14% iron, 21% vit A, 8% vit C, 28% folate.

STREUSEL-TOPPED STRAWBERRY GALETTE ◐

*A crunchy almond streusel takes this show-stopping free-form pie to a higher level.
The flavour and texture of the filling depends on the quality of the fruit you use,
so try to find ripe locally grown strawberries when they are in season.*

HANDS-ON TIME
25 minutes

TOTAL TIME
2 hours

MAKES
10 to 12 servings

INGREDIENTS

GALETTE:

2½ cups	all-purpose flour
6 tbsp	granulated sugar
¼ tsp	salt
¾ cup	cold butter, cubed
¾ cup	ice water (approx)
900 g	strawberries, hulled and halved
⅔ cup	strawberry jam
¼ cup	cornstarch
¼ cup	ground almonds

ALMOND STREUSEL:

½ cup	all-purpose flour
½ cup	granulated sugar
¼ cup	cold butter, cubed
⅓ cup	sliced almonds
1	egg yolk
2 tsp	coarse sugar

DIRECTIONS

GALETTE: In bowl, whisk together flour, 2 tbsp of the sugar and salt. Using pastry blender or 2 knives, cut in butter until mixture resembles large crumbs. Drizzle ice water over flour mixture, tossing with fork and adding up to 2 tbsp more ice water if necessary until ragged dough forms. Shape into disc; wrap and refrigerate for 1 hour.

Toss together strawberries, jam, remaining sugar and cornstarch; set aside.

On large piece of parchment paper, roll out pastry into 17-inch (43 cm) circle. Transfer pastry and paper to large rimmed baking sheet; leaving 3-inch (8 cm) border, sprinkle with almonds. Scrape strawberry mixture onto almonds. Lift pastry edge up and over filling to make 12-inch (30 cm) round, letting pastry fall naturally into folds and leaving centre uncovered. Trim off excess parchment paper.

ALMOND STREUSEL: In bowl, stir flour with sugar. Using fingers, rub in butter until crumbly; stir in almonds. Sprinkle over strawberry mixture.

TO FINISH: Mix egg yolk with 2 tsp water; brush over pastry. Sprinkle with coarse sugar. Bake on bottom rack in 375°F (190°C) oven until golden, 50 to 60 minutes. Let cool on pan on rack.

NUTRITIONAL INFORMATION, PER EACH OF 12 SERVINGS: about 421 cal, 5 g pro, 19 g total fat (10 g sat. fat), 60 g carb, 3 g fibre, 51 mg chol, 165 mg sodium, 194 mg potassium. % RDI: 3% calcium, 15% iron, 14% vit A, 72% vit C, 39% folate.

WARM SPICED APPLE GALETTES ◐
WITH WHISKEY CARAMEL

Cinnamon and allspice give these warm galettes the most inviting aroma. For a restaurant-style finish, serve each one surrounded by a drizzle of sauce on the plate and topped with a dollop of whipped cream.

HANDS-ON TIME
1 hour

TOTAL TIME
2 hours

MAKES
6 servings

INGREDIENTS

GALETTES:

1¾ cups	all-purpose flour
1 tbsp	granulated sugar
½ tsp	salt
½ cup	unsalted butter, cubed
⅓ cup	ice water (approx)
2	tart apples (such as Braeburn or Northern Spy), peeled and chopped
¼ cup	granulated sugar (approx)
¼ tsp	each cinnamon and ground allspice
1	egg

WHISKEY CARAMEL:

¼ cup	unsalted butter
½ cup	packed brown sugar
3 tbsp	whipping cream (35%)
pinch	salt
3 tbsp	whiskey (such as rye or bourbon)
¼ tsp	vanilla

DIRECTIONS

GALETTES: In bowl, whisk together flour, sugar and salt; using pastry blender or 2 knives, cut in butter until mixture resembles coarse crumbs. Stir in ice water all at once with fork, adding up to 2 tbsp more ice water if necessary, just until mixture begins to come together. Shape into disc; wrap and refrigerate for 30 minutes. *(Make-ahead: Refrigerate for up to 24 hours.)*

Divide pastry into sixths; form each into ball. On lightly floured surface, roll out each into 7-inch (18 cm) circle. Arrange on 2 parchment paper–lined rimmed baking sheets.

In bowl, toss together apples, sugar, cinnamon and allspice. Spoon about ½ cup onto centre of each pastry circle. Lift pastry edge up and over filling to form about 4-inch (10 cm) circle, letting pastry fall naturally into folds and leaving centre uncovered. Whisk egg with 1 tsp water; brush over pastry. Sprinkle galettes with about ½ tsp more sugar.

Bake on top and bottom racks in 375°F (190°C) oven, rotating and switching pans halfway through, until pastry is golden and apples are tender, 25 to 30 minutes. Let cool slightly on pan on rack. *(Make-ahead: Lightly cover and set aside on baking sheet for up to 24 hours; warm in 300°F/150°C oven for 10 minutes before serving.)*

WHISKEY CARAMEL: In small saucepan, melt butter over medium heat. Whisk in brown sugar, cream and salt; bring to boil. Boil, whisking, until thickened, about 3 minutes. Remove from heat. Stir in whiskey and vanilla. Drizzle over galettes.

NUTRITIONAL INFORMATION, PER SERVING: about 517 cal, 5 g pro, 27 g total fat (17 g sat. fat), 62 g carb, 2 g fibre, 102 mg chol, 215 mg sodium, 166 mg potassium. % RDI: 4% calcium, 16% iron, 24% vit A, 2% vit C, 36% folate.

SOUR CREAM TART PASTRY

In large bowl, whisk 1¼ cups all-purpose flour with ¼ tsp salt. Using pastry blender or 2 knives, cut in ¼ cup each cold butter and cold lard, cubed, until mixture resembles fine crumbs with a few larger pieces. Whisk 2 tbsp ice water with 2 tbsp sour cream; drizzle over flour mixture, tossing with fork and adding a little more water, 1 tsp at a time, if needed until ragged dough forms. Shape into disc. Wrap and refrigerate until chilled, about 30 minutes. *(Make-ahead: Refrigerate for up to 3 days or freeze for up to 1 month.)*
MAKES 1 batch, enough for 12 tarts

APPLE CRISP TARTS

Enjoy all the pleasures of crumble-topped apple pie in a delightful hand-held size. Serve warm with vanilla ice cream for an even more scrumptious dessert.

HANDS-ON TIME
35 minutes

TOTAL TIME
2¼ hours

MAKES
12 tarts

INGREDIENTS

TARTS:

1	batch Sour Cream Tart Pasty (opposite)
2	Cortland apples (about 450 g)
¼ cup	granulated sugar
2 tbsp	all-purpose flour
2 tsp	lemon juice
¼ tsp	cinnamon
pinch	salt

CRUMBLE TOPPING:

1 cup	quick-cooking rolled oats (not instant)
½ cup	packed brown sugar
⅓ cup	all-purpose flour
¼ tsp	nutmeg
⅓ cup	butter, melted

DIRECTIONS

TARTS: On lightly floured surface, roll out pastry to generous ⅛-inch (3 mm) thickness. Using 4-inch (10 cm) round cutter, cut out 12 circles, rerolling and cutting scraps. Fit into muffin cups; refrigerate for 30 minutes.

Meanwhile, peel and quarter apples. Cut each quarter lengthwise into thirds; thinly slice each third crosswise. Toss together apples, sugar, flour, lemon juice, cinnamon and salt. Divide apple mixture among tart shells.

CRUMBLE TOPPING: In small bowl, whisk together oats, brown sugar, flour and nutmeg; stir in butter until combined. Sprinkle over apple filling.

Bake on bottom rack in 375°F (190°C) oven, covering with foil if topping darkens too quickly, until pastry and topping are golden and filling is tender, 40 to 45 minutes.

Run knife around edges of tarts to release. Let cool in pan on rack for 10 minutes; transfer tarts to rack and let cool.

NUTRITIONAL INFORMATION, PER TART: about 283 cal, 4 g pro, 15 g total fat (8 g sat. fat), 35 g carb, 2 g fibre, 29 mg chol, 117 mg sodium, 93 mg potassium. % RDI: 2% calcium, 9% iron, 8% vit A, 2% vit C, 13% folate.

BUTTER TARTS ✪

We've used very Canadian maple syrup for the more common corn syrup in these gooey, custardy tarts. Plus, we've included variations that will satisfy people who like chocolate, pecans, walnuts or raisins hidden inside the delicious filling.

HANDS-ON TIME
25 minutes

TOTAL TIME
2 hours

MAKES
12 tarts

INGREDIENTS

1	batch Sour Cream Tart Pastry (page 362)
¾ cup	packed brown sugar
½ cup	maple syrup (No. 1 medium grade)
⅓ cup	butter, melted
2	eggs
1 tbsp	cider vinegar
½ tsp	salt

DIRECTIONS

On lightly floured surface, roll out pastry to generous ⅛-inch (3 mm) thickness. Using 4-inch (10 cm) round cutter, cut out 12 circles, rerolling and cutting scraps. Fit into muffin cups; refrigerate for 30 minutes.

Whisk together brown sugar, maple syrup, butter, eggs, vinegar and salt. Spoon scant ¼ cup filling into each tart shell. Bake in 350°F (180°C) oven until filling is set and pastry is golden, 20 to 25 minutes.

Run knife around edges of tarts to release. Let cool in pan on rack for 20 minutes; transfer tarts to rack and let cool completely. *(Make-ahead: Store in single layer in airtight container at room temperature for up to 24 hours.)*

NUTRITIONAL INFORMATION, PER TART: about 236 cal, 2 g pro, 12 g total fat (7 g sat. fat), 29 g carb, trace fibre, 57 mg chol, 204 mg sodium, 72 mg potassium. % RDI: 3% calcium, 6% iron, 9% vit A, 9% folate.

VARIATIONS

CHOCOLATE BUTTER TARTS

Divide ½ cup chopped bittersweet chocolate or semisweet chocolate chips among tart shells before spooning in filling.

PECAN BUTTER TARTS

Divide ½ cup chopped pecans among tart shells before spooning in filling.

WALNUT RAISIN BUTTER TARTS

Divide ½ cup chopped walnuts and ¼ cup each dried currants and golden raisins among tart shells before spooning in filling.

LATTICE JAM TART ◗

This Italian-style tart, called a crostata, has a sandy-textured cookie crust that you can also make in a food processor (see tip, below). This is a sensational dessert for showing off your favourite homemade jam (see pages 341 and 342). Serve with softly whipped cream.

HANDS-ON TIME
30 minutes

TOTAL TIME
2¾ hours

MAKES
6 servings

INGREDIENTS

2 cups	all-purpose flour
⅓ cup	granulated sugar
1 tsp	baking powder
¼ tsp	salt
⅔ cup	unsalted butter, cubed
1	egg
1	egg yolk
1 tsp	grated lemon zest
1 cup	jam (such as raspberry, blueberry, mixed berry or peach)

DIRECTIONS

In bowl, whisk together flour, sugar, baking powder and salt. Using pastry blender or 2 knives, cut in butter until mixture resembles coarse crumbs.

Whisk together egg, egg yolk and lemon zest; drizzle over flour mixture, tossing with fork until ragged dough forms. Press together.

Press slightly more than half of the pastry over bottom and up side of 9-inch (23 cm) tart pan with removable bottom; spread with jam. Wrap remaining pastry in plastic wrap; refrigerate pastry and tart shell until firm, about 30 minutes.

On lightly floured surface and using hands, roll remaining pastry into 14 ropes, each 10 inches (25 cm) long.

Place 1 rope across centre of tart. Add 3 more ropes, equally spaced, on each side of centre rope. Press overhang onto pastry at rim to trim off excess and seal. Repeat with remaining ropes, positioning at 45-degree angle over first layer to make diagonal lattice.

Bake in 350°F (180°C) oven until pastry is golden, about 45 minutes. Let cool in pan on rack. *(Make-ahead: Cover with foil; set aside for up to 24 hours.)*

NUTRITIONAL INFORMATION, PER SERVING: about 547 cal, 6 g pro, 23 g total fat (14 g sat. fat), 80 g carb, 2 g fibre, 119 mg chol, 178 mg sodium. % RDI: 5% calcium, 17% iron, 21% vit A, 8% vit C, 51% folate.

TIP FROM THE TEST KITCHEN
To make the pastry in a food processor, pulse the dry ingredients until combined. Add the butter and pulse until the mixture resembles coarse crumbs. Drizzle in the egg mixture and pulse until the dough just starts to clump together. Turn the dough out onto your work surface and press it together.

CROSSOVER APPLE STRUDEL ◐

The yeast in this recipe may make you think of bread, but this is more of a flaky pastry than a bread. This dough is easy to work with and creates a pretty crisscross top over the tender, lightly caramelized apples. Top with whipped cream or crème fraîche.

HANDS-ON TIME
30 minutes

TOTAL TIME
12½ hours

MAKES
2 strudels,
each 10 servings

INGREDIENTS

PASTRY:

¼ cup	warm water (100°F/38°C)
2½ tsp	active dry yeast
½ cup	milk
1	egg
¼ cup	granulated sugar
2½ cups	all-purpose flour
½ tsp	salt
1 cup	cold unsalted butter, cubed

FILLING:

8 cups	sliced peeled (½ inch/1 cm thick) cooking apples (such as Northern Spy)
¼ cup	granulated sugar
2 tbsp	all-purpose flour
2 tsp	grated lemon zest
1 tbsp	lemon juice
¼ tsp	grated nutmeg

GLAZE:

¼ cup	granulated sugar
2 tsp	coarse sugar

DIRECTIONS

PASTRY: Pour warm water into bowl. Sprinkle in yeast; let stand for 3 minutes. Whisk in milk, egg and sugar.

In food processor, pulse flour with salt. Add butter; pulse until combined but chunky, 5 or 6 times. Pour in milk mixture; pulse to make ragged dough, 6 or 7 times. Press together and transfer to bowl; cover and refrigerate for 12 hours.

On lightly floured surface, roll out dough into 16-inch (40 cm) square. Fold one-third over; fold remaining third over top. Fold crosswise into thirds to make square. Repeat rolling out and folding into square once. Wrap and refrigerate for 30 minutes.

Divide dough in half. Working with 1 half at a time, roll out into 15- x 12-inch (38 x 30 cm) rectangle. Fold in half lengthwise. Along long open edge, make 2-inch (5 cm) long cuts into dough at 1-inch (2.5 cm) intervals. Transfer to parchment paper–lined rimmed baking sheet; unfold dough and flatten out strips at edges.

FILLING: While dough is chilling, toss together apples, sugar, flour, lemon zest, lemon juice and nutmeg; set aside.

ASSEMBLY: Leaving 1-inch (2.5 cm) border at short ends, spoon half of the filling along centre of 1 of the pastry rectangles, heaping and pressing together. Starting at 1 short end, fold uncovered border up over filling. Cross first strip of dough over edge of folded pastry and filling, angling slightly; cross opposite strip over to cover end of first strip. Repeat until last 2 strips remain. Fold uncovered end of pastry over apples; cross over last 2 strips, tucking into bottom flap. Transfer to parchment paper–lined rimmed baking sheet. Repeat with remaining pastry and filling.

GLAZE: In small saucepan, bring granulated sugar and 2 tbsp water to boil, stirring; brush over strudels. Sprinkle with coarse sugar.

Bake in 375°F (190°C) oven until golden, about 30 minutes. Let cool on pans on racks.

NUTRITIONAL INFORMATION, PER SERVING: about 201 cal, 3 g pro, 10 g total fat (6 g sat. fat), 27 g carb, 1 g fibre, 34 mg chol, 65 mg sodium. % RDI: 2% calcium, 6% iron, 9% vit A, 3% vit C, 21% folate.

PEAR FRANGIPANE TART ◐

Need a splashy-looking dessert that's quick and easy to make? This tart is it. The not-too-sweet filling is a lovely combination of almonds and pears. Serve it with a drizzle of chocolate sauce or a dollop of whipped cream.

HANDS-ON TIME
20 minutes

TOTAL TIME
3 hours

MAKES
6 servings

INGREDIENTS

FRANGIPANE:

½ cup	blanched almonds
¼ cup	granulated sugar
2 tbsp	all-purpose flour
pinch	salt
3 tbsp	cold butter, cubed
3 tbsp	liquid honey
2	eggs
1 tsp	almond extract

PASTRY:

1½ cups	all-purpose flour
½ tsp	salt
½ cup	unsalted butter, cubed
1	egg yolk
1 tsp	vinegar
	ice water
1½	ripe Bartlett or Bosc pears (about 250 g)

DIRECTIONS

FRANGIPANE: In food processor, pulse together almonds, sugar, flour and salt until finely chopped. Add butter and honey; pulse until mixture resembles fine crumbs. Add eggs, 1 at a time; blend until smooth. Add almond extract. Transfer to bowl; cover and refrigerate for 1 hour.

PASTRY: While frangipane is chilling, in bowl, whisk flour with salt. Using pastry blender or 2 knives, cut in butter until mixture resembles coarse crumbs.

In liquid measuring cup, beat egg yolk with vinegar; pour in enough ice water to make ⅓ cup. Drizzle over flour mixture. Toss with fork, adding up to 2 tbsp more water if necessary, just until dough clumps together. Shape into rectangle. Wrap and refrigerate for 30 minutes.

On lightly floured surface, roll out pastry into 15- x 5-inch (38 x 12 cm) rectangle. Fit into 14- x 4-inch (35 x 10 cm) tart pan with removable bottom; trim pastry even with edges. Cover with plastic wrap; refrigerate for 30 minutes.

Prick pastry all over with fork. Line with foil; fill with pie weights or dried beans. Bake on bottom rack in 400°F (200°C) oven for 15 minutes. Remove weights and foil; bake until golden, about 5 minutes. Let cool in pan on rack.

ASSEMBLY: Spread frangipane in pie shell. Peel and halve pears; cut each half into ⅛-inch (3 mm) thick slices. Gently fan pear slices and place on top of frangipane.

Bake on bottom rack in 375°F (190°C) oven until puffed and golden, 35 to 40 minutes. Serve warm or at room temperature.

NUTRITIONAL INFORMATION, PER SERVING: about 503 cal, 9 g pro, 30 g total fat (15 g sat. fat), 52 g carb, 4 g fibre, 152 mg chol, 260 mg sodium, 204 mg potassium. % RDI: 5% calcium, 17% iron, 22% vit A, 2% vit C, 40% folate.

VARIATION

PEAR HAZELNUT FRANGIPANE TART

Substitute skinned toasted hazelnuts for the almonds.

MINI LEEK AND BACON PIES

HANDS-ON TIME
30 minutes

TOTAL TIME
50 minutes

MAKES
12 servings

*These cute single-serving pies are delicious served hot, as an elegant starter with a salad.
They're also wonderful cold, eaten out of hand with a little HP Sauce.*

INGREDIENTS

2	strips bacon, sliced
4 cups	thinly sliced leeks (white and light green parts only), about 2
2 cups	thinly sliced onion (about 1)
2 tsp	chopped fresh thyme
pinch	each salt and pepper
2 tbsp	balsamic vinegar
1 tbsp	Dijon mustard
1 cup	baby spinach, coarsely chopped
½ cup	frozen peas
1 cup	shredded Gruyère cheese
half	batch Easy-Roll Pie Pastry (page 348)
1	egg yolk

DIRECTIONS

In large skillet, cook bacon over medium heat, stirring occasionally, until browned, about 3 minutes. Stir in leeks, onion, thyme, salt and pepper; cook, stirring occasionally, until starting to brown, about 7 minutes.

Stir in ½ cup water, vinegar and mustard, scraping up browned bits from bottom of pan; cook until onion is caramelized, about 10 minutes.

Stir in spinach and peas; cook until spinach is wilted and peas are hot, about 3 minutes. Stir in ¾ cup of the Gruyère. Let cool slightly.

On lightly floured surface, roll out pastry into 16- x 12-inch (40 x 30 cm) rectangle. Cut into twelve 4-inch (10 cm) squares; press each into muffin cup. Fill each with ¼ cup of the leek mixture, pressing firmly; sprinkle with remaining Gruyère. Fold 4 corners of dough toward centre, pressing lightly to seal.

Whisk egg yolk with 2 tsp water; brush over top of pastry. Bake in 400°F (200°C) oven until pastry is golden and filling is bubbly, about 20 minutes. Let cool in pan on rack for 5 minutes.

NUTRITIONAL INFORMATION, PER SERVING: about 213 cal, 6 g pro, 14 g total fat (7 g sat. fat), 16 g carb, 1 g fibre, 51 mg chol, 158 mg sodium, 119 mg potassium. % RDI: 11% calcium, 11% iron, 11% vit A, 5% vit C, 20% folate.

BEEF AND MUSHROOM PIE

Stewing beef cubes vary in size. If the ones you buy are a lot bigger than bite-size, halve or quarter them to make them more manageable to cook and eat.

HANDS-ON TIME
45 minutes

TOTAL TIME
3¾ hours

MAKES
8 servings

INGREDIENTS

675 g	stewing beef cubes
¼ tsp	each salt and pepper
5 tsp	vegetable oil
3	strips bacon, chopped
225 g	cremini mushrooms, quartered
1	onion, chopped
3	cloves garlic, chopped
2 tsp	chopped fresh thyme
1 cup	sodium-reduced beef broth
1 cup	brown ale
¼ cup	tomato paste
2	bay leaves
1 tbsp	all-purpose flour
1	batch Easy-Roll Pie Pastry (page 348)
1	egg yolk

DIRECTIONS

Sprinkle beef with pinch each of the salt and pepper. In Dutch oven, heat 2 tsp of the oil over medium-high heat; working in batches, brown beef, adding another 2 tsp of the oil as needed. Transfer to plate; drain any fat from pan.

Add bacon to pan; cook for 2 minutes. Add mushrooms; cook until no liquid remains, about 5 minutes. Transfer to plate; cover and refrigerate until needed.

Add remaining oil to pan; cook onion, garlic, thyme, and remaining salt and pepper until onion is softened and light golden, about 5 minutes.

Add broth, ale, tomato paste and bay leaves; bring to boil, stirring and scraping up browned bits from bottom of pan. Return beef and any accumulated juices to pan. Reduce heat, cover and simmer until beef is tender, about 2 hours. Discard bay leaves.

Whisk flour with 1 tbsp water; whisk into stew and cook until slightly thickened, about 5 minutes. *(Make-ahead: Let cool for 30 minutes; refrigerate in airtight container for up to 2 days.)* Stir in reserved bacon mixture; set aside.

On lightly floured surface, roll out half of the pastry to generous ⅛-inch (3 mm) thickness; fit into 9-inch (23 cm) pie plate. Trim edge to leave ¾-inch (2 cm) overhang. Scrape filling into pie shell.

Roll out remaining pastry to generous ⅛-inch (3 mm) thickness. Whisk egg yolk with 2 tsp water; brush some over bottom pastry rim. Centre pastry over filling; trim to leave ¾-inch (2 cm) overhang. Fold overhang under bottom pastry rim and flute edge. Brush top with remaining egg mixture; cut steam vents in top.

Bake on rimmed baking sheet on bottom rack in 425°F (220°C) oven for 20 minutes. Reduce heat to 350°F (180°C); bake until bottom is golden and filling is bubbly, 60 to 65 minutes. Let cool in pan on rack for 10 minutes.

NUTRITIONAL INFORMATION, PER SERVING: about 583 cal, 25 g pro, 40 g total fat (18 g sat. fat), 31 g carb, 2 g fibre, 139 mg chol, 470 mg sodium, 563 mg potassium. % RDI: 4% calcium, 29% iron, 13% vit A, 5% vit C, 31% folate.

VARIATION

BEEF, MUSHROOM AND STILTON PIE

Sprinkle ⅓ cup crumbled Stilton cheese over filling before covering with pastry. Bake as directed.

RÉVEILLON TOURTIÈRE ☘

When it's time for Réveillon (a special feast on Christmas Eve in Quebec), this is the pie that welcomes everyone to the table. The super-flaky crust is filled to the brim with a savoury spiced meat filling. Enjoy a slice with our Classic Chili Sauce (page 338).

HANDS-ON TIME
40 minutes

TOTAL TIME
3½ hours

MAKES
8 to 10 servings

INGREDIENTS

1 tbsp	vegetable oil
900 g	ground pork
3	small onions, finely chopped
3	cloves garlic, minced
2 cups	sliced white mushrooms
1½ cups	sodium-reduced beef broth
1 cup	finely chopped celery
1 tsp	salt
½ tsp	each cinnamon, pepper and dried savory
¼ tsp	ground cloves
1 cup	fresh bread crumbs (see tip, page 27)
½ cup	chopped fresh parsley
1	batch Easy-Roll Pie Pastry (page 348)
1	egg yolk

DIRECTIONS

In large skillet, heat oil over medium-high heat; cook pork, breaking up with spoon, until no longer pink, 7 to 10 minutes. Drain fat from pan.

Stir in onions, garlic, mushrooms, broth, celery, salt, cinnamon, pepper, savory and cloves; bring to boil. Reduce heat to medium-low and simmer, stirring occasionally, until 2 tbsp liquid remains, about 35 minutes.

Stir in bread crumbs and parsley. Transfer to bowl; cover and refrigerate until cold, about 1 hour. *(Make-ahead: Refrigerate for up to 24 hours.)*

On lightly floured surface, roll out half of the pastry to generous ⅛-inch (3 mm) thickness; fit into 9-inch (23 cm) pie plate. Trim edge to leave ¾-inch (2 cm) overhang. Scrape filling into pie shell, pressing down lightly to pack.

Roll out remaining pastry to generous ⅛-inch (3 mm) thickness. Whisk egg yolk with 1 tsp water; brush some over bottom pastry rim. Centre pastry over filling; trim to leave ¾-inch (2 cm) overhang. Fold overhang under bottom pastry rim and flute edge. Cut decorative shapes from pastry scraps. Brush some of the remaining egg mixture over pastry; arrange shapes over top. Brush top all over with some of the remaining egg mixture; cut steam vents in top.

Bake on rimmed baking sheet on bottom rack in 375°F (190°C) oven until filling is bubbly and bottom is golden brown, loosely covering with foil if top is darkening too quickly, about 1 hour. Let cool in pan on rack for 10 minutes.

NUTRITIONAL INFORMATION, PER EACH OF 10 SERVINGS: about 405 cal, 23 g pro, 23 g total fat (9 g sat. fat), 25 g carb, 2 g fibre, 111 mg chol, 572 mg sodium, 435 mg potassium. % RDI: 5% calcium, 21% iron, 12% vit A, 10% vit C, 29% folate.

TIP FROM THE TEST KITCHEN
Make sure to bake the tourtière on a rimmed baking sheet to catch any bubbling juices that overflow. It will save you from a messy oven cleanup.

CLASSIC VANILLA LAYER CAKE
page 383

ULTIMATE CAKES | 15

"At the heart of all my favourite memories, there's a supremely delicious cake. That feeling of closeness that comes when everyone gathers around as you cut the first slice makes it so special—it's much more than just flour, butter, sugar and eggs."

GILEAN WATTS ARTICLES EDITOR, FOOD

PEACH SOUR CREAM COFFEE CAKE ◐

Peaches are one of the most anticipated fruits of the summer. Juicy and ripe, they find a happy home nestled in this rich sour cream coffee cake batter.

HANDS-ON TIME
16 minutes

TOTAL TIME
1¼ hours

MAKES
12 servings

INGREDIENTS

1½ cups	all-purpose flour
1 tsp	baking powder
½ tsp	baking soda
¼ tsp	salt
pinch	nutmeg
½ cup	butter, softened
¾ cup	packed brown sugar
2	eggs
1 tsp	vanilla
⅔ cup	sour cream
2	firm ripe peaches (340 g total), peeled, pitted and cut in 6 pieces each
1 tbsp	icing sugar

DIRECTIONS

Whisk together flour, baking powder, baking soda, salt and nutmeg. Set aside.

In large bowl, beat butter with brown sugar until well combined. Beat in eggs, 1 at a time; beat in vanilla. Stir in sour cream until smooth.

Stir in flour mixture just until smooth; scrape into greased 9-inch (2.5 L) springform pan. Spread batter evenly in pan; smooth top.

Arrange peach slices over batter in circle around edge of pan. Bake in 350°F (180°C) oven until cake tester inserted in centre comes out clean, about 50 minutes.

Let cool in pan on rack for 10 minutes. Transfer cake to rack; let cool completely. Dust with icing sugar.

NUTRITIONAL INFORMATION, PER SERVING: about 220 cal, 3 g pro, 11 g total fat (6 g sat. fat), 29 g carb, 1 g fibre, 56 mg chol, 201 mg sodium, 137 mg potassium. % RDI: 4% calcium, 9% iron, 10% vit A, 2% vit C, 17% folate.

APPLE STREUSEL COFFEE CAKE ◐

This cake is great for brunch on a lazy Sunday morning because it stays flavourful and moist if you bake it a day ahead. Granny Smith apples are tart, so they don't make the cake overly sweet.

HANDS-ON TIME
25 minutes

TOTAL TIME
2½ hours

MAKES
9 servings

INGREDIENTS

CINNAMON STREUSEL:

¾ cup	all-purpose flour
⅓ cup	unsalted butter, melted
¼ cup	each packed brown sugar and granulated sugar
2 tsp	cinnamon

APPLE FILLING:

2¾ cups	thinly sliced peeled Granny Smith apples (2 or 3)
1 tbsp	granulated sugar
1 tbsp	all-purpose flour

CAKE BATTER:

2¼ cups	all-purpose flour
1 cup	granulated sugar
2½ tsp	baking powder
¼ tsp	cinnamon
¼ tsp	salt
2	eggs
1 cup	milk
½ cup	sour cream
½ cup	unsalted butter, melted
½ tsp	vanilla

DIRECTIONS

CINNAMON STREUSEL: Stir together flour, butter, brown sugar, granulated sugar and cinnamon until mixture resembles fine crumbs; set aside.

APPLE FILLING: Toss together apples, sugar and flour; set aside.

CAKE BATTER: In large bowl, whisk together flour, sugar, baking powder, cinnamon and salt. Whisk together eggs, milk, sour cream, butter and vanilla; stir into flour mixture until smooth.

ASSEMBLY: Spread half of the batter in parchment paper–lined 9-inch (2.5 L) square cake pan. Arrange filling over batter. Pour remaining batter over top, spreading evenly to edges of pan; smooth top. Sprinkle with streusel.

Bake in 350°F (180°C) oven until golden and cake tester inserted in centre comes out clean, about 1 hour. Let cool in pan on rack.

NUTRITIONAL INFORMATION, PER SERVING: about 510 cal, 7 g pro, 21 g total fat (13 g sat. fat), 75 g carb, 2 g fibre, 94 mg chol, 184 mg sodium, 180 mg potassium. % RDI: 10% calcium, 18% iron, 19% vit A, 2% vit C, 43% folate.

LEMON POPPY SEED SOUR CREAM CAKES

A rasp grater works well for grating lemon zest into fine shreds, which distribute more uniformly in batters and doughs.

HANDS-ON TIME
25 minutes

TOTAL TIME
2 hours

MAKES
8 cakes

INGREDIENTS

CAKES:

1 cup	granulated sugar
2 tbsp	grated lemon zest
1 cup	unsalted butter, softened
4	eggs
¼ cup	lemon juice
2 cups	all-purpose flour
2 tbsp	poppy seeds
¾ tsp	baking powder
½ tsp	salt
¼ tsp	baking soda
½ cup	sour cream

ICING AND GLAZE:

1 cup	icing sugar
7 tsp	lemon juice (approx)

DIRECTIONS

CAKES: In large bowl and using fingers, rub sugar with lemon zest until fragrant. Beat in butter until light. Beat in eggs, 1 at a time, beating well after each. Beat in lemon juice.

Whisk together flour, poppy seeds, baking powder, salt and baking soda; stir into butter mixture, alternating with sour cream, making 3 additions of flour mixture and 2 of sour cream. Scrape into 8 greased and floured 1-cup (250 mL) mini Bundt pans.

Bake in 325°F (160°C) oven until cake tester inserted in centre comes out clean, about 30 minutes. Transfer pans to rack.

ICING AND GLAZE: In small bowl, stir icing sugar with 5 tsp of the lemon juice until smooth to make icing. Spoon half of the icing into separate bowl; stir in remaining lemon juice to make glaze. Brush glaze over hot cakes.

Transfer cakes to rack; let cool. Drizzle with icing, adding a little more lemon juice to loosen if necessary.

NUTRITIONAL INFORMATION, PER HALF-CAKE: about 273 cal, 4 g pro, 14 g total fat (8 g sat. fat), 33 g carb, 1 g fibre, 80 mg chol, 90 mg sodium, 62 mg potassium. % RDI: 4% calcium, 7% iron, 13% vit A, 7% vit C, 18% folate.

TIP FROM THE TEST KITCHEN

You can also spoon the batter into four 5¾- x 3¼-inch (625 mL) mini loaf pans or one 9- x 5-inch (2 L) loaf pan. The baking time is the same for the mini pans; increase the baking time to 1 hour if you're using the large pan.

PUMPKIN PECAN BUNDT CAKE ⬤

*Small sugar pumpkins yield a sweet purée that is the base of this lovely autumn cake.
If you can't find them, butternut squash is a great substitute. The rum syrup brushed
over the cake adds a little extra zip.*

HANDS-ON TIME
35 minutes

TOTAL TIME
3½ hours

MAKES
10 to 12 servings

INGREDIENTS

CAKE:

¾ cup	chopped pecans
1⅔ cups	packed brown sugar
¼ cup	butter, softened, or vegetable oil
3	eggs
¾ cup	vegetable oil
2 cups	Roasted Pumpkin or Squash Purée (below)
2½ cups	all-purpose flour
2 tsp	baking powder
1¾ tsp	cinnamon
1 tsp	each baking soda and ground ginger
¾ tsp	salt
¼ tsp	each nutmeg and ground allspice

SYRUP:

¼ cup	butter
⅔ cup	packed brown sugar
¼ cup	dark rum

DIRECTIONS

CAKE: On baking sheet, toast pecans in 350°F (180°C) oven until fragrant, about 8 minutes; let cool.

Stir pecans with 2 tbsp of the brown sugar; sprinkle over greased and flour-dusted 10-inch (3 L) Bundt pan.

In large bowl, beat remaining brown sugar with butter; beat in eggs, 1 at a time. Beat in oil until fluffy. Beat in pumpkin until smooth.

Whisk together flour, baking powder, cinnamon, baking soda, ginger, salt, nutmeg and allspice; stir into egg mixture. Scrape into prepared pan; tap pan on counter to remove air bubbles. Smooth top.

Bake in 350°F (180°C) oven until cake tester inserted in centre comes out clean, about 50 minutes. Let cool in pan on rack for 10 minutes. Transfer cake to rack.

SYRUP: In small saucepan, melt butter over medium heat. Stir in brown sugar and 3 tbsp water; boil until sugar is dissolved and syrup is thickened, 3 minutes. Stir in rum; boil for 1 minute. Brush over cake.

NUTRITIONAL INFORMATION, PER EACH OF 12 SERVINGS: about 550 cal, 5 g pro, 28 g total fat (7 g sat. fat), 67 g carb, 3 g fibre, 67 mg chol, 388 mg sodium, 311 mg potassium. % RDI: 8% calcium, 22% iron, 89% vit A, 3% vit C, 30% folate.

ROASTED PUMPKIN OR SQUASH PURÉE

Halve and seed 1 sugar pumpkin (about 1 kg) or 1 butternut squash (about 900 g). Prick skin all over with fork. Roast, cut side down, on rack on foil-lined rimmed baking sheet in 350°F (180°C) oven until flesh is browned and tender, 60 to 75 minutes. Let cool. Scoop out flesh; discard skin. In food processor, purée flesh. *(Make-ahead: Refrigerate in airtight container for up to 2 days or freeze for up to 3 weeks.)* **MAKES** about 2 cups

ANGEL FOOD CAKE
WITH LEMON CURD AND MASCARPONE CREAM

Angel food cake is springy, so a chef's knife will crush the cake as it goes through. To cut neat slices, use a sharp serrated knife instead.

HANDS-ON TIME
1¼ hours

TOTAL TIME
3¼ hours

MAKES
12 servings

INGREDIENTS

ANGEL FOOD CAKE:

1¼ cups	sifted cake-and-pastry flour
1¼ cups	granulated sugar
1½ cups	egg whites (10 to 12)
1 tbsp	lemon juice
1 tsp	cream of tartar
½ tsp	salt
½ tsp	vanilla

LEMON CURD:

4	egg yolks
½ cup	granulated sugar
1 tbsp	grated lemon zest
⅓ cup	lemon juice
⅓ cup	cold butter, cubed

MASCARPONE CREAM:

115 g	mascarpone cheese, at room temperature
½ cup	whipping cream (35%)
1 tbsp	icing sugar
½ tsp	vanilla

GARNISH:

1 cup	quartered hulled strawberries

DIRECTIONS

ANGEL FOOD CAKE: Sift flour with ½ cup of the sugar; sift into clean bowl.

In large bowl, beat egg whites until foamy; beat in lemon juice, cream of tartar and salt until soft peaks form. Beat in remaining sugar, 2 tbsp at a time, until stiff glossy peaks form. One-quarter at a time, sift flour mixture over top and fold in until blended. Fold in vanilla. Scrape into ungreased 10-inch (4 L) tube pan. Run spatula through batter to eliminate any large air bubbles; smooth top.

Bake in 350°F (180°C) oven until cake springs back when lightly touched, 40 to 45 minutes. Turn pan upside down and let hang on legs attached to pan, or on bottle, until completely cooled. Remove from pan. *(Make-ahead: Store in airtight container for up to 2 days.)*

LEMON CURD: While cake is baking, in heatproof bowl, whisk together egg yolks, sugar, lemon zest and lemon juice. Set over saucepan of simmering water; cook, stirring, until thick enough to coat back of spoon, 8 to 10 minutes.

Remove from heat. Stir in butter, 1 piece at a time, until smooth. Strain through fine-mesh sieve into bowl. Place plastic wrap directly on surface. Refrigerate until thick enough to mound firmly on spoon, about 2 hours. *(Make-ahead: Refrigerate for up to 4 days.)*

MASCARPONE CREAM: While lemon curd is chilling, place mascarpone in bowl. In separate bowl, whip together cream, icing sugar and vanilla; fold into mascarpone. *(Make-ahead: Cover and refrigerate for up to 24 hours.)*

ASSEMBLY: Cut cake in half horizontally. Evenly spread lemon curd over cut side of bottom half; top with remaining cake, cut side down. Spread mascarpone cream over top.

GARNISH: Arrange strawberries decoratively over mascarpone cream.

NUTRITIONAL INFORMATION, PER SERVING: about 310 cal, 7 g pro, 14 g total fat (6 g sat. fat), 41 g carb, 1 g fibre, 94 mg chol, 192 mg sodium, 143 mg potassium. % RDI: 2% calcium, 8% iron, 10% vit A, 20% vit C, 12% folate.

TIP FROM THE TEST KITCHEN
Lemon zest curls make a pretty garnish for this cake. Use a citrus zester with a channel cutter to cut the zest into long, slim curls.

STICKY TOFFEE CAKE ⏰
WITH DECADENT TOFFEE SAUCE

HANDS-ON TIME
25 minutes

TOTAL TIME
1¾ hours

MAKES
12 to 16 servings

This cake stays amazingly moist for up to three days. The toffee sauce is gooey and spectacular, and it's even more delicious topped with a dollop of whipped cream.

INGREDIENTS

CAKE:

1	pkg (375 g) dried pitted dates (about 2⅓ cups)
1⅓ cups	granulated sugar
½ cup	unsalted butter, softened
1½ tsp	grated lemon zest
½ tsp	salt
4	eggs
1½ tsp	vanilla
2¾ cups	all-purpose flour
2 tsp	baking powder
2 tsp	baking soda

TOFFEE SAUCE:

¾ cup	unsalted butter
1 cup	granulated sugar
¾ cup	whipping cream (35%)
2 tbsp	lemon juice
pinch	salt
2 tbsp	brandy

DIRECTIONS

CAKE: In saucepan, bring dates and 2½ cups water to boil; let cool. Mash until smooth; set aside.

In large bowl, beat together sugar, butter, lemon zest and salt until light; beat in eggs, 1 at a time. Beat in vanilla. Whisk together flour, baking powder and baking soda; stir into butter mixture. Stir in dates.

Scrape into greased 10-inch (4 L) tube or 10-inch (3 L) Bundt pan. Bake on bottom rack in 350°F (180°C) oven until cake tester inserted in centre comes out clean, about 55 minutes. Let cool in pan on rack for 15 minutes; invert cake onto plate.

TOFFEE SAUCE: While cake is cooling on rack, in saucepan, melt butter over medium heat; whisk in sugar until dissolved. Cook, whisking, until caramel coloured, about 5 minutes. Averting face, whisk in cream, lemon juice and salt; bring to boil. Cook until thickened, 3 to 5 minutes. Whisk in brandy. Pour ¾ cup over warm cake; let stand to absorb.

To serve, slice cake; drizzle with remaining warm sauce.

NUTRITIONAL INFORMATION, PER EACH OF 16 SERVINGS: about 437 cal, 5 g pro, 20 g total fat (12 g sat. fat), 62 g carb, 2 g fibre, 99 mg chol, 290 mg sodium, 196 mg potassium. % RDI: 4% calcium, 10% iron, 18% vit A, 2% vit C, 24% folate.

LAYERED CARROT CAKE ◐
WITH CREAM CHEESE ICING

Meet the one and only carrot cake recipe you'll ever need. The batter comes together in a matter of minutes and makes a flavourful, moist cake with just the right ratio of crushed pineapple to grated carrot. Topped with cream cheese icing, it is a slice of perfection.

HANDS-ON TIME
1 hour

TOTAL TIME
4 hours

MAKES
16 servings

INGREDIENTS

CAKE:

2 cups	all-purpose flour
2 tsp	baking powder
2 tsp	cinnamon
1 tsp	baking soda
¾ tsp	salt
½ tsp	nutmeg
3	eggs
¾ cup	granulated sugar
¾ cup	packed brown sugar
¾ cup	vegetable oil
1 tsp	vanilla
2 cups	grated carrots (about 2 large)
1	can (398 mL) crushed pineapple, drained
½ cup	chopped pecans

CREAM CHEESE ICING:

2	pkg (each 250 g) cream cheese, softened
½ cup	butter, softened
1 tsp	vanilla
6 cups	icing sugar

DIRECTIONS

CAKE: In large bowl, whisk together flour, baking powder, cinnamon, baking soda, salt and nutmeg. Beat together eggs, granulated sugar, brown sugar, oil and vanilla until smooth; stir into flour mixture just until moistened. Stir in carrots, pineapple and pecans until combined. Scrape into 2 greased and floured 8-inch (1.2 L) round cake pans.

Bake in 350°F (180°C) oven until cake tester inserted in centre of each comes out clean, 35 to 38 minutes. Let cool in pans on racks. *(Make-ahead: Cover with plastic wrap and store at room temperature for up to 2 days or overwrap with heavy-duty foil and freeze for up to 2 weeks; thaw before continuing with recipe.)*

CREAM CHEESE ICING: In bowl, beat cream cheese with butter until smooth. Beat in vanilla. Beat in icing sugar, one-third at a time, until smooth.

ASSEMBLY: Cut each cake in half horizontally to make 4 layers. Place 1 layer, cut side up, on cake plate; slide strips of waxed paper between cake and plate. Spread about ¾ cup of the icing over cut side; top with second layer, cut side down. Spread about ¾ cup of the remaining icing over top of stack. Repeat with remaining layers, omitting icing on top of stack.

Using large offset palette knife, spread thin layer of the remaining icing all over cake to seal in crumbs; refrigerate until firm, about 30 minutes.

Using large offset palette knife, spread remaining icing all over cake. Remove waxed paper strips. Refrigerate for 30 minutes before serving. *(Make-ahead: Cover loosely and refrigerate for up to 24 hours.)*

NUTRITIONAL INFORMATION, PER SERVING: about 611 cal, 5 g pro, 31 g total fat (11 g sat. fat), 82 g carb, 2 g fibre, 84 mg chol, 389 mg sodium, 157 mg potassium. % RDI: 7% calcium, 10% iron, 40% vit A, 2% vit C, 16% folate.

VARIATION
CARROT SLAB CAKE WITH CREAM CHEESE ICING
Prepare batter as directed; scrape into greased and floured 13- x 9-inch (3.5 L) cake pan. Bake until cake tester inserted in centre comes out clean, about 40 minutes. Let cool in pan on rack. Top with half-batch of the Cream Cheese Icing.

CLASSIC VANILLA LAYER CAKE ⟲

A gorgeous vanilla layer cake is a timeless recipe-box staple. Remember to spoon dry ingredients into measuring cups and then level them off with the back of a knife. This method gives you the most accurate measurement.

HANDS-ON TIME
45 minutes

TOTAL TIME
2½ hours

MAKES
12 to 16 servings

INGREDIENTS

CAKE:

1 cup	butter, softened
1½ cups	granulated sugar
3	eggs
1 tbsp	vanilla
3 cups + 2 tbsp	all-purpose flour
1 tbsp	baking powder
2 cups	milk

BUTTERY VANILLA ICING:

2 cups	butter, softened
8 cups	icing sugar
½ cup	whipping cream (35%)
1 tbsp	vanilla

DIRECTIONS

CAKE: Grease two 8-inch (1.2 L) round cake pans; line bottoms with parchment paper. Set aside. In large bowl, beat butter with sugar until fluffy; beat in eggs, 1 at a time. Beat in vanilla. Whisk flour with baking powder; stir into butter mixture, alternating with milk, making 2 additions of each, until smooth. Divide between prepared pans. Bake in 350°F (180°C) oven until cake tester inserted in centre of each comes out clean, 35 to 40 minutes. Let cool in pans on racks for 10 minutes. Invert onto racks; peel off paper. Let cool completely.

BUTTERY VANILLA ICING: In bowl, beat butter until light and fluffy; beat in icing sugar, 1 cup at a time, until smooth. Gradually beat in cream and vanilla, scraping down side of bowl occasionally, until fluffy, about 2 minutes.

ASSEMBLY: Cut each cake in half horizontally to make 4 layers. Place 1 layer, cut side up, on cake plate; slide strips of waxed paper between cake and plate. Spread about ¾ cup of the icing over cut side; top with second layer, cut side down. Spread about ¾ cup of the remaining icing over top of stack. Repeat with remaining layers, omitting icing on top of stack. Using large offset palette knife, spread about 1 cup of the remaining icing in thin layer all over cake to seal in crumbs; refrigerate until firm, 30 minutes.

Using large offset palette knife, spread remaining icing all over cake, smoothing sides and top. Run tip of palette knife back and forth loosely across top to form gentle ripples, if desired. Remove waxed paper strips. Refrigerate until firm, 1 hour. *(Make-ahead: Refrigerate for up to 4 hours.)*

NUTRITIONAL INFORMATION, PER EACH OF 16 SERVINGS: about 756 cal, 6 g pro, 39 g total fat (24 g sat. fat), 98 g carb, 1 g fibre, 140 mg chol, 332 mg sodium, 98 mg potassium. % RDI: 8% calcium, 10% iron, 36% vit A, 20% folate.

VARIATIONS

CLASSIC VANILLA CUPCAKES

Divide batter among 24 paper-lined muffin cups. Bake until cake tester inserted in centre of several comes out clean, 18 minutes. Transfer to rack; let cool completely. Top with half-batch of the Buttery Vanilla Icing.

CLASSIC VANILLA SLAB CAKE

Grease 13- x 9-inch (3.5 L) cake pan; line bottom and sides with parchment paper. Set aside. Prepare batter as directed; scrape into prepared pan. Bake until cake tester inserted in centre comes out clean, 30 to 35 minutes. Let cool in pan on rack for 10 minutes. Invert onto rack; peel off paper. Let cool completely. Invert onto cake plate; top with half-batch of the Buttery Vanilla Icing.

CLASSIC CHOCOLATE LAYER CAKE ⟳

If the stomach is indeed the way to a loved one's heart, then this ultra-decadent chocolate cake is sure to seal the deal. Just as easy and versatile as a cake mix—but way more moist and delicious—it's a recipe you'll want to make for all sorts of special occasions.

HANDS-ON TIME
45 minutes

TOTAL TIME
2½ hours

MAKES
12 to 16 servings

INGREDIENTS

CAKE:

3 cups	all-purpose flour
2 cups	granulated sugar
⅔ cup	cocoa powder
2 tsp	baking soda
½ tsp	salt
2 cups	cooled brewed coffee or water
1 cup	vegetable oil
2 tsp	vanilla
3 tbsp	cider vinegar

BUTTERY CHOCOLATE ICING:

2 cups	unsalted butter, softened
⅔ cup	whipping cream (35%)
4 tsp	vanilla
¼ tsp	salt
5 cups	icing sugar
225 g	unsweetened chocolate (8 oz), melted and cooled

DIRECTIONS

CAKE: Grease two 9-inch (1.5 L) round cake pans; line bottoms with parchment paper. Set aside. In bowl, whisk flour, sugar, cocoa powder, baking soda and salt. Whisk in coffee, oil and vanilla. Stir in vinegar. Divide between prepared pans. Bake in 350°F (180°C) oven until cake tester inserted in centre comes out clean, 25 to 30 minutes. Let cool in pans on racks for 10 minutes. Invert onto racks; peel off paper. Let cool completely. *(Make-ahead: Store in airtight container for up to 24 hours.)*

BUTTERY CHOCOLATE ICING: In bowl, beat butter until light and fluffy; beat in cream, vanilla and salt. Beat in sugar, 1 cup at a time, until smooth; beat in chocolate, scraping down side of bowl often, until fluffy, 2 minutes.

ASSEMBLY: Cut each cake in half horizontally to make 4 layers. Place 1 layer, cut side up, on cake plate; slide strips of waxed paper between cake and plate. Spread about ¾ cup of the icing over cut side; top with second layer, cut side down. Spread about ¾ cup of the remaining icing over top of stack. Repeat with remaining layers, omitting icing on top of stack. Using large offset palette knife, spread about 1 cup of the remaining icing all over cake to seal in crumbs. PHOTO A

Refrigerate until firm, about 30 minutes. Using large offset palette knife, spread remaining icing all over cake, smoothing sides and top. Run tip of palette knife back and forth loosely across top to form gentle ripples, if desired. PHOTO B

Remove waxed paper strips. *(Make-ahead: Refrigerate until firm, about 1 hour. Cover loosely with plastic wrap and refrigerate for up to 24 hours.)*

NUTRITIONAL INFORMATION, PER EACH OF 16 SERVINGS: about 760 cal, 6 g pro, 48 g total fat (23 g sat. fat), 86 g carb, 4 g fibre, 73 mg chol, 242 mg sodium, 263 mg potassium. % RDI: 3% calcium, 30% iron, 24% vit A, 19% folate.

VARIATIONS

CLASSIC CHOCOLATE CUPCAKES

Divide batter among 24 paper-lined muffin cups. Bake until cake tester inserted in centres comes out clean, 18 to 20 minutes. Transfer to rack; let cool completely. Top with half-batch of the Buttery Chocolate Icing.

CLASSIC CHOCOLATE SLAB CAKE

Grease 13- x 9-inch (3.5 L) cake pan; line bottom with parchment paper. Set aside. Prepare batter as directed; scrape into prepared pan. Bake until cake tester inserted in centre comes out clean, 30 to 35 minutes. Let cool in pan on rack for 10 minutes. Invert onto rack; peel off paper. Let cool completely. Invert onto cake plate; top with half-batch of Buttery Chocolate Icing.

HERE'S HOW

COCONUT LEMON CREAM SNOW CAKE ◐

You can make the custard and cake two days ahead and assemble the final product at your leisure. Just don't throw away the egg whites—you'll need them for the buttercream.

HANDS-ON TIME
1 hour

TOTAL TIME
3¾ hours

MAKES
12 to 16 servings

INGREDIENTS

LEMON CREAM:

4	egg yolks
½ cup	granulated sugar
1 tsp	grated lemon zest
½ cup	lemon juice
¼ cup	cornstarch
1¾ cups	milk
3 tbsp	unsalted butter

CAKE:

1 cup	unsweetened desiccated coconut
1 cup	unsalted butter, softened
1⅓ cups	granulated sugar
3	eggs
1 tsp	vanilla
2¾ cups	all-purpose flour
2 tsp	baking powder
½ tsp	each baking soda and salt
¾ cup	coconut milk

BUTTERCREAM ICING:

4	egg whites
1 cup	granulated sugar
1¼ cups	unsalted butter, cubed
½ tsp	vanilla
pinch	salt

GARNISH:

1 cup	unsweetened desiccated coconut

DIRECTIONS

LEMON CREAM: In bowl, whisk together egg yolks, sugar, lemon zest, lemon juice and cornstarch.

In saucepan, heat milk over medium heat until bubbles form around edge; gradually whisk half into egg mixture. Whisk back into pan; bring to boil over medium-high heat, whisking constantly. Cook, whisking, until bubbling and thickened, about 3 minutes. Remove from heat; whisk in butter. Place plastic wrap directly on surface; refrigerate until cold, about 2 hours.

CAKE: While lemon cream is chilling, toast coconut on rimmed baking sheet in 350°F (180°C) oven until golden, 3 to 5 minutes. Set aside.

Grease two 9-inch (1.5 L) round cake pans; line bottoms with parchment paper. Set aside.

In large bowl, beat butter with sugar until light. Beat in eggs, 1 at a time; beat in vanilla. Whisk flour, baking powder, baking soda and salt. Stir into butter mixture, alternating with coconut milk, making 3 additions of flour mixture and 2 of coconut milk. Fold in toasted coconut.

Scrape into prepared pans. Bake in 350°F (180°C) oven until cake tester inserted in centre of each comes out clean, about 30 minutes. Let cool in pans on racks for 15 minutes. Invert onto racks; peel off paper. Let cool completely.

BUTTERCREAM ICING: While cake is cooling, in bowl of stand mixer, whisk egg whites with sugar. Place bowl over saucepan of simmering water; cook, whisking, until warm and sugar is dissolved, about 1 minute. Using whisk attachment, beat at medium-high speed until stiff peaks form, about 6 minutes. Beat in butter, 2 tbsp at a time, until satiny (mixture will curdle initially). Beat in vanilla and salt.

ASSEMBLY: Cut each cake in half horizontally to make 4 layers. Place 1 layer, cut side up, on cake plate. Spread with one-third of the lemon cream; repeat layers twice. Top with remaining cake layer, cut side down. Spread one-third of the buttercream over top and side of cake to seal in crumbs; refrigerate for 30 minutes. Spread remaining icing over top and side.

GARNISH: Press coconut onto icing on top and side of cake.

NUTRITIONAL INFORMATION, PER EACH OF 16 SERVINGS: about 615 cal, 7 g pro, 41 g total fat (27 g sat. fat), 59 g carb, 3 g fibre, 162 mg chol, 196 mg sodium, 195 mg potassium. % RDI: 7% calcium, 14% iron, 29% vit A, 7% vit C, 27% folate.

FLOURLESS CHOCOLATE TRUFFLE CAKE ⬤

The lack of flour in this batter creates a dense, fudgy centre, so your cake tester won't come out clean, even when the cake is done. The texture is similar to that of brownies.

HANDS-ON TIME
30 minutes

TOTAL TIME
2¾ hours

MAKES
12 servings

INGREDIENTS

CAKE:

½ cup	unsalted butter
170 g	bittersweet chocolate, chopped
4	eggs
1 cup	granulated sugar
pinch	salt
⅓ cup	ground almonds
1 tsp	instant espresso powder or instant coffee granules
2 tbsp	cocoa powder

CHOCOLATE ESPRESSO GLAZE:

115 g	bittersweet chocolate, chopped
¼ cup	unsalted butter
¼ cup	hot water
¼ tsp	instant espresso powder

DIRECTIONS

CAKE: Grease 9-inch (2.5 L) springform pan; line bottom and side with parchment paper. Set aside.

In heatproof bowl over saucepan of hot (not boiling) water, melt butter with chocolate, stirring until smooth. Let cool.

In large bowl, beat together eggs, sugar and salt until pale and thickened, about 5 minutes. Fold in chocolate mixture, almonds and espresso powder. Sift cocoa powder over top; fold in. Scrape into prepared pan, smoothing top.

Bake in 350°F (180°C) oven until crackly on top and cake tester inserted in centre comes out with a few moist crumbs clinging, 30 to 35 minutes. Let cool. Remove side of pan and paper; place cake on rack over baking sheet.

CHOCOLATE ESPRESSO GLAZE: In heatproof bowl over saucepan of hot (not boiling) water, melt together chocolate, butter, hot water and espresso powder, stirring until smooth. Pour over centre of cake; spread to within 1 inch (2.5 cm) of edge. Refrigerate until set, about 1 hour. *(Make-ahead: Cover loosely and refrigerate for up to 24 hours.)*

NUTRITIONAL INFORMATION, PER SERVING: about 343 cal, 4 g pro, 24 g total fat (7 g sat. fat), 30 g carb, 3 g fibre, 63 mg chol, 122 mg sodium, 203 mg potassium. % RDI: 3% calcium, 14% iron, 24% vit A, 4% folate.

VARIATION

PASSOVER FLOURLESS CHOCOLATE TRUFFLE CAKE

Substitute kosher pareve margarine for the butter, kosher pareve bittersweet chocolate (such as Lieber's) for the regular chocolate and kosher pareve cocoa powder (such as Ghirardelli) for the regular cocoa powder.

CHOCOLATE HAZELNUT MOUSSE CAKE

Crunchy meringue, silky mousse, moist chocolate cake and smooth ganache make this a show-stopping dessert that's well worth the effort. Starting with room-temperature ingredients yields the best results (see Room-Temperature Ingredients for Cakes, opposite).

HANDS-ON TIME
1 hour

TOTAL TIME
4½ hours

MAKES
16 to 18 servings

INGREDIENTS

CAKE:

1½ cups	all-purpose flour
1 cup	granulated sugar
⅓ cup	cocoa powder
1 tsp	baking soda
¼ tsp	salt
½ cup	vegetable oil
1 tsp	vanilla
4 tsp	cider vinegar

MERINGUE:

3	egg whites
pinch	cream of tartar
¾ cup	granulated sugar
½ cup	ground skinned roasted hazelnuts (about ½ cup whole), see tip, opposite
½ tsp	vanilla

MOUSSE:

1	pkg (7 g) gelatin
1 cup	hazelnut chocolate spread (such as Nutella)
2 tbsp	unsalted butter, softened
1½ cups	whipping cream (35%)

GANACHE:

175 g	bittersweet chocolate, chopped
¾ cup	whipping cream (35%)

CANDIED HAZELNUTS:

⅓ cup	granulated sugar
pinch	salt
½ cup	skinned roasted hazelnuts

DIRECTIONS

CAKE: Grease 10-inch (3 L) springform pan; line bottom with parchment paper. Set aside.

In bowl, whisk together flour, sugar, cocoa powder, baking soda and salt. Whisk in 1 cup water, oil and vanilla; stir in vinegar. Scrape into prepared pan.

Bake in 350°F (180°C) oven until cake tester inserted in centre comes out clean, 20 to 22 minutes. Run knife around edge of pan. Invert cake onto rack; peel off paper. Let cool completely. *(Make-ahead: Store in airtight container for up to 24 hours.)*

MERINGUE: Line rimmed baking sheet with parchment paper. Using 10-inch (3 L) springform pan as guide, trace circle onto paper. Turn paper over.

In bowl, beat egg whites with cream of tartar until soft peaks form. Beat in sugar, 2 tbsp at a time, until stiff glossy peaks form. Fold in hazelnuts and vanilla. Spoon onto circle, smoothing top.

Bake on bottom rack in 225°F (110°C) oven until dry and crisp, 1½ to 2 hours. Turn off oven; let cool in oven for 2 hours. *(Make-ahead: Store in airtight container in cool dry place for up to 5 days.)*

MOUSSE: While meringue is cooling, in small bowl, sprinkle gelatin over 2 tbsp water; set aside. In heatproof bowl over saucepan of hot (not boiling) water, melt hazelnut spread with 3 tbsp water, stirring until smooth; stir in butter.

In microwave, warm gelatin on high until dissolved, about 20 seconds; whisk into hazelnut spread mixture. Set aside and keep warm. (Mixture may separate while standing; whisk to combine.)

Whip cream; whisk one-third into hazelnut spread mixture. Fold in remaining whipped cream.

ASSEMBLY: Line bottom of 10-inch (3 L) greased springform pan with parchment paper. Cut cake in half horizontally to make 2 layers. Place bottom layer, cut side up, in pan; spread 1 cup of the mousse over top. Place meringue layer in pan, trimming to fit if necessary; spread 1 cup of the mousse over top. Top with remaining cake layer, cut side down; top with remaining mousse. Cover with plastic wrap; refrigerate until set, about 1 hour. *(Make-ahead: Wrap in plastic wrap and overwrap in foil. Freeze for up to 2 weeks. Thaw overnight in refrigerator; continue with recipe.)*

GANACHE: While cake is chilling, place chocolate in heatproof bowl. In small saucepan, bring cream to boil; pour over chocolate, whisking until smooth. Let stand, whisking occasionally, until slightly thickened, about 20 minutes.

Run knife around edge of cake; transfer cake to rack set over parchment paper. Pour ganache over top, smoothing top and sides with palette knife. Refrigerate until almost set and ganache is still shiny yet no longer jiggles, about 30 minutes. *(Make-ahead: Cover and refrigerate for up to 3 days or freeze for up to 1 month.)*

CANDIED HAZELNUTS: While ganache is setting in refrigerator, in shallow saucepan, dissolve sugar and salt in 3 tbsp water over medium-high heat.

Add hazelnuts; bring to boil. Reduce heat to medium; simmer, stirring occasionally, until liquid is light golden, about 8 minutes. Spread nut mixture on parchment paper–lined rimmed baking sheet. Let cool.

Coarsely chop hazelnuts; sprinkle over top of cake.

NUTRITIONAL INFORMATION, PER EACH OF 18 SERVINGS: about 487 cal, 6 g pro, 31 g total fat (11 g sat. fat), 49 g carb, 3 g fibre, 43 mg chol, 131 mg sodium, 263 mg potassium. % RDI: 6% calcium, 14% iron, 11% vit A, 11% folate.

TIP FROM THE TEST KITCHEN
If you can't find skinned roasted hazelnuts, roast whole hazelnuts in a 350°F (180°C) oven until the skins crack, 8 to 10 minutes. Transfer to a tea towel and rub off as much of the skin as possible.

ROOM-TEMPERATURE INGREDIENTS FOR CAKES

A successful cake starts with room-temperature ingredients, especially the butter, eggs and milk. Simply measure and set them out 2 hours before you need them. But what if you forget or you need a cake ASAP? Here are some tricks to shorten the warm-up time.

BUTTER
Cube cold, hard butter or shred it on the largest holes of a box grater. Spread over the bottom of a mixing bowl and let it soften for about 20 minutes. Avoid the temptation to heat the butter—it will likely melt. When beaten, melted butter won't incorporate enough air into a cake batter to allow it to rise successfully.

EGGS
Place cold eggs in a bowl, cover with warm water and let stand for 10 minutes. If the cake requires separated eggs, it is easier to separate them while they're still cold—so let the yolks and whites come to room temperature in separate bowls set in a shallow pan or sinkful of barely warm water.

MILK
Warm cold milk in the microwave. Heat it for 10 seconds at a time, checking the temperature after each interval, until it's room temperature.

SKY-HIGH CREAMY CHEESECAKE

Our best cheesecake features a high-rising, super-light, velvety filling, a crack-free top and a crisp graham crust—all without the hassle of a water bath. It is so good on its own, but add Sour Cherry Topping (below) or serve with fresh seasonal fruit if you like.

HANDS-ON TIME
25 minutes

TOTAL TIME
11½ hours

MAKES
16 servings

INGREDIENTS

CRUST:

2 cups	graham cracker crumbs
½ cup	granulated sugar
¼ cup	butter, melted
1	egg white

FILLING:

3	pkg (each 250 g) cream cheese, softened
1¼ cups	granulated sugar
4	eggs
4 tsp	lemon juice
2 tsp	vanilla
pinch	salt
4 cups	sour cream

DIRECTIONS

CRUST: In bowl, stir together graham crumbs, sugar and butter until well moistened; press into bottom and 1½ inches (4 cm) up side of greased 10-inch (3 L) springform pan. Bake in 325°F (160°C) oven until firm, about 12 minutes. Let cool completely.

Whisk egg white with 2 tsp water until foamy; drizzle over crust. Using pastry brush, dab and swirl egg mixture to lightly coat crust. Bake in 325°F (160°C) oven until crust appears dry, 7 minutes. Let cool completely.

FILLING: While crust is cooling, in large bowl, beat cream cheese until fluffy. Gradually beat in sugar and continue to beat, scraping down side of bowl twice, until smooth and light.

On low speed, beat in eggs, 1 at a time and scraping down side of bowl often, just until combined. Stir in lemon juice, vanilla and salt. Stir in sour cream, making 2 additions, until smooth. Pour over crust, smoothing top. Bake in 275°F (140°C) oven until surface is no longer shiny and edge is set yet centre still jiggles slightly, about 1¾ hours. Turn off oven; let cheesecake cool in oven for 1 hour.

Transfer pan to rack; run paring knife around edge of cheesecake. Let cool completely. Refrigerate until chilled, about 6 hours. *(Make-ahead: Cover and refrigerate for up to 2 days.)*

NUTRITIONAL INFORMATION, PER SERVING: about 458 cal, 10 g pro, 30 g total fat (16 g sat. fat), 40 g carb, trace fibre, 127 mg chol, 322 mg sodium, 227 mg potassium. % RDI: 13% calcium, 7% iron, 29% vit A, 2% vit C, 11% folate.

SOUR CHERRY TOPPING

In saucepan, combine 3 cups pitted sour cherries, ⅓ cup granulated sugar and 3 tbsp water. Cook over medium heat, stirring often, until cherries are very tender, about 15 minutes. Stir 1 tbsp cornstarch with 1 tbsp water. Whisk into cherry mixture. Cook, stirring, until thickened, about 1 minute. Remove from heat; stir in 2 tsp each grated lemon zest and lemon juice. Let cool completely *(Make-ahead: Cover and refrigerate for up to 2 days.)* **MAKES** 1 cup

TIP FROM THE TEST KITCHEN
Use an oven thermometer to ensure your oven is properly calibrated. Even a small 25-degree fluctuation can cause the cheesecake to puff up and develop surface cracks.

CHOCOLATE CHEESECAKE
WITH CARAMEL PECAN SAUCE

HANDS-ON TIME
30 minutes

TOTAL TIME
6½ hours

MAKES
16 servings

Turtles candy inspired this sumptuous cheesecake. It has all the elements you love about them: pecans, gooey caramel, and lots and lots of rich chocolate.

INGREDIENTS

CRUST:

1 cup	graham cracker crumbs
⅓ cup	finely chopped pecans
¼ cup	butter, melted

FILLING:

¾ cup	packed brown sugar
3	pkg (each 250 g) cream cheese, softened
4	eggs
1 tsp	vanilla
2	bars (each 100 g) 70% dark chocolate, melted
¼ cup	whipping cream (35%)

CARAMEL PECAN SAUCE:

¾ cup	granulated sugar
½ cup	whipping cream (35%)
2 tbsp	butter
⅓ cup	toasted pecan halves, halved
pinch	salt

DIRECTIONS

CRUST: Grease 9-inch (2.5 L) springform pan; line side with parchment paper. Centre pan on large square of heavy-duty foil; bring foil up and press to side of pan.

In bowl, stir together graham crumbs, pecans and butter until well moistened; press onto bottom of prepared pan. Bake in 350°F (180°C) oven until firm, about 10 minutes. Let cool in pan on rack.

FILLING: Press brown sugar through fine-mesh sieve into bowl to remove any lumps. In stand mixer with paddle attachment or in bowl with hand mixer, beat cream cheese with brown sugar at high speed for 5 minutes, scraping down side of bowl. Beat in eggs, 1 at a time. Beat in vanilla.

Mix about 1 cup of the cream cheese mixture with melted chocolate until smooth; return to cream cheese mixture and stir to combine well. Beat in cream. Pour over crust.

Set springform pan in large roasting pan; pour enough hot water into roasting pan to come 1 inch (2.5 cm) up side of springform pan. Bake in 325°F (160°C) oven until set but centre still jiggles slightly, about 1 hour.

Transfer springform pan to rack and remove foil; let cool. Cover and refrigerate until firm, about 4 hours. *(Make-ahead: Refrigerate for up to 24 hours.)*

CARAMEL PECAN SAUCE: While cheesecake is chilling, in heavy saucepan, stir sugar with ¼ cup water over medium heat until dissolved. Bring to boil; boil vigorously, without stirring but brushing down side of pan often, until dark amber, 6 to 10 minutes. Remove from heat.

Standing back and averting face, add cream; whisk until smooth. Whisk in butter until smooth. Stir in pecans and salt. Let cool. *(Make-ahead: Refrigerate in airtight container for up to 24 hours; rewarm to liquefy.)* Serve with cheesecake.

NUTRITIONAL INFORMATION, PER SERVING: about 451 cal, 7 g pro, 34 g total fat (19 g sat. fat), 33 g carb, 2 g fibre, 124 mg chol, 224 mg sodium, 145 mg potassium. % RDI: 7% calcium, 22% iron, 27% vit A, 8% folate.

FLOURLESS MOLTEN CHOCOLATE LAVA CAKES

These molten chocolate lava cakes are always a hit, and the variation (below) makes a version that is wonderful to serve for Passover.

HANDS-ON TIME
30 minutes

TOTAL TIME
3 hours

MAKES
12 servings

INGREDIENTS

340 g	bittersweet or semisweet chocolate, chopped
½ cup	butter, cubed
1	vanilla bean
2 cups	granulated sugar
6	eggs
6	egg yolks
¼ cup	cocoa powder, sifted
pinch	salt
340 g	strawberries, diced
	whipped cream (optional)

DIRECTIONS

In heatproof bowl over hot (not boiling) water, melt chocolate with butter, stirring until smooth. Halve vanilla bean lengthwise; using tip of sharp knife, scrape seeds into chocolate mixture. Stir to combine. Discard vanilla pod or save for another use. Remove chocolate mixture from heat.

Whisk in sugar. Whisk in eggs and egg yolks, 1 at a time. Whisk in cocoa powder and salt. Pour into 12 greased 6-oz (175 mL) ramekins; place on rimmed baking sheet. *(Make-ahead: Cover and refrigerate for up to 24 hours; add 5 minutes to baking time.)*

Bake in 425°F (220°C) oven until edges are set and centres are slightly jiggly when tapped, about 15 minutes. Let cool for 3 minutes. Run knife around edges of cakes; turn out onto plates. Garnish with strawberries, and whipped cream (if using).

NUTRITIONAL INFORMATION, PER SERVING: about 387 cal, 7 g pro, 18 g total fat (8 g sat. fat), 51 g carb, 4 g fibre, 195 mg chol, 108 mg sodium, 132 mg potassium. % RDI: 3% calcium, 16% iron, 16% vit A, 28% vit C, 15% folate.

VARIATION
PASSOVER DAIRY-FREE GLUTEN-FREE
MOLTEN CHOCOLATE LAVA CAKES

Substitute kosher pareve bittersweet chocolate (such as Lieber's) for the regular chocolate, kosher pareve margarine for the butter, kosher pareve cocoa powder (such as Ghirardelli) for the regular cocoa powder, and kosher nondairy whipped topping for the whipped cream (if using).

TIP FROM THE TEST KITCHEN
You can make the batter ahead for convenience, but the cakes are best eaten immediately after baking. Don't pop them into the oven until you're ready for dessert.

GLUTEN-FREE PB & J CUPCAKES

Adding some tart cream cheese to the icing balances the sweetness of the peanut butter.

HANDS-ON TIME
20 minutes

TOTAL TIME
1 hour

MAKES
12 cupcakes

INGREDIENTS

CUPCAKES:

⅓ cup	unsalted butter, softened
1 cup	granulated sugar
2	eggs
2 tsp	vanilla
1¼ cups	gluten-free all-purpose flour blend (such as Bob's Red Mill)
1 tsp	each xanthan gum and baking powder
½ tsp	baking soda
¼ tsp	salt
¾ cup	hot water
½ tsp	cider vinegar
¼ cup	seedless raspberry jam

PEANUT BUTTER ICING:

¼ cup	butter, softened
125 g	cream cheese (half 250 g pkg), softened
2 tbsp	smooth peanut butter
2 cups	icing sugar
1 tbsp	milk
1 tsp	vanilla

DIRECTIONS

CUPCAKES: In bowl, beat butter with sugar until fluffy; beat in eggs and vanilla.

Whisk together flour, xanthan gum, baking powder, baking soda and salt. Stir into egg mixture for 1 minute (batter will thicken). Stir in hot water and vinegar. Spoon into 12 paper-lined muffin cups.

Bake in 350°F (180°C) oven until cake tester inserted in centre of several comes out clean, 32 to 35 minutes. Let cool in pan on rack for 5 minutes. Transfer to rack; let cool completely. *(Make-ahead: Store in airtight container for up to 24 hours.)*

Spoon jam into piping bag fitted with small plain tip. Press tip into centre of each cupcake; pipe in about 1 tsp of the jam.

PEANUT BUTTER ICING: In bowl, beat butter, cream cheese and peanut butter until light; beat in sugar, ½ cup at a time. Beat in milk and vanilla until smooth. Pipe onto cupcakes. *(Make-ahead: Store in airtight container for up to 3 days.)*

NUTRITIONAL INFORMATION, PER CUPCAKE: about 340 cal, 4 g pro, 16 g total fat (9 g sat. fat), 51 g carb, 2 g fibre, 66 mg chol, 217 mg sodium, 152 mg potassium. % RDI: 4% calcium, 9% iron, 13% vit A, 2% vit C, 5% folate.

VARIATION

GLUTEN-FREE CHOCOLATE PB & J CUPCAKES

Reduce gluten-free all-purpose flour to ¾ cup; add ½ cup cocoa powder to flour mixture.

TIP FROM THE TEST KITCHEN
Omit the peanut butter for a school-friendly nut-free treat.

TRIPLE-CHOCOLATE CUPCAKES

HANDS-ON TIME
40 minutes

TOTAL TIME
1½ hours

MAKES
24 cupcakes

The trio of milk, dark and white chocolates makes these cupcakes ultra-decadent. Right before serving, add the white chocolate discs straight from the fridge so they don't soften.

INGREDIENTS

CUPCAKES:

3 cups	all-purpose flour
2 cups	granulated sugar
⅔ cup	cocoa powder, sifted
2 tsp	baking soda
½ tsp	salt
1 cup	vegetable oil
2 tsp	vanilla
3 tbsp	cider vinegar

WHITE CHOCOLATE DISCS:

2	bars (each 100 g) good-quality white chocolate, chopped
	white sugar pearls, chocolate sprinkles and/or chocolate candies (such as Maltesers)

MILK CHOCOLATE ICING:

1 cup	unsalted butter
⅓ cup	whipping cream (35%)
2 tsp	vanilla
2½ cups	icing sugar
1 tbsp	cocoa powder
pinch	salt
1	bar (100 g) good-quality milk chocolate, melted and cooled

DIRECTIONS

CUPCAKES: In large bowl, whisk together flour, sugar, cocoa powder, baking soda and salt. Whisk in 2 cups water, oil and vanilla. Stir in vinegar. Divide batter among 24 large paper-lined muffin cups.

Bake in 350°F (180°C) oven until cake tester inserted into centre of several comes out clean, 18 to 20 minutes. Transfer cupcakes to rack; let cool completely.

WHITE CHOCOLATE DISCS: While cupcakes are cooling, in heatproof bowl over saucepan of hot (not boiling) water, melt white chocolate; let cool slightly.

On parchment paper–lined baking sheet, drop chocolate by level 1 tsp, smoothing to form twenty-four 1-inch (2.5 cm) wide discs, about 1 inch (2.5 cm) apart. Top with pearls, sprinkles and/or candies; refrigerate until firm, about 30 minutes.

MILK CHOCOLATE ICING: While discs are chilling, in large bowl, beat butter until light and fluffy; beat in cream and vanilla. Beat in icing sugar, cocoa powder and salt until smooth; beat in chocolate, scraping down side of bowl occasionally, until fluffy and well combined, about 2 minutes. Spoon into piping bag fitted with ¾-inch (2 cm) star tip; pipe icing onto cupcakes.

TO FINISH: Gently peel white chocolate discs off paper; place on top of icing, pressing lightly to adhere.

NUTRITIONAL INFORMATION, PER CUPCAKE: about 395 cal, 3 g pro, 22 g total fat (9 g sat. fat), 49 g carb, 1 g fibre, 26 mg chol, 166 mg sodium, 125 mg potassium. % RDI: 3% calcium, 9% iron, 8% vit A, 11% folate.

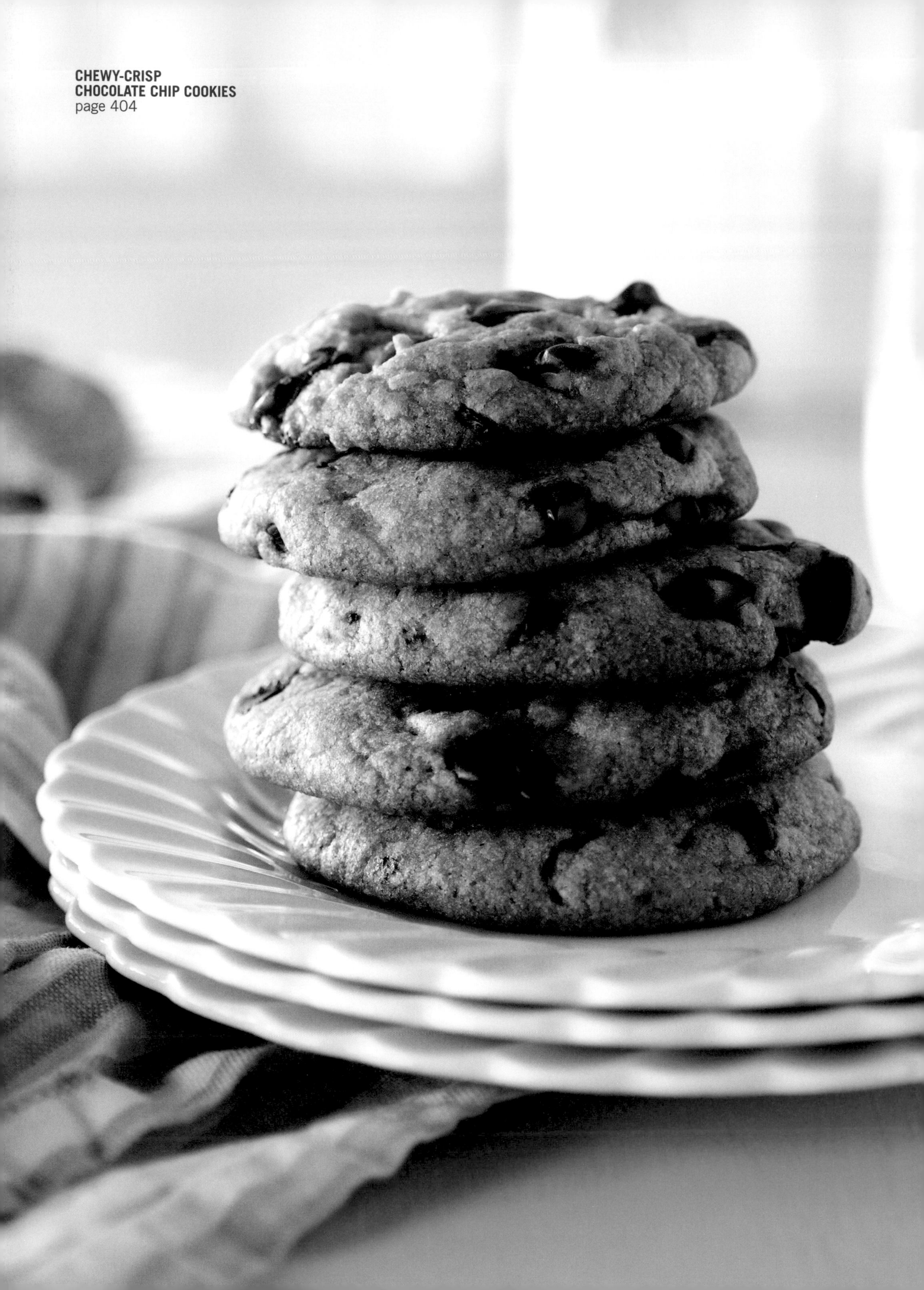

CHEWY-CRISP CHOCOLATE CHIP COOKIES
page 404

ULTIMATE DESSERTS

"There is something wonderful about watching your family's and friends' faces light up when they take a first bite of a really good homemade dessert. You get the feelings of pride, happiness and gratitude all rolled into one."

ANNABELLE WAUGH FOOD DIRECTOR

DATE SQUARES ◔

Chopping the dates for these squares is easier, and less messy, if you use kitchen shears or scissors to cut them.

HANDS-ON TIME
20 minutes

TOTAL TIME
1 hour

MAKES
30 squares

INGREDIENTS

DATE FILLING:

3 cups	chopped dried pitted dates
1 cup	boiling water
¾ tsp	cinnamon
¼ tsp	nutmeg
pinch	salt

CRUST AND TOPPING:

1½ cups	large-flake rolled oats
1¼ cups	all-purpose flour
¾ cup	packed brown sugar
½ tsp	salt
½ tsp	baking soda
⅔ cup	unsalted butter, softened
2 tbsp	cold water
½ cup	chopped almonds

DIRECTIONS

DATE FILLING: In bowl, combine dates with boiling water; cover and let stand for 20 minutes. Stir in cinnamon, nutmeg and salt; mash with fork until smooth.

CRUST AND TOPPING: In food processor, pulse together oats, flour, brown sugar, salt and baking soda until oats are chopped, five to 10 pulses. Pulse in butter until crumbly; pulse in cold water until mixture comes together. Remove one-third of the oat mixture for topping; toss with chopped -almonds.

ASSEMBLY: Press remaining oat mixture into parchment paper–lined 13- x 9-inch (3.5 L) cake pan to make crust; spread filling over crust. Sprinkle topping over filling, pressing lightly.

Bake in 350°F (180°C) oven until light golden, 35 to 40 minutes. Let cool in pan on rack before cutting into squares.

NUTRITIONAL INFORMATION, PER SQUARE: about 140 cal, 2 g pro, 5 g total fat (3 g sat. fat), 23 g carb, 2 g fibre, 10 mg chol, 60 mg sodium, 164 mg potassium. % RDI: 2% calcium, 6% iron, 4% vit A, 5% folate.

VARIATIONS

DATE AND PRUNE SQUARES

In filling, reduce dates to 1½ cups; add 1½ cups chopped pitted prunes.

BLUEBERRY SQUARES

Omit Date Filling. In saucepan, bring 5 cups blueberries and 1 cup granulated sugar to boil; reduce heat and simmer until tender, about 10 minutes. Whisk ⅓ cup orange juice with 3 tbsp cornstarch until smooth; whisk into blueberry mixture and boil, stirring, until thickened, about 1 minute. Scrape into bowl; place plastic wrap directly on surface. Refrigerate until chilled, about 2 hours. Assemble and bake as directed. Let cool to room temperature; refrigerate until set before cutting into squares.

THE BEST CHOCOLATE TOFFEE BROWNIES

These brownies have become the Test Kitchen's secret weapon for parties, showers, gifts and other occasions. The combination of rich dark chocolate and a subtle crunch from chopped toffee bars is what makes them the best brownies you'll ever make.

HANDS-ON TIME
20 minutes

TOTAL TIME
3 hours

MAKES
24 bars

INGREDIENTS

115 g	semisweet or other dark chocolate, chopped
28 g	unsweetened chocolate, chopped
½ cup	butter, cubed
1 cup	granulated sugar
2 tsp	vanilla
2	eggs
½ cup	all-purpose flour
pinch	salt
3	bars (each 39 g) chocolate-covered toffee bars (such as Skor), chopped

DIRECTIONS

In saucepan, melt together semisweet chocolate, unsweetened chocolate and butter over medium-low heat, stirring occasionally; let cool for 10 minutes.

Whisk in sugar and vanilla. Whisk in eggs, 1 at a time. Stir in flour and salt; fold in chopped chocolate bars. Scrape into parchment paper–lined 8-inch (2 L) square cake pan; smooth top.

Bake in 350°F (180°C) oven until cake tester inserted in centre comes out with a few moist crumbs clinging, about 25 minutes. Let cool in pan on rack. Cut into bars. *(Make-ahead: Layer between waxed paper in airtight container and refrigerate for up to 3 days or freeze for up to 3 weeks.)*

NUTRITIONAL INFORMATION, PER BAR: about 137 cal, 1 g pro, 8 g total fat (5 g sat. fat), 17 g carb, 1 g fibre, 28 mg chol, 49 mg sodium, 43 mg potassium. % RDI: 1% calcium, 4% iron, 4% vit A, 3% folate.

TIP FROM THE TEST KITCHEN

Brownies are best when baked until just cooked but still moist in the centre. You may find these brownies look a little underbaked at the recommended time, but rest assured they'll continue to cook after they come out of the oven. They will firm up nicely when cooled.

CLASSIC NANAIMO BARS ✿ ◐

The pride of Nanaimo, B.C., these bars have a coconutty crumb crust layered with a creamy custard filling and a smooth chocolate topping. Best served at room temperature, the bars keep well refrigerated or frozen.

HANDS-ON TIME
20 minutes

TOTAL TIME
2¾ hours

MAKES
25 bars

INGREDIENTS

CRUMB CRUST:

1 cup	graham cracker crumbs
½ cup	sweetened shredded coconut
⅓ cup	finely chopped walnuts
¼ cup	cocoa powder
¼ cup	granulated sugar
⅓ cup	butter, melted
1	egg, lightly beaten

FILLING:

¼ cup	butter, softened
2 tbsp	custard powder
½ tsp	vanilla
2 cups	icing sugar
2 tbsp	milk (approx)

TOPPING:

115 g	semisweet chocolate, chopped
1 tbsp	butter

DIRECTIONS

CRUMB CRUST: In bowl, stir together graham crumbs, coconut, walnuts, cocoa powder and sugar. Drizzle with butter and egg, stirring until combined.

Press into parchment paper–lined 9-inch (2.5 L) square cake pan. Bake in 350°F (180°C) oven until firm, about 10 minutes. Let cool in pan on rack.

FILLING: In bowl, beat together butter, custard powder and vanilla. Beat in icing sugar, alternating with milk, making 3 additions of sugar and 2 of milk, adding up to 1 tsp more milk if too thick to spread. Spread over cooled base. Refrigerate until firm, about 1 hour.

TOPPING: In heatproof bowl over saucepan of hot (not boiling) water, melt chocolate with butter; using offset palette knife, spread over filling. Refrigerate until chocolate is almost set, about 30 minutes.

With tip of sharp knife, score into bars; refrigerate until chocolate is completely set, about 30 minutes. *(Make-ahead: Wrap and refrigerate for up to 4 days or overwrap in foil and freeze for up to 2 weeks.)* Cut into bars.

NUTRITIONAL INFORMATION, PER BAR: about 150 cal, 1 g pro, 9 g total fat (5 g sat. fat), 19 g carb, 1 g fibre, 20 mg chol, 65 mg sodium, 62 mg potassium. % RDI: 1% calcium, 4% iron, 4% vit A, 2% folate.

CITRUS MADELEINES

*These buttery little sponge cakes are feather-light and eaten like cookies.
Instead of brushing them with the glaze, you can dip them halfway into melted
bittersweet chocolate or dust them with icing sugar.*

HANDS-ON TIME
15 minutes

TOTAL TIME
1 hour

MAKES
24 madeleines

INGREDIENTS

MADELEINES:

3	eggs
½ cup	unsalted butter, melted
2 tsp	each grated lemon, lime and orange zest
¼ tsp	vanilla
¾ cup	all-purpose flour
½ cup	granulated sugar
⅓ cup	ground almonds
½ tsp	salt

GLAZE:

¾ cup	icing sugar
1 tbsp	lemon juice

DIRECTIONS

MADELEINES: In large bowl, whisk together eggs; butter; lemon, lime and orange zests; and vanilla. Whisk together flour, sugar, almonds and salt; whisk into egg mixture.

Spoon by heaping 1 tbsp into each mould of 2 well-greased 12-mould madeleine pans. Bake in 350°F (180°C) oven until edges are golden brown, 12 to 15 minutes. Loosen with tip of knife. Invert onto rack; let cool.

GLAZE: Whisk icing sugar with lemon juice; brush over cooled madeleines. *(Make-ahead: Store in airtight container for up to 24 hours or freeze for up to 1 week.)*

NUTRITIONAL INFORMATION, PER MADELEINE: about 96 cal, 2 g pro, 5 g total fat (3 g sat. fat), 11 g carb, trace fibre, 33 mg chol, 56 mg sodium. % RDI: 1% calcium, 2% iron, 4% vit A, 2% vit C, 5% folate.

TIP FROM THE TEST KITCHEN
You will need a special madeleine pan to bake these tiny cakes. They are available at most kitchen supply stores.

CHEWY-CRISP CHOCOLATE CHIP COOKIES

No matter how you like your chocolate chip cookies—soft, crisp or perfectly in between— our best-in-class take on this classic treat is buttery, chocolaty and totally satisfying.

HANDS-ON TIME
20 minutes

TOTAL TIME
1½ hours

MAKES
about 60 cookies

INGREDIENTS

1 cup	butter, softened
1¼ cups	packed brown sugar
¾ cup	granulated sugar
2	eggs
2 tsp	vanilla
3 cups	all-purpose flour
1 tsp	salt
1 tsp	baking powder
¼ tsp	baking soda
3 cups	good-quality semisweet chocolate chips or chunks

DIRECTIONS

In large bowl, beat together butter, brown sugar and granulated sugar until fluffy. Beat in eggs, 1 at a time; beat in vanilla. Whisk together flour, salt, baking powder and baking soda; stir into butter mixture. Fold in chocolate chips. *(Make-ahead: Shape into disc, wrap in plastic wrap and refrigerate for up to 3 days or freeze in resealable freezer bag for up to 1 month. Let come to room temperature.)*

Roll by 2 tbsp into balls. Arrange, about 3 inches (8 cm) apart, on parchment paper–lined rimless baking sheets; flatten slightly.

Bake, 1 sheet at a time, in 350°F (180°C) oven until tops are no longer shiny, 13 to 15 minutes.

Let cool on pan on rack for 2 minutes; transfer to rack and let cool completely. *(Make-ahead: Store in airtight container for up to 3 days.)*

NUTRITIONAL INFORMATION, PER COOKIE: about 123 cal, 1 g pro, 6 g total fat (4 g sat. fat), 17 g carb, 1 g fibre, 15 mg chol, 75 mg sodium, 48 mg potassium. % RDI: 1% calcium, 4% iron, 3% vit A, 5% folate.

VARIATIONS

CRISP CHOCOLATE CHIP COOKIES

Decrease all-purpose flour to 2½ cups. Roll dough by 2 tbsp into balls. Arrange on baking sheets as directed; flatten to ½-inch (1 cm) thickness. Bake as directed.

SOFT CHOCOLATE CHIP COOKIES

Prepare dough and arrange on baking sheets as directed (do not flatten). Refrigerate until firm, about 30 minutes. Transfer directly to 350°F (180°C) oven; bake until tops are no longer shiny, about 12 minutes.

TIP FROM THE TEST KITCHEN

Baking sheets vary in thickness and finish, which affect the doneness of cookies. A heavy, shiny uncoated baking sheet will allow the cookies to bake the most evenly.

TOP TO BOTTOM:
CRISP CHOCOLATE CHIP COOKIES
CHEWY-CRISP CHOCOLATE CHIP COOKIES
SOFT CHOCOLATE CHIP COOKIES

CRISSCROSS PEANUT BUTTER COOKIES

HANDS-ON TIME
25 minutes

TOTAL TIME
1¼ hours

MAKES
about 42 cookies

With their distinctive crisscross tops and salty-sweet taste, peanut butter cookies are classic treats. This recipe includes chopped peanuts for a little extra crunch in each bite.

INGREDIENTS

½ cup	butter, softened
½ cup	granulated sugar
½ cup	packed brown sugar
1	egg
1 cup	smooth peanut butter
½ tsp	vanilla
1½ cups	all-purpose flour
½ tsp	salt
½ tsp	baking soda
1 cup	unsalted roasted peanuts, coarsely chopped

DIRECTIONS

In large bowl, beat together butter, granulated sugar and brown sugar until fluffy; beat in egg, peanut butter and vanilla. Whisk together flour, salt and baking soda; stir into peanut butter mixture in 3 additions. Stir in peanuts.

Drop by 1 tbsp, 2 inches (5 cm) apart, onto 2 parchment paper–lined rimless baking sheets; using fork and dipping in flour if necessary to prevent sticking, press crisscross pattern into tops of cookies.

Bake on top and bottom racks in 375°F (190°C) oven, rotating and switching pans halfway through, until light golden brown, about 10 minutes.

Let cool on pan on rack for 2 minutes. Transfer to racks; let cool. *(Make-ahead: Layer between waxed paper in airtight container and store at room temperature for up to 4 days or freeze for up to 1 month.)*

NUTRITIONAL INFORMATION, PER COOKIE: about 111 cal, 3 g pro, 7 g total fat (2 g sat. fat), 10 g carb, 1 g fibre, 10 mg chol, 89 mg sodium. % RDI: 1% calcium, 3% iron, 2% vit A, 8% folate.

TIP FROM THE TEST KITCHEN
Instead of plain peanuts, you can use honey-glazed peanuts to create a slightly sweeter cookie.

CLASSIC OATMEAL COOKIES ◐

These oatmeal cookies are crisp and delicious, with a light caramel taste from the brown sugar. This straight-up version is excellent, and we've included three variations (below) for people who like to dress up their cookies a little more.

HANDS-ON TIME
25 minutes

TOTAL TIME
1½ hours

MAKES
about 36 cookies

INGREDIENTS

⅔ cup	butter, softened
1 cup	packed brown sugar
1	egg
1 tbsp	vanilla
1½ cups	large-flake rolled oats
1 cup	all-purpose flour
½ tsp	cinnamon
½ tsp	each baking powder and baking soda
¼ tsp	salt

DIRECTIONS

In large bowl, beat butter with brown sugar until fluffy; beat in egg and vanilla. Whisk together oats, flour, cinnamon, baking powder, baking soda and salt; stir into butter mixture.

Drop by heaping 1 tbsp, about 2 inches (5 cm) apart, onto greased or parchment paper–lined rimless baking sheets.

Bake, 1 sheet at a time, in 375°F (190°C) oven until golden, about 10 minutes. Let cool on pans on racks for 2 minutes. Transfer to racks; let cool completely.

NUTRITIONAL INFORMATION, PER COOKIE: about 95 cal, 1 g pro, 4 g total fat (2 g sat. fat), 15 g carb, 1 g fibre, 14 mg chol, 67 mg sodium. % RDI: 1% calcium, 4% iron, 3% vit A, 4% folate.

VARIATIONS

OATMEAL RAISIN COOKIES

Add 1 cup raisins just before stirring flour mixture into butter mixture.

CHOCOLATE PECAN OATMEAL COOKIES

Omit vanilla and cinnamon. Add ¾ cup chocolate chips and ½ cup chopped pecans just before stirring flour mixture into butter mixture.

TRAIL MIX OATMEAL COOKIES

Omit vanilla and cinnamon. Add ⅓ cup each raisins, slivered almonds and sweetened shredded coconut just before stirring flour mixture into butter mixture.

BUTTERY SHORTBREAD COOKIES ◔

The holidays (and plenty of other times) wouldn't be complete without sweet, buttery shortbread, and this is the Test Kitchen's tried-and-true classic to enjoy at those moments. These cookies have a crispy snap but still melt delicately in your mouth.

HANDS-ON TIME
20 minutes

TOTAL TIME
1¾ hours

MAKES
24 cookies

INGREDIENTS

1 cup	unsalted butter, softened
¾ cup	icing sugar
½ tsp	vanilla
¼ tsp	salt
2 cups	all-purpose flour
2 tsp	granulated sugar

DIRECTIONS

In stand mixer with paddle attachment, or in bowl using wooden spoon, beat together butter, icing sugar, vanilla and salt until light and fluffy; stir in flour just until combined.

Press dough into parchment paper–lined 9-inch (2.5 L) square cake pan. Using palm of hand, flatten to make smooth, even surface. Sprinkle with granulated sugar. Using knife, score surface of dough into 24 rectangles; prick each cookie several times with fork. Refrigerate until firm, about 30 minutes.

Bake in 300°F (150°C) oven until firm and pale golden, about 55 minutes. Let cool for 5 minutes; cut through score lines. Let cool completely in pan. *(Make-ahead: Store in airtight container for up to 1 week or freeze for up to 1 month.)*

NUTRITIONAL INFORMATION, PER COOKIE: about 122 cal, 1 g pro, 8 g total fat (5 g sat. fat), 12 g carb, trace fibre, 20 mg chol, 25 mg sodium, 13 mg potassium. % RDI: 4% iron, 7% vit A, 7% folate.

VARIATIONS

BUTTERY SHORTBREAD ROUNDS

On lightly floured surface, roll out dough to ⅓-inch (8 mm) thickness. Using 2-inch (5 cm) round cookie cutter, cut out shapes. Arrange, 1 inch (2.5 cm) apart, on parchment paper–lined rimless baking sheets. Sprinkle with granulated sugar. Refrigerate until firm, about 30 minutes. Bake, 1 sheet at a time, in 300°F (150°C) oven until firm and pale golden, about 20 minutes.

BUTTERY SHORTBREAD WEDGES

Press dough into parchment paper–lined 8-inch (1.2 L) round cake pan; using palm of hand, flatten to make smooth, even surface. Sprinkle with granulated sugar. Using knife, score surface of dough into 16 wedges. Bake as directed.

CHOCOLATE CHUNK SHORTBREAD

Add 55 g bittersweet chocolate (2 oz), chopped, just before stirring flour into butter mixture.

HOT AND FRESH APPLE FRITTERS ⊘

Apple fritters aren't just a treat to enjoy during harvest time—they're a welcome indulgence any time of year. These fritters are best served warm, so gather everyone in the kitchen to enjoy them as soon as they're ready.

HANDS-ON TIME
40 minutes

TOTAL TIME
3¼ hours

MAKES
16 to 18 fritters

INGREDIENTS

1⅓ cups	all-purpose flour
2 tbsp	granulated sugar
1 tsp	baking powder
½ tsp	cinnamon
¼ tsp	salt
1 cup	soda water
2 tbsp	unsalted butter, melted
2	eggs, separated
3	sweet baking apples (such as Royal Gala, Golden Delicious or Pink Lady)
	vegetable oil (such as canola, safflower or sunflower oil) for deep-frying,
2 tbsp	icing sugar

DIRECTIONS

In large bowl, whisk together 1¼ cups of the flour, granulated sugar, baking powder, cinnamon and salt; whisk in soda water. Whisk in butter and egg yolks; cover and let stand for 2 hours. *(Make-ahead: Refrigerate for up to 12 hours.)*

In separate bowl, beat egg whites until stiff but not dry peaks form; fold into batter. Place bowl in larger bowl of ice water; let stand until cold, about 15 minutes.

Peel and cut apples into ½-inch (1 cm) cubes. Toss with remaining flour; fold into batter.

Meanwhile, pour enough oil into deep fryer, wok or wide deep saucepan to come about 2 inches (5 cm) up side; heat until deep-fryer thermometer reads 350°F (180°C).

Using ¼ cup for each, pour in batter to make 4 fritters. Cook, turning once, until golden, 3 to 4 minutes. Using slotted spoon, transfer to paper towel–lined plate; let drain. Repeat with remaining batter.

Sprinkle fritters with icing sugar; serve warm.

NUTRITIONAL INFORMATION, PER EACH OF 18 FRITTERS: about 139 cal, 2 g pro, 10 g total fat (2 g sat. fat), 12 g carb, 1 g fibre, 24 mg chol, 59 mg sodium, 38 mg potassium. % RDI: 1% calcium, 4% iron, 2% vit A, 2% vit C, 10% folate.

CLASSIC VANILLA CRÈME BRÛLÉE ⬤

It's hard to find someone who doesn't like this rich, crackly sugar–topped custard dessert. The trick to creating the perfect glassy, crunchy surface is to combine granulated and brown sugars.

HANDS-ON TIME
15 minutes

TOTAL TIME
4¾ hours

MAKES
6 servings

INGREDIENTS

VANILLA CUSTARD:

1	vanilla bean
1 cup	milk
1 cup	whipping cream (35%)
pinch	salt
5	egg yolks
3 tbsp	granulated sugar

TOPPING:

2 tbsp	granulated sugar
2 tbsp	packed brown sugar

DIRECTIONS

VANILLA CUSTARD: Halve vanilla bean lengthwise. In saucepan, combine vanilla bean, milk, cream and salt; bring to boil over medium heat. Remove from heat; cover and let stand for 10 minutes. Discard vanilla bean.

In heatproof bowl, whisk egg yolks with sugar until pale and thickened, about 2 minutes. Stirring constantly with heatproof spatula, add milk in slow steady stream. Strain through fine-mesh sieve into clean bowl.

Divide egg mixture among six 6-oz (175 mL) ramekins; arrange ramekins in shallow roasting pan. Pour in enough warm water to come halfway up sides of ramekins.

Bake in 350°F (180°C) oven until skin forms on surfaces, edges are lightly set and custards are still slightly jiggly in centre, 25 to 30 minutes.

Remove ramekins from pan; let cool on rack. Cover and refrigerate for 4 hours. *(Make-ahead: Refrigerate for up to 24 hours.)*

TOPPING: Mix granulated sugar with brown sugar; sprinkle evenly over tops of custards. Place ramekins on baking sheet; broil, 6 inches (15 cm) from heat, watching carefully, until sugar is melted and caramel colour, 2 to 4 minutes. Let cool before serving.

NUTRITIONAL INFORMATION, PER SERVING: about 265 cal, 5 g pro, 19 g total fat (11 g sat. fat), 18 g carb, 0 g fibre, 224 mg chol, 39 mg sodium, 127 mg potassium. % RDI: 9% calcium, 4% iron, 20% vit A, 11% folate.

SILKY CHOCOLATE MOUSSE ◔

HANDS-ON TIME 25 minutes

TOTAL TIME 4¾ hours

MAKES 6 servings

INGREDIENTS

115 g	milk chocolate, chopped
55 g	dark chocolate (70%), chopped
1½ cups	whipping cream (35%)
4	egg yolks
3 tbsp	granulated sugar
pinch	salt
½ tsp	vanilla

DIRECTIONS

In heatproof bowl over saucepan of hot (not boiling) water, melt milk chocolate and dark chocolate, stirring until smooth. Set aside.

In small saucepan, heat ½ cup of the cream over medium-high heat just until tiny bubbles form around edge of pan. In separate heatproof bowl, whisk together egg yolks, sugar and salt; slowly whisk in hot cream. Place bowl over saucepan of gently simmering water; cook, stirring, until instant-read thermometer reads 160°F (71°C) and mixture is thick enough to coat back of spoon, about 15 minutes. Remove from heat.

Whisk in melted chocolate and vanilla. Place plastic wrap directly on surface; let cool, about 15 minutes.

Whip remaining cream; fold one-quarter into chocolate mixture. Fold in remaining whipped cream. Divide among 6 dessert dishes; cover and refrigerate until set, about 4 hours. *(Make-ahead: Cover and refrigerate for up to 24 hours.)*

NUTRITIONAL INFORMATION, PER SERVING: about 413 cal, 5 g pro, 34 g total fat (20 g sat. fat), 24 g carb, 2 g fibre, 209 mg chol, 43 mg sodium, 201 mg potassium. % RDI: 9% calcium, 14% iron, 27% vit A, 10% folate.

VARIATION

SILKY MOCHA MOUSSE

Heat 2 tbsp instant coffee granules with cream.

LUSCIOUS LEMON MOUSSE ◔

HANDS-ON TIME 25 minutes

TOTAL TIME 1½ hours

MAKES 10 servings

INGREDIENTS

6	egg yolks
2	eggs
1 cup	granulated sugar
¾ cup	lemon juice
1½ cups	whipping cream (35%)
1 tsp	vanilla

DIRECTIONS

In large heatproof bowl, whisk together egg yolks, eggs, sugar and lemon juice. Set over saucepan of simmering water; cook, stirring constantly, until thick enough to mound on spoon and mixture holds its shape when spoon is drawn through it, 10 to 12 minutes.

Strain through fine-mesh sieve into clean large bowl. Place plastic wrap directly on surface; refrigerate until cold, about 1 hour.

In separate bowl, beat cream with vanilla until fluffy medium-firm peaks form. Gently stir one-third of the whipped cream into the lemon mixture; fold in remaining whipped cream. *(Make-ahead: Cover and refrigerate for up to 24 hours.)*

NUTRITIONAL INFORMATION, PER SERVING: about 250 cal, 4 g pro, 17 g total fat (9 g sat. fat), 22 g carb, trace fibre, 205 mg chol, 33 mg sodium, 71 mg potassium. % RDI: 4% calcium, 4% iron, 19% vit A, 5% vit C, 11% folate.

VANILLA BEAN RICE PUDDING ◐

HANDS-ON TIME 45 minutes

TOTAL TIME 45 minutes

MAKES 4 servings

INGREDIENTS

half	vanilla bean
2½ cups	homogenized milk
2 tbsp	butter
½ cup	short-grain rice
2 tbsp	granulated sugar
2 tbsp	sliced dried apricots
¼ cup	toasted slivered almonds or slivered dried apricots

DIRECTIONS

Halve vanilla bean lengthwise; scrape seeds into small saucepan. Reserve pod for another use. Add milk to pan; heat just until bubbles form around edge of pan.

In separate saucepan, melt butter over medium heat; stir in rice. Stir in milk mixture and sugar; bring to boil. Reduce heat, cover and simmer, stirring often, until creamy, most of the liquid is absorbed and rice is tender, about 25 minutes.

Stir in apricots. *(Make-ahead: Let cool; refrigerate in airtight container for up to 24 hours. Reheat before serving, if desired.)* Serve sprinkled with slivered almonds.

NUTRITIONAL INFORMATION, PER SERVING: about 309 cal, 8 g pro, 14 g total fat (7 g sat. fat), 37 g carb, 1 g fibre, 36 mg chol, 118 mg sodium. % RDI: 18% calcium, 4% iron, 11% vit A, 2% vit C, 5% folate.

■VARIATION■
VANILLA EXTRACT RICE PUDDING

Omit vanilla bean. Stir in 1½ tsp vanilla along with apricots.

VANILLA BEAN PUDDING ◐

HANDS-ON TIME 20 minutes

TOTAL TIME 4¼ hours

MAKES 6 servings

INGREDIENTS

½ cup	granulated sugar
2 tbsp	cornstarch
half	vanilla bean
2¼ cups	homogenized milk
2	eggs
1 tbsp	unsalted butter, cubed
1 tsp	vanilla
pinch	salt

DIRECTIONS

In saucepan, whisk sugar with cornstarch. Halve vanilla bean lengthwise; scrape seeds into sugar mixture. Add vanilla pod to pan. Whisk in milk; cook over medium heat, stirring, until steaming.

In heatproof bowl, whisk eggs; whisk in half of the hot milk mixture in slow steady stream. Gradually whisk back into pan; cook over medium heat, whisking constantly, until bubbly and thickened, 5 to 8 minutes. Whisk in butter, vanilla and salt.

Strain through fine-mesh sieve into clean bowl; place plastic wrap directly on surface. Refrigerate until chilled, about 4 hours. *(Make-ahead: Refrigerate for up to 2 days; whisk before serving.)*

NUTRITIONAL INFORMATION, PER SERVING: about 175 cal, 5 g pro, 7 g total fat (3 g sat. fat), 24 g carb, 0 g fibre, 75 mg chol, 58 mg sodium, 153 mg potassium. % RDI: 10% calcium, 2% iron, 7% vit A, 6% folate.

■VARIATIONS■
DARK CHOCOLATE PUDDING

Omit vanilla bean. Whisk ⅓ cup cocoa powder with sugar and cornstarch. Add 55 g dark chocolate (2 oz), chopped, with butter; whisk until smooth.

CHAI SPICE PUDDING

Omit vanilla bean. Decrease vanilla to ½ tsp. Add 4 whole cloves, 2 cardamom pods and 1 cinnamon stick with milk. Discard whole spices before whisking in butter, vanilla and salt.

PROFITEROLES ◐

This impressive bakery specialty is easier to make than it looks. And once you've mastered choux pastry, you can pipe it into a number of different shapes to make éclairs and other tasty treats.

HANDS-ON TIME
1 hour

TOTAL TIME
2¼ hours

MAKES
24 pieces

INGREDIENTS

CHOUX PASTRY:

½ cup	milk
⅓ cup	unsalted butter
1 tsp	granulated sugar
¼ tsp	salt
1 cup	all-purpose flour
4	eggs

VANILLA PASTRY CREAM:

4	egg yolks
2 cups	milk
¾ cup	granulated sugar
¼ cup	cornstarch
1 tsp	vanilla

CHOCOLATE GLAZE:

60 g	bittersweet chocolate, finely chopped
2 tbsp	unsalted butter
2 tsp	corn syrup

DIRECTIONS

CHOUX PASTRY: In saucepan, bring ½ cup water, milk, butter, sugar and salt to boil over medium-high heat until butter is melted. Using wooden spoon, stir in flour until mixture forms ball and film forms on bottom of pan. **PHOTO A**

Cook, stirring, for 1 minute. Transfer to stand mixer or bowl. Beat for 30 seconds to cool. Beat in 3 of the eggs, 1 at a time, beating well after each addition until smooth and shiny.

Line 2 rimless baking sheets with parchment paper. Using piping bag fitted with ½-inch (1 cm) plain tip (or spoon), pipe (or spoon) dough into twenty-four 1½-inch (4 cm) wide mounds onto prepared baking sheets. Whisk remaining egg with 1 tbsp water; using pastry brush, brush mixture over mounds, gently flattening any peaks in dough. **PHOTO B**

Bake in 425°F (220°C) oven until puffed and golden, about 15 minutes. Reduce heat to 375°F (190°C); bake until golden and crisp, about 10 minutes. Turn off oven; let stand in oven for 25 minutes to dry.

Transfer to rack; using tip of knife, poke hole in bottom of each profiterole. Let cool completely. *(Make-ahead: Store in airtight container for up to 24 hours. Recrisp in 350°F/180°C oven for 5 minutes; let cool before filling.)*

VANILLA PASTRY CREAM: In bowl, whisk together egg yolks, ½ cup of the milk, the sugar and cornstarch. In heavy-bottomed saucepan, heat remaining milk over medium heat just until bubbles form around edge; gradually whisk into egg yolk mixture. Return to saucepan; cook, whisking, until thick enough to mound on spoon, about 5 minutes.

Strain through fine-mesh sieve into clean bowl; stir in vanilla. Place plastic wrap directly on surface; refrigerate until chilled, about 3 hours. *(Make-ahead: Refrigerate in airtight container for up to 24 hours.)*

CHOCOLATE GLAZE: In heatproof bowl over saucepan of hot (not boiling) water, melt together chocolate, butter and corn syrup, stirring until smooth. Remove from heat, leaving bowl over saucepan to keep warm.

ASSEMBLY: Using piping bag fitted with ¼-inch (5 mm) plain tip, pipe pastry cream into each profiterole through hole in bottom. Dip tops into glaze. Let stand until set, about 20 minutes. *(Make-ahead: Refrigerate for up to 4 hours.)*

NUTRITIONAL INFORMATION, PER PIECE: about 126 cal, 3 g pro, 6 g total fat (3 g sat. fat), 14 g carb, trace fibre, 75 mg chol, 49 mg sodium, 66 mg potassium. % RDI: 4% calcium, 4% iron, 8% vit A, 8% folate.

WHITE CHOCOLATE AND RASPBERRY TIRAMISU ⟁

HANDS-ON TIME
30 minutes

TOTAL TIME
12½ hours

MAKES
12 to 16 servings

To keep the ladyfingers from getting soggy in this revamp of tiramisu, dip them in the coffee mixture for just half a second per side.

INGREDIENTS

115 g	white chocolate
6	egg yolks
¾ cup	granulated sugar
1	pkg (500 g) mascarpone cheese
1 tsp	vanilla
2 cups	whipping cream (35%)
½ cup	strong brewed coffee, at room temperature
¼ cup	crème de cacao liqueur
36	ladyfinger cookies (about 4 x 1 inches/ 10 x 2.5 cm)
3	pkg (each 170 g) fresh raspberries

DIRECTIONS

Finely chop 85 g of the white chocolate; set aside.

In large heatproof bowl, whisk egg yolks with ½ cup of the sugar. Place bowl over saucepan of simmering water; cook, whisking, until thickened and mixture leaves ribbon when whisk is lifted, about 6 minutes. Stir in chopped white chocolate until smooth, about 1 minute. Remove from heat; let cool slightly.

Whisk mascarpone and vanilla into egg mixture until smooth. Whip cream with remaining sugar; fold into mascarpone mixture until combined.

In shallow dish, stir coffee with crème de cacao. Quickly dip both sides of each ladyfinger in coffee mixture. Arrange half of the ladyfingers in 13- x 9-inch (3 L) baking dish. Spread with half of the mascarpone mixture; top with raspberries. Repeat with remaining ladyfingers, coffee mixture and mascarpone mixture. Cover and refrigerate for 12 hours. *(Make-ahead: Refrigerate for up to 24 hours.)*

Shave remaining white chocolate; sprinkle over top.

NUTRITIONAL INFORMATION, PER EACH OF 16 SERVINGS: about 395 cal, 8 g pro, 28 g total fat (17 g sat. fat), 30 g carb, 2 g fibre, 192 mg chol, 61 mg sodium, 121 mg potassium. % RDI: 11% calcium, 7% iron, 22% vit A, 13% vit C, 14% folate.

JUICY FRUIT CRUMBLE

Almost any fruit makes a good base for a juicy crumble. Our filling variations (below) give you plenty of options so you can enjoy this dessert year-round.

HANDS-ON TIME
15 minutes

TOTAL TIME
55 minutes

MAKES
6 servings

INGREDIENTS

1 cup	large-flake rolled oats
½ cup	all-purpose flour
⅓ cup	packed brown sugar
¼ tsp	cinnamon
pinch	salt
⅓ cup	butter, softened
	fruit filling (variations, below)

DIRECTIONS

In bowl, whisk together oats, flour, brown sugar, cinnamon and salt. Using fork, mash in butter until crumbly.

Spread fruit filling evenly in greased 8-inch (2 L) square baking dish; sprinkle oat mixture over filling.

Bake in 350°F (180°C) oven until bubbly, fruit is tender and topping is crisp and golden, 40 to 60 minutes.

NUTRITIONAL INFORMATION, PER SERVING (WITH APPLE CINNAMON FILLING): about 347 cal, 4 g pro, 12 g total fat (7 g sat. fat), 60 g carb, 4 g fibre, 27 mg chol, 79 mg sodium. % RDI: 3% calcium, 13% iron, 9% vit A, 7% vit C, 14% folate.

VARIATIONS

APPLE CINNAMON FILLING

Toss together 8 cups sliced peeled apples, ¼ cup granulated sugar, 2 tbsp all-purpose flour and ½ tsp cinnamon.

APPLE QUINCE FILLING

Toss together 5 cups sliced peeled apples, 3 cups thinly sliced peeled quinces, ¼ cup granulated sugar, 1 tbsp all-purpose flour and 1 tbsp lemon juice.

BUMBLEBERRY FILLING

Toss together 3 cups diced peeled apples; 2 cups quartered hulled strawberries; 1 cup each raspberries, blueberries and blackberries; ¼ cup granulated sugar; and 3 tbsp all-purpose flour.

PEAR CRANBERRY FILLING

Toss together 6 cups diced peeled pears, 2 cups fresh or thawed frozen cranberries, ¼ cup granulated sugar and 3 tbsp all-purpose flour.

APPLE PLUM FILLING

Toss together 4 cups sliced plums, 2 cups sliced peeled apples, ⅓ cup packed brown sugar, 2 tbsp all-purpose flour and ¼ tsp each nutmeg and cinnamon.

BLUEBERRY PEACH FILLING

Toss together 6 cups sliced peeled peaches, 2 cups blueberries, ¼ cup granulated sugar, 3 tbsp all-purpose flour and 1 tbsp lemon juice.

MINCEMEAT PEAR FILLING

Stir together 1 jar (700 mL) all-fruit mincemeat; 2 firm ripe pears, peeled and grated; 1 cup chopped dried figs or whole golden raisins; and 1 tsp grated orange zest.

STRAWBERRY RHUBARB FILLING

Toss together 6 cups sliced fresh rhubarb (or thawed frozen sliced rhubarb), 2 cups sliced strawberries, ½ cup granulated sugar, 3 tbsp all-purpose flour and ½ tsp finely grated orange zest.

CHOOSING THE RIGHT COOKING AND BAKING EQUIPMENT
pages 421 to 423

THE CANADIAN LIVING TEST KITCHEN LEFT TO RIGHT:
AMANDA BARNIER FOOD SPECIALIST; **GILEAN WATTS** ARTICLES EDITOR, FOOD;
ANNABELLE WAUGH FOOD DIRECTOR; **JENNIFER BARTOLI** FOOD SPECIALIST;
AND **IRENE FONG** SENIOR FOOD SPECIALIST

ULTIMATE KITCHEN REFERENCE

WHAT TESTED TILL PERFECT MEANS

You love to cook, so creating delicious, trustworthy recipes is the top priority for us in the Canadian Living Test Kitchen. Our team is composed of industry professionals and food experts from different backgrounds—we are chefs, home economists, recipe developers and food writers. Every year, we work together to produce approximately 1,000 Tested-Till-Perfect recipes. So what does Tested Till Perfect mean? It means we follow a rigorous process to ensure you'll get the same results in your kitchen as we do in ours.

Here's What We Do

1 In the Test Kitchen, we use the same everyday ingredients and equipment that you use in your own kitchen.

2 We start by researching ideas and brainstorming as a team.

3 We write up the recipe and go straight into the kitchen to try it out.

4 We taste, evaluate and tweak the recipe until we really love it.

5 The recipe then gets handed off to a separate food specialist for another test and another tasting session.

6 We meticulously test and retest each recipe as many times as it takes to make sure it turns out as perfectly in your kitchen as it does in ours.

7 We carefully weigh and measure all ingredients, record the data and send the recipe out for nutritional analysis.

8 The recipe is then edited and rechecked to ensure all the information is correct and it's ready for you to cook.

ABOUT OUR NUTRITION INFORMATION

To meet nutrient needs each day, moderately active women 25 to 49 need about 1,900 calories, 51 g protein, 261 g carbohydrate, 25 to 35 g fibre and not more than 63 g total fat (21 g saturated fat). Men and teenagers usually need more. Canadian sodium intake of approximately 3,500 mg daily should be reduced, whereas the intake of potassium from food sources should be increased to 4,700 mg per day.

The percentage of recommended daily intake (% RDI) is based on the values used for Canadian food labels for calcium, iron, vitamins A and C, and folate.

Figures are rounded off. They are based on the first ingredient listed when there is a choice and do not include optional ingredients or those with no specified amounts.

ABBREVIATIONS

cal = calories   **pro** = protein   **carb** = carbohydrate   **sat. fat** = saturated fat   **chol** = cholesterol

Canadian Living Recipe Assumptions

Before you cook a Test Kitchen recipe, it's important to know our assumptions about ingredients and techniques. Before you start, always read the entire recipe, checking to make sure you have all the ingredients and equipment. Unless otherwise specified in an ingredient list or recipe method, the following are our assumptions.

- Ovens are preheated
- Salt is regular table salt
- Pepper is black and freshly ground
- Lemon and lime juices are always freshly squeezed
- Vegetables and fruits are medium-size, washed and prepared (peeled, seeded, pitted or hulled) as appropriate
- Eggs are large; they should be at room temperature for baking
- Butter is salted
- Milk and yogurt are 2%
- Baking is done on the middle rack in the oven
- Foods are cooked uncovered
- Packaged broth is usually specified as sodium-reduced in recipes; you can substitute full-sodium packaged broth or good-quality powdered broth by mixing it at a 1:1 ratio with water to avoid oversalting a dish
- If a choice of ingredients is offered (such as "fresh cilantro or parsley"), the first is preferred but the second is a reasonable alternative—though it may create a slightly different taste in the finished dish
- Ingredients are prepared and measured before starting to bake or cook

TABLES OF EQUIVALENTS

Canadian Living uses standard imperial table measurements in recipes to reflect how Canadians measure and cook. We call for weights in metric to match how items are packaged and sold in supermarkets in Canada.

WEIGHT

30 g	1 oz	1/16 lb
55 g	2 oz	1/8 lb
115 g	4 oz	1/4 lb
225 g	8 oz	1/2 lb
450 g	16 oz	1 lb
675 g	24 oz	1 1/2 lb
900 g	32 oz	2 lb
1 kg	36 oz	2 1/4 lb
1.8 kg	64 oz	4 lb

LIQUID AND DRY MEASUREMENTS

pinch (dry only)	1/8 tsp
dash (liquid only)	1/8 tsp
3 tsp	1 tbsp
2 tbsp	1 fluid oz
4 tbsp	1/4 cup
1/4 cup	2 fluid oz
5 tbsp + 1 tsp	1/3 cup
8 tbsp	1/2 cup
1/2 cup	4 fluid oz
10 tbsp + 2 tsp	2/3 cup
12 tbsp	3/4 cup
3/4 cup	6 fluid oz
16 tbsp	1 cup
1 cup	8 fluid oz

Trust Your Senses

Oven and burner temperatures differ slightly from appliance to appliance. That's why we often provide a range of cooking times in our recipes, such as "25 to 30 minutes." We also give visual and/or textural cues to help you determine doneness, such as "until golden brown and crisp." Always check for these signs of doneness throughout the cooking process, starting before the first specified time, and trust your senses more than your timer.

How to Measure

DRY INGREDIENTS

Such as flour, granulated sugar and cornstarch

Lightly spoon the ingredient into a dry measuring cup or a measuring spoon until heaping, without packing or tapping the cup or spoon. Level off the top with the straight edge of a knife. When measuring brown sugar, pack it down lightly until it holds the shape of the cup or spoon when turned out.

THIN LIQUID INGREDIENTS

Such as milk, oil and water

Place a liquid measuring cup on a flat surface. Pour in liquid to the desired level, and then bend down so that your eye is level with the lines on the measure to check for accuracy.

FATS AND THICK LIQUID INGREDIENTS

Such as butter, shortening, lard, cream cheese and sour cream

Cut off the desired amount using the markings on the package, or press or spoon the ingredient firmly into a dry measuring cup and then level off the top with the straight edge of a knife.

COOKING EQUIPMENT 101

While you don't need absolutely every item listed here, these tools will set you up
for success in the kitchen. If you want to splurge on any tools, an excellent chef's knife and
paring knife (see below) are great first purchases; so are a couple of high-quality saucepans.

MEASURING TOOLS

MEASURING CUPS AND SPOONS: Stock your kitchen with at least one graduated set of dry measuring cups, liquid measuring cups and measuring spoons. Slim metal measuring spoons are excellent for spooning spices out of skinny bottles. For step-by-step instructions for accurate measuring, see opposite.

KITCHEN SCALE: A digital kitchen scale is ideal for checking weights (even tiny ones). Look for one that has a tare button—it allows you to set a container on the scale and zero the display so the scale weighs only the contents of the container.

INSTANT-READ THERMOMETER: This tool takes the guesswork out of judging the doneness level of meats and poultry. See Meat Doneness Temperatures & Visual Cues (page 427).

DEEP-FRYER AND CANDY THERMOMETER: This is another handy measuring instrument, which ensures you fry or boil at the correct temperature. It allows you to monitor fluctuations and adjust the heat as necessary.

PREP TOOLS

COLANDERS AND SIEVES: These are essential for separating solids from liquids. A big colander is helpful for making pasta and draining all sorts of large items. A fine-mesh sieve works well for straining delicate sauces and purées.

CUTTING BOARDS: You'll need at least one of these to protect your counters and your knives, but having a few on hand makes chopping, slicing and mincing easy. Cutting boards come in an array of materials (wood, bamboo and plastic), sizes and shapes. Choose whatever works best for you.

MIXING BOWLS: Have a selection of sizes on hand. We like stainless steel (which conducts heat well and whips egg whites to glossy peaks) and glass or Pyrex (for combining acidic mixtures and foods that may react with metal).

WHISKS: These tools make it easy to combine both dry and liquid ingredients so they are uniformly blended. Invest in a few, in a number of sizes.

KNIVES

CHEF'S KNIFE: This knife has a wide blade near the handle and tapers to a point. It is available with an 8-inch (20 cm), 10-inch (25 cm) or 12-inch (30 cm) blade. High-carbon stainless steel is the optimal material for a knife—it stays sharp and will not rust. Choose a heavy, well-balanced knife with a riveted wood or moulded plastic handle, and a full-tang blade, which extends through the handle to the butt. Buy a knife that feels solid and comfortable in your hand.

PARING KNIFE: This small, pointed knife is used to cut and peel fruits and vegetables. It's a good idea to keep more than one on hand, because you'll use them often.

SERRATED KNIFE: The long, toothed blade on this knife is great for cutting breads, cakes and tomatoes into neat slices without tearing.

SLICING KNIFE: A long, slim knife with a rounded tip, this tool works well when carving ham and other cooked meat or slicing fish, fruits and vegetables.

SHARPENING STEEL: Sharp knives keep your fingers safe because they don't slip. This simple tool makes blades straight and true. Choose a 12-inch (30 cm) medium-grained sharpening steel with a protective guard at the top of the handle. To use, place the steel, tip side down, on your counter. Run the length of the blade downward along one side of the steel at about a 20-degree angle. Now switch sides: hone the opposite side of your blade on the opposite side of the steel. Repeat four or five times on each side.

KNIFE CARE

Wash knives by hand. Putting them in the dishwasher will dull the blades and may damage the handles.

Store knives in a wooden knife block or on a magnetic wall strip to keep the blades protected and sharp.

STOVE-TOP PANS

SAUCEPANS: Saucepans are usually sold by capacity, either in quarts or litres or both. You'll generally need two or three, ranging from 1 to 4 quarts (1 to 4 L), each about 4 inches (10 cm) deep. Buy the best-quality pans you can afford—they will last a lifetime. Look for pans with heavy bases, tight-fitting lids and ovenproof handles. Stainless steel is a good material as long as the base encloses a thick pad of aluminum or copper for proper heat distribution. Some saucepans come with a double-boiler or steamer insert, which is useful.

DUTCH OVEN: This large, deep pot with a tight-fitting lid works on the stove top and in the oven. It is handy for many tasks, including preserving, stir-frying and braising. Choose a heavy-bottomed one with a 6-quart (6 L) capacity. A stainless-steel Dutch oven with an enclosed aluminum core is a reliable choice. An enamelled cast-iron Dutch oven is pricey, but it conducts heat well and will last for decades.

SKILLETS: These shallow pans are great for pan-frying, sautéing and simmering. They often range in diameter from small (6 inches/15 cm) to large (12 inches/ 30 cm), and some brands offer even larger diameters. It's helpful to have a few skillets in different sizes and materials, such as nonstick, cast iron and heavy-bottomed stainless steel. A high-sided skillet can always stand in for a wok (see below).

STOCKPOT: This large, tall pot is great for making stock, cooking pasta and boiling cobs of corn. An 8- to 10-quart (8 to 10 L) stockpot is a good all-purpose size.

GRILL PAN: Essentially a skillet with raised grill-like ribs on the bottom, this pan allows you to grill year-round. Look for nonstick and cast-iron versions.

WOK: A flat-bottomed wok with one or two handles is superb for stir-frying because it has an extra-large capacity. Carbon steel is the most popular material because it heats quickly and to a very high temperature, but some equally good woks are made of stainless steel (with or without a nonstick coating). A wok with a lid is ideal for braising and steaming, too.

OVENWARE

CASSEROLES: These round, oval, square or rectangular baking dishes with tight-fitting lids are made of many materials; it's good to have at least one or two large ones, and a medium and small one on hand. They come in a range of sizes: 6 cups (1.5 L), 8 cups (2 L), 10 cups (2.5 L), 12 cups (3 L) and 20 cups (5 L).

GRATIN DISHES: Wide and shallow with sloping or straight sides, these are most often used for scalloped potatoes or baked pastas. They come in a range of sizes; 4-cup (1 L) or 6-cup (1.5 L) capacity dishes are good all-purpose choices.

ROASTING PAN: Buy a stainless-steel or enamelled-steel roasting pan with 2-inch (5 cm) high sides and a rack, which allows you the raise the meat off the bottom of the pan so the heat can circulate freely around it. Choose a pan to suit the size of roasts or poultry you typically make: Too large a pan will let the wonderful juices on the bottom of the pan burn; too small a pan won't permit proper heat circulation. For an average-size chicken, you need a 14- x 10-inch (35 x 25 cm) pan; for a typical turkey or a large brisket, a 17- x 12-inch (42 x 30 cm) pan will work.

SOUFFLÉ DISHES: These straight-sided round dishes are made of porcelain or stoneware; many have the traditional fluted design around the exterior. Soufflé dishes are sold in 6-cup (1.5 L) or 10-cup (2.5 L) capacities. There are also mini-soufflé dishes that hold 12 oz (350 mL) for making individual portions.

CHECK THE SIZE

To measure a skillet, pie plate, baking dish or cake pan, measure it across the top, from inside edge to inside edge.

To check the volume capacity of a baking dish or pan (in cups, quarts or litres), fill it with water, then pour the water into a liquid measuring cup, emptying the cup and refilling with the pan contents as many times as necessary.

COOKING EQUIPMENT 201

Once you have the basics, there are plenty more amazing kitchen tools you can add to your collection. These are just some of the machines, utensils and gadgets you might want to consider.

blender (countertop and/or immersion) • box grater • bulb baster • food mill
food processor • juicer • kitchen shears • ladles • melon baller • metal, wood or bamboo skewers
mixer (hand-held or countertop stand mixer) • pepper grinder • potato masher
rasp grater • salad spinner • skimming spoon • slotted spoons • timer
tongs • vegetable peelers • zester

BAKING EQUIPMENT 101

Below are the pans you'll need to make the baked goods in this book. Invest in good-quality equipment, because it will last for years and give the best results.

BAKING DISHES

These glass dishes are usually square or rectangular with sides that are about 2 inches (5 cm) high. They are sold in a variety of sizes: 8-inch (2 L) square, 11- x 7-inch (2 L), 13- x 9-inch (3 L) are the most common.

PIE PLATES

Generally, our pies are made in 9-inch (23 cm) pie plates, but it's handy to have a 10-inch (25 cm) pie plate for deep-dish variations. Buy either glass or dark metal ones to create crisp pie crusts.

MUFFIN PANS

You'll need these 12- and 24-cup tins to make muffins, cupcakes and tarts. Stock up on paper muffin cups, too, to ensure easy cleanup.

SPECIALTY CAKE PANS

It's good to have a few of these. Invest in a 9- or 10-inch (2.5 or 3 L) springform pan, a 10-inch (4 L) tube pan and/or a 10-inch (3 L) Bundt pan so you can make a variety of baked goods.

BAKING SHEETS

Rimmed baking sheets are great for all sorts of tasks, including baking, roasting and even catching spills under juicy pies in the oven. For cookie baking, invest in rimless baking sheets—the absence of sides lets heat circulate more easily and allows the cookies to slide right off when baked. We recommend buying shiny, light-coloured baking sheets; dark ones cause food to brown too quickly.

TART PANS

These metal pans have removable bottoms and fluted sides that create beautiful tarts and quiches. Round tart pans are available in a number of sizes ranging from mini (4 inches/10 cm) to large (12 inches/ 30 cm). There are also rectangular pans in multiple sizes.
Hint: Wash tart pans by hand in hot soapy water to keep them perfectly seasoned. Do not put them in the dishwasher.

LOAF PANS

These pans are essential for quick breads, yeast breads and meat loaves. The most common sizes are 8 x 4 inches (1.5 L)—perfect for typical bread recipes or a meat loaf recipe that calls for 450 g ground meat—and 9 x 5 inches (2 L). These pans come in glass or metal, and some also have built-in drainers that reduce the amount of fat in meat loaves.

PLAIN CAKE PANS

These metal pans come in many sizes: 8-inch (1.2 L) round, 8-inch (2 L) square, 9-inch (1.5 L) round, 9-inch (2.5 L) square and 13- x 9-inch (3.5 L) rectangular are some of the most common. **Hint:** If you use a glass baking dish when a recipe calls for a metal cake pan, reduce the baking temperature by 25°F (10°C) and check the item 5 minutes before the suggested time.

BAKING EQUIPMENT 201

Below are some other tools you will find handy if you're taking on more advanced techniques or doing lots of baking on a regular basis.

cookie cutters • **custard cups** (¾ cup/175 mL is a good all-purpose size)
metal cooling racks • **offset spatulas** (small and large) • **pastry blender** • **pie weights**
piping bags (at least 10 inches/25 cm long) • **piping tips** (with a variety of openings and a coupler)
ramekins • **rolling pin** • **rubber spatulas** (including a high heat–resistant one)
wooden spatulas • **wooden spoons**

SUBSTITUTIONS SAVE THE DAY

There's nothing more frustrating than being ready to bake or cook only to discover you are missing one essential ingredient. Here's a list of substitutions that will save you a last-minute dash to the store.

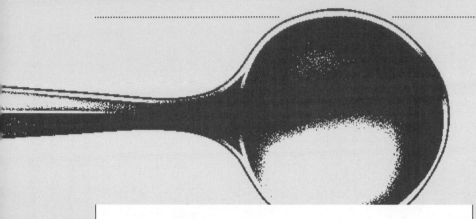

FLOUR & BAKING STAPLES

1 cup sifted cake-and-pastry flour
= ⅞ cup all-purpose flour
(1 cup less 2 tbsp)

1 cup unsifted all-purpose flour
= 1 cup + 2 tbsp sifted
cake-and-pastry flour

1 cup self-rising flour
= 1 cup all-purpose flour
+ 1 tsp baking powder + ¼ tsp salt

for thickening
1 tbsp all-purpose flour
= 1½ tsp cornstarch

1 tsp baking powder
= ½ tsp cream of tartar
+ ¼ tsp baking soda

for stabilizing egg whites
1 tsp cream of tartar
= 1 tsp vinegar or lemon juice

¼ cup dried bread crumbs
= 1 slice dry bread, ground

SUGAR & SWEETENERS

1 cup granulated sugar
= 1 cup packed brown sugar **or**
= 1 cup packed dark brown sugar
(has a more pronounced
molasses flavour)

1 cup superfine or berry sugar
= 1 cup granulated sugar,
ground in food processor

for muffins and quick breads
1 cup granulated or brown sugar
= 2 cups icing sugar

1 cup corn syrup
= 1 cup fancy molasses **or**
= 1 cup liquid honey

for dessert sauces
1 cup corn syrup
= 1¼ cups granulated or packed
brown sugar
+ ¼ cup more of the liquid called
for in the recipe

High-Altitude Baking

Baking at high altitudes poses a few unique challenges. These guidelines outline how different ingredients react, and will help you adapt our recipes to suit.

• Leavening agents such as baking powder, baking soda and yeast release more and larger gas bubbles. These expand rapidly and—before the heat of the oven can firm them up—collapse, causing cakes and breads to fall. When you're making a cake batter, reduce the baking powder or baking soda by ⅛ tsp for each 1 tsp called for in the recipe. You won't need to alter cookie recipes because they usually include small amounts of leavener.

• Yeast doughs rise quickly, so rely on visual cues more than on suggested times to make sure the dough has risen until doubled in bulk. If breads rise for too long, large air pockets may develop, which will cause the bread to fall.

• Moisture evaporates at a lower temperature, so baked goods can come out drier. Line pans with parchment paper or greased waxed paper to combat this.

• Cakes take longer to complete than the time specified in the recipe. Increase the baking time by a few minutes, but do not alter the oven temperature; watch carefully for doneness cues.

• Excessive sugar weakens a cake's structure, and high altitudes can worsen this problem. If the recipe calls for an amount of sugar that's more than half the amount of the flour in the recipe, reduce the sugar by 1 tbsp for every 1 cup called for in the ingredient list.

CITRUS JUICE & ZEST

1 tsp grated lemon zest
= ¾ tsp grated lime zest

1 tsp lemon juice = ¾ tsp lime juice

1 tsp lemon juice = 1 tsp vinegar

EGGS & DAIRY

for baking
1 egg white
= 2 tbsp pasteurized egg white

for muffins and quick breads
1 egg
= ½ tsp baking powder
+ ¼ cup more of the liquid called
for in the recipe

1 cup 2% or homogenized milk
= ½ cup evaporated milk
+ ½ cup water

1 cup milk
= ⅓ cup powdered milk + enough
water to fill measure to 1 cup (this
is generally the proportion; follow
package instructions if different)

1 cup buttermilk
= 1 tbsp lemon juice or vinegar
+ enough milk to make 1 cup;
let stand for 5 minutes to thicken

*for muffins, quick breads
and pancakes*
1 cup buttermilk or sour cream
= 1 cup plain yogurt

for simple cheesecakes
1 cup cream cheese
= 1 cup cottage cheese
puréed until very smooth
+ ¼ cup butter or margarine

1 cup butter
= 1 cup firm margarine
(substituting soft margarine in
baking will affect texture)

for icings
1 cup whipping cream (35%)
= ¾ cup whole milk
+ ⅓ cup butter

for sauces
1 cup light cream
= 1 cup homogenized milk

**1 cup shredded old
Cheddar cheese**
= 1 cup shredded mild cheese
+ ¼ tsp Worcestershire sauce
+ ⅛ tsp dry mustard

TOMATOES

1 cup tomato juice
= ½ cup tomato sauce
+ ½ cup water

1 cup tomato sauce
= ½ cup tomato paste
+ ½ cup water

1 cup ketchup or chili sauce
= 1 cup tomato sauce
+ ¼ cup granulated sugar
+ 2 tbsp vinegar

DRIED FRUITS

1 cup raisins
= 1 cup dried currants **or**
= 1 cup dried cherries **or**
= 1 cup dried cranberries

CHOCOLATE

30 g unsweetened chocolate
= 3 tbsp cocoa powder
+ 2½ tsp butter

30 g semisweet chocolate
= 15 g unsweetened chocolate
+ 1 tbsp granulated sugar
+ 1 tbsp butter **or**
= 3 tbsp cocoa powder
+ 1 tbsp granulated sugar
+ 1 tbsp butter

1 cup chocolate chips
= 1 cup chopped chocolate
(Note: You can't always substitute
chocolate chips for chopped
chocolate because stabilizers affect
how chocolate chips melt)

**1 cup chopped
bittersweet chocolate**
= 1 cup chopped semisweet
chocolate or dark chocolate

ALCOHOL

for sauces and gravies
½ cup dry white wine
= ½ cup chicken broth **or**
= 7 tbsp chicken broth
+ 1 tbsp wine vinegar

for sauces and gravies
½ cup dry red wine
= ½ cup beef broth
(reduce salt in recipe)

1 cup beer
= 1 cup nonalcoholic beer **or**
= 1 cup broth (any type)

SEASONINGS

1 cup chopped leeks or shallots
= 1 cup chopped onions

1 tbsp finely chopped fresh chives
= 1 tbsp finely chopped green parts
of green onions

1 tbsp chopped fresh herbs
= 1 tsp crushed dried herbs (start
with less for strongly flavoured,
assertive herbs like rosemary)

1 tbsp minced fresh ginger
= 1 tsp ground ginger

for wet mixtures
1 tsp dry mustard
= 1 tbsp Dijon mustard

1 tbsp prepared mustard
= 1 tbsp dry mustard
+ 1 tsp each vinegar, cold water and
granulated sugar; when volume
as well as flavour is important,
as in a dressing, let mixture stand
for 15 minutes to thicken

dash hot pepper sauce
= pinch cayenne pepper or
hot pepper flakes

2 tbsp soy sauce
= 1 tbsp Worcestershire sauce
+ 2 tsp water
+ pinch salt

1 tbsp Worcestershire sauce
= 1 tbsp soy sauce
+ dash each hot pepper sauce
and lemon juice
+ pinch granulated sugar

2 tbsp hoisin sauce
= 2 tbsp oyster sauce or fish sauce
(if less than 2 tbsp hoisin sauce is
called for, it can be omitted;
if more than 2 tbsp, the flavour is
too important to substitute)

1 tbsp balsamic vinegar
= 1 tbsp red wine vinegar
+ pinch granulated sugar

1 tsp curry powder
= 1 tsp curry paste

1 clove garlic, minced
= ¼ tsp garlic powder

FOOD SAFETY

Here are basic strategies for keeping harmful foodborne bacteria at bay.

WHEN SHOPPING

- Always examine packages carefully before buying. Avoid swollen or dented cans or damaged packages; their contents may have been exposed to harmful bacteria.

- Pick up frozen and perishable items (such as meat, poultry, seafood, produce and dairy products) last, just before you check out. When you get home, put them away first.

- In hot weather, bring a cooler and ice packs to the market so you can transport perishables safely.

- Buy fish and shellfish from a reputable source with high turnover.

- Even acidic foods, such as fruit juices, are susceptible to cross-contamination if they have not been pasteurized. Pasteurization removes any doubt by killing all bacteria with high heat.

- Never reuse grocery bags or meat trays that once contained raw meat, seafood or poultry.

- Do not buy frozen food that has thawed.

WHEN PREPPING

- Before you start to prep or cook, wash your hands thoroughly with warm water and soap. Scrub for 20 seconds and then rinse them well. Wash your hands again after using the toilet, blowing your nose or handling raw meat, poultry, seafood or eggs.

- Keep a clean kitchen. Bacteria from raw foods is easily transferred onto countertops, sponges and dishcloths, and from cutting boards onto utensils. When in doubt, clean the counter and use a fresh cloth or sponge that has been laundered in hot, soapy water.

- Invest in two different cutting boards. Use one exclusively for raw meat, seafood and poultry; use the other only for ready to-eat foods, such as breads, fruits and vegetables.

- After working with raw meat, seafood or poultry, wash cutting boards and utensils well, and then soak in a solution of 1 tbsp chlorine bleach and 4 cups water before rinsing. Bacteria can seep in through cracks in wood and plastic, so discard old or scarred cutting boards.

- Wash your can opener after every use. Food and bacteria can get stuck on the cutting blade.

- Rinse fresh fruits and vegetables before eating or cooking them. Wash salad greens and drain them well in a colander or use a salad spinner to remove the rinse water.

- Completely thaw frozen meat, poultry or fish before cooking. Never thaw at room temperature. Thaw food on a plate on top of a rimmed baking sheet on the bottom shelf of the refrigerator—the sheet will catch any juices and keep them away from other foods. Calculate five hours per every 450 g of food. To quick-thaw a wrapped frozen item, immerse it in cold water for 1 hour per every 450 g, changing the water every hour.

- Never refreeze partially thawed meat without cooking it first.

WHEN COOKING

- Cook meat and poultry to the proper doneness level. Use an instant-read thermometer to make sure the food has reached a safe internal temperature (see Meat Doneness Temperatures & Visual Cues, opposite).

- Don't put cooked meat, seafood or poultry on a plate that has come into contact with raw meat, poultry or seafood. The same goes for any utensils that touched these ingredients when raw. Use clean tongs and lifters to turn and remove cooked food from the skillet, oven or barbecue.

- Don't attempt to cook food in stages, letting it cool for a long time in between, as this encourages bacteria to multiply.

WHEN STORING

- Keep hot foods hot, above 140°F (60°C), and cold foods cold, below 40°F (4°C).

- Refrigerate leftovers as soon as possible. Never let cooked foods stand at room temperature for longer than 2 hours.

- To quick-chill made-ahead or leftover items, divide large amounts into small, shallow, uncovered containers. Refrigerate them, leaving enough space around each container to allow cold air to circulate around the food. Cover the containers when the food is cold.

- Cool large quantities of very hot food on the counter for 30 minutes before refrigerating to keep from overburdening the refrigerator's cooling system.

- Periodically check your refrigerator and freezer temperatures; refrigerators should be set at 40°F (4°C) or below, and freezers should be set at 0°F (−18°C) or below.

- Store eggs in their cartons in the coldest part of your refrigerator, not in the door tray. Always discard cracked eggs and respect the best-before dates.

WHEN OUTDOORS

- Keep serving times outdoors as short as possible.

- If you're having a picnic, chill the food before packing it and always keep it covered and chilled inside coolers that have been well stocked with ice or ice packs. Place the coolers in the shade to help them stay cool for as long as possible.

- Plan amounts carefully to avoid leftovers; discard any uneaten meat, poultry, seafood, salads or dairy products.

MEAT DONENESS TEMPERATURES & VISUAL CUES

Our recipes for beef, pork, lamb, veal and poultry always ask you to look for a specific internal temperature, visual cue and/or textural cue to ensure the meat is fully cooked. Ovens, barbecues and stove-top burners can vary widely, so start checking for signs of doneness before the shortest suggested time in the recipe.

	RARE	MEDIUM	WELL-DONE	VISUAL CUE
BEEF, LAMB AND VEAL (not ground)	140°F (60°C)	160°F (71°C)	170°F (77°C)	**RARE** bright red in centre with brown just near surface **MEDIUM** light pink in centre and brown through remainder **WELL-DONE** brown throughout
PORK (not ground)		160°F (71°C)		juices run clear when pork is pierced and just a hint of pink remains inside
GROUND MEATS (BEEF, PORK, LAMB AND VEAL)			160°F (71°C)	no longer pink
WHOLE CHICKEN AND TURKEY (unstuffed)			185°F (85°C)	juices run clear when thickest part of thigh is pierced
CHICKEN AND TURKEY PIECES (including chunks for stews or kabobs)			165°F (74°C)	**THIGHS AND WINGS** juices run clear when thickest part is pierced **BREASTS** no longer pink inside
GROUND CHICKEN AND TURKEY			165°F (74°C)	no longer pink

USE A THERMOMETER

The best way to determine meat doneness is to use an instant-read thermometer. Invest in a reliable brand and always keep it handy. Insert the probe into the thickest part of roasts or into the centre of meat loaves and burgers to get an accurate internal temperature. Avoid touching bones, because they will give you a false reading. Some meats can be cooked to your desired doneness level; others need to be cooked to a specific temperature to be safe to eat. If just one temperature is listed in the chart above, that is the only safe option for that particular cut.

Carryover Cooking

Meat and poultry will continue to cook after they are removed from the heat. Generally, their internal temperature will increase by 5 to 10°F (2.5 to 5.5°C) as they rest. Remember that thickness is a factor, especially when grilling steaks. The temperature of steaks thinner than ¾ inch (2 cm) will increase by about 10°F (5.5°C) after they come off the grill. The temperature of steaks that are ¾ inch (2 cm) or thicker will go up by about 5°F (2.5°C). The cooking times in our charts take this carryover cooking into consideration.

COOKING MEAT & POULTRY: BASIC HOW-TOS

In these tables, we've included general guidelines for cooking a variety of cuts of beef, lamb, pork, veal and poultry without using one of our recipes. When you're barbecuing or broiling especially, watch carefully for signs of burning or charring, and turn down the heat if you need to.

BEEF

PREMIUM OVEN ROASTS prime rib, rib eye, top sirloin	Roast in 325°F (160°C) oven for 20 minutes per each 450 g for rare; 25 minutes per each 450 g for medium; or 30 minutes per each 450 g for well-done.
PREMIUM OVEN ROASTS tenderloin	Roast in 450°F (230°C) oven for 10 to 15 minutes per each 450 g for rare to medium-rare.
OVEN ROASTS inside round, outside round, eye of round, sirloin tip, rump roast	Pour enough water into roasting pan to come 1 inch (2.5 cm) up side. Place 1 to 2 kg roast on rack in pan so it is above water level. Roast in 500°F (260°C) oven for 30 minutes. Reduce heat to 275°F (140°C); roast for 25 to 35 minutes per each 450 g for rare to medium-rare.
POT ROASTS cross rib, boneless blade, shoulder, brisket, short rib	In lightly oiled Dutch oven over medium-high heat, brown on all sides if desired. Cover and simmer on stove top or braise in 325°F (160°C) oven, in enough cooking liquid to come halfway up roast, until tender, about 3 hours.
SIMMERING STEAKS blade, top blade, bottom blade, cross rib	In lightly oiled Dutch oven over medium-high heat, brown on both sides. Cover and simmer on stove top or braise in 325°F (160°C) oven, in enough cooking liquid to come halfway up steak, until tender, about 1¼ hours.
STEWING CUTS simmering short ribs, boneless and bone-in, stewing cubes	In lightly oiled Dutch oven, brown on all sides. Cover and simmer on stove top or braise in 325°F (160°C) oven, in enough cooking liquid to cover, until tender, 1½ to 2 hours.
QUICK-SERVE CUTS stir-fry strips, fast-fry minute steaks, grilling kabobs, fondue cubes	Season to taste (do not add salt). In lightly oiled skillet or wok, cook over medium heat for 2 to 3 minutes for strips, or 2 to 4 minutes per side for steaks.

LAMB

LEG boneless rolled	Roast in 325°F (160°C) oven for 25 to 30 minutes per each 450 g for rare; 30 to 35 minutes per each 450 g for medium; or 35 to 40 minutes per each 450 g for well-done.
LEG bone-in, 2.2 to 3.15 kg	Roast in 325°F (160°C) oven for 20 to 25 minutes per each 450 g for rare; 25 to 30 minutes per each 450 g for medium; or 30 to 35 minutes per each 450 g for well-done.
LEG bone-in, 3.15 to 4 kg	Roast in 325°F (160°C) oven for 15 to 20 minutes per each 450 g for rare; 20 to 25 minutes per each 450 g for medium; or 25 to 30 minutes per each 450 g for well-done.

STEAKS & CHOPS

BEEF GRILLING STEAKS
rib, rib eye, T-bone, strip loin,
top sirloin, tenderloin

BEEF MARINATING STEAKS
inside round, outside round,
eye of round, sirloin tip, flank

LAMB CHOPS
rib and loin

VEAL CHOPS

- For ½-inch (1 cm) thick steaks or chops: Grill over medium-high heat or broil, turning once, for 3 minutes for rare; 4 minutes for medium-rare; 5 minutes for medium; or 6 minutes for medium-well.

- For ¾-inch (2 cm) thick steaks or chops: Grill over medium-high heat or broil, turning once, for 4 to 5 minutes for rare; 6 to 7 minutes for medium-rare; 8 to 9 minutes for medium; or 10 to 12 minutes for medium-well.

- For 1-inch (2.5 cm) thick steaks or chops: Grill over medium-high heat or broil, turning once, for 8 to 9 minutes for rare; 10 to 11 minutes for medium-rare; 12 to 13 minutes for medium; or 14 to 16 minutes for medium-well.

- For 1½-inch (4 cm) thick steaks or chops: Grill over medium-high heat or broil, turning once, for 14 to 15 minutes for rare; or 16 to 19 minutes for medium-rare. For higher levels of doneness: Grill over medium-high heat or broil, turning once, for 16 minutes, and then transfer to 375°F (190°C) oven for 6 to 9 minutes for medium; or 10 to 14 minutes for medium-well.

- For 2-inch (5 cm) thick steaks or chops: Grill over medium-high heat or broil, turning once, for 18 to 22 minutes for rare. For higher levels of doneness: Grill over medium-high heat or broil, turning once, for 18 minutes, and then transfer to 375°F (190°C) oven for 6 to 7 minutes for medium-rare; 9 to 10 minutes for medium; or 15 to 18 minutes for medium-well.

PORK

LOIN ROAST
bone-in centre-cut rack of pork,
boneless single loin, crown roast
(unstuffed)

LEG ROAST
boneless inside and outside

Roast in 325°F (160°C) oven until juices run clear when pork is pierced and just a hint of pink remains inside, 20 to 25 minutes per each 450 g.

LOIN ROAST
boneless tenderloin end,
boneless rib end

SHOULDER ROAST
bone-in shoulder butt or picnic

Roast in 325°F (160°C) oven until juices run clear when pork is pierced and just a hint of pink remains inside, 25 to 30 minutes per each 450 g.

LOIN ROAST
boneless double loin

SHOULDER ROAST
boneless shoulder butt or picnic

Roast in 325°F (160°C) oven until juices run clear when pork is pierced and just a hint of pink remains inside, 30 to 35 minutes per each 450 g.

TENDERLOIN

Roast in 375°F (190°C) oven until juices run clear when pork is pierced and just a hint of pink remains inside, 30 to 35 minutes total.

CHOPS
¾ inch (2 cm) thick

Grill over medium-high heat or broil, turning once, until juices run clear when pork is pierced and just a hint of pink remains inside, 8 to 12 minutes total.

POULTRY

WHOLE CHICKEN AND TURKEY
unstuffed

Roast on greased rack in roasting pan in 325°F (160°C) oven until juices run clear when thickest part of thigh is pierced, 20 minutes per each 450 g.

FRUIT & VEGETABLE BUYING GUIDE

- The fruits and vegetables in our charts are based on commonly available sizes found at the supermarket. Where there is a range, we have based amounts on the first figure; for example, if 450 g = 2 or 3 apples, we have used 2 apples.

- For chopped or sliced fruits and vegetables, we assume that have been trimmed, pitted, stemmed and peeled as appropriate.

- The peak periods reflect either Canadian in-season dates (when local versions of these foods are most available) or the times when these foods are commonly found in abundance in Canadian markets. Some types of produce—such as English cucumbers, sweet peppers and citrus fruits—are on sale year-round because they're flown in or grown in hothouses. Others, such as apples, are available from cold storage at nonpeak times. Availability varies according to location and weather.

- You can buy good-quality frozen fruits and vegetables year-round, such as cranberries, wild blueberries, strawberries, raspberries, rhubarb, peas, corn, beans and broccoli.

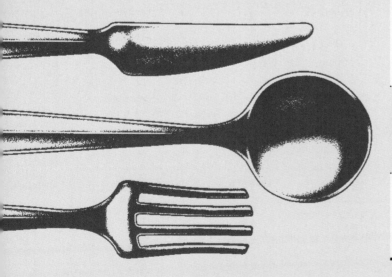

FRUIT	PEAK PERIOD
Apples 450 g = 2 or 3 apples 1 apple = 1 cup grated or chopped, or 1½ cups sliced	late August to April
Apricots 450 g = 5 to 7 apricots 1 apricot = ½ cup sliced	July and August
Avocado 450 g = 2 avocados 1 avocado = 1 cup sliced or cubed, or ½ cup mashed	April to August
Bananas 450 g = 4 bananas 1 banana = 1 cup sliced, or ¾ cup mashed	year-round
Blueberries 340 g = 1 pint 1 pint = 2 cups	July to September
Cantaloupe 1.35 kg = 1 cantaloupe 1 cantaloupe = 7 cups chopped	July to September
Cherries 450 g = 50 cherries, or 3 cups (unpitted) 450 g = 2 cups pitted	late June to early August
Cranberries 340 g = 1 bag 1 bag = 3 cups	September to December
Grapefruit 450 g = 1 to 3 grapefruits 1 grapefruit = 1 cup sections, or ¾ cup juice	year-round; peak in winter

FRUIT	PEAK PERIOD
Grapes 450 g = 3 cups stemmed	August to early October
Honeydew 2.45 kg = 1 honeydew 1 honeydew = 12 cups chopped	July to September
Kiwifruit 450 g = 4 to 6 kiwifruit 1 kiwifruit = ½ cup sliced or chopped	year-round; peak in fall and winter
Lemons 450 g = 2 or 3 lemons 1 lemon = 1 tbsp grated zest and ¼ cup juice	year-round; peak in winter
Limes 450 g = 4 limes 1 lime = 2 tsp grated zest and 3 tbsp juice	year-round; peak in fall
Mandarins 450 g = 3 or 4 mandarins 1 mandarin = 1 cup sections, or 2 tsp grated zest and ⅓ cup juice	November to January
Nectarines 450 g = 4 nectarines 1 nectarine = 1 cup sliced or chopped	August to mid-September
Oranges 450 g = 2 or 3 oranges 1 orange = 1 cup sections, or 1 tbsp grated zest and ⅓ cup juice	year-round; peak in winter
Peaches 450 g = 2 to 4 peaches 1 peach = 1 cup sliced, chopped or diced	mid-July to mid-September

FRUIT	PEAK PERIOD
Pears 450 g = 2 or 3 pears 1 pear = 1 cup sliced or chopped	August to November
Pineapple 1.125 kg = 1 pineapple 1 pineapple = 5 cups chopped	year-round; peak in winter
Plums 450 g = 5 plums 1 plum = ½ cup chopped or sliced	mid-July to September
Raspberries 340 g = 1 pint 1 pint = 2 cups whole raspberries, 1 cup puréed or ⅓ cup seeded puréed	July (some available until September)
Rhubarb (forced) 450 g = 10 stalks, trimmed 1 stalk, trimmed = ½ cup chopped	January to April
Rhubarb (outdoor) 450 g = 10 stalks, trimmed 1 stalk, trimmed = ½ cup chopped	May to July
Strawberries 675 g = 1 quart, or 30 strawberries 1 quart = 4 cups sliced or chopped 4 cups hulled = 2½ cups puréed	June to July (some available until September)
Watermelon 6.25 kg = 1 medium-large watermelon 450 g = 3½ cups cubed	August and September

Canned fruits and vegetables are another option if fresh or frozen aren't available. Canned peaches, pears, pineapple, apricots, applesauce, tomatoes, beets, corn and legumes are all handy pantry staples.

VEGETABLE	PEAK PERIOD	VEGETABLE	PEAK PERIOD
Artichokes 340 g = 1 large artichoke	spring and fall	**Celery** 675 g = 1 bunch 1 stalk = ½ cup sliced, or 6 celery sticks	August and September
Asparagus 450 g = 1 bunch, or 24 stalks 1 bunch = 3 cups chopped	April to June	**Corn** 225 g = 1 cob 1 cob = 1 cup kernels	late July to September
Beans (green/yellow wax) 450 g = 6 cups whole, or 4 cups chopped	July to September	**Cucumber, English** 450 g = 1 English cucumber 1 English cucumber = 4 cups sliced, or 2½ cups chopped	year-round
Beets 450 g = 1 bunch, or 3 or 4 beets 1 bunch = 2 cups quartered, or 2⅓ cups chopped or sliced	July to mid-October	**Cucumber, field** 450 g = 2 to 8 small field cucumbers	June to early September
Broccoli 450 g = 1 bunch 1 bunch = 4 cups chopped florets and 2 cups sliced peeled stems	July to October	**Eggplant** 450 g = 1 large eggplant, or 7 cups sliced or cubed 170 g = 1 Asian eggplant, or 2 cups sliced or cubed	August and September
Brussels sprouts 450 g = 24 brussels sprouts, or 4 cups	September to November	**Garlic** 55 g = 1 head 1 head = 10 cloves 1 clove = 1 tsp minced	August to October
Cabbage, green 1.8 kg = 1 large green cabbage 450 g = 6 cups shredded	July to November	**Green onions** 115 g = 1 bunch, or 6 green onions 1 bunch = 1½ cups chopped (white and trimmed green parts)	July to September
Carrots 450 g = 4 large carrots 1 large carrot = ¾ cup chopped or sliced, or ⅔ cup grated	July to September	**Leeks** 450 g = 1 bunch, or 3 or 4 leeks 1 leek = 1 cup sliced (white and light green parts only)	August to November
Cauliflower 1.2 kg = 1 large cauliflower 1 large cauliflower = 12 cups trimmed florets	August to October	**Lettuce, Boston** 450 g = 1 head 1 head = 11 cups torn	June to September

VEGETABLE	PEAK PERIOD
Lettuce, iceberg 565 g = 1 head 1 head = 12 cups torn	July to September
Lettuce, romaine 675 g = 1 head 1 head =14 cups torn	June to September
Mushrooms, button 450 g = 30 mushrooms 450 g = 6 cups sliced	year-round
Onions, cooking 450 g = 3 or 4 onions 1 onion = 1½ cups sliced, or 1 cup chopped	August to May
Onions, red 450 g = 2 onions 1 onion = 2 cups chopped, or 1¼ cups sliced	August to October
Onions, Spanish and other large, sweet varieties 450 g = 1 onion 1 onion = 3 cups sliced, or 2 cups chopped	August to October
Parsnips 450 g = 3 to 5 parsnips 1 parsnip = 1 cup chopped, or ⅓ cup mashed cooked	September to November
Peas 450 g fresh peas in pods = 1⅓ cup shelled peas	mid-June to late July
Potatoes 450 g = 3 or 4 potatoes 1 potato = 1 cup sliced, ¾ cup chopped or ½ cup mashed cooked	late August to late October

VEGETABLE	PEAK PERIOD
Potatoes (new/mini) 450 g = 15 potatoes	July to September
Potatoes, sweet 450 g = 2 or 3 sweet potatoes 1 sweet potato = 2½ cups sliced, 2 cups cubed or 1 cup mashed cooked	late summer
Radishes 450 g = 2¼ bunches, or 27 radishes 1 bunch = 12 radishes, or 1½ cups sliced	June to September
Rutabaga 1.125 kg = 1 rutabaga 1 rutabaga = 5 cups cubed 1 cup cubed = ½ cup mashed cooked	October to December
Spinach 300 g = 1 bag, or 19 cups lightly packed trimmed or 10 cups packed trimmed 340 g = 1 bunch, or 16 cups lightly packed trimmed or 8 cups packed trimmed	June to October
Squash, butternut 1.35 kg = 1 large butternut squash 1 large butternut squash = 11 cups cubed 1 cup cubed = ½ cup mashed cooked	September to November
Sweet peppers 450 g = 2 to 4 peppers 1 pepper = 1½ cups sliced, or 1¼ cups chopped	August to September (local); year-round (hothouse)
Tomatoes 450 g = 2 or 3 tomatoes 1 tomato = 1 cup chopped	late July to September
Zucchini 450 g = 4 zucchini 1 zucchini = 2 cups halved and sliced, or 1½ cups chopped	July to September

THANK YOU

When you put the word *ultimate* on the cover of a book, you better mean it. The team that made this book—this beautiful, comprehensive, packed-with-deliciousness book—definitely let that concept be its guiding principle.

First, I'd like to thank the Canadian Living Test Kitchen: they are the heart and soul of this operation. Food director Annabelle Waugh, senior food specialist Irene Fong, food specialists Amanda Barnier and Jennifer Bartoli, and food articles editor Gilean Watts are champions of good taste and constantly strive for perfection. Special thanks also go to Rheanna Kish and Leah Kuhne, two Test Kitchen alumnae, who were instrumental in bringing this particular book into being. Rheanna sifted through hundreds of recipes with Annabelle, searching for just the right ones—the ultimate ones—and Leah retested and updated many of our recipes to ensure they were the very best versions we could share with you. Thanks to all of these talented women, editing this book was a pleasure.

Second, I'd like to thank Colin Elliott, our art director and my nearly constant companion in the months that led up to the printing of this book. I appreciate his creative solutions to problems, his flawless sense of style and his deep knowledge of design and typography. I also treasure his ability to laugh even under intense pressure—all 448 pages of it!

Gratitude goes next to the photographers and stylists who worked with us to create beautiful images to show off our ultimate recipes. Special thanks to the dream team that shot lovely new images for this volume: photographers Jodi Pudge and Maya Visnyei; food stylists David Grenier and Claire Stubbs; and prop stylist Catherine Doherty (who did double duty dashing between studios). For a complete list of the talented photographers and stylists who contributed to these pages, see page 448.

Next up, I'm always grateful for Lisa Fielding, our copy editor, who cleans up grammar and style points after I'm done editing, making sure every page is just so. I'm also indebted to our indexer, Beth Zabloski, who reads every single line of copy and creates the handy index that helps you (and me) navigate through the many, many recipes in this book. Thanks also to Sharyn Joliat of Info Access, who created the nutrient analysis for all of the recipes.

I also owe a big thank-you to our teams at Juniper Publishing and Simon & Schuster Canada for their work behind the scenes on this and many other books. I appreciate their insight, hard work and help in making this book a success across the country.

Last, a round of applause for Jacqueline Loch, Canadian Living's vice-president and group publisher; Sandra E. Martin, our editor-in-chief; and Jessica Ross, our content director, multiplatform editions, books and special issues, for their vision and collaboration on this book. It was a huge undertaking, and their confidence in us made it worth the effort.

TINA ANSON MINE
PROJECT EDITOR

INDEX

Credits

RECIPES

All recipes were developed by the **CANADIAN LIVING TEST KITCHEN**.

PHOTOGRAPHY

RYAN BROOK p. 274 and 332.

JEFF COULSON p. 5, 6, 11, 20, 39, 50, 55, 58, 61, 65, 77, 82, 84, 87, 91, 103, 111, 126, 131, 150, 152, 155, 159, 165, 173, 176, 184, 203, 210, 216, 225, 230, 238, 244, 249, 252, 257, 263, 271 (A and B), 278, 283, 292, 298, 304, 321, 340, 349 (main), 354, 359, 362, 368 and 420 (food).

YVONNE DUIVENVOORDEN p. 78, 98, 116, 123, 147, 160, 187, 301, 308, 309 and 335.

JOE KIM p. 168 (A and B).

STEVE KRUG p. 206.

EDWARD POND p. 15, 16, 25, 235 (A and B), 330, 331, 375 and 415 (A and B).

JODI PUDGE p. 31, 42 (main and A), 92, 106, 139, 190, 195, 198, 213, 235 (main), 271 (main), 281, 289, 297, 313, 318, 349 (A and B), 380, 400 and 410.

RYAN SZULC p. 8, 42 (B), 47, 120, 134, 226 and 260.

JAMES TSE p. 390, 396 and 405.

MAYA VISNYEI p. 32, 36, 68, 73, 115, 142, 168 (main), 181, 221, 241, 266, 284, 324, 346, 372, 385, 399 and 415 (main).

DAVID WILE p. 4 and 420 (portrait).

FOOD STYLING

ASHLEY DENTON p. 47, 84, 91, 152, 159, 330 and 331.

MICHAEL ELLIOTT/JUDYINC.COM p. 390, 396 and 405.

DAVID GRENIER p. 6, 31, 42, 92, 106, 139, 176, 190, 195, 198, 213, 226, 235 (main), 260, 271 (main), 281, 289, 297, 313, 318, 332, 349 (A and B), 354, 380, 400 and 410.

ADELE HAGAN p. 39, 65 and 77.

HEATHER HOWE p. 415 (A and B).

LUCIE RICHARD p. 15, 16, 25, 123, 301, 308, 309 and 375.

CHRISTOPHER ST. ONGE p. 238 and 249.

HEATHER SHAW p. 58, 216, 283 and 420 (food).

CLAIRE STUBBS p. 5, 8, 20, 32, 36, 50, 68, 73, 78, 98, 103, 115, 116, 126, 142, 147, 150, 155, 160, 168 (main), 173, 181, 184, 187, 203, 206, 210, 221, 235 (A and B), 241, 252, 266, 284, 324, 335, 346, 372, 385, 399 and 415 (main).

MELANIE STUPARYK p. 82, 87, 168 (A and B), 225, 244, 263, 274, 278, 292, 321, 349 (main), 359 and 368.

NOAH WITENOFF p. 11, 55, 61, 111, 131, 165, 257 and 340.

NICOLE YOUNG p. 120, 134, 230, 298, 304 and 362.

PROP STYLING

LAURA BRANSON p. 39, 47, 58, 65, 77, 103, 173, 176, 216, 283 and 420 (food).

AURELIE BRYCE p. 6, 8, 55, 82, 131, 230, 263, 278, 298, 304, 321, 340 and 354.

ALANNA DAVEY p. 206.

CATHERINE DOHERTY p. 5, 15, 16, 25, 31, 32, 36, 42 (main and A), 68, 73, 78, 87, 92, 98, 106, 115, 116, 123, 139, 142, 147, 150, 155, 160, 168 (main), 181, 190, 195, 198, 210, 213, 235 (main), 241, 252, 266, 271 (main), 281, 284, 289, 292, 297, 301, 308, 309, 313, 318, 324, 330, 331, 346, 349, 359, 368, 372, 375, 380, 385, 399, 400, 410 and 415 (main).

JENNIFER EVANS p. 390, 396 and 405.

MADELEINE JOHARI p. 11, 20, 42 (B), 50, 61, 120, 126, 134, 184, 225, 226, 244, 257, 260 and 362.

KAREN KIRK p. 168 (A and B), 274 and 332.

SABRINA LINN p. 111.

SASHA SEYMOUR p. 84, 91, 152, 159, 165, 238 and 249.

OKSANA SLAVUTYCH p. 235 (A and B) and 335.

PAIGE WEIR/JUDYINC.COM p. 221.

GENEVIEVE WISEMAN p. 187 and 203.